PROGRESS IN PREVENTING AIDS?
DOGMA, DISSENT AND INNOVATION
Global Perspectives

Edited by
David Buchanan and George Cernada

BAYWOOD PUBLISHING COMPANY, INC.
AMITYVILLE, NEW YORK

Library of Congress Catalog Number: 97-1804
ISBN: 0-89503-176-0 (Cloth)

Library of Congress Cataloging-in-Publication Data

Progress in preventing AIDS? : dogma, dissent, and innovation : global
  perspectives / edited by David Buchanan and George Cernada.
      p.   cm.
   Includes bibliographical references and index.
   ISBN 0-89503-176-0 (cloth)
   1. AIDS (Disease)- -Prevention.   2. AIDS (Disease)- -Social aspects.
   3. AIDS (Disease)- -Political aspects.   I. Buchanan, David Ross.
   II. Cernada, George Peter.
   RA644.A25P7655   1998
   362. 1'969792- -dc21   97-1804
                                                               CIP

Cover Photo Credits
Community Health Education in the Field: 3 Continents

TOP	Bangladesh	Photo by Dan Gerber University of Massachusetts, Amherst
MIDDLE	Rural Zimbabwe	Photo by George Cernada
BOTTOM	Urban U.S.A.	Photo by Carmen Claudio Centro de Educacion Prevencion y Accion Holyoke, Massachusetts

Preface

This state-of-the-art volume provides the reader with twenty-one pivotal articles on global AIDS prevention. Both policy and research are highlighted in these topical and sometimes controversial contributions from experienced professionals in some nine countries on four continents.

Professors Buchanan and Cernada, the editors, who combine some fifty years of community health education experience in national and international arenas, have collected these readable articles and provided a comprehensive introductory overview and an easily grasped framework comprised of:

I   *The Science of Prevention: Doctrine and Dogma;*
II   *Voices of Dissent;* and
III   *Innovations in Field Practice.*

The first section examines current scientific approaches to assessing preventive needs. Social and behavioral approaches useful for large-scale field programs are presented in terms of meeting public needs, particularly those of youth, the disenfranchised, the marginalized.

The second section provides the dissenting view: skeptics and dissenters call attention to the politics of AIDS. They question the commitment of governments, double standards of sexual conduct, even the whole idea of progress in AIDS prevention and the dominant AIDS causality paradigm.

Innovative community approaches to AIDS education and prevention highlight the third section of the book. Traditional healers, the use of drama and songs, community-controlled planning and program intervention and culturally and ethnically relevant themes are the focus of this diverse collection of articles.

This important contribution to our understanding of AIDS education and prevention is *must* reading for concerned professionals. It is unique in bringing to focus recent empirical community-based research and policy and in exposing the reader to the diverse views of health education and social change practitioners from around the world. It also would be an appropriate text for community health and social science students, since Buchanan's and Cernada's masterful analysis of the practices and theories underlying the twenty-one articles on AIDS, has implications and is relevant to health problems other than AIDS. For public health students majoring in health education or behavioral science, this text should be required reading. We need more health education publications similar to this one: creative in their approach to important health issues, but anchored by sound research practices and interpretations.

William Griffiths
Professor Emeritus
University of California, Berkeley

Table of Contents

Introduction and Overview
Progress in Preventing AIDS?

David Buchanan and George Cernada

INTRODUCTION

AIDS has been with us now at least since the late 1970s. It has reached pandemic proportions. With no immunization nor proven accessible medical treatment, how are we to respond to AIDS—as individuals and as a society? Where do we turn for progress in preventing more people from becoming infected? Are we on the right track? Is it only a matter of time until we find the keys to prevention, the power to block transmission? Is there a program of scientific research in progress that will discover what needs to be done? If not science, where do we look for hope? Is behavior change our only choice? What types of educational interventions have made sense?

Progress in Preventing AIDS? Dogma, Dissent and Innovation assesses our current situation. It explores the results, gains, and limits of the standard program—the application of a rigorous methodical scientific process of testing hypotheses through observation and experiments designed to separate fact from fiction, true knowledge from wishful thinking. We have collected a series of six articles representative of this approach. They stand as testimony to the fruits of this system.

We then turn to the dissenters—the skeptics, the challengers, the naysayers, those who would call into question the whole idea of progress in preventing AIDS. Do we really know and fully understand what causes AIDS? Can we rely on the government to keep us fully informed? Are condoms really the only way short of abstinence to stop sexual transmission? What are we to make of the epidemic's far disproportionate toll on marginalized peoples? Mere coincidence? Can we rely on the government to make or maintain a commitment to fight AIDS

1

if it becomes any further concentrated among the powerless? Are we blaming the victim again? Do experts really know better than the affected groups themselves what is in their best interest? What if they're wrong? To whom do you listen? Whom do you trust? And why? The dissenters give us pause. They force us to reexamine our assumptions. They want to disturb our complacency. We have collected here seven articles that ask us to take nothing for granted.

And then we move on; the paralysis of doubt cannot be tolerated for long. What innovations in practice are there? Are there truths about preventing AIDS that do not necessarily have scientific proof for their recommendation? Can we proceed on our best judgment and intuitive insight into human nature without further warrant? How do you decide when an idea is worth repeating, or when it is a waste of time? Some seven articles are presented here.

We open with a brief profile of the epidemic in the United States and in the international arena both to describe the dimensions of the challenge and to set the context for understanding the task facing prevention programs. These introductory remarks then explain the scientific process of developing effective prevention programs, a program of research that has the official endorsement and recommendation of government funding agencies (such as the Centers for Disease Control) and the biomedical scientific community (such as the World Health Organization and the scientific review panel members of the National Institutes of Health). The chapter concludes with an overview of the book, the criteria used for selecting articles, and highlights from each of the twenty chapters that follow.

PROFILE OF AN EPIDEMIC IN
THE UNITED STATES

November 1995 marked another milestone in the AIDS epidemic in America: more than one-half million confirmed cases had been reported to the Centers for Disease Control and Prevention [1]. Of these, 311,381 (62%) were dead. To put this number in perspective, it is more than all casualties suffered by Americans in World War II and more than five times the number of U.S. deaths sustained during the decade of war in Viet Nam. Almost one-quarter of a million people were diagnosed with AIDS in the last three years. Another 630,000 to 900,000 Americans are now estimated to be infected with HIV [2]. AIDS is now the leading cause of death among persons twenty-five to forty-four in the United States. Since 1990, the total number of new cases diagnosed each year has plateaued, at about 60,000 people per year. The dimensions of this tragedy are staggering. If or until a cure can be found, one-half million souls and counting stand in solemn witness to the urgent need for prevention.

The face of the epidemic has changed since its first appearance in the United States in 1981. During the first six years, 1981-1987, 92 percent of reported cases were men, only 8 percent women. Since 1993, the percentage of women with the disease has more than doubled, climbing to 17.5 percent of all reported cases over the last three years. In the 1981-87 period, 59.8 percent of all people with AIDS (PWA) were white; since 1993, 57.4 percent of all PWAs are people of color. (As a point of reference, people of color were approximately 24% of the total U.S. population in the 1990 census.) In 1994, AIDS rates per 100,000 population were 101 for African Americans, 51 for Latinos, 17 for Whites, 12 for Native Americans, and 6 for Asians. The age distribution has remained relatively stable in comparisons of these two periods, with a small decline in the percentage of pediatric AIDS cases and a small increase in the number of people over the age of forty. These changes in the demography of AIDS reflect more significant changes in the mode of transmission over time.

During the first years of the epidemic, nearly two-thirds (64%) of all cases were attributed to men having sex with other men. The ramifications of this particular route of infection are well known, from its early labeling as Gay-Related Immune Disease (GRID) to the unconscionable delays by then-President Reagan in calling the nation's attention to the epidemic. Over the last three years, the percentage of cases due to male homosexual transmission has dropped to less than half (44.9%), although this vector continues to account for the largest portion of cases. During the 1993-1995 period, whites were more likely to have been infected through having sex with other men (accounting for approximately 51% of all infections among whites) than were people of color (approximately 32%). The decline reflects both the strides taken by the gay community in preventing the further spread of infection and the rise in the number of cases due to other modes of transmission, especially injection drug and heterosexual contact. The percentage attributed to injection drug use has jumped from 17.2 percent in the 1981-87 period to more than one-quarter (27.3%) of all cases over the last three years. The rates of infection due to heterosexual contact have quadrupled, from 2.5 percent to 10 percent, with almost 25,000 people diagnosed with AIDS through heterosexual sex in the last three years.

There are major implications for prevention due to these shifts in the modes of transmission and concomitant changes in the demographic profile of PWAs. First, despite impressive gains, men who have sex with other men continue to be those who are at highest risk of infection. Second, people who inject drugs, especially people of color who inject drugs, are now engaging in the fastest growing category of behaviors that put people at risk. Finally, heterosexual contact is putting more and more women at risk. Thus, prevention programs in the United States need to continue to reach out to the gay community. Prevention efforts also need to focus increasingly on outreach to people who inject drugs, particularly in communities of color. And programs need to pay more attention to educating women.

The juxtaposition of the continuing and more recently rising risk behaviors presents both threats and opportunities for the future of prevention efforts. To the extent that the epidemic is seen to pose a growing threat to women and heterosexuals, public sympathy and taxpayer support will likely continue and indeed perhaps expand. To the extent that the epidemic becomes increasingly identified with injection drug users who, moreover, also happen to be people of color, there is reason to be concerned about the potential withdrawal of public support for the resources necessary to maintain and strengthen ongoing prevention/education activities. These threats are magnified exponentially when we turn to the international scene.

AIDS INTERNATIONAL

Hardly more than a decade ago, a number of countries acted and spoke in public as if they had immunity to HIV and AIDS. Major geographic areas reported few cases. In most of the world, women and children "seemed to be on the periphery of the AIDS epidemic" [3].

No longer is this the case. AIDS has reached pandemic proportions. The World Health Organization (WHO) estimates that 4.5 million people have contracted AIDS since the late 1970s. In Uganda, AIDS is reported to be the leading cause of death with an estimated 1.5 million people infected with HIV—about 10 percent of its population. WHO estimated that in late 1995, there were 20 million HIV-positive people: 13 million in Africa, 4 million in South and Southeast Asia as well as 2 million in the Americas [4].

Today, women and children have joined men as being "at the center of our concern," according to WHO [4]. Worldwide, as many women as men contract the AIDS virus and in Africa "women now account for 55% of all new cases of HIV" [5]:

> In some areas of Africa, 25 to 30% of pregnant women attending antenatal clinics are HIV-positive. One in three of their babies will be born with the virus. All will develop AIDS and most will die before the age of five. So far, approximately 1 million children have been infected and half a million have already died—almost all of them in Africa [5].

And what has become increasingly more obvious about the extent of the epidemic in Africa is also becoming evident in Asia. For example, a rate of one of fifty adults in Thailand being HIV-positive has been reported. The estimate of new infections in 1995 for Southeast Asia is 2.5 million [5].

In a global context where WHO has estimated that more than 250 million sexually transmitted disease cases occur each year, the prospects for a continuing increase in HIV infections are daunting [6]. Given that sexually transmitted disease (STD) infection rates are high globally, their even higher rate in so-called "developing" countries where access to health services is limited does not suggest a hopeful scenario for AIDS prevention. For example two-thirds of all new cases are believed by international agencies to be occurring in Africa. UNICEF reports that, because of AIDS in Africa, some "9 million children will be orphaned in the 1990's" [5].

International sources are predicting some 26 million people infected by the end of the century and annual deaths of almost two million [7]. Given then that there is relatively widespread recognition that AIDS is reaching pandemic proportions—indeed, that AIDS deaths may even drastically affect population growth rates in some urban African areas—how much has been done to prevent the problem? If little, why?

To respond to the above questions, the following points seem relevant:

1. There is no immunization to prevent this disease. Treatment is insufficient. Behavioral change is the only option;
2. The social and cultural context of the different geographic regions determine much of the epidemiology of the disease and often provide formidable barriers to prevention programs;
3. The behavioral change being requested by prevention efforts involves sex education and adolescent sexuality. Most new HIV infections occur among persons ages fifteen to twenty-four.
4. Economic considerations greatly influence sexual and AIDS-related behavior, particularly in the developing countries: injections for drug users in Southeast Asia, rising numbers of younger women working in factories away from their families, double standards for sexual conduct, commercial sex workers in tourist areas, etc., are often indicators of inequitable distribution of income by class and gender.
5. There are few, if any, real epidemiologically controlled studies to pinpoint the effectiveness of specific educational interventions;
6. Only recently have there been signs of progress, e.g., declines in the increase of HIV infection among gay males in the United States; a downturn in prevalence among recruits to the Royal Thai Army [8, 9].

It is less surprising in the context of the above to find that of the $2 billion UNICEF estimates to be spent each year on AIDS prevention, only 10 percent reaches the developing world.

Why then is only one-tenth of the AIDS prevention budget going to that part of the world where an estimated 85 percent of the infections are? One obvious answer is that this is simply indicative of where *most* of the international economic resources are being distributed since most of the control is exerted by the economically developed countries (a North vs. South phenomenon).

A less obvious answer is that the enormity of the AIDS pandemic as viewed, say from Geneva or New York, is far less likely to be as significant as from a "developing" country's capital city. Simply put, the sheer numbers of deaths in the developing world, not to mention disabilities, due to other health-related factors, still are considerably greater than those occurring from AIDS. For example, some 17 million people were killed by infectious diseases in 1995, including 9 million from clearly preventable causes such as diarrhea and pneumonia. Although the view from WHO in Geneva may be that the increasing numbers of AIDS-related deaths predicted by the year 2000, particularly in the developing world, should make countries panic, the enormity of the other existing health problems to be dealt with now are still the focus of attention. And these seem to have workable solutions, e.g., immunizations, ORT, etc.

A recitation of some of the litany of annual deaths caused by health problems other than AIDS remains impressive:

3,000,000 persons: TB
3,000,000 children: diarrhea;
4,000,000 children: pneumonia/acute lower respiratory infections;
500,000 infants: neonatal tetanus; and
5-600,000 maternal mortalities: pregnancy, abortion, and childbirth [10].

Given the levels of poverty, armed conflicts, inadequate distribution of social and economic resources, lack of access to safe water, to adequate sanitation and to health services, and the inadequate budgets allocated for other development activities, the prognosis for effective AIDS prevention is not optimistic.

Faced with an array of daunting challenges, the modern world has increasingly placed its faith in the power of science to discover the forces that will enable us to tame those elements of the natural world that bring harm to humankind. From antibiotics to vaccines to heart transplants, the triumphs of modern science are impressive to the point of awe. Can not the same science tell us how to tame those noxious elements of human behavior? The jury is out. The application of the tenets and methods of the natural sciences model to predict and control human behavior has given rise to a number of ethical and epistemological concerns.

COMMUNITY HEALTH EDUCATION APPLICATIONS
OF SOCIAL AND BEHAVIORAL THEORY

A fractious debate has arisen about the current direction of the field of community health education [11]. The predominant view is that health education is the social and behavioral science wing of public health, and as such, the purpose of health education is to import social scientific theories developed in psychology, social psychology, and other social science disciplines to assist public health professionals in achieving public health goals. Specifically, for those modern public health problems that have a behavioral etiology, health education is supposed to provide explanatory models that will enable practitioners to intervene and prevent the complicit behaviors from being enacted.

The development of these theories is modeled on the experimental, hypothesis-testing paradigm used in the natural sciences. The ultimate test of the validity of a theoretical model entails a double-blind trial with random assignment of subjects to treatment and control groups (exactly like the trials of new medications). An alternative view of the field is that community health education is an inherently ethical and political activity, and as such, the work of practitioners should be guided by principles reflecting respect for the dignity and autonomy of each individual. The validity of this type of health education practice is evidenced by the felt capacities of the individuals to lead their lives more fulfilled, less blindly, more courageously, with greater integration, awareness and insight.

In the dominant view, researchers have developed and tested a relatively well-defined set of theories that have demonstrated certain predictive power. The names of these theories are familiar to anyone in the field: the Health Belief Model, Social Learning Theory, the Theory of Reasoned Action, the Diffusion of Innovations, Cognitive Dissonance Theory, the Theory of Protective Motivation, the Transtheoretical Model, Social Marketing, Social Support, and so on. Each of these theories has identified a small number of discrete independent variables (typically 4-6) that have been shown to stand in a causal relationship to the dependent variable of interest, which in the social sciences is usually people's behavior. That is, researchers have hypothesized—and by now repeatedly demonstrated—that a change in the independent variables of these theories will cause a predictable change in the dependent variable. To give a concrete example using the Health Belief Model, researchers have shown that increasing people's "perceived susceptibility" (their perception of the likelihood that they will contract a given disease) will result in a behavior change, such as taking action to decrease their susceptibility. The implications for putting theory into practice are obvious, with one small caveat.

In the natural sciences, including the bio-medical sciences, there are definite, absolute cause-and-effect relationships between different objects. In the germ theory of disease, researchers discovered the micro-organisms that were the necessary and sufficient causes of disease (e.g., diphtheria, cholera, pertussis, pneumonia, etc.). In the same way, bio-medical researchers now think that the Human Immunodeficiency Virus (HIV) is the necessary and sufficient cause of AIDS and they are searching for pharmaceutical drugs that will kill this biological agent absolutely, all the time in all people.

But, while it once may have been hoped that social science theories could account for comparably high levels of the variability in human behavior, it is now accepted that the identified independent variables are not absolutely determinate, but rather are more accurately characterized in terms of probabilities. It is not definitely, absolutely certain that a change in perceived susceptibility will cause a precise predictable amount of change in behavior, but rather such a change is now regarded as just making a change in behavior *more likely*. In this, the social and behavioral sciences have arrived at the same point as the modern foundations of epidemiology, where etiological conditions are now largely viewed as *risk factors.* Just as it is not certain that smoking, cholesterol, and hypertension will inevitably result in a heart attack but only that they make it more likely, so the variables identified and defined by the various social scientific theories are now understood as "risk factors" which make certain behaviors more or less likely.

To apply theory, the prevailing view recommends (or more strongly, directs) that the practitioner conduct a baseline assessment of the specified independent variables defined in a given theory to determine the most promising points for intervention. To put the Health Belief Model into practice, the practitioner should conduct a pre-intervention survey of the model's six independent variables: perceived susceptibility to AIDS, perceived severity of AIDS, perceived barriers to changing behaviors, perceived benefits to changing behaviors, cues to action (socio-environmental prompts, such as a doctor's advice), and, with its recent incorporation into the model, perceived self-efficacy. From the baseline survey of the target population, practitioners can find out where to intervene. For example, in a given population, they might learn that their perceptions of the severity of AIDS are quite high, but their perceived susceptibility to AIDS and perceived self-efficacy in using condoms (or cleaning needles) are low. From this information, they then know that, in designing an educational intervention for this population, they do not need to increase their perception of the severity of AIDS (since it is already high), but instead would be better off focusing on increasing their sense of susceptibility and self-efficacy.

After completing this type of needs assessment, the practitioners then need to design an educational intervention that will have an impact on the variables that emerge in the baseline survey. So, they might invite someone who is HIV+ to attend who has many characteristics in common with the target audience so that they can see that someone just like themselves got infected, and thereby, increase their sense of susceptibility. (The idea for bringing in someone like the target audience is borrowed from the Diffusion of Innovations theory, where researchers have demonstrated that *homophilous* speakers are more effective in producing changes than people who are unlike [*heterophilous*] the target audience.) And they might line up someone to demonstrate how to use a condom and ask the audience to practice at home (before the need arises) to increase their sense of self-efficacy, or confidence in their ability, to carry out the desired new behavior. (The concepts of *modeling* and *behavioral rehearsal* are taken from Social Learning Theory.)

To evaluate the effectiveness of the educational intervention, the practitioners should then conduct a follow-up survey. From the follow-up survey, they can learn three things. First, they will find out if the educational intervention had its intended impact: did the target audience's perceived susceptibility and perceived self-efficacy increase when compared to the results of the baseline survey? If there is no change, then they know they need to go back and redesign the educational program. Second, they may learn something about the magnitude of

the change. For example, a common measure of things like perceived susceptibility and perceived self-efficacy is a 7-point scale, running from 1—"Not
at all" susceptible (or confident) to 7—"Very susceptible" (or "extremely confident"). A program that causes a 3-point shift in people's responses (say, from an
average of 2.5 at the time of baseline to 5.5 after the intervention) can be
considered more effective and more likely to be successful in producing behavior
change than a program that causes a half-point shift. Finally, they will learn if the
changes in the targeted variables produce the desired changes in behavior. At
baseline and follow-up, they can ask people how frequently they use condoms,
for example. They may then assess how effectively they used the condoms. If
effective condom use has gone up as predicted by increases in susceptibility and
self-efficacy, then the program is considered a success. Producing this type of
behavior change is ultimately the whole point of utilizing social and behavioral
theories. It is the science of prevention.

So, what then is the problem? The *first* problem with the *dominant perspective*
on community health education approaches to prevention is that it has repeatedly
been shown that these theories account for only a small amount of the variability
in people's behaviors. The best have explained 40 percent of the variance at most
in statistical models. Hence, the application of these theories produces quite
modest results.

Second, critics suggest that these theories do little more than dress up
common sense in arcane, academic jargon. They question whether we need a
scientifically-proven Theory to tell us that people who think they are more
likely to contract a disease are more likely to do something about it than
people who do not think they are as likely to get the disease. Or that people
who think it is more serious are more likely to do something than people who
do not think it is very serious. Or that people who feel more confident are
more likely to take action than those who do not feel so confident. As a colleague
of ours once remarked, it seems here "The purpose of research is to document
the obvious."

Third, because the scientific paradigm seeks the common, generalizable,
universal features of situations, these theories are not sensitive to cultural variations. Indeed, the value of this kind of theorizing is considered directly propor-
tional to the degree to which they can be applied across the broadest range of
situations, e.g., the Health Belief Model can be used no matter what the age,
gender, race, ethnicity, or religion of the target population. None of these theories
regard race or ethnicity as an independent variable of interest (because they
cannot be manipulated, and hence, their effect tested, of course); rather, they are
treated as control conditions about which researchers' major concern is the
"noise" they introduce into the equations. Thus, their application becomes particularly problematic when "majority" practitioners are working with minority
populations; they do not tell the practitioner anything about what is appropriate or
relevant in interactions with minorities.

Fourth, critics are concerned that the dominant view has an inherent tendency toward *victim-blaming*. Because of the complexity of the social world, it is extraordinarily difficult to test hypotheses that go much beyond the individual level. It is much more feasible to conduct experiments examining a discrete set of variables at the individual level than it is to test hypotheses about open dynamic social systems. Hence, the vast majority of scientifically-validated theories used in health education today come from the psychology and social-psychology of individual behavior, with few, if any, comparably representative theories from the sociology or anthropology of populations and cultures. Because of this bias, the target of change is almost invariably located in the individual, rather than in environmental conditions, when these theories are applied. If behavior is a function of the interaction of person and environment, as Lewin propounded, then much more attention to the latter variable remains needed.

Fifth, as many of the readings presented here in the section *Innovations in Practice* show, programs that have not restricted themselves to the relatively small set of confirmed, conclusively-proven causal independent variables have produced better results. The most recent documented signs of tangible progress, i.e., declines in HIV infection rates, seem to have been among gay males in the United States and among recruits in the Royal Thai Army. The clear correlation of effective educational interventions to change sexual behavior (e.g., the "100 percent condom" campaign in northern Thailand) with these declines in infection suggest the value of such interventions. In the case of the United States, they demonstrate the value of community action and peer educational approaches. In the face of a global epidemic of tragic proportions, practitioners have felt it necessary to go well beyond what are perceived to be the relatively feeble, banal targets offered by social scientific theories to try more creative approaches that resonate more deeply with their experience and understanding of the needs of those at risk.

Sixth, scientific theories are not well-equipped to help practitioners operate in a contentious political environment. The AIDS epidemic brings together sex, drugs, homosexuality, youth, people of color, and other issues that push people's buttons. Prevention programs are not put forward in a vacuum. The "objective," "value-neutral" stance of the dominant view ill-prepares health educators to respond to the value-laden, moral and political claims raised by opponents of AIDS education programs.

Finally, the scientific model has encountered resistance from the very populations it is ostensibly intended to save. People reject being treated as guinea pigs. While critics have been more vociferous with respect to drug trials, where the stakes are much higher, more and more communities are objecting to the idea of being randomly allocated to treatment or control groups in the name of a science over which they have no control. There is a growing sense of distrust about whose interests are being served. And with revelations about the vacillations, backtracking and political maneuverings that characterized the early years in the official fight against the epidemic, those populations at highest risk have developed a deep cynicism and healthy distrust of government-sponsored programs. Thus, the science of prevention is not proceeding as smoothly as advocates once hoped in the quest for conclusively effective prevention techniques. Yet the task cannot wait. *So let us now take a closer look.*

BOOK OVERVIEW

The twenty-one articles in this book cover AIDS prevention programs and issues in some nine countries and four continents. Seven articles deal with five African countries: Ghana, Nigeria, Sierra Leone, Zambia, and Zimbabwe. Another covers Africa more broadly. Two are set in the Caribbean and Latin America (Mexico and Trinidad) and one in Asia (Singapore). Eight articles are U.S. based. The others are more globally focused. Three of the U.S. articles deal with minority groups: Asian and Pacific Islanders, Black communities, and migrant Hispanic farmworkers.

Most of the articles were written during the 1990s and their authors come from a wide range of public health, social work, cultural, social, and behavioral science experience and backgrounds. Some are expatriates serving in resident advisory capacities; others are university professors carrying out behavioral baseline survey research. Local and region non-governmental and public sector social and health agency managers and program implementors constitute the remainder.

These twenty-one articles, excepting the introductory essay, were selected from the several dozen articles on AIDS prevention which appeared primarily in Volumes 10 through 16 of the journal, *International Quarterly of Community Health Education* [12] published by Baywood Publishing (USA). The articles were selected by two of its editors on the basis of their readability and relevance to the programs, problems, issues, and context of global AIDS education as treated in the *Journal*. Choice also was influenced by the desire to provide a *Reader on AIDS Prevention* which could be useful to social scientists and public health, social welfare, and development specialists—as well as serve as useful supplementary text for students in an undergraduate or graduate course on public health or AIDS prevention and education.

Each article needed to be included in one of the three sections of the book:

1. *The Science of Prevention: Doctrine and Dogma;*
2. *Voices of Dissent;* and
3. *Innovations in Field Practice.*

The first section, comprising six articles, examines current scientific approaches to determining preventive needs. It represents the traditional view. Social, cultural and behavioral approaches relevant to large-scale field programs are discussed in terms of meeting public needs, particularly those of youth and the disenfranchised. Some of the more prevalent uses of traditional behavioral and educational models are examined in program context.

The second section provides seven articles in which some of the skeptics and dissenters call attention to the politics of AIDS (even the accepted paradigm of causation), plead for program decision-making roles for minorities and women, and question the commitment of specific governments and the international agencies, even the whole idea that there has been progress in AIDS prevention.

The third section, with seven articles, highlights innovative community approaches to AIDS education and prevention: involving traditional healers; using drama and songs in community education; community-based and controlled planning.

The extent to which this collection of articles serves its purpose is both enhanced and hindered by the editorial judgment of its editors who were free to choose what they wanted for this edition as well as the universe of the *Journal* from which the articles were selected.

SECTION I:
THE SCIENCE OF PREVENTION: DOCTRINE AND DOGMA

The articles in the first section are arranged in rough approximation of the recommended order of scientific research. In an ideal, textbook world, researchers should start with *exploratory* studies, seeking to discover unknown causes as they embark on new areas of research. If little is known about a new problem, one needs to keep an open mind to all possible influences. The first two chapters in this section are examples of exploratory research. From this exploration, researchers can then move on to examine the more promising possibilities in more systematic fashion.

In *descriptive* studies, the researchers formulate hypotheses about causal relationships between independent factors—identified in the first (exploratory) stage of the research program—and the dependent variable of interest (viz., risky behaviors). Researchers "operationalize" the variables to define and measure them in a rigorous (objective, reliable, and valid) process, e.g., through the development of scales on survey questionnaires. The next three chapters here are representative of descriptive research. If statistically significant correlations are uncovered, researchers can then progress to the most important test of whether or not the hypothesized factor is truly a cause of behavior, namely, *experimental* research. Subjects are randomly assigned to treatment and control groups and the experimental group is exposed to an intervention designed to manipulate the hypothesized cause to see if this experiment leads to the predicted results. The final chapter in this section provides an excellent example of this type of experimental research design now commonly used in the behavioral sciences. Highlights of each article follow.

The *Science of Prevention* section opens with "Sexual Practices That May Favor the Transmission of HIV in a Rural Community in Nigeria." As indicated, it is exploratory research, not hypothesis-testing. Using focus groups and in-depth interviews, the researchers were interested in uncovering information about the sexual practices of local residents that could promote the transmission of the virus in small relatively isolated communities. They found that the frequent recourse to prostitutes due to taboos about intercourse while one's wife is breastfeeding and the common practice of engaging in extra-marital affairs as a step toward polygamous unions were the most common sexual behaviors that would put villagers at high risk for infection.

In another thought-provoking exploratory study, "Perceived Barriers to HIV Prevention among University Students in Sierra Leone, West Africa," almost one-fifth of the respondents agreed with the statement, "There is no real threat of AIDS in Africa; rather, there is a conspiracy to keep Africans from having sex and children." Reflecting cultural norms, 59 percent thought it was the male's responsibility to bring up the issue of "safer sex," with men twice as likely as women to agree with this. In addition, fully 90 percent of these college students did not know that the greatest number of AIDS cases have occurred in Africa. The implications for educational interventions are apparent.

The third chapter, "AIDS-Related Knowledge, Attitudes, Beliefs, and Behavioral Intentions of Adolescents in Trinidad: A Pilot Study," employs one of the most basic theories in health education, the KAP, or Knowledge—Attitudes—Practices, model. Here, the theory is that a change in people's knowledge (information) will cause a change in their attitudes (feelings), which in turn will cause a change in their behavior. The task of health education would be much simpler if the causes of human behavior were indeed structured so straightforwardly. But, as discovered in countless other studies, the researchers found little relationship between the amount of information or knowledge that students had about AIDS and their intentions to engage in safer sexual practices (like limiting their number of partners, waiting until marriage to have sex, and discussing condom use with their partner). Ironically, results such as these provide a sort of backhanded justification for further scientific research and expert professional interventions. If the naive belief that, if people know how the disease is transmitted, then they will protect themselves, turns out *not* to be true, then we must seek to discover the more subtle arcane causes that are actually motivating people's behavior. By extension, these can only be found through the rigorous application of highly technical sophisticated scientific methods designed and executed by qualified researchers.

The fourth chapter is titled "Preventing HIV Infection among Juvenile Delinquents: Educational Diagnosis using the Health Belief Model." The research focuses on a youthful population at very high risk for infection and makes use of the Health Belief Model—perhaps the most widely cited scientific theory in the public health education literature—to try to discover strategic points of intervention. Based on measures of current levels of factors identified in the Health Belief Model (i.e., perceived susceptibility, perceived severity, etc.), the study asks and answers which factors need to be targeted to cause these high-risk youth to change their behavior. Consistent with a vast body of literature, the results show that those youth who do not perceive themselves to be susceptible to infection (e.g., 92% agreed with the statement, "I am too young to get an HIV infection") and who perceive significant barriers to initiating safer sex practices (e.g., 62% agreed that "Condoms decrease pleasure during sex") are more likely to state that they do not intend to use condoms during sex than those who feel they are susceptible and the barriers less daunting. The implications from this research are that practitioners need to increase these youths' sense of their own susceptibility and reduce their perceptions of the barriers to practicing safer sex. Interestingly, contrary to the theory's predictions, those youth who express a high level of self-efficacy with respect to condom use (e.g., "I am able to make sure a condom is used with a new sex partner") expressed a low level of intention to use condoms consistently. The contradictory findings—the lack of support for the hypothesized relationship between self-efficacy and intentions—are quite common in this type of research. From these contradictory results, practitioners are left largely to draw their own conclusions.

The fifth chapter, "Use of Health Belief Model to Predict Condom Use among University Students in Nigeria," returns to the popular Health Belief Model. The research demonstrates the *generalizability* of the theory, yielding results comparable to those found when it is applied to subjects in the United States. The results of this research show statistically significant correlations between the model's independent variables of benefits, barriers, and cues to action and intention to use condoms. These statistically significant correlations range from a high of .28 to a low of .13. Gender (female) was also correlated at .25. The study also found significant differences in levels of the independent variables for benefits, barriers and cues to action between those who had used condoms in the past and those who had not. The modest results—the strongest correlation was .28 and comparable to the impact of demographic control variables like gender—are likewise typical of findings generated in this type of research.

The final chapter in this section, "The Role of Threat and Efficacy in AIDS Prevention," uses a fully experimental research design. This study examines the long-fascinating use of fear in motivating behavior change. Drawing on Rogers's Protection Motivation Theory, the study confirms that fear—in and of itself—is insufficient and indeed somewhat counterproductive in stimulating people to mend their ways. Fear alone paralyzes people. But when messages about the threat of disease are combined with information about the steps necessary to reduce the threat, the combination produces high levels of change, as shown again in this research.

SECTION II: VOICES OF DISSENT

The lead chapter of this section, "The Viral Model for AIDS: Paradigmatic Dominance, Politics, or Best Approximation of Reality?" opens up the forum for dissension. It brings again to public attention continuing questions about the etiology of AIDS as well as the consequences if the generally accepted HIV viral causal hypothesis is incorrect. Why is it that a single explanation for the epidemic of immune system suppression has dominated scientific discourse on AIDS despite viewpoints of other proponents?

The next and eighth chapter, "AIDS Communication: What Predicts Health Professionals' Decisions?" is a fascinating study of what theoretical perspectives predominate in AIDS communication practice and why? U.S. college students, medical professionals, and health educators were asked to design an AIDS communication program for a student audience. The dangers of using a "naive psychology" and fear appeals in designing programs are reviewed as well as the skills-oriented approach of health educators using interactive educational involvement.

"Another Crack in the Mirror: The Politics of AIDS Prevention in Mexico," the ninth chapter, is a well-documented piece of research which traces the emergence of AIDS prevention efforts in Mexico. It critically examines the problems of "importing" programs from the United States to a country where social and political conditions are quite different. Possible directions for future development of AIDS prevention in the specific social context of Mexico are provided.

Asian and Pacific Islanders are the fastest growing cultural groups in the United States. This tenth chapter, "HIV/AIDS in Asian and Pacific Islander Communities in the U.S.: A Review, Analysis and Integration" uses an AIDS Risk Reduction Model as an integrating framework to review the state of knowledge, attitudes, beliefs and behaviors associated with HIV/AIDS among Asian and Pacific Islanders living in the United States. Implications for culturally specific community health education programs are discussed.

"Sociology of AIDS Within Black Communities: Theoretical Considerations" is the next selection. This retrospective review of the AIDS crisis among Black Americans during the 1980s tries to provide theoretical orientations to help health educators better serve Black communities at risk during the 1990s. Conflict, functionalist, and interactionist theories are used to examine "economic stratification," "social dysfunction and marginality," and "deviance and labeling" respectively. Policy considerations and recommendations are provided to make AIDS prevention programs more relevant.

Chapter 12, "AIDS in the African Press," is a content analysis of AIDS coverage of government-owned newspapers in Kenya, Nigeria, Senegal, Togo, and Uganda over 1985-89. The political and psychological progression over time from stages of denial, scapegoating, and blame to responding constructively to the AIDS epidemic are chronicled.

The last contribution to this section on dissent is "Women and the Risk of HIV Infection in Nigeria: Implications for Control Programs." It focuses on ethical and cultural issues relating to gender that need attention in social sector planning. The susceptibility and degree of vulnerability of Nigerian women to STD infection are emphasized. Social, cultural, and economic inequities related to gender are presented in terms of their effect on women's susceptibility to AIDS, e.g., existing double standards for male and female sexual activity and economic conditions pressing women into commercial sex work. Suggestions to reduce risk are made.

SECTION III:
INNOVATIONS IN FIELD PRACTICE

The opening chapter under this section, "Theory and Action for Effective Condom Promotion: Illustrations from a Behavior Intervention Project for Sex Workers in Singapore," describes a unique AIDS/STD education program for female sex workers in Singapore. Low self-efficacy, inadequate negotiation skills, and employment security concerns were identified as barriers to brothel-based workers getting clients to use condoms. A community health education theoretical framework is used and tested which increased workers' capabilities in promoting safe sex. Included are cartoons used in the educational program.

Research findings from a baseline survey of farm workers, Paulo Freire's Social Change Theory and the Ecological Model for Health Promotion are integrated to develop a participatory intervention for HIV-AIDS prevention in Zimbabwe in our next and fifteenth chapter, "Using Theory to Design an Intervention for HIV/AIDS Prevention for Farm Workers in rural Zimbabwe." The first stage of the intervention uses innovative methods to encourage appraisal of HIV/AIDS vulnerability. The second stage emphasizes developing cognitive and attitude change. Self-protective behavior was encouraged through condom use and increased self-efficacy in negotiating safe sex. The last stage developed a climate for behavior maintenance.

The sixteenth chapter, "Was the Intervention Implemented as Intended?: A Process Evaluation of an AIDS Prevention Intervention in Rural Zimbabwe," describes the process evaluation of the HIV/AIDS education program above. The reader learns what happened and how. Highlighted is the way in which social issues outside the scope of the educational intervention may affect the program's successes and failures.

The seventeenth chapter, "The Potential of Drama and Songs as Channels for AIDS Education in Africa: A Report on Focus Group Findings from Ghana," provides a detailed account of the effectiveness of drama and songs in carrying out AIDS education in Ghana. Focus groups are used to evaluate the impact of one drama troupe on AIDS knowledge, attitude, and behavior.

"Needle Sharing for the Use of Therapeutic Drugs as a Potential AIDS Risk Behavior Among Migrant Hispanic Farmworkers in the Eastern Stream" explores knowledge of AIDS, patterns of sexual behavior, and self-injection for therapeutic reasons through interviews with Hispanic migrant workers in the Eastern United States. Ways for AIDS health education to address the cultural pattern of therapeutic self-injection are suggested.

Traditional healers in Zambia once provided little support to the nationwide AIDS education program. This nineteenth chapter, "Enlisting the Support of Traditional Healers in an AIDS Education Campaign in Zambia," chronicles the successful efforts of the health education unit of the Ministry of Health to implement a workshop on AIDS for such traditional medicine practitioners.

The last chapter in this section, "The CEPA Project: A New Model for Community-Based Program Planning," describes an innovative HIV prevention program model for Puerto Ricans living in Massachusetts. It is based on models of critical thinking, empowerment and participatory education. The basic philosophy of the CEPA Project is to narrow the gap between program developers and program recipients to the greatest extent possible. Successes and challenges in approaching this ideal are reviewed.

REFERENCES

1. Morbidity and Mortality Weekly Report (MMWR), "First 500,000 AIDS Cases—United States, 1995," *MMWR, 44*:6, pp. 49-853, U.S. Department of Health and Human Services, Public Health Service, November 24, 1995.
2. P. Rosenberg, Scope of the AIDS Epidemic in the United States, *Science, 270,* pp. 1372-1375, November 24, 1995.
3. World Health Organization, *WHO Global Programme on AIDS,* Geneva, September 1993.
4. World Health Organization, *The World Health Report: 1996,* Geneva, 1996.
5. UNICEF, *The State of the World's Children,* Oxford University Press, Oxford, 1995.
6. World Health Organization, *Global AIDS News, 2,* pp. 1-3, 1995.
7. World Vision, *Partners, 5*:4, p. 2, 1996.
8. B. G. Weniger and T. Brown, Editorial: The March of AIDS through Asia, *New England Journal of Medicine, 335*:6, pp. 343-344, 1996.
9. K. E. Nelson et al., Changes in Sexual Behavior and a Decline in HIV Infection among Young Men in Thailand, *New England Journal of Medicine, 335*:6, pp. 297-303, 1996.
10. World Health Organization, *Implementation of the Global Strategy for Health for All by the Year 2000: Second Evaluation,* Vol. 1, Geneva, 1993.
11. M. Minkler, Health Education, Health Promotion and the Open Society: An Historical Perspective, *Health Education Quarterly, 16*:1, pp. 17-30, 1989.
12. *International Quarterly of Community Health Education,* Vols. 10-16, 1989-96.

I

THE SCIENCE OF PREVENTION: DOCTRINE AND DOGMA

CHAPTER 1

Sexual Practices that May Favor the Transmission of HIV in a Rural Community in Nigeria

Ademola J. Ajuwon, Oladimeji Oladepo,
Joshua D. Adeniyi, and William R. Brieger

Acquired Immune Deficiency Syndrome (AIDS) and its causative agent, Human Immunodeficiency Virus (HIV), pose serious public health problems in Nigeria. Since 1986, when the first cases of AIDS were reported in the country, the number of persons infected with HIV has increased rapidly. In 1988, only twelve (0.23%) of 5,238 people screened nationwide were seropositive [1]. By May 1992, of the 233,710 screened, 3,519 (1.5%) were seropositive [2]. Although HIV and AIDS have been reported among different segments of the population including apparently healthy persons [1], clients of sexually trans-mitted diseases (STDs) clinics, pregnant women attending antenatal clinics, and tuberculosis patients, the highest risk group remains commercial sex workers (CSWs) [3].

In Nigeria, several governmental and non-governmental organizations have initiated AIDS campaigns, which have raised the level of public awareness about the problem in recent years [4]. Despite greater awareness among the population, AIDS risk practices remain widespread throughout the country. For example, the prevalence of unprotected sexual networking has been reported to be high in both urban and rural areas [5] as well as along major trucking routes between urban centers [6]. Prostitution flourishes in most urban areas [7]. Under this situation and considering the pattern of the AIDS epidemic in other sub-saharan African countries, AIDS is likely to have a profound impact in Nigeria in the next few years [3].

In the absence of a known cure or vaccine, the most feasible way of preventing further spread of AIDS is modification of high risk behaviors through education. Bringing about such change requires in-depth information, not only about the nature of the behaviors, but also the social and cultural factors that facilitate them [8]. This understanding is crucial since sexual behaviors, the principal mode of HIV transmission, are especially difficult to influence due to the taboos and social pressures surrounding them [9].

Although AIDS has been primarily an urban phenomenon in Nigeria to date [10], its spread to rural areas is highly likely [5]. Unfortunately, not enough is currently known about the nature and degree of risky sexual practices and the belief system underlying them in Nigeria, particularly in rural areas, where health care, education, and social service systems are weakest. This study therefore has begun to address the gap in knowledge about rural sexual patterns through an explorative, in-depth study of potential HIV transmission behaviors and their cultural context in a rural Yoruba community in northern Oyo State.

THE STUDY AREA

Ago-Are, the site for this study, is a rural community situated approximately 150 kilometers north of Ibadan, the capital of Oyo State, Nigeria, and is inhabited by approximately 15,000 residents. In Ago-Are, the basic social unit is the extended family compound, which physically consists of a cluster of houses occupied by paternally related persons, their spouses and children. Although Christianity and Islam are the dominant religions, the African traditional value system dictates patterns of relationships. There is a strong allegiance to the kinship system based on blood and marriage ties. Polygyny flourishes in the community.

Although Ago-Are is inhabited primarily by Yorubas, there are other Nigerian ethnic groups found in the area as well as migrants from Ghana and Benin Republic. These non-indigenes are, for the most part, seasonal farm laborers. Subsistence farming is the major occupation of the local male citizens, while women are mainly petty traders.

As in most rural communities in Nigeria, the bulk of the young, educated citizens work outside the community in urban centers scattered across the country. In spite of their prolonged physical absence from their traditional homes, a majority of these urban-based citizens still maintain strong relationships with family members and friends in Ago-Are. This is manifested in annual visits during holidays and for ceremonies such as funerals and weddings. In addition, these urban residents also belong to social and other organizations based in Ago-Are, and come home for occasional meetings.

A variety of indigenous and modern health care options are available in Ago-Are. There is a local government maternity center/dispensary, three private clinics and ten patent medicine stores. However, government clinics are known for chronic drug shortages, and private clinics for their exorbitant fees. Thus, the patent medicine shops enjoy the highest patronage as a source of modern medicine, and in addition to the prepackaged remedies that they are legally allowed to sell, many prescribe antibiotics, dress wounds, and administer injections.

Indigenous health care providers are of three types. There are itinerant herbalists who hawk herbs and concoctions said to be a cure for ailments ranging from gonorrhoea to dysentery. Home-based healers provide both curative and preventive services, the latter of which is often in the form of charms and prophylactic herbal mixtures. There are also the local surgeons, known as *olólà*, who visit the town to perform circumcisions and scarification. The implications for such practices on HIV transmission was also explored [11], and will be presented in a future article.

METHODS

Qualitative research methods were used in Ago-Are for two reasons. First, by their nature, qualitative methods are well suited for the collection of in-depth information required to plan culturally appropriate health education programs aimed at influencing sexually risky behaviors such as those involved in AIDS transmission [8, 9, 12]. Second, the sensitive nature of the subject makes it difficult to elicit truthful responses from formal quantitative surveys, whereas a qualitative approach can ensure a harvest of valid data [13]. This was considered imperative given the existence of Yoruba taboos regarding sex. Public discussion about sexual intercourse is considered obscene, and reference to it, when it is deemed absolutely necessary, is usually euphemistic [14-16].

Data was collected from three study populations, opinion leaders as key informants, female CSWs, and the general population of reproductive age. Opinion leaders included the heads of the biggest male and female voluntary associations (membership of 50 and 40 married people respectively), three religious leaders (Christian, Moslem, and African), and two honorary chiefs (1 male and 1 female). In-depth interviews with the key informants were conducted by the principal author in the Yoruba language using an open-ended guide. Background information on Ago-Are was sought as was insight into sexual practices involving multiple partners and the social and cultural context of these practices.

The key informants identified the CSWs in Ago-Are. Given the central role played by CSWs in HIV transmission in Africa [17, 18], plans were made to observe their activities and interview them. Unobtrusive observation of their clientele was done for two hours daily (1 morning, 1 evening) on Mondays, Wednesdays, and Sundays for a period of one month at a local hotel where some CSWs were based. Informal interviews were used to obtain CSWs' history of prostitution and any measures they may have taken to prevent STDs.

Focus Group Discussions (FGDs) were conducted among the general population of reproductive age (≥ 15 years) to gain further insight into the nature and cultural aspects of sexual practices identified by the key informants. To encourage free discussion, small, demographically homogeneous groups were formed [19]. A theoretical sampling process was used [20], based on the variables of marital status and sex. Five of the approximately fifty family compounds were randomly selected for the recruitment of FGD participants. Each of the five selected compounds was visited, and the names, sex, and marital status of eligible persons was recorded. From this list of names, six-eight persons were selected to form twelve discussion groups, three for married males, three for married females, and three each for females and males who had never married.

A discussion guide was developed based on the key informant interviews. The guide contained items on the social and cultural factors influencing pre-marital and extra-marital sexual relationships, prostitution, and the participants' level of awareness of the risks associated with these practices. Six male and female residents with at least a high school education were trained as moderators. Sessions were conducted in the Yoruba language, recorded on tape and later transcribed.

FINDINGS

The results of the study are presented under four main headings, those concerning commercial sex work, pre-marital sexual relationships, extra-marital sexual relationships, and marriage customs. Perceived risks from these activities are mentioned.

Commercial Sex Work

All key informants agreed that prostitution is a socially disapproved behavior. As a Moslem leader said, "It is shameful for a decent Yoruba man to patronize these prostitutes."

Nine CSWs were identified in Ago-Are at the start of the study. Seven were Nigerians (including 1 Yoruba), and two were from Ghana. They had been in their business an average of three years, and resident in Ago-Are on average nine months. All had worked in other places including metropolitan areas like Lagos, large towns like Oyo and Shaki, and smaller nearby towns like Tede and Irawo. The CSWs were observed to be quite mobile. Two left town during the study, and another two arrived to replace them.

Five of the CSWs solicited and lived in a hotel, while the remainder rented houses in town. The hotel charged them N2.00[1] per night, and they in turn charged their clients N2.00 per encounter. All night service cost N10.00. During weekdays, these five CSWs averaged three clients each and five on Sundays.

---

[1] This amount is approximately US $0.20.

Clients were said to include local residents, men from nearby towns and migrant farm laborers. The latter were the majority, especially on Sundays when they were free to come to town from the surrounding farms. Not all CSWs were very discerning about their clientele. As one of the women from Ghana said,

> It is hard to tell (who your clients are), because working is like being in a market where you sell to a lot of people. So, how can you know all the people who buy something from you? Sometimes, it is night, and you cannot see who it is. You are working; you do not look at people's faces before you provide service.

When asked about their awareness of the risk involved in prostitution, all the women mentioned gonorrhoea, but none said AIDS. To limit their risk from STDs, three women reported taking "capsules" as prophylaxis, while two others received weekly "injections" from patent medicine sellers. None of the women reported ever insisting that a client use a condom during sexual intercourse.

Participants in the FGDs were aware that the CSWs were not indigenes of the town and that few local men were clients. Migrant workers and drivers were two groups singled out as customers of the CSWs. It was said of drivers who come to Ago-Are to obtain agricultural produce that, "While they wait for their vehicles to load, the drivers visit prostitutes to relax."

Local men were said to use CSW services discretely and generally at night, while clients from other areas demanded sex at any time. One member discerned the pattern of patronage as follows:

> In terms of not hiding it, not being ashamed and regarding it as normal, the non-indigenes stand out as the clients of prostitutes in (the hotel). They regard visiting the prostitutes as normal, even in the morning. But with we Yoruba, we may delay our visits until night time when we go there secretly. But to go there in broad daylight! Only a few Yoruba men will attempt that, except he is a visitor from another town.

Participants were split along gender lines in their interpretation of reasons why men seek the services of CSWs. Male respondents pointed to the fact that the majority of clients were migrant workers, and being separated from their wives for long periods of time, found prostitutes a cheap and convenient outlet for meeting their sexual needs. Local men and those from nearby were said to seek out CSWs to satisfy a need for sexual variety.

Female respondents implicated the traditional post-partum sexual abstinence period as the major factor. This is based on the belief that sexual intercourse will spoil breastmilk and make the new baby sick. They explained that few men could abstain for up to two years, and if they did not have other wives, they would go to CSWs to satisfy their sexual desires until they could resume normal relations with their wives. "Convenience" was the term used to describe why non-indigenous men patronized CSWs. That is it was easier for them to meet CSWs than local Ago-Are women.

All respondents agreed that risks were involved in having sexual intercourse with CSWs, especially STDS, but AIDS was mentioned in only three groups. Two types of *àtòsi* (gonorrhoea) were described, *àtòtsi ègbe* (dry gonorrhoea) and *àtòsi elèro* (wet gonorrhoea). The former was associated with pain on urination and likely to lead to death, but has no visible symptoms. It might stay in the body, even after treatment, and could relapse anytime. The wet type was recognized by discharge like water drops. Tuberculosis was also thought to be spread through relations with CSWs. Female participants added further that association with CSWs could lead men to adopt other unhealthy behaviors such as cigarette smoking and abuse of alcohol.

Pre-marital Sexual Relationships

All key informants noted that while pre-marital sexual activities are common in the town, this is contrary to custom. Religious leaders lamented increased sexual activity among young people, commenting on young girls (unnamed) having illegitimate babies because the paternity was disputed. Related problems included increased abortions and drop out from secondary school. Reasons elicited for why custom was no longer observed included love of money by young girls, the corrupting influence of Western civilization, lack of control by parents and lack of restraint by adolescents.

FGD participants also agreed that sexually active unmarried young people are a problem in the community. Many participants spoke nostalgically about sexual norms in their youthful days when virginity and chastity were highly valued. Older, married respondents often spoke thus, "In our days, we went to farm early in the morning and returned late in the evening, tired and exhausted. Where was the energy to run after girls?" Or as another said, "In our days, if you are not fully grown up, your parents must *not* find you playing with a girl, much less 'sleeping' with one."

Young, unmarried participants had another perspective. "When I ask for something from my parents, maybe I need money to buy a blouse or something that my friends already have, and my parents cannot give me the money, then I have to go to the person who can give me the money, and I know that boys do not give something for nothing, so I cooperate with them."

Unmarried people blamed their parents using the proverb, "*Esin iwájú ni tii ééyìn nwò sáré*," or a horse takes its cue from the horse ahead of it. In this case they were blaming their parents for setting a bad example. They also blamed their peers. Some young, unmarried women said their friends would call those who observed chastity and virginity as "old fashioned" and "uncivilized." Another proverb expressed the perceived outcome of peer pressure—"*Agùntán tó nb'ájá rin yóó jè gbéé,*" or the sheep that befriends a dog will certainly consume rubbish like the dog.

The exposure to risk and pressure was noted by all because it is now common for young people, during their school holidays, to travel to the cities to visit relatives. Married respondents identified several factors that increased the risk of pre-marital sex. Some said that today, female children were hardly ever satisfied with what their parents could provide. Others noted the lack of job opportunities for young people to keep them busy. The actual risks perceived by the unmarried respondents included unwanted pregnancies among the females and gonorrhoea and AIDS among the males.

Extra-marital Sexual Relationships

Key informants agreed that extra-marital sexual relationships were common in Ago-Are. The other person, whether male or female, is termed *àlè*. Informants explained that the practice was largely based on the customary post-partum sexual abstinence. While both sexes could have expected to be more discrete, men were expected to provide cash or material support for their *àlè*. Relations were expected to occur strictly away from the matrimonial home. Some informants claimed that some women use the customary abstinence period observed by their husbands to find *àlè* for themselves.

One traditional way of preventing extra-marital relationships was mágùn. This is a charm/curse placed on married women such that any other man who engages in sexual intercourse with her meets an untimely death, often on the spot. The husbands themselves have immunity from the curse. Key informants claimed that today more emphasis is placed on suing adulterers in Customary Court.

FGD respondents agreed also on the need for greater discretion among women during extra-marital relationships. Married female respondents said that inadequate care from husbands pushed women into extra-marital affairs, especially in today's times of economic hardship. As one commented, "Sometimes we are unable to leave our poor husbands and marry men who are better off because we do not want to abandon our children. Instead, we have *àlè* who can assist us financially." In the Yoruba patrilineal society, children belong to the father, and women who divorce their husbands are expected to leave the children with him.

One female participant spoke metaphorically, "*Obìnrin tó lo ko tí ò lálè kòlè ní aso t'égbé ní,*" that is, a married woman without an *àlè* cannot buy the dress used by her social group. Another was blunt about the sexual double standard. "You know that a Yoruba woman cannot have two husbands at the same time. That is impossible. She will have to hide one of them."

Interestingly, while agreeing that some husbands could not care adequately for their wives, the unmarried women's groups blamed certain married women as bad influences on their peers. They cited anonymous examples of married people in the town who had àlè.

The male FGD participants felt that CSWs served as a negative example to married women because of their ostentatious living. Men also blamed women for extra-marital affairs, saying they lacked restraint and were easily seduced by money. A few even claimed that some women even befriend àlè in order to throw lavish parties (during ceremonies like funerals) to impress their peers. Unmarried men blamed husbands who engaged in extra-marital affairs for setting a bad example for their wives.

Extra-marital relationships were said by all groups to be the forerunner to polygamous marriages. Risks of extra-marital relationships mentioned by the FGDs were mágùn, STDs and another sexually transmitted cultural disease known as jèrí jèrí, which presents as severe genital pains.

Key informants described another form of sexual activity that may be either pre-marital or extra-marital, but was characterized as "casual" in nature, as distinct from having àlè or boy/girlfriends. Casual sex was reported to occur during festival periods (e.g., Easter, Id el Kabir, New Year, traditional Masquerades). During this period, citizens working in far away urban areas would come home. These returnees would often bring extra spending money, and during the merriment of the season engage local residents or CSWs in brief sexual encounters.

Finally, extra-marital sexual relations cannot be separated from the issues of polygamy, the status of wives in the family, and divorce. While both key informants and FGD participants agreed that polygamy was more common among Moslem residents, they said that it may be practiced among any person in the town. As noted above, many FGD respondents felt that extra-marital relationships may be a prelude to another marriage in the polygamous standard of the community. The operative word in the preceding statement is "may," as there were clear implications that extra-marital experimentation does not necessarily lead to marriage.

Marriage Customs

There are various aspects of traditional marriage customs that directly or indirectly lead to exposure to additional sexual partners and possible extra-marital sexual activities. An example of the former is the tradition of wife inheritance. After a five-month period of mourning the death of a husband, the husband's brother(s) could make it known to the head of the extended family that he wished to inherit the widow. Women who were not interested in this proposal could refund the bride price to the family before she can remarry outside. Key informants were split on whether this practice is still common in Ago-Are.

All key informants and FGD participants agreed that polygamy is widely practiced, but were divided on whether it was more common among Moslems or cut across all groups. On a related note, male FGD members explained that religion was not really the issue, but that the current hard economic times were a deterrent to polygamy. As one man said,

> In the past, polygamy was something prestigious. But responsibilities were not as burdensome then as they are today. In those days, people go to farms, and there was no schooling, and feeding was not a problem. But today, polygamy is no longer attractive because of the responsibilities involved.

This statement must be viewed in the context of other statements concerning men's desires for sexual variety. In particular, there are implications that if today's financial situation does not permit sexual exploration to evolve into an additional marriage, there may be more longer term extra-marital relationships.

The customary practice of divorce was also considered. The Clerk of the Customary Court served as an additional key informant on this matter. Customary Courts were established in the colonial period and headed by the head chief of the community. They heard disputes related to transactions related to indigenous laws and customs. In theory either the husband or wife can initiate divorce proceedings, but since there is greater financial costs to men (child support until the woman remarries and denial of the right to reclaim the bride price), more women actually initiate proceedings.

In the 134 divorces heard before the Customary Court in Ago Age between 1982 and 1988 (exclusive of 1985 for which records were not available) 96.5 percent were initiated by women. The most common reasons given by these women were "lack of care" (52%), "frequent fighting" (26%) and "no more love or interest" (16%). The only two charges of adultery were initiated by men. The Court Clerk explained that it is difficult for a woman to charge and prove adultery on the part of their husbands, because men could always claim that they were planning marriage with the other women.

When a man sues for divorce, the woman's reputation is severely tarnished, such that she may decide to leave town. Therefore, instead of jeopardizing the woman's future prospects, a man who is dissatisfied with the marriage will ignore the wife. She may ask family members to intervene, but may eventually get the message and ask for a divorce. The implication is that during this period the husband will be engaging in extra-marital relations in the search for a new partner, assuming that such a search has not already taken place and is the reason why he has lost interest in the current wife.

Likewise, when the woman gets the message that a divorce is desired, she must plan how she will refund the bride wealth. This would be most likely paid by a future husband, so she too must be looking around for likely suitors or àlè. Another alternative for the woman is simply to return to her natal family, but such a woman is labeled with the derogatory term, *adálémosú*, which means that she has set up another home and neglected her husband. Marital separation is socially disapproved as it symbolizes an inability to persevere with the normal troubles of married life. Comments about such women, on return to their natal compound include, "*Ilémosú dalérú*," or that they have come to disturb (*dalérú*) the peace of the family and terrorize the other married women there.

Key informants believed that *adálémosú* are sexually active and change partners frequently, since, "They are not under control of any man." Key informants were also divided on whether there were many of these women in town, or only a few.

FGD participants outlined additional problems related with divorce. A key reason for divorce found in court records, "lack of care," was strongly echoed in the responses of married women. This may result in several moves, since as one participant explained,

> A woman may divorce and remarry today and discover that conditions in her new husband's house are worse than those in her former husband's home. Eventually, she has to try another place until she gets a good place, where she remains.

Male participants blamed polygamy for divorce, saying that not only would a polygamous man be unable to provide adequate care for all wives, but he also would not worry much about losing one wife. In contrast they noted that the monogamous man,

> . . . will not want to lose (his wife). He will do all in his power to cater for the woman so as not to lose her, because if the woman divorces him, people will ridicule him saying, "How shameful! He has only one wife, and he cannot cater for her."

FGD respondents observed that while divorce is still common in the community, few people resort to use of Customary Court. This arises from a change in the mode of marriage. According to one married man,

> There is no formal ceremony these days. The woman merely moves into the man's house and packs out when she is no longer satisfied with the man. A majority of divorce cases (heard at the Court) involve marriages that were formalized long ago.

DISCUSSION

Of the sexual practices identified in this study, commercial sex work carries the highest risk of transmitting HIV. Although few of their clients are reported to be local men, they themselves and most of their other clients (i.e., drivers and migrant farm laborers) are quite mobile [5, 21], increasing the likelihood that HIV would enter the community, especially from urban areas [1], and from neighboring countries with higher reported HIV and AIDS prevalence [22]. Generally in Nigeria, CSWs have the highest reported prevalence rates of HIV [3], and in addition are responsible for the transmission of other STDS that facilitate HIV transmission [17, 23].

Casual sexual encounters among community members, especially during holidays and festivals when Ago-Are indigenes living in larger urban centers come home, represents another behavior that could facilitate the spread from urban to rural areas as has been observed in Zambia [24]. Should HIV become established in a rural community through CSWs and visitors, the practice of extra-marital sexual relations would provide opportunity for faster internal spread of the disease. Men have been observed to engage in such relations more frequently than women in other small Yoruba communities [25], in part because the traditional post-partum sexual abstinence taboo for lactating mothers is still observed [6].

It would be worth further study to learn if there are differences in the number of extramarital relationships between monogamous men and those in polygamous unions, where an alternative wife is available if one is breastfeeding, but comments from FGD respondents imply that the practice of extra-marital relations does not likely predominate in one sector of society. An extra-marital liaison in a monogamous marriage may be the forerunner to a polygamous marriage for the man or a divorce by the wife. The relative informality of divorce in present day society is certainly another potential facilitating factor for HIV transmission within the community.

The findings of this study provide a foundation for developing appropriate health education for rural communities. Multiple strategies have been shown to be effective in influencing AIDS risk behaviors [26], and seems the most logical approach given the variety of risk groups identified in this study. The first priority would be the CSWs because they potentially link many groups in Ago-Are in a "common sex pool" [27]. Peer education among CSWs has been demonstrated to be a successful approach in other countries [22, 25] and could be instituted by local health authorities in rural districts.

The local religious and social associations would be the ideal focus for educational efforts to prevent HIV spread within the community. These would even reach the urban dwelling indigenes because they retain their membership in such associations, and association meetings often take place during festivals when many people are home. Although at present little is known about the HIV prevalence in the multitude of rural communities in Nigeria, that is no reason for local and national health authorities to delay health education programming for those areas.

REFERENCES

1. A. Mohammed, J. O. Nassidi, E. E. Chickwem, T. O. Williams, G. O. Harry, O. O. Okafor, S. A. Ajose-Coker, P. Ademiluyi, K. M. Tukei, K. M. De-Cork, and T. P. Monath, HIV Infection in Nigeria, *AIDS, 2*, pp. 61-62, 1988.
2. Federal Ministry of Health, *Official Statement on HIV Prevalence Rate in Nigeria*, Lagos, May 1992.
3. *Nigeria Bulletin of Epidemiology, 2*, pp. 2-16, 1992.
4. Development Research Bureau, *Report of a Survey on Knowledge, Attitude and Practice of Secondary School Students and Adults on AIDS in the Traditional Areas of Ibadan*, Ibadan, 1992.
5. I. O. Orubuloye, P. Caldwell, and J. C. Caldwell, The Role of High-risk Occupations in the Spread of AIDS: Truck Drivers and Itinerant Market Women in Nigeria, *International Family Planning Perspectives, 19*:2, pp. 43-48, 1993.
6. I. O. Orubuloye, J. C. Caldwell, and P. Caldwell, Experimental Research on Sexual Networking in the Ekiti District of Nigeria, *Health Transition Working Paper, 3*, pp. 1-19, 1980.
7. J. O. Chickwem, T. O. Oyebode, W. Gasdhau, S. D. Chickwem, B. Bajami, and S. Mambula, Impact of Health Education on Prostitutes' Awareness and Attitudes to Acquired Immune Deficiency Syndrome (AIDS), *Public Health, 102*, pp. 439-445, 1988.
8. E. Green, AIDS in Africa: An Agenda for Behavioural Scientists, in *AIDS in Africa: The Social and Policy Impact*, The Edwin Mellen Press, New York, 1988.
9. J. H. Hubley, AIDS in Africa: A Challenge to Health Education, *Health Education Research, 3*, pp. 41-47, 1988.
10. A. O. Williams, *AIDS: An African Perspective*, CRC Press, Boca Raton, Florida, 1992.
11. A. J. Ajuwon, *Socio-cultural Practices that May Favour the Transmission of Acquired Immunodeficiency Syndrome 'AIDS' in a Rural Yoruba Community: Implications for Health Education*, a dissertation in the Department of Preventive and Social Medicine, University of Ibadan, Nigeria, 1990.
12. B. G. Schoepf, R. Nkera, C. Schoepf, W. Enugunda, and P. Ntosomo, AIDS and Society in Central Africa: A View from Zaire, in *AIDS in Africa: The Social and Policy Impact*, The Edwin Mellen Press, New York, 1988.
13. J. Ramakrishna and W. R. Brieger, The Value of Qualitative Research: Health Education in Nigeria, *Health Policy and Planning, 2*, pp. 171-175, 1987.
14. A. O. Demehin, Sexual Attitudes in Traditional and Modern Yoruba Society, *International Quarterly of Community Health Education, 4*, pp. 231-238, 1993-94.
15. Z. A. Ademuwagun, Problems of Interview Methods and Techniques in Health Education, *Journal of the Society of Health (Nigeria), 11*, pp. 91-99, 1976.
16. P. O. Olusanya, The Educational Factor in Human Fertility: A Case Study of Residents of a Sub-urban Area in Ibadan, Western Nigeria, *The Nigerian Journal of Economic and Social Studies, 8*, pp. 151-163, 1967.
17. W. Cameron, L. D'costa, G. M. Maitha, M. Cheung, P. Piot, J. N. Simonsen, A. L. Ronald, M. N. Gakinya, J. O. Ndinya-Achola, R. C. Brunham, and F. A. Plummer, Female to Male Transmission of Human Immunodeficiency Virus Type I: The Risk Factors for Sero Conversion in Men, *The Lancet, II*, pp. 403-407, 1989.

18. J. K. Kreiss, D. Koech, F. A. Plummer, K. K. Holmes, M. Lightfoote, P. Piot, A. R. Ronald, J. O. Ndinya-Achola, L. J. D'costa, P. Roberts, E. N. Ngugi, and T. C. Quin, AIDS Virus Infection in Nairobi Prostitutes, Spread of the Epidemic to East Africa, *The New England Journal of Medicine, 314*, pp. 414-418, 1986.
19. E. Folch-Lyon and J. F. Frost, Conducting Focus Group Sessions, *Studies in Family Planning, 12*, pp. 443-448, 1981.
20. R. A. Krueger, *Focus Groups: A Practical Guide for Applied Research*, Sage Publications, Newbury Park, California, 1988.
21. D. Brokensha, K. M. MacQueen, C. Stess, T. Patton, and F. Conant, *Social Factors in the Transmission of and Control of AIDS in Africa*, report prepared for the Directorate for Health, Bureau of Science and Technology, U.S. Agency for International Development, Washington, 1987.
22. A. Yeboah-Afari, Helping Prostitutes in Accra, *AIDS Watch, 4*, pp. 4-5, 1988.
23. W. Cameron, L. D'Costa, G. M. Maitha, M. Cheung, P. Plot, S. N. Simunsen, A. L. Ronald, M. N. Gakinya, J. O. Ndinya-Achola, R. C. Brunham, and F. A. Plummer, Female to Male Transmission of Human Immunodeficiency Virus Type I: The Risk Factors for Sero-conversion in Men, *The Lancet, II*:8660, pp. 403-407, 1989.
24. C. Lowe-Murna, Public Awareness and the New AIDS Culture, *Africa Health, 11*, pp. 32-33, 1989.
25. T. T. A. Elemile, *Epidemiology of Sexually Transmitted Diseases in a Rural Area, Ilora, Oyo State, Nigeria*, Fellowship of Nigeria Medical College of Health Dissertation, 1982.
26. E. N. Ngugi, J. N. Simunsen, M. Bosire, A. R. Ronalds, F. A. Plummer, D. W. Cameron, P. Waiyaki, and J. O. Ndinya-Achola, Prevention of Transmission of Human Immunodeficiency Virus in Africa: Effectiveness of Condom Promotion and Health Education among Prostitutes, *The Lancet, II*:8616, pp. 887-890, 1988.
27. V. De Grutolla, K. Mayer, and W. Bennett, AIDS: Has the Problem Been Adequately Assessed? *Review of Infectious Diseases, 8*, pp. 295-305, 1986.

CHAPTER 2

Perceived Barriers to HIV Prevention among University Students in Sierra Leone, West Africa

Thomas J. Stewart and Donna L. Richter

THE AIDS ENVIRONMENT IN SIERRA LEONE

Prior to 1990 Sierra Leone faced circumstances common to a number of other West African nations (with the exception of Nigeria): confirmed AIDS cases, although small numbers at first, were increasing annually (1989 data provided to WHO indicated 23 diagnosed cases and 80 HIV+ individuals; 1991 data reported 40 confirmed cases of AIDS and 166 HIV+). Sierra Leone, like The Gambia, Liberia, Guinea, Senegal and other states in the region, was vulnerable to both HIV+ 1 and HIV+ 2.

A National AIDS Programme (NAP) was formed in 1988 and a field staff of six were charged to conduct educational programs for a nation the size of South Carolina with a population of 4,000,000. Laboratory facilities were limited to Freetown, the nation's capital and only urban center. A nationwide five-year plan was developed and forwarded for action at the federal level. Groups believed to be engaging in high risk activities, such as prostitutes in Freetown and long distance truck drivers, were targeted for special prevention efforts. By 1990 NAP staff reported significant progress in the implementation of educational efforts: good results had been achieved in alerting traditional ethnic leaders and health care providers such as local midwives about the HIV transmission risks involved in use of unsterilized instruments in scarification and circumcision. Other informal educational efforts were undertaken by the Sierra Leone AIDS Prevention Society aimed at illiterate young men and women [1]. Creative print and media campaigns for condom utilization were before the public in Freetown.

Early efforts also involved the distribution of free condoms to hotel managers for circulation to clients and staff. In the late 1980s it was widely believed in several West African countries that European tourists had introduced HIV/AIDS into West Africa [1, 2]. Substantial technical and training support were being provided by the Canadian United Service Organization (CUSO), the U.S. Peace Corps, and Volunteer Service Organization (VSO) of the United Kingdom.

Sierra Leone was less able to withstand the anticipated epidemic than its sister states along the Western coast: although Sierra Leone had occupied a place of economic and political prominence in West African affairs at an early point following its independence from Great Britain in the 1960s, it had sustained a precipitous decline economically in the 1970s and 1980s. At the beginning of the 1990s Sierra Leone was among the least developed nations in the world. The declining economic situation contributed to a dire public health situation: in 1989 Sierra Leone held the dubious position of having the lowest life expectancy rate in sub-Saharan Africa (a ranking shared with Ethiopia) and was second only to Mali in the rates of infant mortality [3]. Tuberculosis and lassa fever have been major public health challenges for several decades. The circumstances described for the entire continent of Africa were particularly evident in Sierra Leone:

> A broader look at African health issues is helpful in understanding the context in which AIDS is viewed by Africans. In countries' where malaria is a constant scourge and new strains continue to resist available drugs and weaken immunity developed over decades, and where diarrheal disease kills hundreds of thousands of both young and elderly each year it has been reasonable for governments to pay more attention to traditional health threats than to a new, relatively unknown or unheard-of disease [4].

In a very important sense it was difficult to mobilize federal policy and resources to focus specifically on AIDS when so many other public health issues demanded attention as well. That so much was accomplished in the early stages of the AIDS era in Sierra Leone was a tribute to the commitment and energy of a small group of professionals.

In the early stages, Sierra Leone and most other West African states did not have to address the substantial population movements which seemed to be affecting the spread of AIDS in other parts of sub-Saharan Africa (East and Central Africa particularly). Traditional migrations by members of particular ethnic groups (such as the Fula, Madingo, and others) occurred between Guinea, Liberia, and Sierra Leone primarily for purposes of trade, but these typically involved small numbers of people. The nature of population movements in the region changed radically in December 1989 with the outbreak of the Liberian civil war. Although the Liberian civil war has received less international media attention than the recent war in Rwanda, its effects in the long run will be almost as devastating and disruptive.

The impact of that war on Sierra Leone was immediate: refugees from adjacent areas of Liberia began flowing into Sierra Leone. As the situation deteriorated in 1991, U.S. armed forces assisted with the evacuation of Monrovia, the capital of Liberia, with most refugees passing through or remaining in Sierra Leone. Thousands of Liberians affected by the fighting migrated into Sierra Leone and entered displacement camps.

The civil war in Liberia spawned a rebellion in Sierra Leone as a by-product. Charles Taylor, one of the principals in the Liberian war, established a former Sierra Leonean noncomissioned officer as "governor" in a region along the border between the two countries. Eventually a full scale internal war raged in the Eastern and Southern Provinces of Sierra Leone, the country's most productive agricultural and mineral areas. It is estimated that over 200,000 Sierra Leoneans were dislocated into neighboring Guinea and 300,000 resettled internally [5]. Liberia had an estimated 600,000 displaced internally and 750,000 displaced out of country in Sierra Leone, Guinea, and Cote d'Ivoire [6]. Large international troop contingents (15,000 and more) from the military component (ECOMOG) of the Economic Council of West African States (ECOWAS) were assigned to combat and police duty in both Liberia and Sierra Leone during the period 1989-1993.

In Sierra Leone a new government, established following a coup d'état in April 1992, has regained a larger portion of the land lost in this rebellion and the fighting which continues is mostly renegade action. Yet, the legacy of this disruptive period will be felt for many years. Increased population risk for AIDS will be one of the residuals of this population disturbance. For instance, all of the international military units were from West African countries with much higher AIDS prevalence rates (such as Nigeria). Virtually the entire population of Monrovia's prostitutes with the financial means to do so relocated to Freetown. A significant portion were absorbed into the local population.

The National AIDS Programme has designed most of interventions to 1994 without much baseline data. Interviews with NAP Program Director indicated that most interventions were based upon anecdotal evidence and the experiences of staff. A two-stage data collection strategy was discussed and approved by the Ministry of Health and NAP. The first stage, reported here, was designed as a pilot project to assess field work and methodological issues (such as survey instrument design, language considerations, etc.) for a broader survey to be conducted in 1994.

METHODOLOGY

Study Population and Sample

The staff of the National AIDS Programme and the sitting Minister of Health recommended that the pilot project population be university students. There was interest in determining the extent to which media campaigns had reached this group. A report from Cameroon indicated that university students were among the most skeptical about AIDS and were highly vocal about labeling AIDS as an externally driven conspiracy [7]. An earlier UNESCO study of drug abuse in Sierra Leone had cited university students as a special population in drug abuse [8]. Some evidence from other sub-Saharan countries pointed to higher HIV prevalence rates among those of higher socioeconomic status and education levels [6].

Students at Fourah Bay College were selected as the first target survey group. Fourah Bay College, the oldest institution of higher education in sub-Saharan Africa and located in Freetown, has had singular impact upon the educated elite in Sierra Leone. Most professionals and the majority of the white collar labor force in Freetown have been Fourah Bay College graduates.

During the 1992 academic year at Fourah Bay College, approximately 1600 students were enrolled, with females composing about one-fourth of the total. Class lists from which a random sample could be drawn were not available at the time the survey was implemented because a series of three strikes had affected university operations. Therefore, geographic sampling of student hostels (dormitories) was utilized in two waves at different times. Students living off campus were captured in a sampling of students enrolled in three required core courses. Of the 120 surveys distributed, eighty-nine completed anonymous questionnaires were returned and two of these were excluded because they were completed by American exchange students. The response rate for distributed surveys was 74.2 percent and the sample represented an estimated 5.3 percent of the total population.

Questionnaire Design

A large portion of the questionnaire was constructed using items from previous surveys conducted in the United States, particularly those tested with university populations. Items unique to Sierra Leone and its university student population were generated from the literature on AIDS field studies in sub-Saharan Africa and from exploratory interviews.

Extensive interviews were conducted with twenty students regarding the following issues: AIDS knowledge; perceptions of AIDS patient populations; risk factors in their own lives; social and cultural factors influencing the transmission of AIDS and their own sexual attitudes; and assessments of their comfort level exploring sexual content. Additionally, these students were queried about phrasing and interpretations of selected questionnaire items. The exploratory interviews convinced the research team that it would be advisable to use English entirely, rather than attempting to incorporate a mix of Krio, the lingua franca of Sierra Leone, and English, the country's official language.

The questionnaire included an HIV/AIDS knowledge section with both multiple choice and true/false responses. Other questions addressed beliefs and attitudes related to HIV/AIDS and elicited a scaled response from "strongly agree" to "strongly disagree."

Statistical analysis included calculation of means and chi-square analysis of variance.

DATA ANALYSIS

Respondent Profile

Female respondents comprised 19.5 percent of the total, a proportion approximating the percentage of all females in the student body (Table 1). The mean age of all respondents was 24.9 years of age (it should be noted that university students in sub-Saharan Africa tend to be older by several years than American students in that they spend at least two more years in secondary education before entry into universities). Approximately 30 percent came from Freetown and the remainder of the sample were originally from rural areas. All ethnic groups of the country were represented in the sample, with the majority from the two most populous ethnic groups (Mende and Temne). Christian students made up 53.5 percent of the sample and 46.5 percent were Islamic. To determine the degree to which students had participated in traditional cultures, they were asked if they had undergone puberty rites in the secret societies of their ethnic groups (most ethnic groups in Sierra Leone maintain traditional societies). Approximately 60 percent were initiates, a subgroup which was almost exclusively from rural areas.

Results

The political, social and ideological responses to AIDS in Africa have been widely discussed [9-11]. In preliminary interviews with students, it was determined that they felt a significant portion of peers viewed AIDS as a "sham" epidemic or a conspiracy to reduce African birth rates. The survey asked students if they agreed with the proposition that AIDS was not a public health threat, but actually was a conspiracy. Interestingly, 19.8 percent (Table 2) agreed with this statement and this subgroup was all male. No women agreed with the conspiracy theory. Neither religion nor traditional cultural participation had any measurable influence on responses to this item.

Two-thirds of the respondents were convinced that HIV/AIDS posed a serious immediate threat to them. There was no variable which demonstrated a relationship with the propensity to believe or disbelieve this. When asked hypothetically if the average Sierra Leonean would use condoms if they were convinced that AIDS was an immediate threat to them, 61 percent thought that most people would still *not* utilize a condom.

One of the traditional views about the discussion of sexual matters is that women who are willing to bring up sexual matters with their partners are considered "loose women." Almost 59 percent of this sample agreed that it was "a

Table 1. Demographic Characteristics of Survey
Participants ($N = 87$)

Gender	79.3%	Male
	19.5%	Female
Age	range =	18-36 years
	mean =	25 years
Religion	53.5%	Christian
	46.5%	Muslim
Birthplace	29.4%	Freetown/Western Area
	28.2%	Eastern Province
	20.0%	Southern Province
	17.6%	Northern Province
	4.7%	Outside Sierra Leone
Ethnic Background	35.7%	Mende
	19.0%	Temne
	14.2%	Krio
	31.1%	Other (8 ethnic groups)
Participated in Initiation	58.8%	Yes
	36.5%	No
	4.7%	Did not answer
Current Sexual Activity	24.4%	Intercourse rarely/Not at all
	5.8%	Frequent intercourse, No regular partner
	29.1%	One regular partner
	10.5%	Two regular partners
	4.7%	Three or more regular partners
	25.6%	Unwilling to answer question
Source of AIDS Information	58.1%	Newspapers/Magazines
	18.6%	Other people
	11.6%	Radio
	8.1%	Posters
	3.5%	School/College presentations
Frequency of Discussing AIDS with Peers	1.1%	Never
	13.8%	Not often
	66.7%	Sometimes
	18.4%	Often

Table 2. HIV/AIDS-related Attitudes

Statement	% Agree	% Disagree	% Unsure
There is no real threat of AIDS in Africa; rather, there is a conspiracy to keep Africans from having sex and children.	19.8	67.5	12.8
Most Sierra Leoneans are convinced that AIDS is a serious threat to them if they do not practice "safer sex."	66.7	17.2	16.1
Even if most people in Sierra Leone were convinced that using a condom while having sexual intercourse would protect them from getting AIDS, they *would not* use condoms.	60.9	24.1	14.9
When a man and a woman are starting a new sexual relationship, it is the man's responsibility to bring up the issue of "safer sex."	58.6	29.8	11.5
If I were to raise the issue of AIDS with a new sexual partner, they would become upset or vexed with me.	48.2	23.5	28.2
Sometimes I wonder if someone I am having a sexual relationship with might be infected with the AIDS virus.	51.9	48.1	0.0
If I were beginning a relationship with a new sexual partner, I would discuss the prevention of AIDS or sexually-transmitted diseases with them.	38.1	8.3	53.6
If I were presenting my child for initiation ceremonies, I would try to find out if the society uses sterile techniques for scarification or circumcision.	55.4	13.3	31.4

man's responsibility to bring up the issue of safe sex" among sexual partners in a heterosexual relationship. Men were twice as likely as women to agree with this statement. Younger students (those below the sample mean age) were less likely to believe that it was the man's primary responsibility.

One of the most critical scaled responses had to do with the consequences of discussing the matter of safer sex. Almost half of the sample agreed with the proposition that if they raised the issue of safer sex and the utilization of condoms, their sexual partner would become upset with them. Again, women were less likely to think that this would be a sensitive matter for discussion with a sexual partner.

Students were requested to describe their personal attitudes toward sexual intercourse: 18.4 percent indicated that they thought intercourse was for the purpose of procreation only; 46 percent described it as a "normal part of a relationship between a man and a woman"; only 6.9 percent viewed intercourse as an important expression of love; and, 12.6 percent expressed a view of sexuality as pleasurable. Slightly over 16 percent of the total chose not to respond to this item, and, over 53 percent of the women did not respond.

Reported sexual activity patterns revealed that 24.4 percent had intercourse rarely or not at all. Of those reporting more frequent sexual relations, 5.8 percent had one regular sexual partner; 29.1 percent had two regular sexual partners and 10.4 percent had three or more regular partners. This question elicited a high non response rate with almost 41 percent of women and 28 percent of men electing not to answer.

Only 15.1 percent reported starting a sexual relationship with a new partner in the past three months. There was a significant relationship between respondent gender and this item, with no women reporting a new relationship. A traditional orientation was also shown to be significantly related to this variable: those who had been initiated into a traditional society were much more likely than the uninitiated to have taken on a new sexual partner in the past three months.

Slightly over half of the respondents had wondered at one time if a sexual partner was HIV infected. Those with the more traditional background were more likely to wonder if their partners were infected with the virus.

Each respondent was asked how likely it was that they would bring up the matter of AIDS and any other sexually transmitted disease in the beginning of a new relationship: 8.3 percent reported they absolutely would not bring up such a matter; 41.7 percent thought they probably would discuss the topic; 38.1 percent indicated that they absolutely would discuss the matter; and, 12 percent were uncertain how they would handle this. Age was significantly related to this variable with younger students showing a greater degree of uncertainty than older students. Gender and religion were also determined to be significant here: female respondents were either certain they would discuss the issue or were not sure. Those who were Christian said it was probable or certain they would discuss the matter.

Table 3 demonstrates that this sample was generally well informed about HIV/AIDS. Ten of the knowledge items were answered correctly by over 90 percent of the respondents. These items included most means of transmission and prevention. The items for which the level of knowledge was more modest were the belief that AIDS can be transmitted by a mosquito bite and the perception that AIDS was a worldwide phenomenon. Almost 90 percent of the respondents did not know that the highest number of diagnosed cases of AIDS occurred in Africa.

DISCUSSION

The findings of this study reveal several barriers to HIV prevention which must be considered in the design and implementation of AIDS education and prevention programs. These barriers include a persistent belief in conspiracy theory, an ambivalence among women students regarding sexuality issues, a lack of familiarity with the parameters of the epidemic in Africa, and a belief that condom use behavior is not amenable to change.

Persistence of Belief in Conspiracy Theory

Even among this highly educated population, 20 percent were convinced that AIDS posed no real threat, but that it was a conspiracy to keep Africans from having sex and children. It was an all male group which subscribed to the conspiracy theory—no women supported this perspective.

Ambivalence of Women Students Regarding Sexuality Issues

The reluctance of women students in this survey to answer questions relating to their own sexual behavior is clear in the data: 58 percent of women did not respond to the question regarding their personal attitude toward sexual intercourse, 41 percent of women did not respond to the question regarding current sexual activity, and no women reported beginning a new sexual relationship recently. Although women were reluctant to discuss their own sexuality, they were willing to express opinions related to the propriety of discussing safer sex with partners. In fact, women were less worried than men about a partner becoming vexed about discussion of the issue of safer sex. These results seem to indicate that among highly educated women, there is an awareness of the need to communicate with their partners about the issue of safer sex, but that these women still retain the traditional unwillingness to discuss their own sexual behavior. Because of the size of the subsample of women, caution is urged in making generalizations about the larger population of college-educated women in Sierra Leone. We also conclude that a survey is not the optimum means of assessing the extent and nature of sexual behavior for educated women in Sierra Leone.

Table 3. HIV/AIDS Knowledge

Statement	% Answering Correctly
AIDS can be transmitted by a blood transfusion from a person who has AIDS.	100
Having sexual intercourse with a person who has AIDS is one of the most common means of getting AIDS.	98.9
AIDS is *not* a fatal or killing disease.	96.5
There are drugs available that can cure AIDS.	95.2
If a pregnant woman has AIDS, it can be passed to her fetus.	94.3
AIDS stands for Acquired Immune Deficiency Syndrome.	94.2
Of those people who become infected with AIDS, 75 percent do so through sexual relations.	92.9
The use of condoms during sexual intercourse is an effective means of preventing AIDS.	91.8
Drinking from a cup used by a person with AIDS can give you AIDS.	90.6
There is some risk that AIDS can be transmitted in initiation ceremonies if knives and other tools are not sterilized after each use.	90.5
AIDS can be passed from one person to another by a mosquito bite.	68.8
AIDS is a disease which occurs world wide.	64.4
The greatest number of AIDS cases have occurred in Africa.	10.5

Other strategies need to be considered and explored, such as personal interviews by field staff.

Lack of Knowledge about Parameters of the Epidemic in Africa

Few respondents to this survey were aware that the largest number of AIDS cases have occurred in Africa. This finding may reflect a lack of familiarity with the epidemiologic aspects of the pandemic, or may be a reaction to the way AIDS in Africa has been presented in the American and European media [6, 10].

Belief that Condom Use Behavior Will Not Change

The fact that a clear majority of respondents (61%) believed that most Sierra Leoneans would refuse to use condoms even if they knew condoms would protect them from contracting HIV is consistent with some of the continent-wide findings [4]. This finding also reinforces the notion that a daunting challenge faces those working to promote safer sex practices.

CONCLUSIONS

This study reflects the perspectives of those who are highly educated and likely to assume positions of influence in a nation still shaping its destiny in many areas, including the AIDS epidemic. While relatively well-informed about HIV transmission and prevention, the respondents' pessimistic assessment of their fellow countrymen's willingness to take prevention measures involving the use of condoms is cause for concern. Their assessment may be correct, but tacit acceptance of this barrier to prevention will do nothing to alleviate the spread of HIV. Current programs of the NAP model a positive response to this perceived barrier. NAP staff are involved in training individuals in rural areas to serve as "condom promoters." These condom promoters are charged with educating their neighbors about condoms and with distributing condoms from a supply provided to them by the NAP.

Since women in this study appeared more open to discussion of safer sex with their partners, education and prevention programs might be targeted at providing women with skills for eroticizing condom use and negotiating for condom use. These findings are somewhat different from those reported by Harrell-Bond in a 1970s contraceptive use study which included university students: this group in the current study seemed to be more forthright and knowledgeable about use of condoms [12]. Further research is needed which focuses on a broader spectrum of the population of Sierra Leone, including the majority who are not literate.

REFERENCES

1. K. A. Sarpong, AIDS Control in Action, *West Africa, 3878*, p. 71, 1992.
2. P. daCosta, Keeping the Vigil Alive, *West Africa, 3892*, pp. 675-676, 1992.
3. T. Goliber, Africa's Expanding Population: Old Problems, New Policies, *Population Bulletin, 44*, pp. 5-48, November 1989.
4. D. Weeks, The AIDS Pandemic in Africa, *Current History, 91*, pp. 208-213, 1992.
5. M. Butscher, Things Falling Apart, *West Africa, 3888*, pp. 494-495, 1992.
6. T. Barnett and P. Blaikie, *AIDS in Africa*, Guilford Press, New York, 1992.
7. T. Lucas, Battle Against AIDS, *West Africa, 3727*, p. 187, 1989.
8. K. A. Sarpong, Drug Alert in Freetown, *West Africa, 3768*, pp. 180-181, 1989.
9. B. Akakpo, Africa, AIDS and Race, *West Africa, 3878*, p. 71, 1992.
10. P. J. Hilts, Dispelling Myths about AIDS in Africa, *Africa Report, 33*, 1988.
11. N. Schmidt, *Resources for Teaching about the Social Impact of AIDS in Africa*, paper presented at the Annual Meeting of the African Studies Association, Atlanta, Georgia, November 5, 1989.
12. B. Harrell-Bond, Some Influential Attitudes about Family Limitation, in *Population Growth and Socioeconomic Change in West Africa*, J. C. Caldwell (ed.), Columbia University Press, New York, 1975.

CHAPTER 3

AIDS-Related Knowledge, Attitudes, Beliefs, and Behavioral Intentions of Adolescents in Trinidad: A Pilot Study

Naomi N. Modeste, Claudette Francis, and Dumiso Matshazi

Globally, the HIV/AIDS pandemic has reached catastrophic proportions, affecting men, women, and children. Certain cultural and social conditions may encourage the problem, especially in some developing countries. There is an urgent need to determine the attitudes and beliefs among adolescents with regard to AIDS since they form a high-risk segment of the population.

The AIDS epidemic has been rapidly increasing in the Caribbean region. Since the first reported case in Trinidad in 1983, there has been an alarming increase in both males and females. While the majority (73%) of the reported cases occurred among young adults between the ages of twenty and forty-four years, the number of pediatric cases has also been steadily rising. The percentage of AIDS cases contracted through heterosexual contact increased from zero (or no reported cases) in 1983 to 47 percent by 1987. An important factor contributing to this abrupt rise was the high number of bisexual males with multiple female partners [1-3].

Adolescents form an age group of increasing significance in the AIDS epidemic. They have views and values of the world that appear quite different from those of adults. They generally have low perceptions of vulnerability to any risks, and are often complacent about the magnitude and devastating effects of AIDS. This group certainly needs knowledge of how the virus can be contracted and what preventive measures they can take, but knowledge alone is insufficient to motivate them to act in a healthful manner. Beliefs, attitudes, and family values frequently play an important role in motivating people to adopt certain behaviors [4].

Attention has been recently directed at adolescents and their risk of AIDS. The rate of AIDS and other sexually transmitted diseases in adolescents continues to rise, and misconceptions about preventing these diseases still exist [5, 6]. However, there is a surprising lack of relevant information on adolescents.

A study of Canadian youth aged eleven to twenty-one years regarding knowledge, attitudes, and behaviors related to AIDS and other sexually transmitted diseases indicates that most know how the HIV virus is transmitted. However, the majority of youth did not believe that their sexual behaviors put them at risk, nor did they seriously contemplate protecting themselves or abstaining from such behaviors [7].

According to a report from the Centers for Disease Control, 21 percent of known AIDS cases are in the age group twenty-one to twenty-nine, most of whom may have been exposed to the virus in their teen years. Even in the face of such knowledge, adolescents still perceive themselves as invincible and tend to deny possible dangers of AIDS [8, 9].

Although AIDS education is provided to children in some elementary and secondary schools, many teens are involved in risk-taking behaviors that could lead to HIV infection [10]. After one year of intensive AIDS health information among San Francisco teenagers, a survey conducted to assess their knowledge, attitudes, and use of condoms showed an increase in AIDS knowledge, but a decrease in intention to use protection (i.e., condom). The authors suggested that understanding teenagers attitudes may help in efforts aimed at prevention [11]. Another AIDS-related study in the same geographic area on minorities (Black and Latino adolescents) produced similar findings, but revealed more misconceptions about the disease [12].

A study of foreign-born (mostly Caribbean and Latin-American) high school students in Boston revealed that immigrant students were more likely than American students to hold misconceptions about how the virus is transmitted. Immigrant or foreign-born students were less likely than American students to talk about their risk taking behaviors, but more likely to worry about getting AIDS [13].

METHODS

Sample

The study population consisted of students in Forms III, IV, and V (equivalent to the last three grades of U.S. high school) who were randomly selected from three high schools in the Island Republic of Trinidad, in the Caribbean. The schools were selected on the basis of their geographic location, their willingness to participate in the survey and the fact that one was an all boys institution, one, all girls, and one co-educational. Age ranged from thirteen to eighteen with a mean age of 14.8 years. Thirty-nine percent were male and 61 percent were female.

Of the sixty students initially selected, 85 percent participated in the survey. Questionnaires were administered to students present on a day determined for the survey. Students who were absent or did not consent to take part in the survey were excluded. The information was self-reported and responses were kept confidential.

Instrumentation

The survey instrument was a structured questionnaire, developed and pretested in the population under study, to assess adolescents knowledge, attitudes, beliefs, and behavioral intentions about AIDS. After pretesting the questionnaire, appropriate revisions were made. In developing the questionnaire, relevant research studies on AIDS-related knowledge, attitudes, and beliefs among adolescents were critically evaluated and items adapted from survey instruments by Hingson [13], and DiClemente [12]. A 4-point Likert scale was used to assess attitudes and beliefs toward AIDS. Categorical data items (true and false statements) were used for the knowledge section, and a three-category response for intentions and self-efficacy. The questionnaire consisted of five sections: knowledge, attitudes, beliefs, behavioral intentions and demographics. There were eighteen questions: four in the knowledge section including fifteen true or false statements, two in the attitudes section, four in the beliefs section, four in the behavioral intentions section, and the rest were demographical data such as age, gender, and education.

Internal reliability was determined for all Likert scales by calculating the reliability coefficient (Cronbach's Alpha) for each construct. The Cronbach's Alpha values (internal reliability) for the sub-scales of self-efficacy, such as their perceived ability to abstain from sex within the next year ($\alpha = .7096$) and intention to engage in AIDS risk reducing behaviors ($\alpha = .7343$) indicated good reliability.

Data Collection

Approximately three months prior to the survey consent was obtained from the principal of each selected school and time was designated for the data collection. In the first quarter of 1993 the questionnaire was administered to selected subjects after explaining the nature and anonymity of the survey, and assuring confidentiality of the reports. Classroom teachers were absent from the room while the data were being collected. Completed questionnaires were placed in a sealed envelope until time for data entry and analysis.

Data Analysis

Data were analyzed using the statistical package for the social sciences (SPSS/PC+). Descriptive statistics were calculated for all variables. Frequencies and percentages were done for categorical data. Chi square statistics, Pearson correlation coefficients, and t-tests were computed to assess associations among variables tested.

RESULTS

Of the fifty-one students surveyed, twenty (39%) were males and thirty-one (61%) were females, and the majority (59%) were fourteen and fifteen years old. Nineteen (37%) were in form III, fifteen (30%) were in Form IV, and seventeen (33%) in Form V.

A greater percentage (96% and 98%, respectively) of adolescents were knowledgable about the cause and mode of transmission of AIDS and that a vaccine was not available. However, 26 percent said that AIDS can be acquired from insect bites (Table 1).

Students were asked about where they got most of their information about AIDS and were given a list of possible sources. Eighty-six percent listed the television as the major source of AIDS knowledge with clubs and churches as the lowest source (Figure 1). However, when looking at their knowledge level and source of information, there was a significant relationship ($p < .05$) between knowledge level and newspapers or magazines as sources of knowledge. Those with higher levels of AIDS knowledge were more likely to acquire it from newspapers or magazines.

Students were asked to indicate their belief about a number of factors that can cause HIV/AIDS. All (100%) believed that they can get AIDS from having sex with a prostitute. Ninety-seven percent believed that sex between men and men was a cause of AIDS. However, only 53 percent believed that sex between men and women was an important cause of AIDS. Eighteen percent believed they can get AIDS from a toilet seat.

Thirty students (59%) thought they were at risk for getting AIDS and twenty-one (41%) thought they were not at risk. They were to state by writing out their answers, why they thought they were or were not at risk. Forty-seven percent said they were not at risk because they were not sexually active, and 6 percent felt they were not at risk because if they decided to have sex they would use a condom. Twenty-one percent said they felt helpless and at risk because the disease is everywhere and there is nothing they can do to prevent themselves from getting it. Nine percent felt they were at risk because at sometime in their life they may need a blood transfusion. Only two students (4%) indicated they were at risk because they were sexually active. However, the majority of students responding felt it was not likely they would get AIDS.

Table 1. Student AIDS Knowledge (*n* = 51)

Questionnaire Statements	Responses (*n* = 51) (Percent)	
	True	False
Stress can cause AIDS.	4	96
AIDS is caused by a virus.	96	4
People with AIDS die from the disease.	86	14
You cannot get AIDS from insect bites.	74	26
You cannot get AIDS from blood transfusion.	96	4
AIDS can be transmitted by mother to unborn baby.	98	2
You can tell a person has AIDS by looks.	4	96
AIDS can be transmitted through sexual contact.	100	0
A person with the AIDS virus may not show symptoms.	94	6
An AIDS vaccine is available.	2	98
There is no cure for AIDS.	98	2
AIDS is transmitted by semen.	86	14
AIDS is transmitted by vaginal fluids.	82	18
AIDS is not a serious disease.	0	100
The AIDS virus is carried in saliva.	33	67

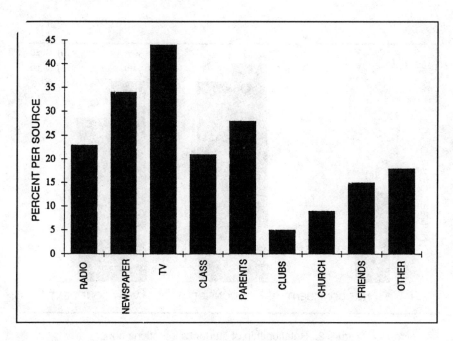

Figure 1. Source of AIDS information.

Teenagers in the lower forms (III and IV) and younger age group (13 through 15) expressed a greater likelihood of safe sexual behavior than those in Form V. This may be largely a reflection on the age of the students. As people get older, they tend to become more experienced, and hence, have a better understanding of safer sexual practices and which ones they are likely to follow.

There was a significant ($p < .05$) relationship between teenagers in the all girls' school and behavioral intention about sexual partners—having only one sexual partner, waiting until after marriage to have sex, discussing condom use with partner, not having sex with someone who is pressuring them to do so, avoid having sex with someone they just fell in love with or knew for a short time, or who has been "shooting up" drugs, when compared with the all boys' and coeducational schools. More girls than boys were confident about their behavior intentions, but those in the all girls' school showed the highest level of confidence (Figure 2). In comparing teenagers attending all boys school with those attending all girls schools, and their behavioral intentions, there was also a significant ($p < .05$) relationship with being in an all girls school (Figure 3).

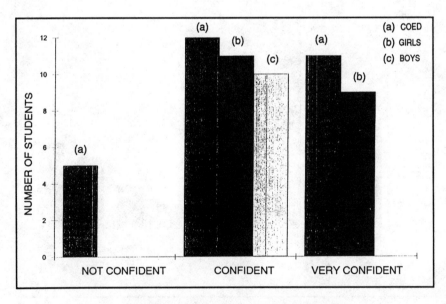

Figure 2. Relationship of student's intentions about
sexual partners and type of school.

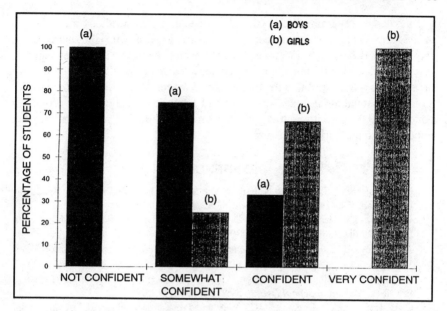

Figure 3. Comparison of behavioral intentions in
all boys vs. all girls schools.

DISCUSSION

This pilot study of adolescents on the island of Trinidad was limited by
the small sample size of respondents. Although findings cannot be generalized,
information gained suggests the need for additional in-depth studies of a larger
scale. Adolescents in the study population were aware of the AIDS problem, and
the important modes of transmission, but there is still some misconception with
regards to the role of insect bites and toilet seats in the spread of the disease,
though not in the majority of respondents. A larger study, however, may reveal
more misconceptions. These findings are similar to results from the Boston study
by Hingson and colleagues, indicating that foreign-born (mostly Caribbean and
Latin-American) students were more likely to hold misconceptions about the
disease [13].

Our study showed that knowledge did not seem to have a major effect on
behavioral intention, a finding that supports the observations of Montauk and
colleagues among American adolescents [10]. Although knowledge or education
about the disease does not necessarily result in prevention, type of knowledge may
well be distorted if it is gained mainly through television. It was observed in
our study that the majority of students got their knowledge of AIDS from the
television or newspaper.

Knowledge regarding HIV/AIDS is increasing, but methods of effective AIDS prevention do not appear to be keeping pace with the increase. A larger study is indicated since much has not been done in this important segment of the population. Additional surveys of adolescents are needed to help identify areas of misconceptions and explore effective means of avoiding HIV transmission. Understanding attitudes and beliefs of adolescents may help in providing education and preventive strategies that are more focused and suited to that population in the Caribbean region.

REFERENCES

1. C. Bartholomew, C. Raju, and N. Jankey, The Acquired Immune Deficiency Syndrome in Trinidad, *West Indian Medical Journal, 32*, p. 177, 1983.
2. T. C. Quin, J. P. Narain, and F. R. K. Zacarias, AIDS in The Americas: A Public Health Priority for the Region, *AIDS, 4*, pp. 709-724, 1990.
3. J. D. Farley, *AIDS in The CAREC Member Countries,* a conference presentation, April 1993.
4. C. Basch, Preventing AIDS through Education: Concepts, Strategies, and Research Priorities, *Journal of School Health, 59*:7, pp. 296-299, 1989.
5. C. B. Boyer and S. Kegeles, AIDS Risk and Prevention among Adolescent, *Social Science and Medicine, 33*:1, pp. 11-21, 1991.
6. C. Croft and M. C. Sorrentino, Physician Interaction with Families on Issues of AIDS: What Parents and Youth Indicate they Desire, *Health Values, 15*:6, pp. 13-22, 1991.
7. D. L. Kerr, AIDS Update: The Canada Youth and AIDS Study, *Journal of School Health, 59*:2, pp. 86-88, 1989.
8. L. Lawrence, S. Levy, and L. Rubinson, Self-efficiency and AIDS Prevention for Pregnant Teens, *Journal of School Health, 60*:1, pp. 19-24, 1990.
9. D. Holtzman, J. E. Anderson, and L. Kann et al. HIV Instruction, HIV Knowledge and Drug Injection among High School Students in the United States, *American Journal of Public Health, 81*:12, pp. 1596-1601, 1991.
10. S. L. Montauk and D. M. Scoggin, AIDS: Questions from Fifth and Sixth Grade Students, *Journal of School Health, 59*:7, pp. 291-295, 1989.
11. S. M. Kegeles, N. E. Adler, and C. E. Irwin, Sexually Active Adolescents and Condoms: Changes Over One Year in Knowledge, Attitudes and Use, *American Journal of Public Health, 78*:4, pp. 460-461, 1988.
12. R. J. DiClemente, C. B. Boyer, and E. S. Morales, Minorities and AIDS: Knowledge, Attitudes, and Misconceptions among Black and Latino Adolescents, *American Journal of Public Health, 78*:1, pp. 55-57, 1988.
13. R. W. Hingson, L. Strunin, and M Grady et al., Knowledge about HIV and Behavioral Risks of Foreign Born Boston Public School Students, *American Journal of Public Health, 81*:12, pp. 1638-1641, 1991.

[The authors wish to express their appreciation to the Loma Linda University Center for Health Research for providing funding and technical assistance.]

CHAPTER 4

Preventing HIV Infection among Juvenile Delinquents: Educational Diagnosis Using the Health Belief Model

Kathleen M. Lux and Rick Petosa

Between October 1989 and October 1990, the number of identified AIDS cases in adolescents increased 35 percent [1]. The number of cases attributed to heterosexual contact with infected persons also significantly increased. Adolescent cases are more likely than adult cases to be females (14% versus 7%) and more likely to be heterosexually acquired (9% versus 4%) [2-4]. Although the incidence of AIDS cases among adolescents is low, it is doubling every fourteen months [5, 6]. Some authorities speculate that adolescents who engage in high risk sexual and drug use behaviors such as runaways, sex offenders, and juvenile delinquents are at high risk for contracting HIV [7-9]. High risk adolescents are understudied so empirical evidence to support these claims is meager.

PURPOSE OF THE STUDY

The purpose of this study was to describe the health beliefs and safer sex intentions of incarcerated youths between the ages of thirteen to eighteen years residing in state supported training schools within Ohio. An enhanced version of the Health Belief Model (HBM) was used as the conceptual framework for the study. The survey examined: perceived barriers to condom use, perceived social barriers to safer sex intentions, perceived susceptibility to HIV infection, perceived severity of HIV infection, perceived benefits of safer sex intentions, perceived social norms for safer sex intentions, self-efficacy for condom use, self-efficacy for sexual discussion, self-efficacy for self-disclosure of high risk behaviors which may be considered socially unacceptable, and cues to action for safer sex intentions. Carmel [10] and Rosenstock [11] recommend inclusion of self-efficacy and social norms as constructs of the HBM. The assessment of these theory-based constructs provide the basis for an educational diagnosis to assist in the design of effective HIV prevention efforts with this population.

REVIEW OF THE LITERATURE

Ohio leads the nation in the number of juveniles put behind bars at both the state and local level, and ranks second to California in the number of juvenile delin-quents incarcerated [12]. Ohio's rate of institutionalizing its youth is five times higher than Pennsylvania, the closest state with a similar population. Incarcerated youths caught in the web of delinquent behavior find it difficult to extricate themselves from the juvenile justice system in spite of judicial, medical, and psychological/educational efforts to support them [13, 14]. Forty percent of youths referred to juvenile courts become repeat offenders [15]. According to the Office of Juvenile Justice and Delinquency Prevention (OJJDP), with each repeat offense, delinquent youth get more and more involved in aberrant behaviors and their risks for a variety of problems, including HIV infection, increase [15].

Indirect markers of HIV risk behavior, such as pregnancy rates, rates of sexually transmitted diseases (STD) and injection drug use (IVDU) rates for incarcerated youths suggest juvenile delinquents are indeed at high risk for HIV infection. Incarcerated youths have rates above the national average for pregnancy, STDs and IVDU [14, 16, 17]. Hence, it is logical to infer that juvenile delinquents would be at high risk for HIV infection.

The assumption that risky behaviors reflect lack of knowledge, misinformation or deficiencies in understanding which can be eliminated by education is prevalent [18-21]. However, studies in the adolescent HIV literature which have analyzed the relationship between knowledge and risk behavior suggest that adolescents' behavior change needed to reduce the risk of HIV infection is not related to knowledge [22-24]. The adolescent HIV literature indicates teens do have some understanding of how HIV is transmitted, but many ignore or deny their inherent vulnerability.

Previous surveys of adolescents both within school systems and detention facilities reflect a lack of theory [25]. Variables measured were limited to factual content about HIV/AIDS and lifestyle practices. Current theories in health educa-tion emphasize the importance of psychosocial variables which help explain the likelihood of preventive actions. The incorporation of theory into research design of educational needs assessments could provide valuable insights for improving health education program effectiveness.

No studies were located in the adolescent HIV literature which investigated the health beliefs and safer sex intentions of juvenile delinquents. Among adolescents within school systems, the literature is sparse but what is there appears to indicate a relationship between health beliefs and HIV prevention behaviors for teens [26]. Seigel et al. found belief in condom effectiveness correlated with reported condom use among adolescents [27].

INSTRUMENT DEVELOPMENT

Considerable effort was expended to develop valid and reliable measures of HBM variables and dependent measures. The instrument had three main sections—items to measure each of the seven HBM variables (52 items), safer sex intentions (6 items) and sexual behaviors (17 items). A pool of 132 items was constructed using a review of the literature. The draft instrument was reviewed by a panel of eight nationally recognized experts—three HBM experts, three instrumentation experts and two adolescent HIV prevention experts. After revision based on the comments of the panel of experts, 124 items were used in a pilot and field test with thirty female and thirty male juvenile delinquents. Further revisions were made to the instrument as a result of the pilot and field testing due to Cronbach alpha scores and subject comments. The study instrument had 110 items which was administered to the accepting sample. A principal factor exploratory factor analysis using orthogonal rotation was done to identify factors. Exploratory factor analysis is a means of explaining underlying dimensions [28]. It is an expedient way of ascertaining the minimum number of hypothetical factors which account for decreased covariation. Review of the literature showed that factor analysis of study instruments based on the HBM had rarely been done. Exploratory factor analysis had not been processed on HBM constructs to establish their existence. Thus, an exploratory factor analysis was done to establish the presence of HBM constructs.

Ten factors with an eigenvalue greater than one were retained. Factor loading criteria of .35 was used to retain items. Each of the factors was studied to determine if all items which loaded on each factor made theoretical sense. Then the content of the items which loaded on each factor was studied to determine a theoretical name for each factor. Originally, items were developed to measure the seven main HBM constructs: perceived susceptibility, perceived severity, perceived barriers, perceived benefits, social norms, self-efficacy, and cues to action. Exploratory factor analysis revealed ten HBM constructs. Two HBM constructs broke down into more than one factor. Perceived barriers became perceived barriers to condom use and perceived social barriers to safer sex intentions. Self-efficacy became self-efficacy for condom use, self-efficacy for sexual discussion and self-efficacy for self-disclosure of high risk behavior which may not be considered socially acceptable.

Using the items identified as loading on each factor from the exploratory factor analysis, a confirmatory factor analysis was run. A principal factor analysis was done using each factor identified by exploratory factor analysis. No rotation was done as it is not possible to rotate only one factor. The eigenvalue for each factor was greater than or equal to one. Factor scores were created by finding the average of the item means which loaded on each factor. The same confirmatory factor analysis technique was run on the six items measuring safer sex intentions. The results show one factor with an eigenvalue of 1.7577. The factor loadings of the items for this factor were all greater than .3500.

The alpha coefficients for the subscales on the final 75-item instrument ranged from .79-.57. The alpha coefficient values were: perceived susceptibility was .72, perceived severity was .62, perceived social barriers .63, perceived barriers to condom use .57, perceived benefits .61, self-efficacy for self-disclosure of high risk behaviors .72, self-efficacy for condom use .63, self-efficacy for sexual discussion .79, safer sex intentions .64, perceived social norms .56, cues to action .75 and sexual behaviors .57.

SAMPLE

The population for this study consisted of a census of juvenile delinquents residing in three state supported training schools and a sample of fifty youths (out of 150) from the fourth state supported training school. Access to juvenile delinquents was controlled by the state Department of Youth Services based on staffing and crowding conditions of the nine institutions available for possible study. Informed assent was obtained from all adolescents before participation in the study. An incentive of a candy bar was offered to all study participants. Surveys were read by a health educator to those subjects who had difficult reading. Parental consent was obtained for all teens under the age of eighteen through assumed consent procedures. A total of forty (8.7%) juvenile delinquents were excluded from the study due to parental refusals. Data were collected over a two-week period during February 1992. The accepting sample was 458, the data sample was 452 (99%). In this study, 51 percent of youths were African Americans, 37 percent were White and 12 percent were Other. The study sample was primarily male (88.9%). The average age of subjects was sixteen with a range from thirteen to nineteen years of age. One-third of the juvenile delinquents in this study completed ninth grade. Five percent of youths had completed high school and no youths had less than a fourth grade education. Sixty-four percent of the youths had received some type of formal education about HIV prevention. For study participants, the average length of incarceration was 6.09 months (*s.d.* = 8.46).

RESULTS

Perceived Susceptibility of an HIV Infection

Depending on the specific item, only 8 to 26 percent of the sample reported personal susceptibility to HIV infections (Table 1). Seventy-six percent agreed that people like them were not likely to get HIV infections. Similarly, 77 percent

Table 1. Perceived Susceptibility of an HIV Infection
(Percent)

	Disagree	Mildly Disagree	Mildly Agree	Agree
People like me do not get HIV infections.	12.2	11.8	16.2	59.9
I am very healthy so my body can fight off an HIV infection.	12.6	9.0	16.4	61.5
I am too young to get an HIV infection.	4.4	4.2	7.7	86.7
I am not worried that I might get an HIV infection.	14.4	11.5	23.1	51.0
People my age are too young to get an HIV infection.	4.2	4.2	7.8	83.8
People my age do not get HIV infections.	3.8	4.2	9.8	82.2

agreed they were healthy so their bodies could fight off an HIV infection. Seventy-four percent agreed that they do not worry about getting HIV infections. And, 91.6 percent believed people their age are too young to get HIV infections. Finally, 92 percent agreed people their age do not get HIV infections. It is interesting to note that the three items which made personal references to the subject had lower perceived susceptibility rates than did the three items measuring perceived susceptibility of others.

The level of perceived susceptibility reported by juvenile delinquents is approximately the same as those reported in the literature for adolescents attending middle or high school. In the early study conducted by Price, Desmond, and Kulula in Ohio, 73 percent of subjects responded they were not worried about contracting HIV [29]. A later study reported 49 percent of subjects felt they were not likely to get HIV infections [30]. Two other studies reported 50 to 74 percent of adolescents worried about contracting HIV [31, 32]. In contrast, Barling and Moore reported that 63 percent of adolescents felt no concern for AIDS as their friends were not the types to be carriers [33].

Perceived Severity of an HIV Infection

About 30 to 67 percent reported social consequences to HIV infection (Table 2). Thirty-six percent agreed that their family relationships would change if they had an HIV infection. Fifty-five percent believed no one would date them if they had an HIV infection. About one-third (31%) agreed that their friends would remain their friends if they had an HIV infection. And, 55 percent agreed that people would avoid them if they had an HIV infection. Similar measures of perceived severity of an HIV infection are not reported in the literature so comparisons cannot be made.

Perceived Barriers to Condom Use

A considerable number of subjects reported barriers to condom use (Table 3). Sixty-two percent agreed that condoms decreased pleasure during sex and 46 percent agreed that using condoms during sex is a hassle. Finally, 46 percent agreed that they would rather use some other kind of birth control than condoms. Hingson, Strunin, and Berlin reported that 50 percent of Massachusetts' teens believed condoms reduced sexual pleasure [31]. This rate is similar to the one reported by juvenile delinquents in this study. Further barriers to condom use identified by the Massachusetts study were: upsetting a partner by asking them to use a condom and believing condoms were difficult to use.

Table 2. Perceived Severity of an HIV Infection
(Percent)

	Disagree	Mildly Disagree	Mildly Agree	Agree
If I had an HIV infection, my family relationships would get worse.	43.7	19.8	21.0	15.4
If I had an HIV infection, no one would date me.	21.1	23.6	21.3	34.1
If I had an HIV infection, my friends would still be my friends.	40.3	27.7	15.1	16.3
People would avoid me if I had an HIV infection.	22.5	22.3	30.5	24.7

Table 3. Perceived Barriers to Condom Use
(Percent)

	Disagree	Mildly Disagree	Mildly Agree	Agree
Condoms decrease pleasure during sex.	19.7	17.7	22.0	40.4
Using condoms during sex is a hassle.	29.2	24.1	26.0	20.8
I would rather use some other kind of birth control than condoms.	36.9	17.0	17.7	28.4

Perceived Social Barriers for Safer Sex

Twenty-four percent agreed that they feel pressure from friends to have sex. Thirty-six percent reported that having sex makes them feel more mature. About 29 percent reported pressures from friends to have sex or to have more than one sex partner (Table 4). Clearly, an important minority of subjects experience social pressures regarding sexual risk behavior. Similar measures of perceived social barriers to safer sex intentions are not reported in the literature so juvenile delinquent's responses cannot be compared to other groups of adolescents.

Perceived Benefits of Safer Sex Intentions

About 80 percent of study respondents perceived benefits of safer sex intentions (Table 5). And, 85 percent believed using condoms would decrease their chances of getting an HIV infection. Eighty percent agreed that using condoms would decrease their worry about HIV infection. Almost 80 percent agreed they worry less when not having sex. Similar measures of perceived benefits are not reported in the literature so study participants cannot be compared to other groups of adolescents.

Self-Efficacy for Condom Use

A high percentage of the sample reported capability to acquire and use condoms (Table 6). Juvenile delinquents express high to moderate levels of self-efficacy for condom use. Eighty-seven percent agreed condoms were easy to use. Seventy-eight percent agreed condom use indicates they care about their health. Subjects believed they knew where to buy condoms (93% agreed). And, 93 percent agreed they knew how to use condoms during intercourse. An amazing 86 percent agreed they would use condoms with a new sex partner. On average, 11 percent of the

Table 4. Perceived Social Barriers for Safer Sex
(Percent)

	Disagree	Mildly Disagree	Mildly Agree	Agree
I feel pressure from my friends to have sex.	56.6	19.4	13.6	10.5
Having sex makes you feel more mature.	32.3	23.3	22.7	13.4
I feel pressure from my friends to have more than one sex partner.	51.1	20.3	15.9	12.8

Table 5. Perceived Benefits of Safer Sex Intentions
(Percent)

	Disagree	Mildly Disagree	Mildly Agree	Agree
If I use a condom when having sex, I will lessen my chances of getting an HIV infection.	9.1	5.0	12.9	72.3
If I use a condom when having sex, I will worry less about getting an HIV infection.	8.4	11.5	19.8	60.3
I worry less about getting an HIV infection when I am not having sex.	9.3	10.4	19.9	60.0

subjects reported low self-efficacy for condom use. Similar measures of self-efficacy for condom use are not available in the literature for comparison purposes.

Self-Efficacy for Sexual Discussion

Subjects reported low levels of self-efficacy for sexual discussion (Table 7). Thirty-five percent reported it would be difficult to ask their sex partners about past partners. Yet, 75 percent believed they could discuss condom use with their

Table 6. Self-Efficacy for Condom Use
(Percent)

	Disagree	Mildly Disagree	Mildly Agree	Agree
Condoms are easy to use.	6.0	7.3	11.1	75.6
Using condoms when having sex tells my partner I care about my health.	7.5	13.8	21.3	57.1
I am able to buy condoms.	4.2	2.7	7.2	85.8
I know where to get condoms.	1.9	2.2	3.5	92.2
I am able to carry condoms with me on a date in case I decide to have sex.	5.9	3.8	13.9	76.3
I know how to use a condom when I have sex with someone.	2.6	4.6	4.7	88.0
I am able to make sure a condom is used with a new sex partner.	4.4	9.6	18.7	67.3

sex partners. Twenty-eight percent reported difficulty in telling their partners about their past sex partners. Somewhat lower rates of confidence to discuss sexual histories were found among South Carolina adolescents in school systems [32]. Fifty percent reported it would be difficult to discuss sexual histories with a partner.

Self-Efficacy for Self-Disclosure of High Risk Behavior Which May Be Socially Unacceptable

The rate of subjects who reported ability to discuss socially unacceptable behavior was much lower (Table 8). Eighty-one percent did not believe they would tell their partners if they used IV drugs or had anal sex. In contrast, 38 percent did not believe they could tell their partners if they had ever had sex with another man. No similar measures of self-efficacy for self-disclosure of high risk behaviors were found in the literature for comparison purposes.

Table 7. Self-Efficacy for Sexual Discussion
(Percent)

	Disagree	Mildly Disagree	Mildly Agree	Agree
It is hard to ask a sex partner about other people they have had sex with.	39.1	15.6	15.1	19.8
It is hard to ask someone if they have had sex with more than one person in the last year.	49.8	16.4	14.6	18.9
I am able to discuss the use of condoms with my sex partner.	8.2	16.1	24.3	51.4
I am able to ask my sex partner how many people they have had sex with before me.	8.7	11.7	20.5	69.1
I am able to ask my sex partner(s) if they have ever had anal sex.	23.7	13.3	16.9	46.0
I am able to ask my sex partner(s) if they have ever used IV drugs.	7.9	8.0	15.5	68.5
I am able to ask my sex partner(s) if they have ever had sex with another man.	11.1	8.2	12.7	68.1
I am able to tell my sex partner(s) how many people I have had sex with before him or her.	14.0	14.2	21.2	51.5

Perceived Social Norms for Safer Sex Intentions

Subjects report low social norms for safer sex intentions (Table 9). Only 15 percent agreed their friends were still virgins. Similarly, 70 percent reported that their sexually active friends were not monogamous. Finally, 69 percent believed their friends would not wait until marriage to have intercourse. No similar measures of perceived social norms toward safer sex intentions were found in the literature for comparison purposes.

Table 8. Self-Disclosure of High Risk Behavior which May
Be Socially Unacceptable
(Percent)

	Disagree	Mildly Disagree	Mildly Agree	Agree
I am able to tell my sex partner(s) if I have ever used needles to inject drugs.	69.8	11.5	8.2	10.6
I am able to tell my sex partner(s) if I have had anal sex.	69.8	11.5	8.2	10.6
I am able to tell my sex partner(s) if I have had sex with another man.	32.2	5.5	8.5	53.5

Table 9. Perceived Social Norms toward Safer Sex Intentions
(Percent)

	Disagree	Mildly Disagree	Mildly Agree	Agree
Most of my friends are still virgins.	70.9	13.5	9.5	5.8
Most of my friends who are sexually active only have one sexual relationship at a time.	49.0	20.5	13.7	16.7
I have friends who do not plan on having a sexual relationship until they are married.	53.6	15.5	12.9	18.0

Safer Sex Intentions

Subjects reported low safer sex intentions (Table 10). Sixty-eight percent agreed they would make sure a condom was used during sex. Fifty-five percent disagreed they would be monogamous. They also disagreed (84%) that they would wait until they were married to have intercourse and that they would wait until age eighteen before having intercourse (88%). Finally subjects agreed (55%) they would have sex with someone who refuses to use a condom.

Table 10. Safer Sex Intentions
(Percent)

	Disagree	Mildly Disagree	Mildly Agree	Agree
I will make sure a condom is used when I have sex.	11.6	20.3	33.3	34.7
I will only have one sexual relationship at a time.	32.5	22.0	13.4	32.1
I do not plan on having sex until I am married.	73.1	10.7	8.4	7.5
I would only have sex with a person who I have a long-term relationship with.	36.8	21.5	15.2	26.4
I will not have sex with someone who refuses to use a condom.	19.6	25.2	18.7	36.1
I do not plan on having sex until I am at least eighteen years old.	77.6	10.9	5.1	6.4

Three studies have considered safer sex intentions of adolescents within school systems. Sixty-three to 89 percent of adolescents reported they intended to use condoms in future sexual encounters compared to 68 percent of juvenile delinquents [25, 33, 34]. Seventy percent of school adolescents indicated they intended to refrain from having multiple sexual partners compared to only 45.5 percent of juvenile delinquents. Fifty-seven percent of school adolescents intended to have intercourse before marriage compared to 83.8 percent of juvenile delinquents. And, 41 percent of school adolescents thought they would have intercourse before graduation from high school compared to 88.5 percent of juvenile delinquents. Juvenile delinquents in this study have lower reported rates of safer sex intentions than adolescents within school systems.

Cues to Action for Safer Sex Intentions

Study subjects had low cues to action for safer sex intentions (Table 11). Almost half the subjects have never talked with a sex partner (47.5%), a family member (47.8%), a doctor or nurse (48.9%) or a friend (43.3%) about how to prevent an HIV infection. Seventy-four percent have talked about HIV prevention in school and 84 percent have read books or magazines about HIV prevention at least one

Table 11. Cues to Action for Safer Sex Intentions
(Percent)

	0 Times	1 Time	2 Times	3 Times	4 or More
How many times have you talked with a friend about how to prevent an HIV infection?	43.3	16.2	12.0	5.1	23.1
How many times have you talked with someone in your family about how to prevent an HIV infection?	47.8	14.0	0.2	5.3	22.4
How many times have you talked with a sex partner of yours about how to prevent an HIV infection?	47.5	14.0	12.7	7.1	18.4
How many times have you talked to a doctor or nurse about how to prevent an HIV infection?	48.9	14.9	14.4	6.4	15.3
How many times have you talked about how to prevent an HIV infection in school?	25.6	12.9	13.8	8.4	39.3
How many times have you read about how to prevent an HIV infection in books and magazines?	16.0	10.4	14.7	8.0	50.9

time. Similar measures of cues to action for safer sex behaviors were not found in the literature for comparison purposes.

CONCLUSIONS/RECOMMENDATIONS

In this study the HBM was used to gain insight into the HIV education needs of juvenile delinquents. By conducting an educational diagnosis using the HBM, programs can be tailored specifically to the health beliefs of this group. The vast majority of the subjects reported low susceptibility to HIV infection. Most believed that they were too young and healthy to contract HIV. They did not believe that "people like them" were susceptible and they were not worried about infection. Juvenile delinquents' lack of perceived susceptibility to HIV infection in this study is consistent with the literature on adolescent development. Elkind suggests teenagers believe in a "personal fable" [35]. They do not think bad things can or will happen to them; they are personally invulnerable. This perceived invulnerability may be reinforced by the fact that the majority of the sample have been sexually active. Many have had intercourse and not experienced negative health consequences. Such experience is likely to reinforce feelings of personal invulnerability and decrease perceived susceptibility to HIV infection. The personal fable has been interpreted in the health education literature as a perceived lack of susceptibility to HIV infection [36]. The findings of this study support this interpretation.

Researchers suggest adolescents are capable of perceiving the severity of health risk [37, 38]. However, in this study juvenile delinquents did not report high levels of negative social consequences from HIV infection. These findings may be due to the difficulty juvenile delinquents have in conceptualizing realistic consequences. HIV is a health threat that is usually thought to be far in the future and juvenile delinquents have little or no personal experience with medical conditions related to HIV infections. Lack of perceived severity of an HIV infection may relate to juvenile delinquents' poor understanding of the physical and social consequences of HIV infection caused by lack of health education and/or low general educational levels. The adolescent HIV literature shows adolescents tend to score low on perceived severity [31, 32, 39]. Juvenile delinquents in this study are consistent with the adolescent HIV literature.

Three studies located in the literature have identified barriers to condom use as an important factor in HIV risk behavior [22, 31, 40]. A large number of juvenile delinquents reported that condoms: reduce pleasure, are a hassle and would prefer to use another form of birth control. Social barriers for safer sex were also studied. About 25 percent of the sample reported social pressures to have sex and to have more than one partner. Over one-third reported that having sex makes them feel more mature. Elkind observes that adolescents are constructing a sense of identity in a social context [41]. Thus, adolescents define themselves as group members as well as individuals. Adolescents are heavily influenced by group behaviors, beliefs, and norms. Importantly, adolescents may not be consciously aware of the influence of group behaviors, beliefs and norms on their own behavior. Sexual behaviors are likely to be strongly influenced by these norms. The 25 to 35 percent who reported social pressures may only be those consciously aware of this influence. Clearly, barriers to condom use and social barriers to safer sex create significant obstacles to safer sex behavior. Prevention programs should directly address these perceptions and social pressures.

Perceived benefits of safer sex behavior were reported by over 80 percent of the sample. Reported benefits include: condoms reduce risk of HIV, condoms reduce worry over HIV infection and not having sex reduces worry. These high rates of perceived benefits are inconsistent with low reported rates of safer sex intention. It is possible that perceived benefits are overwhelmed by other factors which reduce safer sex intentions. Since most juvenile delinquents are aware of these perceived benefits, little instructional time in prevention programs seems warranted for this HBM construct.

Self-efficacy has been related to frequency and consistency of condom use [42, 43]. About 90 percent of juvenile delinquents report the ability to buy, carry, and use condoms. Within the limitations of the present study it is unclear if perceived efficacy for condom use is actually related to skill or performance. It is clear that rates of reported efficacy are much higher than rates of intent to use condoms. Barriers to condom use (i.e., decrease pleasure, prefer other type of birth control) may help explain the disparity. Subjects report lower levels of self-efficacy for sexual discussion and self-disclosure of high risk behavior which may not be considered socially acceptable. About one-third agreed that it was difficult to discuss sexual histories. About 80 percent are not likely to self-disclose high-risk behavior. So while most believe they are capable of discussing risk history with sex partners, a large majority are not likely to disclose high-risk behavior. As a consequence, discussion of sexual histories among juvenile delinquents is not likely to be effective in reducing risk of HIV infection. Prevention programs for juveniles should emphasize the barriers to honest risk disclosure and not consider discussion of sexual history an effective risk-reducing behavior. Or, prevention programs should focus on increasing juveniles' sense of self-efficacy about disclosing their sexual histories.

Juvenile delinquents' safer sex intentions place them at high risk for HIV infection. This finding is consistent with the HIV risk literature on incarcerated youth [44, 45]. As expected, juvenile delinquents beliefs and intentions place them at higher risk than unincarcerated youth [36, 42]. Clearly, HIV prevention programs for incarcerated youth must be tailored to their high-risk lifestyle. Eighty-nine percent do not intend to abstain from sexual intercourse until age eighteen. Over half indicated they would have sex with someone who refuses to use a condom and 32 percent would not make sure a condom was used during sex. Almost 58 percent indicated a willingness to have sex outside of a long-term relationship.

The low levels of safer sex intentions reported by juvenile delinquents reinforces the need for effective prevention programs for this population. Cues to Action for Safer Sex Intentions suggest that this population is lacking exposure to HIV prevention messages. The low levels of discussion with friends (43% report no discussions) about HIV prevention suggests that this issue is not a prime concern for this high-risk group. Only 22 percent reported four or more exposures to HIV prevention from family members. For this population, health care providers do not appear to be an avenue of HIV instruction. Forty-nine percent reported no HIV discussion with a doctor or nurse. Most important, 39 percent reported four or more exposures on HIV instruction in the schools. The most frequent reported source of information about HIV prevention was books and magazines. Fifty-one percent reported four or more exposures through this channel. This is consistent with other adolescent HIV literature. The most frequently reported source of HIV prevention information was the mass media [46-48]. Overall, these low levels of exposure to HIV prevention messages suggest that this population is hard-to-reach and could benefit from sound, systematic instruction.

Juvenile delinquents' sexual behavior places them at high risk for HIV infection. Conducting an educational diagnosis based on the HBM has identified specific motivational targets which enable the design of effective prevention programs. Barriers to condom use and social barriers to safer sex appear to be of particular importance. It is critical that studies focus on identifying the most effective approaches to modifying health beliefs and determining the amount of health belief change necessary to substantially reduce HIV risk through behavior change.

REFERENCES

1. Centers for Disease Control, *National HIV Seroprevalence Surveys. Summary of Results. Data from Seroprevalence Activities through 1989* (2nd Edition), DHHS, HIV/CID/9-90/006, Atlanta, Georgia, 1990.
2. M. Caldwell and M. Rogers, Epidemiology of Pediatric HIV Infection, *Pediatric Clinics of North America, 38*:1, pp. 1-16, 1991.
3. Centers for Disease Control, Guidelines for Effective School Health Education to Prevent the Spread of AIDS, *Morbidity and Mortality Weekly Report Supplement, 37*:5-2, pp. 1-13, 1988.
4. H. Gayle, M. Rogers, and S. Manoff, *Demographic and Sexual Transmission Differences between Adolescent and Adult AIDS Patients*, paper presented at the Fourth International Conference on AIDS, Stockholm, June 12-16, 1988.
5. N. Gibbs, Teens: The Rising Risk of AIDS, *Time, 138*:9, pp. 60-61, 1991.
6. L. Strunin, Adolescents' Perceptions of Risk for HIV Infection: Implications for Future Research, *Social Science and Medicine, 32*:2, pp. 221-228, 1991.
7. J. Brooks-Gunn, C. Boyer, and K. Hein, Preventing HIV and AIDS in Children and Adolescents: Behavioral Research and Intervention Strategies, *American Psychologist, 43*, pp. 958-964, 1988.
8. K. Hein and M. Hurst, Human Immunodeficiency Virus Infection in Adolescents: A Rationale for Action, *Adolescent Pediatric Gynecology, 1*, pp. 73-82, 1988.
9. D. Wendell, I. Onorato, E. McCray, D. Allen, and P. Sweeney, Youth at Risk: Sex, Drugs, and Human Immunodeficiency Virus, *American Journal of Diseases of Children, 146*, pp. 76-81, 1991.
10. S. Carmel, The Health Belief Model in the Research of AIDS-related Preventive Behavior, *Public Health Review, 18*, pp. 73-85, 1990.
11. I. Rosenstock, The Health Belief Model: Explaining Health Behavior through Expectancies, in *Health Behavior and Health Education*, K. Glanz, F. Lewis, and B. Rimer (eds.), Jossey-Bass, San Francisco, California, pp. 39-62, 1990.

12. M. Berens, Teen Prison System a Nightmare, *The Columbus Dispatch*, 1A-2A, May 17, 1992.

13. M. Berens, Juvenile Judges Left without Choices: Youth Services Only Place for Serious Offenders, *The Columbus Dispatch*, 4B-5B, May 17, 1992.

14. J. Mangos, T. Doran, B. Aranda-Naranjo, Y. Rodriguez-Escobar, A. Scott, J. Setzer, J. Sherman, and S. Kossman, Pediatric AIDS: Adolescence, Delinquency, Drug Abuse and AIDS, *Journal of Texas Medicine, 86*:7, pp. 100-103, 1990.

15. Office of Juvenile Justice and Delinquency Prevention, Update on Research: Study Sheds New Light on Juvenile Offender, *Juvenile Justice Bulletin*, Office of Juvenile Justice and Delinquency Prevention, Washington, D.C., August 1988.

16. K. Hein, A. Marks, and M. Cohen, Asymptomatic Gonorrhea: Prevalence in a Population of Urban Teenagers, *Journal of Pediatrics, 90*, pp. 634-635, 1977.

17. K. Hein, M. Cohen, and A. Marks, Age at First Intercourse among Homeless Adolescent Females, *Journal of Pediatrics, 93*, pp. 147-148, 1978.

18. Centers for Disease Control, Results of a Gallup Poll on Acquired Immunodeficiency Syndrome—New York City, United States, *Morbidity and Mortality Weekly, 34*, pp. 513-514, 1985.

19. National Academy of Sciences, *Confronting AIDS: Directions for Public Health, Health Care, and Research*, National Academy Press, 1986.

20. Surgeon General, *The AIDS Crisis*, Surgeon General's Office, 1986.

21. U.S. Department of Education, *AIDS and the Education of Our Children: A Guide for Parents and Teachers*, Department of Education, 1987.

22. R. DiClemente, Predictors of HIV-Preventive Sexual Behavior in a High-Risk Adolescent Population: The Influence of Perceived Peer Norms and Sexual Communication on Incarcerated Adolescents' Consistent Use of Condoms, *Journal of Adolescent Health, 12*, pp. 385-390, 1991.

23. M. Rotheram-Borus and C. Koopman, Sexual Risk Behaviors, AIDS Knowledge and Beliefs about AIDS among Runaways, *American Journal of Public Health, 81*:2, pp. 208-210, 1991.

24. L. Strunin and R. Hingson, Acquired Immunodeficiency Syndrome and Adolescents: Knowledge, Beliefs, Attitudes and Behaviors, *Pediatrics, 79*:5, pp. 825-828, 1987.

25. R. Petosa and J. Wessinger, Using the Health Belief Model to Assess the HIV Education Needs of Junior and Senior High School Students, *International Quarterly of Community Health Education, 10*:2, pp. 135-143, 1990.

26. C. Koopman, M. Rotheram-Borus, R. Henderson, J. Bradley, and J. Hunter, Assessment of Knowledge of AIDS and Beliefs about AIDS Prevention among Adolescents, *AIDS Education and Prevention, 2*:1, pp. 58-70, 1990.

27. D. Seigel, N. Lazarus, F. Krasnovsky, M. Durbin, and M. Chesney, AIDS Knowledge, Attitudes and Behavior among Inner City, Junior High School Students, *Journal of School Health, 61*:4, pp. 160-165, 1991.

28. J. Kim and C. Mueller, *Introduction to Factor Analysis. What It Is and How To Do It*, Sage, Newbury Park, California, 1978.

29. J. Price, S. Desmond, and G. Kukulka, High School Students' Perceptions and Misperceptions of AIDS, *Journal of School Health, 55*:3, pp. 107-110, 1985.

30. L. McGill, P. Smith, and T. Johnson, AIDS: Knowledge, Attitudes and Risk Characteristics of Teens, *Journal of Sex Education and Therapy, 15*:1, pp. 30-35, 1989.

31. R. Hingson, L. Strunin, and B. Berlin, Acquired Immunodeficiency Syndrome Trans-
    mission: Changes in Knowledge and Behaviors among Teenagers, Massachusetts
    Statewide Surveys, 1986 to 1988, *Pediatrics, 85*:1, pp. 24-29, 1990.
32. R. Petosa and J. Wessinger, The AIDS Educational Needs of Adolescents: A Theory-
    based Approach, *AIDS Education and Prevention, 2*:1, pp. 127-136, 1990.
33. N. Barling and S. Moore, Adolescents' Attitudes towards AIDS Precautions and
    Intention to Use Condoms, *Psychological Reports, 67*, pp. 883-890, 1990.
34. L. Dusenbury, G. Botvin, E. Baker, and J. Laurence, AIDS Risk Knowledge, Attitudes
    and Behavioral Intentions among Multiethnic Adolescents, *AIDS Education and
    Prevention, 3*:4, pp. 367-375, 1991.
35. D. Elkind, Egocentrism in Adolescence, *Child Development, 38*, pp. 1025-1034, 1967.
36. R. Petosa and K. Jackson, Using the Health Belief Model to Predict Safer Sex Inten-
    tions among Adolescents, *Health Education Quarterly, 18*:4, pp. 463-476, 1991.
37. C. Irwin and S. Milstein, Biopsychosocial Correlates of Risk-taking Behavior during
    Adolescence, *Journal of Adolescent Health Care, 7*:6, pp. 582-596, 1986.
38. G. Melton, G. Koocher, and M. Saks (eds.), *Children's Competence to Consent*,
    Plenum, New York, 1983.
39. H. Walters, R. Vaughan, M. Gladis, D. Ragin, S. Kasen, and A. Cohall, Factors
    Associated with AIDS Risk Behaviors among High School Students in an AIDS
    Epicenter, *American Journal of Public Health, 82*:4, pp. 528-532, 1992.
40. J. Hernandez and F. Smith, Sensation Seeking and STD Control, *Journal of Health
    Education, 22*:5, pp. 307-312, 1991.
41. D. Elkind, *All Grown Up and No Place To Go: Teenagers in Crisis*, Addison-Wesley,
    Reading, Massachusetts, 1984.
42. R. Ahia, Compliance with Safer-sex Guidelines among Adolescent Males: Application
    of the Health Belief Model and Protection Motivation Theory, *Journal of Health
    Education, 22*:1, pp. 49-52, 1991.
43. K. Basen-Enquist and G. Parcel, Attitudes, Norms and Self-Efficacy: A Model of
    Adolescents' HIV-related Sexual Risk Behavior, *Health Education Quarterly, 19*:2,
    pp. 263-277, 1992.
44. M. Lanier, R. DiClemente, and P. Horan, HIV Knowledge and Behaviors of Incar-
    cerated Youth: A Comparison of High and Low Risk Locales, *Journal of Criminal
    Justice, 19*, pp. 257-262, 1991.
45. J. Rolf, J. Nanda, and L. Thompson, J. Mamon, A. Chandra, J. Baldwin, and
    M. Delahunt, Issues in AIDS Prevention among Incarcerated Offenders, in *Troubled
    Adolescents and HIV Infection: Issues in Prevention and Treatment*, D. Woodruff,
    D. Doherty, and J. Athey (eds.), Georgetown University Child Development Center,
    Washington, D.C., pp. 56-69, 1989.
46. R. Fennell, Knowledge, Attitudes and Beliefs of Students Regarding AIDS: A Review,
    Journal of Health Education, 21:4, pp. 20-26, 1990.
47. E. Goodman and A. Cohall, Acquired Immunodeficiency Syndrome and Adolescents:
    Knowledge, Attitudes, Beliefs and Behaviors in a New York City Adolescent Minority
    Population, *Pediatrics, 84*:1, pp. 36-42, 1989.
48. S. Helgerson, L. Petersen, and The AIDS Education Study Group, Acquired Immuno-
    deficiency Syndrome and Secondary School Students: Their Knowledge is Limited
    and They Want to Learn More, *Pediatrics, 81*:3, pp. 350-355, 1988.

References Not Cited in the Text

Associated Press, Poll Examines Magic's Revelation, *Cleveland Plain Dealer*, p. 10, November 29, 1991.

A. Bandura, Self-efficacy: Toward a Unifying Theory of Behavioral Change, *Psychological Review, 84*:2, pp. 191-215, 1977.

A. Bandura, Self-efficacy Determinants of Anticipatory Fears and Calamities, *Journal of Personal and Social Psychology, 45*, pp. 464-469, 1983.

L. Kirsch, Efficacy Expectations or Response Predictor: The Meaning of Efficacy Ratings as a Function of Task Characteristics, *Journal of Personal and Social Psychology, 42*, pp. 132-136, 1982.

I. Kirsch, Self-efficacy and Expectancy: Old Wine with New Labels, *Journal of Personal and Social Psychology, 49*, pp. 824-830, 1985.

G. Melton, Adolescents and Prevention of AIDS, *Professional Psychology: Research and Practice, 19*:4, pp. 403-408, 1988.

J. Stiener, D. Sorokin, D. Schiedermayer, and T. Van Susteren, Are Adolescents Getting Smarter about Acquired Immunodeficiency Syndrome? *American Journal of Diseases of Children, 144*, pp. 302-306, 1990.

V. Stretcher, M. DeVellis, M. Becker, and I. Rosenstock, Self-efficacy and the Health Belief Model, *Health Education Quarterly, 13*, pp. 73-92, 1986.

R. Warren, G. Konglan, and M. Sabri, *The Certainty Method: Its Application and Usefulness in Developing Empirical Measures in Social Sciences*, Rural Sociology Rep. No. 82, Iowa State University, Ames, 1969.

CHAPTER 5

Use of Health Belief Model to Predict Condom Use among University Students in Nigeria

Christiana Udo Edem and S. Marie Harvey

Acquired Immunodeficiency Syndrome (AIDS) continues to be a major global public health issue. Projections to the year 2000 anticipate that between thirty-eight million and 110 million adults and more than ten million children will be infected [1]. This pandemic warrants global mobilization and coordinated strategies at national and international levels. In this mobilization, the study of sexual behavior and the prevention of sexual risk-taking behavior both deserve high priority. An effective vaccine may be years away and will most certainly not be available to all the world for many years. Thus, health education activities directed at reducing high-risk behaviors and promoting safe sex remain the only way forward.

Sexual behavior is central to the epidemic spread of HIV and acquired immuno-deficiency syndrome (AIDS). As of January 1992, an estimated 71 percent of HIV infection around the world was due to heterosexual behavior [1]. In Sub-Saharan Africa, the pattern of behavior that encourages the spread of AIDS/HIV is different from that in Europe or the United States. For example, AIDS/HIV is spread in this region mainly through heterosexual activities, such as direct exposure to multiple sexual partners and infected prostitutes, rather than through homosexual and drug use activities [2].

While the greatest impact of the AIDS epidemic has been felt in East and Central Africa, the numbers of HIV-1 and HIV-2 infected individuals and those with AIDS in West Africa have increased dramatically in recent years [3]. In Nigeria, the first AIDS case was reported around 1984/85. Following the initial report, a few cases were detected among prostitutes in Lagos and Anambra States. As of August 1992, a total of 436 AIDS cases had been reported to the National AIDS/STD Control Programme (NASCP) [4]. Moreover, according to the Federal Ministry of Health and Human Services, Nigeria is in the " 'exponential' or very rapid growth phase of the HIV/AIDS epidemic" [5]. The rate of HIV infection in blood donors has doubled every year in some state hospitals, an indication of this rapid growth rate. Various studies in Nigeria have also shown that the average age of first sexual intercourse is as early as fifteen years in males and most likely lower in females. Special attention, therefore, needs to be focused on this most sexually active age group (15-30 years old), when interventions are being considered [4].

The dramatic rise in morbidity and mortality rates associated with HIV infection in Nigeria has created an urgent demand for the development of prevention programs, particularly for this high risk group. Unfortunately, very few or no studies have been conducted in Nigeria to examine knowledge, beliefs, attitudes, and behaviors related to AIDS/HIV. Moreover, an important issue for health education research in Africa is the cross-cultural validity of behavioral models such as the Health Belief Model [6, 7], the Theory of Reasoned Action [8], and the PRECEDE framework [9]. These models have been developed and tested mainly in the context of industrialized countries and need careful scrutiny for relevance to the African setting [2].

The purpose of this study is, therefore, to use the concepts of the Health Belief Model (HBM) to predict the adoption of safer sex behaviors to reduce risk of HIV infection among university students in Nigeria. The variables perceived susceptibility, perceived severity, perceived barriers and benefits, cues to action, knowledge, age and gender will test the ability of the HBM to predict self-reported condom use, past and intended, among university students in Nigeria.

A comprehensive review of studies found the HBM valuable in understanding preventive actions and recommended its use in health education program planning [10]. In addition, the specific set of beliefs described in the Health Belief Model has been hypothesized [11] and used [12, 13] to predict whether someone will adopt behaviors to avoid HIV transmission. Derived from value expectancy theory, the components of the HBM hypothesize that preventive behavior is a function of two factors: the value an individual places on health and the individual's belief that specific preventive actions will achieve the desired goal. As applied in this study, both actual and intended condom use are influenced by personal beliefs regarding the susceptibility to AIDS and severity of the disease. In addition, the HBM hypothesizes that the perceived benefits of condom use are weighed against the perceived barriers to condom use. Finally, the HBM proposes that a specific stimulus or a cue to action is often necessary to trigger the decision-making process.

METHODS

Participants and Procedures

Participants were 395 second year students (171 women and 221 men) who were enrolled in a university required course during the 1991/92 academic year at the University of Uyo in Akwa Ibom State of Nigeria. The required nature of the course ensured that the characteristics of the sample approximated those of the population of undergraduates enrolled at the university.

The students ranged in age from eighteen to twenty-four years, with the majority (74.4%) aged between nineteen and twenty-two years. Participating students were predominantly protestants (57.0%), single (84.3%), and from Akwa Ibom State (72.0%) where the university is located. Nearly two-thirds (65.3%) of the study population (61.7% of females and 68.1% males) had engaged in sexual intercourse. Of those students who were sexually active nearly 40 percent had never used condoms (44.3% of females and 34.9% of males).

During the first semester of the 1991/1992 academic year, a self-administered questionnaire was distributed to 450 students in a classroom setting. Participants were instructed to complete the questionnaire outside of the classroom, place the completed survey in the attached envelope and return the sealed envelope to the departmental office. Three hundred and ninety-five questionnaires were completed and returned for a response rate of 73.2 percent.

Survey Questionnaire

An instrument was developed to elicit AIDS/HIV related knowledge, beliefs and attitude as well as intentions and behaviors regarding condom use. The HBM was used as the conceptual framework for the development of the instrument. Subscales were developed to measure perceived susceptibility to and seriousness of AIDS, benefits of condom use, barriers to condom use, cues to action and AIDS knowledge. The questionnaire was a modification of three existing instruments on AIDS/HIV. Modification was based on what was considered relevant to the culture of Nigeria, the scope of the present study and the elimination of overlapping items from the three sources. Wording of some of the items was revised following a pilot study with twenty Nigerian students to determine readability and comprehension.

Health Belief Model Variables

The independent variables in the study were perceived susceptibility/severity, perceived benefits, perceived barriers, cues to action, age and gender.

Perceived Susceptibility/Severity

This variable consisted of eight items that tested perception of individual susceptibility to AIDS/HIV, and the seriousness of contracting AIDS/HIV. Four of the items tested susceptibility, while the remaining four tested severity. Variable items required respondents to state their level of agreement or disagreement with such statements as "There is no cure for AIDS," "AIDS can reduce body's natural immunity," "Someone with AIDS will eventually die from the disease," and "An infected person can pass the virus to a sex partner during sexual intercourse." Response options were on a 4-point Likert scale ranging from strongly agree to strongly disagree or from very likely to not at all likely. These options were summed into index scores ranging from eight to thirty-two, with a higher score representing higher perceptions of susceptibility/severity.

Perceived Benefits

This variable consists of five items that suggest, among other things, that condoms are an effective way of preventing the transmission of the AIDS virus, sexually transmitted diseases, and of preventing unwanted pregnancies. The response options were on a 4-point Likert scale ranging from strongly agree to strongly disagree. Responses were summed into index scores ranging from five to twenty, with a higher score indicating higher perception of benefits.

Perceived Barriers

This variable also consisted of five items, which, among others, suggested that buying or using condoms is embarrassing, expensive, and indicates mistrust. The items requested respondents to rate their level of agreement or disagreement with such statements as "I would feel insulted if a sex partner wanted to use a condom" and "Using condoms suggests that you do not trust your sex partner." Response options were on a 4-point Likert scale ranging from strongly agree to strongly disagree, with higher score representing higher perception of barrier. The index scores ranged from five to twenty.

Cues to Action

Four items were included in this variable which required respondents to state whether or not they have ever discussed AIDS/HIV with adult family members, health professionals and friends or received instructions on the subject in their university. Response options were yes or no, where yes was coded as "one" and no was coded as "zero." The index scores ranged from four to eight, with the higher score representing exposure to more cues.

Knowledge of AIDS/HIV

The knowledge scale consisted of thirteen questions that focused mainly on the transmission and prevention of AID/HIV. Some of the transmission items required respondents to state how likely they thought that a person will get the AIDS virus from sharing an injection needle with someone who has the AIDS virus, using the public toilet, or sharing a scarification knife with someone who is infected with the virus. Preventive questions sought to elicit how much respondents knew about AIDS/HIV prevention. For example, respondents were asked how likely the use of condoms, birth control pills, abstinence, douching after sexual intercourse, or withdrawal can protect someone from getting AIDS/HIV. Response options were arranged on a 4-point Likert scale of strongly agree to strongly disagree or very likely to not at all likely. The most correct response was assigned four points while the least correct had one point. The score index ranged from thirteen to fifty-two.

Reliability for the five HBM concepts, computed using Cronbach's alpha, was moderate to good: perceived susceptibility/severity, .59; perceived benefits to condom use, .73; perceived barriers to condom use, .69; cues to action, .52; and AIDS/HIV knowledge, .83 (Table 1).

Dependent Variables: Measures of Condom Use

Intentions to Use Condoms

All students, regardless of past sexual experience, were asked about their intentions to use condoms in the future. They responded to the following question: "If you have sex within the next month, how likely is it that you would use a condom?" Responses ranged from very likely to very unlikely.

Table 1. Health Belief Model (HBM) Variables, Means, Number of Items, and Cronbach Alphas

HBM Variable (Range of Subscale)	Mean (SD)	No. of Items	Cronbach Alpha
Susceptibility/Severity (8 to 32)	27.7 (3.2)	8	.59
Barriers to Condom Use (5 to 20)	11.5 (3.2)	5	.69
Benefits of Condom Use (5 to 20)	14.7 (3.1)	5	.73
Cues to Action (4 to 8)	2.5 (1.3)	4	.52
AIDS/HIV Knowledge (13 to 52)	37.6 (6.4)	13	.83

Condom Use

To determine what percentage of respondents had ever used condoms during sexual intercourse, sexually active students were asked, "Have you ever used a condom during sexual intercourse?" This was a dichotomous variable that required a "yes" or "no" response.

RESULTS

To examine the bivariate relationships of the Health Belief Model concepts to condom use, both intended and past, Pearson correlations and t-test analyses were performed. Pearson correlations between predictor variables and the dependent variable, intentions to use condoms, are presented in Table 2. Three HBM variables were significantly correlated to intentions to use condoms. Results indicate that condom benefit beliefs ($p < .001$) and cues to action ($p < .01$) are positively associated with intentions to use condoms while condom barrier beliefs ($p < .05$) are negatively correlated with the dependent variable.

Results from the t-test analyses indicate that the same three HBM variables are significantly associated with past condom use (Table 3). Sexually active students who perceive higher benefits to condom use ($p < .001$) and report more cues to action ($p < .001$) are significantly more likely to report condom use. Those who perceive more barriers to condom use are significantly ($p < .001$) less likely to report past condom use.

Since some of the predictor variables are intercorrelated, making bivariate relationships difficult to interpret and because the major objective of this study was to determine which HBM variables are significant predictors of condom use, multivariate analyses were performed for each of the dependent variables. Two forms of regression analyses were used. Multiple regression analysis was

Table 2. Correlations between Health Belief Model (HBM)
Variables and Intentions to Use Condoms

HBM Variable	Correlation Coefficient
Susceptibility/Severity	−.02
Benefits	.28**
Barriers	−.13*
Cues	.16**
Knowledge	−.09
Age	−.11*
Gender (Female)	−.25**

*$p < .05$
**$p < .01$

Table 3. Means For and Significant Differences on Health Belief
Model (HBM) Variables by Condom Use Status

HBM Variable	Used Condoms	Never Used Condoms
Susceptibility/Severity	27.6	27.7
Benefits	15.5	14.1***
Barriers	15.6	18.3***
Cues	2.8	2.2***
Knowledge	52.4	53.6
Age	21.5	21.6

***$p < .01$

conducted to determine which of the variables were significant predictors of intentions to use condoms. Logistic regression analysis was employed in the examination of the categorical dependent variable, condom use. In both regression analyses, the major Health Belief Model variables (susceptibility/severity, benefits, barriers, and cues to action) were entered first into the analysis, knowledge was entered second and age and gender were entered third. This ordering was employed to test whether the subsidiary variables of the model (knowledge and demographics) significantly contributed to the prediction of condom use after controlling for the major HBM concepts.

Three variables emerged as significant predictors of future condom use (Table 4): perceived barriers to condom use ($p < .001$), perceived benefits to condom use ($p < .001$), and gender ($p < .001$). Condom barrier beliefs was negatively associated with intentions to use condoms while perceived benefits to condom use positively predicted future intentions. In addition, men were significantly more likely to report they intended to use condoms than were women. The combined variables accounted for 16 percent of the variance in the sample.

A logistic regression analysis was conducted using the Health Belief Model constructs as independent variables and condom use as the dependent variable. For this analysis, ever used condoms was coded as one and never used condoms was coded as zero. Results indicate that perceived benefits to condom use ($p < .01$), perceived barriers to condom use ($p < .001$), cues to action ($p < .001$), AIDS knowledge ($p < .05$), and male gender ($p < .01$) are significant predictors of condom use (Table 5). Condom barrier beliefs were negatively associated with condom use while perceived benefits of condom use positively predicted condom use. Cues to action was positively related to condom use indicating that students who discuss AIDS/HIV with significant others and/or who have received classroom instructions on the subject were more likely than others to use condoms. Knowledge negatively predicted condom use indicating that student with less knowledge about AIDS were more likely to use condoms. Finally, the results indicate that men were more likely than women to report condom use.

Table 4. Regression Analysis Predicting Intentions to Use Condoms

Step	Predictor Variable	Beta Value	T
1.	Susceptibility/Severity	−.0273	0.61
	Benefits	.1996	3.65***
	Barriers	−.1987	−3.71***
	Cues	.0603	1.12
2.	Knowledge	−.0839	−1.56
3.	Age	−.0636	−1.20
	Gender	−.2759	−5.14***

Multiple regression: Adjusted R square = .16
***$p < .001$

Table 5. Logistic Regression Analysis Predicting Condom Use

Step	Predictor Variable	B	Exp. (B)
1.	Susceptibility/Severity	−.05	.95
	Benefits	.17	1.18**
	Barriers	−.23	.88***
	Cues	.45	1.58***
2.	Knowledge	−.04	.96*
3.	Age	.05	1.05
	Gender (Female)	−.66	.52**

Note: Dependent variable is coded: Ever used condoms = 1, Never used condoms = 0.
*$p < .05$
**$p < .01$
***$p < .001$

DISCUSSION

The Health Belief Model was used as a framework for exploring condom use behavior and intentions among University students in the south eastern corner of Nigeria. The model has been used successfully in Western cultures to predict preventive health behaviors and intentions [13-15], but has not been systematically applied, so far, in studies conducted in sub-Saharan Africa. The present study is a preliminary attempt to assess the applicability of this Model to an African population. All major constructs of the model were used in this study and results indicate that some beliefs about HIV transmission and AIDS identified in the Health Belief Model predict whether university students in Nigeria use condoms or intend to use condoms. More specifically, the major HBM variables (perceived benefits of condom use, perceived barriers to condom use, and cues to action) together with AIDS knowledge and male gender significantly predicted condom use. Similarly, perceived benefits of condom use, perceived barriers to condom use and male gender predicted future condom use.

As would be expected, barriers to condom use was negatively associated with condom use and intentions to use condoms indicating that students who perceived barriers to condom use neither intend to nor use condoms during sexual intercourse. Barriers to use include financial cost of buying condoms and/or the psychological cost of being identified with buying or using condoms as a young, unmarried individual. In Nigeria, young people are still expected to abstain from sex until they are married. Moreover, condoms sold at subsidized rates are channelled through maternal and child welfare clinics where they are often inaccessible and difficult for young, unmarried individuals to obtain.

Perceived benefits of condom use, as predicted in the model, were positively associated with intentions and actual condom use. Benefits of condom use include prevention of pregnancy as well as protection against the transmission of HIV and STDs. In south eastern Nigeria where this study was conducted, unmarried individuals would primarily use condoms to prevent an unwanted pregnancy. In this culture, pregnancy outside of marriage continues to be a social stigma for the young woman and her family and a reason for serious repercussions for the male partner. At the present time the prevention of STDs and AIDS has not yet become a major priority in this culture. For this reason, women who use other forms of contraception to prevent pregnancy may not feel the need to simultaneously use condoms. This behavior is consistent with results from studies in the United States which suggest that the use of oral contraceptives are negatively correlated with condom use [16]. This finding highlights the importance of promoting condom use for HIV prevention when another method of pregnancy prevention is used.

Cues to action, another HBM variable, positively predicted condom use. Cues in this study consisted of discussions of AIDS/HIV with family, health professionals and friends as well as taking a university course on HIV/AIDS. According to the model, cues create a force leading to action. This finding emphasizes the need for opportunities that constitute cues and give students the chance to discuss more openly issues regarding HIV/AIDS.

Of particular interest is the finding that knowledge about HIV was inversely related to condom use and was not a significant predictor of intentions to use condoms. Clearly, HIV knowledge is necessary for young adults to identify behaviors which are effective in reducing the risk of HIV transmission. However, the present findings are in concert with numerous U.S. studies [11, 17] which indicate that HIV knowledge, in and of itself, is not sufficient to motivate the adoption and maintenance of HIV preventive behaviors including condom use.

It is noteworthy that a higher percentage of women than men reported that they had never used condoms and that female gender was negatively related to condom use. This gender difference in condom use is consistent with other studies conducted in Africa [18, 19]. The finding is alarming for several reasons. First, studies of gender-related risk of HIV infection through heterosexual contact have shown that transmission of HIV from men to women is more efficient than from women to men [20, 21]. Moreover, women are more biologically vulnerable than men to STD and HIV infections. STDs are particularly serious for women because women and their offspring bear a disproportionate share of the complications from them, including pelvic inflammatory disease, infertility, tubal pregnancy, congenital syphilis and HIV [22]. As the number of women with AIDS increases, so does the number of infected young children, who generally acquire the disease before or during birth.

Many other factors not explored in this study and not directly related to health benefits about condoms and AIDS/HIV may influence whether university students in Nigeria use or intend to use condoms. Of particular concern are interpersonal factors such as the ability to discuss contraception with sexual partners and the imbalances of power in the relationships between women and men. Condoms to prevent conception and condoms to prevent STDs are viewed differently. Introduction of condom use for STD prevention with a regular partner can bring up issues of infidelity [23]. Recent findings from studies conducted in the United States indicate that women often suffer abandonment, physical violence as well as accusations of infidelity when they insist on or even suggest condom use [24-26]. These findings highlight the urgent need for the development and distribution of effective and acceptable female-controlled methods for preventing the transmission of HIV and other agents that cause STDs.

In summary, this study suggests that certain components of the Health Belief Model provide a useful set of beliefs about AIDS to explore among university students in Nigeria and to target in efforts to increase condom use. Education programs will need to address students' misconceptions about condoms and to identify groups of students unlikely to use condoms because of negative beliefs about them. In contrast to pregnancy prevention, women and men have no choice about which method to use to prevent the transmission of HIV and STDs. Therefore, innovative approaches to promote condom use remain essential. Finally, findings from this study suggest that prevention efforts to promote condom use among this population need to target women and to be gender specific if their effectiveness is to be maximized.

REFERENCES

1. A. A. Ehrhardt, Trends in Sexual Behavior and HIV Pandemic, *American Journal of Public Health, 82*, pp. 1459-1461, 1992.
2. J. H. Hubley, AIDS in Africa—A Challenge to Health Education, *Health Education Research: Theory and Practice, 3*, pp. 41-47, 1988.

3. K. M. DeCock, F. Brun-Vezinet, G. Adjorlolo, et al., Risk of Tuberculosis in Patients with HIV-1 and HIV-2 Infections in Abidjian, *British Medical Journal, 302*, pp. 496-499, 1991.
4. Nigerian Federal Ministry of Health and Human Services in Collaboration with the World Health Organization, *Global Program on AIDS*, November 1992.
5. Nigerian Federal Ministry of Health and Human Services, Ministerial Press Briefing (1992), reprinted in *Daily Times, AIDS and STD Control*, January 14, 1993.
6. M. H. Becker, *The Health Belief Model and Personal Health Behavior*, Slack, Thorofare, New Jersey, 1974.
7. I. M. Rosenstock, The Health Belief Model and Preventive Health Behavior, *Health Education Monograph, 2*, pp. 354-386, 1974.
8. I. Ajzen and M. Fishbein, *Understanding Attitudes and Predicting Social Behavior*, Prentice Hall, Englewood Cliff, New York, 1980.
9. L. W. Green, L. W. Kreuter, S. G. Deeds, and K. B. Partridge, *Health Education Planning—A Diagnostic Approach*, Mayfield, Palo Alto, California, 1980.
10. N. K. Janz and M. H. Becker, The Health Belief Model: A Decade Later, *Health Education Quarterly, 11*, pp. 1-47, 1984.
11. M. H. Becker and J. Joseph, AIDS and Behavioral Change to Avoid Risk: A Review, *American Journal of Public Health, 78*, pp. 384-410, 1988.
12. R. W. Hingson, L. Strunin, B. M. Berlin, and T. Heeren, Beliefs about AIDS, Use of Alcohol and Drugs, and Unprotected Sex among Massachusetts Adolescents, *American Journal of Public Health, 80*, pp. 295-299, 1990.
13. R. Petosa and K. Jackson, Using the Health Belief Model to Predict Safer Sex Intentions among Adolescents, *Health Education Quarterly, 18*, pp. 463-476, 1991.
14. J. A. Stein, S. A. Fox, P. J. Murata, and D. E. Morisky, Mammography Usage and the Health Belief Model, *Health Education Quarterly, 19*, pp. 447-462, 1992.
15. M. Eisen, G. Zellman, and A. McAlister, A Health Belief Model Approach to Adolescents' Fertility Control: Some Pilot Program Findings, *Health Education Quarterly, 12*, pp. 185-210, 1985.
16. D. M. Grimley, G. E. Riley, J. M. Bellis, and J. O. Prochaska, Assessing the Stages of Change and Decision-making for Contraceptive Use for the Prevention of Pregnancy, Sexually Transmitted Diseases, and Acquired Immunodeficiency Syndrome, *Health Education Quarterly, 20*, pp. 455-470, 1993.
17. R. J. DiClemente, Predictors of HIV Preventive Sexual Behavior in a High-risk Adolescent Population: The Influence of Perceived Peer Norms and Sexual Communication on Incarcerated Adolescents' Consistent Use of Condoms, *Journal of Adolescent Health, 12*, pp. 385-390, 1991.
18. J. T. Bertrand, B. Makani, S. E. Hassig, and K. L. Nivembro, Sexual Behavior and Condom Use in 10 Sites of Zaire, *The Journal of Sex Research, 28*, pp. 347-364, 1991.
19. S. J. Forster and K. E. Furley, 1988 Public Awareness Survey on AIDS and Condoms in Uganda, *AIDS, 3*, pp. 147-154, 1989.
20. P. G. Miotti, J. D. Chiphangwi, and H. A. Dellabetta, The Situation in Africa, *Bailliere's Clinical Obstetrics and Gynaecology, 6*, pp. 165-186.
21. N. S. Padian, S. C. Shiboski, and N. P. Jewell, Female-to-male Transmission of Human Immunodeficiency Virus, *Journal of the American Medical Association, 266*, pp. 1664-1667.

22. M. J. Rosenberg and E. L. Gollub, Commentary: Methods Women Can Use that May Prevent Sexually Transmitted Diseases, Including HIV, *American Journal of Public Health, 82*, pp. 1473-1478, 1992.
23. C. Elias, Sexually Transmitted Diseases and the Reproductive Health of Women in Developing Countries, *Working Paper, No. 5*, The Population Council, New York, 1991.
24. D. Worth, Sexual Decision-making and AIDS: Why Condom Promotion among Vulnerable Women is Likely to Fail, *Family Planning Perspectives, 20*, pp. 297-307, 1989.
25. R. Dixon-Mueller, The Sexuality Connection in Reproductive Health, *Studies in Family Planning, 24*, pp. 269-282, 1993.
26. W. Chavkin, J. Cohen, A. Ehrhardt, M. Fullilove, and D. Worth, Women and AIDS, *Science, 251*, pp. 359-360, 1991.

CHAPTER 6

The Role of Threat and Efficacy in AIDS Prevention

Kim Witte

THE PROBLEM: AIDS AND YOUNG PEOPLE

Until recently, AIDS was relatively rare among young adults and adolescents. Depending on the population group (e.g., street youth, urban, rural, etc.), some surveys suggest that "from 70 in 1,000 to three in 1,000 teenagers" are infected with the AIDS virus [1, p. A8]. Two out of every 1,000 college students tested were infected with HIV in a study utilizing anonymous blood samples from student health centers at campuses around the nation [2]. This compares with the United States military which recently found that one in every 3,000 teenage recruits tested HIV positive [3]. Teenagers appear to be contracting HIV at a faster rate than other population groups [1].

AIDS is an unusual disease in that, for many people, it is 100 percent preventable. Sexual intercourse appears to be the primary transmission route for adolescents and young adults, although intravenous drug use constitutes a significant HIV pathway [4-6]. Adolescents and college students know how people contract AIDS (e.g., sexual intercourse, IV drug use), but are less likely to know how AIDS is *not* transmitted (e.g., shaking hands, sharing a glass) [7-13].

Alarmingly, even though teens are knowledgeable about AIDS prevention measures, many of them do little to prevent it or other sexually transmitted diseases (STDs) [10, 13-16]. For example, many young people rule out the option of abstinence as an AIDS-prevention method. Manning, Balson, Barenberg, and Moore [17, p. 69] found that study participants repeatedly made it clear that giving up sexual intercourse to prevent AIDS would be "impossible." In addition, though young people believe that condoms effectively prevent STDs [18], only small proportions of college students have adopted safer sex measures such as condom use [13, 15, 16]. Strunin and Hingson found that only "15 percent of sexually active adolescents reported changing their sexual practices to avoid contracting AIDS, and only 20 percent of those who changed mentioned truly effective precautions" [16, p. 825]. Similarly, Thurman and Franklin [13] reported that of college students surveyed, 97 percent knew that condoms were effective in preventing infection, yet nearly three-fifths of the sample did not change their behaviors to prevent AIDS. Thus, knowledge about how to prevent AIDS is relatively high, but AIDS-preventive practices are low [9-12, 15, 17].

At least two explanations for young adults' and adolescents' lack of self-protective behaviors exist. Perceived invulnerability may cause many adolescents or young adults to disregard the threat of AIDS [19]. For example, many teens are convinced that harm or injury will happen to other young people, but not to themselves [10]. King et al. found that many young adults and adolescents focused on short-term gains (i.e., sexual gratification) instead of long-term health considerations (e.g., risk of AIDS; "the protection wasn't there, and she was" [10, p. 105]). A second explanation for lack of self-protective behavior among young people is that fear of AIDS may generate avoidance strategies when individuals are faced with the threat of AIDS. Numerous studies of young adults and teens have found high levels of fear toward AIDS. For example, Katzman, Mulholland, and Sutherland found that 95.2 percent of Arizona State college students believed that AIDS would spread among "the nation's college students/young adults" [15, p. 129]. More than 60 percent of Thurman and Franklin's college sample feared a campus-wide epidemic [13]. In San Francisco, 78.7 percent of adolescents surveyed reported "being afraid of getting AIDS," 73.7 percent were "worried about contracting the disease," and about half (50.6%) of the teenagers surveyed would rather contract "any other disease than AIDS" [8, pp. 1443-1444].

Thus, adolescents and young adults know about AIDS, and know how to prevent it, yet they don't. Perceived invulnerability and fear of AIDS may partly explain these findings. Young persons may deny the threat of AIDS because they do not believe they are truly susceptible to the disease (e.g., "only white gay men get AIDS"). On the other hand, they may be so fearful of their chances of getting AIDS that they may defensively avoid thinking about AIDS. In either case, the result is a failure of young persons to protect themselves against the disease. One class of literature that addresses both of these issues—perceived invulnerability and fear, and their relation to behavior change—is the fear appeal literature. Fear appeals, or the use of "scare tactics," is one controversial persuasive message strategy that has been used in several preventive health domains. Though much of the work on fear or threat appeals conducted during the 1970s and 1980s suggests that the relationship between threat and behavior change is positive and linear (see Rogers [20], for summary), many researchers still conclude that too much fear or threat in a persuasive message causes a boomerang behavioral response (i.e., people do the opposite of what is advocated) [e.g., 21-23]. The low levels of self-protective behavior and the rise in HIV transmission among young adults and teens necessitates research into effective behavior change methods. Because threat appeals focus on *motivating* and *enabling* behavior change, they may be appropriate tools in the fight against AIDS. Thus, the goal of this study was to examine the effectiveness of scare tactics, or more precisely, the effectiveness of threat appeals on AIDS prevention. Following a brief review of the threat appeal theoretical literature, a study designed to test threat appeal principles in the context of AIDS prevention will be presented.

THREAT APPEALS

Some of the first scientific attempts at persuading people to change their health-related behavior were through persuasive messages known as threat or fear appeals. A threat appeal is hypothesized to arouse fear in order to motivate people to change their behavior. The Extended Parallel Process Model (EPPM) is the most recent threat appeal theory offered [24]. It is an integration of past theoretical perspectives [e.g., 20, 25-28] and its goal was to reconcile the diverse threat appeal literature (i.e., explain why and when threat appeals work, and why and when they do not work).

The EPPM (Figure 1) proposes that when a person is presented with a threatening message, two appraisals occur that initiate either fear control or danger control processes [27]. First, persons appraise a persuasive message to determine whether they are susceptible to a severe threat (i.e., perceived threat) and whether they are able to effectively prevent the threat from occurring (i.e., perceived efficacy) [20, 25]. Second, they weigh (either deliberately or automatically) perceived threat against perceived efficacy in a *joint appraisal process* to determine whether anything can be done to prevent the threat. As long as perceived efficacy is greater than perceived threat (e.g., "I know that AIDS is a terrible threat, but if I use condoms correctly, I can protect myself"), danger control processes will dominate. But, when perceived threat outweighs perceived efficacy (e.g., "I'm at-risk for this terrible disease and there's no way I can effectively prevent it"), then fear control processes will dominate. Danger control processes are cognitive processes. They refer to how individuals think about, evaluate, and deal with the danger. For example, in the case of AIDS, people might think of ways to prevent HIV transmission (e.g., become monogamous, avoid sexual intercourse, use condoms). Thus, *cognitive* danger control processes generate protection motivation, which stimulates *adaptive* actions such as attitude, intention, or behavior changes that reduce or diminish the *threat*. People 1) realize they are at risk for a hazard *and* believe they can prevent it, 2) become motivated to protect themselves, and 3) deliberately and cognitively confront the danger (e.g., "When I'm with my boyfriend next time I'm going to talk to him about using condoms"). These analyses suggest that:

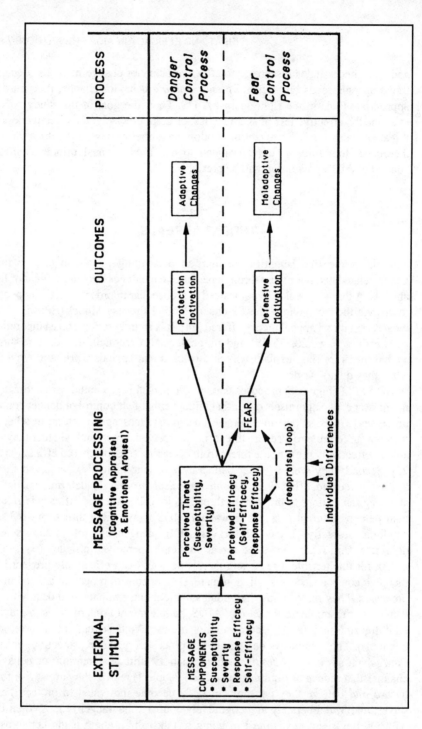

Figure 1. The Extended Parallel Process Model (EPPM).

H1. When efficacy is high (i.e., young adults believe that they are able to use condoms to effectively prevent AIDS), the relationship between threat (i.e., perceptions of susceptibility to AIDS and severity of AIDS) and attitudes toward condom use, intentions to use condoms, and reported use of condoms (behavior), will be positive and linear.

Maximum message acceptance will occur as threat increases when efficacy is high because danger control responses dominate (i.e., perceived efficacy exceeds perceived threat).

Conversely, when people think that they cannot prevent a serious threat from occurring, either because they believe the response is ineffective or because they believe they are incapable of performing the recommended response (i.e., fear control responses), then they will become so frightened that defensive motivation takes over, and fear control processes dominate, resulting in maladaptive actions (Figure 1). Fear control processes are emotional processes where people become motivated to cope with, and get rid of, their *fear*—not the danger. They are more automatic and involuntary in nature, sometimes occurring outside our conscious awareness [29]. Dealing with fear appears to be an unintentional occurrence induced by feelings of helplessness when threat is high and efficacy is low. In fact, boomerang effects (i.e., doing the opposite of what is advocated) become more likely as the focus shifts from dealing with the danger to dealing with the fear. Individuals strive to diminish their fear by reacting against the communicator or message (i.e., perceiving manipulation, derogating the message) or suppressing thoughts of the danger (defensive avoidance). Thus:

H2. When efficacy is low (i.e., young adults feel unable to perform an effective response to prevent AIDS), the relationship between threat (i.e., perceptions of susceptibility to AIDS and severity of AIDS) and attitudes toward condom use, intentions to use condoms, and reported use of condoms (behavior), will be negative or boomerang.

Minimal message acceptance will occur when efficacy is low and threat is high because fear control responses will dominate (i.e., perceived threat exceeds perceived efficacy).

Overall, fear control responses (defensive avoidance, reactance) are expected to interfere with danger control responses (attitude, intention, behavior change) [24, 30]. If an individual is denying the threat of AIDS (controlling one's fear), then he or she will not ask a partner to use condoms (control the danger). This suggests:

H3. Maladaptive responses (defensively avoiding the threat of AIDS, derogating the AIDS-prevention message, or perceiving manipulation) and adaptive responses (attitudes toward condoms, intentions to use condoms, condom-related behaviors) will be inversely related.

METHODS

Design and Subjects

The focus of the experiment was to persuade young adults to use condoms to prevent AIDS. Threat and efficacy were manipulated in a 3 (high, moderate, low threat message) × 2 (high, low efficacy message) factorial design with one no-message control group. The control group served as a baseline comparison of attitudes and beliefs toward AIDS and condom use. The dependent variables were attitudes toward "my using condoms," intentions to use condoms, behaviors, defensive avoidance, and perceived manipulation. The dependent variables were assessed immediately following the experiment, and six weeks later in a follow-up questionnaire.

Subjects were screened prior to the study to ensure they were sexually active, unmarried, and relatively uninformed about AIDS. (The persuasive messages targeted this population.) Thus, only those people who were not in long-term monogamous relationships, who had had sexual intercourse, and who had not taken a course on AIDS or human sexuality were eligible for the study. Approximately 8 percent of all students screened were eligible for the study.

One hundred forty-six undergraduates received extra credit for their participation in part 1 of the study (the immediate posttest). Each experimental condition consisted of approximately equal numbers of males and females. Ninety-three percent of the study participants were between ages seventeen to twenty-four and the average number of sexual partners in the previous six months was 1.4. Most participants were heterosexual (97%) and 66.4 percent were White, 17.8 percent were Asian, 11 percent were Hispanic, and 0.7 percent were African-American.

Attrition was approximately 21 percent, leaving 115 subjects who participated in the follow-up six weeks later. Chi-square tests revealed no differential attrition across cells, $\chi^2(6, N = 146) = 2.25, p = .90$).

Procedure

Pre-screened subjects were run in groups ranging up to twelve persons and were randomly assigned to the experimental conditions and no-message control. Participants were exposed to combinations of the independent variables by reading written messages with five pictures each. The experiment was described as a study to evaluate AIDS education materials. Subjects were told that the materials were in the early stages of development and that their reactions to the messages were needed in order to refine them. Participants were directed to read the messages carefully and to underline important passages to ensure close attention [31]. Then, subjects immediately completed the posttest questionnaire. Six weeks later subjects returned to complete the follow-up questionnaire. Anonymity was ensured by having subjects develop their own secret code to match the posttest and six-week follow-up questionnaires. Participants were asked not to discuss the messages with classmates or roommates until they had completed the follow-up questionnaire. When the follow-up questionnaire was completed, participants were debriefed as to the purpose of the study and given an AIDS prevention brochure provided by the campus AIDS education director.

Stimulus Materials

Both the messages and the questionnaire items were designed to correspond in their level of specificity [32, 33]. Each message manipulation consisted of 1) a core message based on a public health service message ("*What you should know about AIDS*"), 2) a case study of a fictitious AIDS patient, and 3) a message about the effectiveness of condoms. Four photos were imbedded in the core message and the case study. Threat was varied in the first two sections (core message and case study); efficacy was manipulated in the last section. The case studies were of male AIDS victims because the photos were of male AIDS victims. The variations in the message manipulations are outlined in Table 1.

Each message contained verbatim passages from several HIV textbooks and government and private documents [e.g., 34-40]. All of the information in the messages was totally true; each message simply emphasized different issues (e.g., condoms work most of the time; condoms fail some of the time). The low condom efficacy message was taken directly from public health service materials targeted toward high school students [40, p. 16]. Messages and measures were pilot-tested extensively in three phases (process analysis, validation of messages, complete trial run of study).

Message Validation

Messages were equated for length, order of the arguments, and number of pictures. Subjects were asked to rate the accuracy, objectivity, ease of reading, whether they understood the message, and whether they learned from the message. Both the threat and efficacy message manipulations were validated in the main study.

MEASURES

Seven-point Likert-type response formats were used to assess participants' perceptions for each item, except where noted. Items representing the same construct were averaged for a composite score. Internal consistency of these composites is given in Table 2. All measures are described briefly.

Table 1. Differences between Messages (the Manipulations)

Threat Messages	Low Threat	Moderate Threat	High Threat
I. Photographic Component (Emphasizing increased threat, especially severity)	Black and white photos	Color photos	Color photos
	Photos of clinical lab results, assays	Photos of Kaposi's sarcoma on upper body, swollen lymph gland, lymph node lab slide, chart of AIDS increase	Photos of emaciated victim, perianal ulcer, tumors on penis, lesions on foot caused by Kaposi's sarcoma
Potential confounders	Gender neutral	Photos of males	Photos of males
	No body parts shown	Disease on "public" body parts shown (neck, chest)	Disease on genitals shown (penis, anus)
To diminish confounding	Analyze males and females separately; Covary if necessary	→	→
	1 picture of frontal nudity on cover of each message	→	→
II. Written Component	Neutral language	Moderately personalistic and vivid language	Very personalistic and vivid language
	AIDS in Africa stressed	AIDS in heterosexual population stressed	AIDS in college students stressed
	Other risk groups stressed	Heterosexual risk stressed	Your personal risk stressed
Examples of susceptibility manipulations	"A 35-year-old male prostitute admitted to the Central London Hospital"	"A 27-year-old male grocery clerk admitted to the Chicago Regional Hospital"	"A 19-year-old male UCI college student (heterosexual) admitted to the UCI Medical Center"
Examples of severity manipulations	"On admission, the patient complained of fatigue and a rash"	"On admission, the patient complained of fatigue and lumps on the neck"	"On admission, the patient complained of fatigue and bleeding, oozing sores all over his body"

Efficacy Messages	Low Efficacy	High Efficacy
Written Component	Both response and self-efficacy at low levels	Both response and self-efficacy at high levels
	Emphasizes that condoms fail some of the time	Emphasizes that condoms work most of the time
	Highlights problems of using condoms (have to be used correctly to prevent AIDS)	Role-plays specific questions and answers to increase self-efficacy
	Lists typical excuses people give for not using condoms	Emphasizes ease of use, other benefits of using condoms
	No refutation of these beliefs (simply states these beliefs may not be true)	Attacks and refutes beliefs that condoms decrease spontaneity, reduce pleasure, etc.

Demographic Variables

Gender, age, ethnicity, sexual orientation, prior intravenous drug use, and sexual practices (e.g., condom use, monogamous, many partners, sex with IV drug user) were assessed. Sexual orientation and practices items were taken from the Rutgers University Sexual Health Program "College Health Survey." These items have been pilot-tested and validated via interviews with pilot subjects by researchers in the Rutgers' project.

Manipulation Checks

Threat was operationalized as susceptibility to threat and severity of threat. Efficacy was operationalized as response and self-efficacy. Although suscep-tibility and severity are conceptually distinct, when combined they create the

Table 2. Reliability of the Measures

Index	Alpha
Fear	.88
Susceptibility	.81
Follow-up susceptibility	.81
Severity	.51
Follow-up severity	.68
Response efficacy	.81
Follow-up response efficacy	.66
Self-efficacy	.75
Follow-up self-efficacy	.73
Attitude	.82
Follow-up attitude	.84
Condom intentions	.83
Defensive avoidance	.71
Confound check: Learning	.90
Message derogation (Reactance)	.78
Perceived manipulation (Reactance)	.66
Self-report behavior (Follow-up)	.69

overall construct of threat. Similarly, response and self-efficacy are conceptually distinct, but together they create the overall construct of efficacy. These conceptually distinct variables were measured separately with at least two items and served as manipulation checks: 1) susceptibility (e.g., "How possible is it for you to get AIDS?"—"not at all possible" to "extremely possible"); 2) severity (e.g., ranking of several diseases or harmful outcomes (including AIDS) in terms of their seriousness, painfulness, etc.); 3) self-efficacy (e.g., "A sex partner(s) and I are able to use condoms to prevent AIDS"—"strongly disagree" to "strongly agree"); and 4) response efficacy (e.g., "I think that condoms prevent AIDS"— "strongly disagree" to "strongly agree").

Confound Checks

Participants rated the accuracy, objectivity, and whether they understood the message on a 7-point scale from "strongly disagree" to "strongly agree." A three-item learning scale also assessed whether subjects thought they learned a lot about "AIDS," "AIDS prevention," or "condom use" from the message.[1]

Fear

Fear arousal was measured by having subjects rate the following mood objectives ("not at all" to "very much"): frightened, tense, nervous, anxious, uncomfortable, and nauseous. These items frequently have been used in other threat appeal studies [31, 41, 42].

Dependent Variables

The dependent variables were attitudes toward condoms, intentions to use condoms, self-reported condom use, defensive avoidance, message derogation, and perceived manipulation (see Appendix 1). Defensive avoidance was measured in the follow-up questionnaire, because defensive avoidance is a delayed phenomena [43]. Reactance was measured by assessing the degree to which subjects derogated the message (i.e., reacted against the message) and the degree to which subjects perceived that the message was trying to manipulate them. Each dependent variable was measured with at least three items. One attitude item ("safe"—"not safe") was dropped from the composite measure in the follow-up, due to lack of variance.

---

[1] If subjects learned more from one message over another, then attitude or intention change may have occurred because subjects learned more from one message over another.

RESULTS

Overview

Manipulation checks for the threat constructs (i.e., susceptibility, severity), efficacy constructs (i.e., response efficacy, self-efficacy), and fear were computed. Hypotheses 1 and 2 were tested using a 3 (low, moderate, high threat) by 2 (low, high efficacy) analysis of covariance design with demographic variables treated as covariates when significant.[2] Hypothesis 3 was tested with Pearson correlations. Statistical power exceeded .85 for all tests [44].

Evaluation of assumptions of normality, homogeneity of variances, and linearity indicated that all were satisfactory except for the normality assumption for posttest attitudes and intentions (significant skewness for all, $p < .001$). However, Tabachnick and Fidell [45] and Hays [46] note the robustness of statistical tests if normality assumptions are violated. Therefore, transformations were not performed. No within cell outliers were detected using Mahalanobis' distance ($p < .001$).

Manipulation Checks

Severity

A significant main effect for threat was found on the severity measure, $F(2, 123) = 10.72, p < .001$. No other significant main effects of interactions were found (i.e., being in a high or low efficacy group did not significantly affect perceptions of severity). Subjects exposed to the high threat message believed AIDS was a more serious disease ($M = 5.27$) than those exposed to the moderate threat message ($M = 4.55$), and those exposed to the low threat messages ($M = 3.90$). A Duncan multiple-range test ($p < .05$) revealed that the high threat message induced significantly stronger severity of AIDS beliefs than the moderate threat message, which induced significantly greater severity beliefs than the low threat message. Dunnett's test to compare experimental means against control means indicated that participants in the high threat group believed AIDS to be more severe than participants in the control condition ($M = 4.2, p .05$). Severity of AIDS beliefs for the moderate and low threat subjects did not differ significantly from the control subjects.

For the follow-up (6 weeks later), a significant main effect for threat was obtained on the follow-up severity measure $F(2, 93) = 5.032, p < .01$. No other significant main effects or interactions were found. Subjects exposed to the high

---

[2] MANCOVAs were run initially to check for multivariate effects while controlling for chance due to number of dependent variables. There was a significant multivariate effect for all dependent variables (i.e., attitudes, attitude change, intentions, and behaviors). Therefore, univariate statistics are presented, as is typical in the persuasion literature.

threat message believed AIDS was a more serious disease ($M = 5.16$) than those exposed to the moderate threat message ($M = 4.89$), who in turn, thought AIDS was more serious than those reading the low threat message ($M = 4.19$). A Duncan multiple-range test ($p < .05$) showed that the high and moderate threat messages produced significantly stronger severity of AIDS beliefs than the low threat message. The difference between the high and moderate threat messages was not significant. Dunnett's test revealed no significant differences between any of the threat messages and the control ($M = 4.54$).

Susceptibility

A significant main effect for threat was found on the susceptibility measure, $F(2, 123) = 3.38$, $p < .05$. No other significant main effects or interactions were found. Subjects exposed to the high threat message believed they were more susceptible to AIDS ($M = 3.85$) than those exposed to the moderate threat message ($M = 3.60$), who in turn believed themselves to be more susceptible to AIDS than subjects reading the low threat message ($M = 3.23$). However, significant differences appeared between the high threat and low threat subjects only (Duncan multiple-range test, $p < .05$). The Dunnett test revealed no significant differences between any of the experimental groups and the control group.

For the follow-up (6 weeks later), no significant main effects or interactions were found. However, the means were ordered in the expected direction with high threat subjects perceiving greater susceptibility to AIDS ($M = 3.77$), than moderate threat subjects ($M = 3.29$) and low threat subjects ($M = 3.2$). Dunnett's test revealed no differences between the experimental groups and the control ($M = 3.48$).

Response Efficacy

A significant main effect for efficacy was obtained on the response efficacy measure, $F(1, 124) = 62.5$, $p < .0001$. No other significant main effects or interactions were found. Stronger beliefs in the efficacy of using condoms to prevent AIDS were found among the high efficacy subjects ($M = 6.08$) when compared to the low efficacy subjects ($M = 4.27$). High efficacy subjects did not differ significantly from control subjects ($M = 5.4$). However, control subjects indicated significantly stronger condom response efficacy beliefs than did low efficacy subjects ($p < .05$).

For the follow-up (6 weeks later), a significant main effect for efficacy was obtained on the response efficacy measure, $F(1, 95) = 14.30$, $p < .01$. No other significant main effects or interactions were found. High efficacy subjects believed condoms were more effective in preventing AIDS ($M = 5.93$) than low efficacy subjects ($M = 5.18$). Neither high nor low efficacy subjects differed significantly from the controls ($M = 5.0$).

Self-Efficacy

A significant main effect for efficacy was obtained on the self-efficacy measure, $F(1, 124) = 7.89$, $p < .01$. No other significant main effects or interactions were found. Those subjects in the high efficacy condition had stronger beliefs that they were able to use condoms to prevent AIDS ($M = 5.53$) than subjects in the low efficacy condition ($M = 4.83$). There were no significant differences between the high and low efficacy groups compared to the control group ($M = 4.97$).

For the follow-up (6 weeks later), no significant main effects or interactions were found. Experimental subjects ($M = 5.22$) perceived greater self-efficacy than control subjects ($M = 4.86$), but the difference was not significant.

Fear

A significant main effect for threat was obtained on the fear measure, $F(2, 121) = 20.10$, $p < .0001$. No other significant main effects or interactions were found. Participants in the high threat group ($M = 4.57$) were more fearful of AIDS than moderate threat participants ($M = 3.38$), who in turn were more fearful of AIDS than low threat participants ($M = 3.02$). A Duncan multiple-range test ($p < .05$) indicated that the difference between high and moderate threat subjects was significant ($p < .05$), as was the difference between the high and low threat subjects ($p < .05$). The difference between the moderate and low threat subjects was not statistically significant.

Confound Checks

No differences were detected across threat or efficacy level for objectivity, learning of the message, or understanding of the message. However, there was a significant main effect for efficacy on the accuracy measure ($F(1, 120) = 5.995$, $p = .016$). Subjects who read the high efficacy message ($M = 5.76$) rated it as more accurate than those subjects who read the low efficacy message ($M = 5.14$).

Hypotheses 1 and 2

Posttest Attitudes toward Condoms

A significant main effect for efficacy was detected, $F(1, 118) = 14.33$, $p < .0001$. Significant covariates for attitudes were prior condom use ($F(1, 118) = 24.33$, $p < .0001$) and number of sexual partners during the last six months ($F(1, 118) = 9.99$, $p < .01$). No other significant main effects or interactions were found. Those in the high efficacy condition had more favorable attitudes toward using condoms (adjusted $M = 5.69$) than those in the low efficacy group (adjusted $M = 5.02$). There were no differences between the experimental means when compared to control means.

Attitude Change toward Condoms

Attitudes changed significantly due to efficacy condition over the six weeks from the posttest to the follow-up (change scores used) $F(1, 95) = 4.08, p < .05$. Over the 6-week period, low efficacy subjects developed less favorable attitudes toward condoms (low threat $M = .357$, moderate threat $M = .183$, high threat $M = .001$) and high efficacy subjects developed more favorable attitudes toward condoms (low threat $M = .338$, moderate threat $M = .534$, high threat $M = .835$). Figure 2 shows attitude change by threat and efficacy condition. The experimental means did not differ significantly from the control mean $(M = .273)$.

Intentions to Use Condoms

A significant main effect for threat was obtained on the condom intentions measure, $F(2, 113) = 3.27, p < .05$. Significant covariates for intentions were prior condom use $(F(1, 113) = 52.66, p < .0001)$, age $(F(1, 113) = 7.86, p < .01)$, and whether the participant and his/her partner(s) were monogamous, had many partners, etc. $(F(1, 113) = 9.02, p < .01)$. No other significant main effects or interactions were found. High threat subjects intended to use condoms more (adjusted $M = 5.93$) than moderate threat subjects (adjusted $M = 5.8$), who intended to use condoms more than low threat subjects (adjusted $M = 5.33$). Figure 2(b) shows condom intentions by threat conditions. There were no differences between the experimental and control means.

Condom-Related Behavior Changes

A significant threat x efficacy interaction was found for self-report behavior, $F(2, 45) = 4.50, p < .017$. Significant covariates for self-report behavior were prior condom use $(F(1, 45) = 19.41, p < .001)$ and age $(F(1, 45) = 4.11, p < .05)$. No other significant main effects were found. As threat increased for those in the low efficacy condition, a boomerang effect emerged (participants reported doing the opposite of what was advocated) (low threat $M = 3.85$, moderate threat $M = 3.79$, high threat $M = 3.25$).[3] Conversely, as threat increased for those in the high efficacy condition, so did behavior change (low threat $M = 3.20$, moderate threat $M = 4.15$, high threat $M = 4.49$). Figure 2(c) shows self-reported condom-related behavior by threat and efficacy condition. The no-message control group reported no behavior change during the past six weeks $(M = 3.2)$.

---

[3] The message advocated the use of condoms to prevent AIDS and those with a score of less than 4 (on a scale of 1 to 7) said they did not use condoms (from varying degrees of "never planned to use them" to "thought about it briefly"). Thus, people did the opposite of what was advocated in the message if they had a score of less than 4.

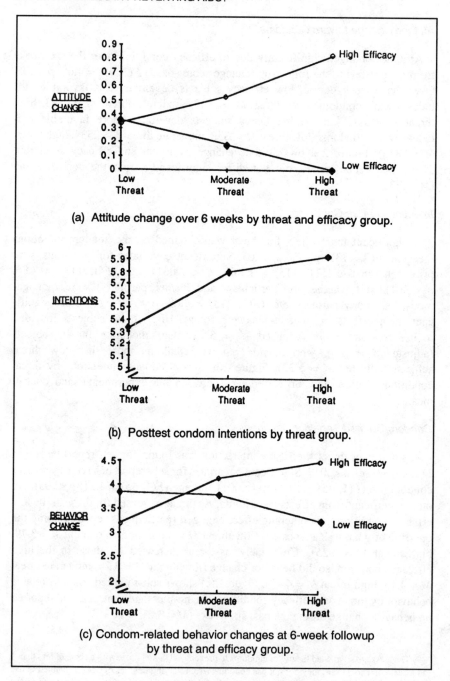

(a) Attitude change over 6 weeks by threat and efficacy group.

(b) Posttest condom intentions by threat group.

(c) Condom-related behavior changes at 6-week followup by threat and efficacy group.

Figure 2. Results from hypotheses 1 and 2.

Hypothesis 3

Message derogation had an inverse relation to attitudes, and was unrelated to attitude change, intentions, and behavior change. The more subjects derogated the message, the less favorable their attitudes toward condoms ($r = -.19$, $p < .02$, $N = 126$). Perceived manipulation had a positive relation to behavior change (opposite the expected direction), and was unrelated to attitudes, attitude change, or intentions. The more people perceived manipulation, the more they changed their behaviors ($r = .28$, $p < .02$, $N = 53$). Defensive avoidance was inversely related to attitudes, intentions, and behaviors, and unrelated to attitude change. The more people defensively avoided AIDS prevention, the less favorable attitudes ($r = -.32$, $p < .001$, $N = 93$), intentions ($r = -.22$, $p < .02$, $N = 89$), and the fewer behavior changes they made ($r = -.31$, $p < .01$, $N = 51$).

DISCUSSION

Overall Findings

Sexual behaviors are notoriously difficult to change given the interrelation between drives, emotions, cognitions, contexts, prior beliefs, interpersonal relationships, desires, etc. However, even in the face of this extraordinarily difficult task, this study demonstrated that "scaring" people into changing their behaviors works—*under certain conditions*. Specifically, if public health practitioners are to use threatening messages to motivate individuals to change their behaviors, *they also must present recommended responses that are perceived as effective and easy to do*.

In this study, when college students were depicted as being very susceptible to the severe disease AIDS, but told when, how, and why condoms were the best protection against AIDS barring celibacy (high threat/high efficacy), they reported using condoms more often and their attitudes toward condoms became more favorable over time. Increasing threat in the persuasive message, while providing individuals the means to protect themselves against AIDS, served to break down perceived invulnerability barriers characteristic among many young adults. This high threat/high efficacy combination resulted in an effective persuasive message that led to attitude and behavior change.

In contrast, this study also demonstrated that if too much fear is aroused, then avoidance strategies will be generated. For example, when college students were depicted as very susceptible to the severe disease AIDS, and condoms were portrayed as *failing* some of the time (high threat/low efficacy), participants reported having sex *without* condoms more often and their attitudes became even less favorable toward condoms. Thus, fear of AIDS in the high threat/low efficacy condition appeared to generate avoidance strategies and caused individuals to do the opposite of what was advocated; they used condoms less.

Overall, a fine line is trod between making individuals feel susceptible to a threat, but also making them feel that they can do something to effectively avert the threat. As the EPPM proposes, it appears that as long as perceived efficacy outweighs perceived threat (e.g., "AIDS is a terrible threat that I'm at-risk for, but I know that condoms prevent AIDS and I'm able to easily use condoms"), then behavior change will occur and people will protect themselves. Conversely, when individuals are made to feel vulnerable to a severe threat but perceive no effective response to avert the threat, then they will cope with their fear—because coping with the danger would be a futile exercise (e.g., "There's nothing I can do to prevent the threat anyway, so I might as well not think about it").

Fear and Danger Control Processes

The test of the relation between fear control and danger control responses resulted in additional support for the EPPM's predictions. Specifically, this study revealed that when individuals coped with their fear (fear control processes), they failed to manage the danger of AIDS (danger control processes). For example, the more participants defensively avoided the threat of AIDS, the less favorable their attitudes toward condoms, the less likely they were to intend to use condoms, and the less likely they were to actually report using condoms. Similarly, the more people criticized and derogated the AIDS-prevention message, the less favorable their attitudes toward condoms.

An exception to these findings is the case of perceived manipulation. The more participants thought they were being manipulated at the immediate posttest, the greater their behavior change at the six-week follow-up. However, the data also indicated that perceived manipulation disappeared a the six-week follow-up. One explanation for these findings centers on the message appraisal process. Initially fear may directly cause perceived manipulation (fear control process) and interfere with adaptive responses, similar to defensive avoidance and message derogation. For example, posttest perceived manipulation was unrelated to any of the immediate posttest measures of adaptive responses (i.e., attitudes and intentions). However, over the six-week period, people may cognitively reappraise the message (see the reappraisal loop in Figure 1), become less concerned with whether they were manipulated, and make behavior changes. Indeed, in this study, perceptions of manipulation nearly disappeared over the six- week period, while behavior changes were made. This cognitive reappraisal of the threat appears to occur for perceived manipulation—which entails cognitive thought (e.g., "I think that message was trying to manipulate me"), but not for defensive avoidance or message derogation, which are more affectively-based enterprises. As Leventhal [27] notes, short-term effects of fear appeals result in fear control strategies while long-term effects result in danger control strategies. Thus, in this study, the threat appears to have been reappraised over time, causing perceived manipulation to disappear, and behavior changes to be made.

Limitations

The confound checks yielded the expected results in most cases. The messages were equally objective and understandable and subjects learned the same information from each. However, the high efficacy subjects rated their message as more accurate than the low efficacy subjects. Subjects' prior knowledge about condoms may have contributed to this result. For instance, the no-message control group had high response and self-efficacy perceptions in regard to condoms. These high efficacy baseline rates suggest that college students think that condoms are effective in preventing AIDS. With these high efficacy baseline perceptions, college students may evaluate a message as less accurate if evidence is presented to the contrary.

Weinstein's criticism of self-protective behavior models, including PMT and the EPPM, is relevant here. He notes that these models "focus on a single threat and on a single preventive response" [47, p. 357]. Thus, the predictive power of these models is less than optimal because issues such as time, interpersonal relations, cultural issues, etc., are not addressed. In terms of this study, sexual behavior is complex. To change one's sexual behaviors, one must have interpersonal skill, impulse control, be able to delay gratification, have planning skills, etc. In addition, to prevent AIDS, one must use a condom consistently. Thus, even if people change their behaviors, recidivism may be high [48]. One persuasive strategy to prevent AIDS might be to persuade people to use condoms until they are sure they are safe (i.e., both partners tested)—although some people who are HIV positive may not test positive due to the lag time between infection and seroconversion. Careful attention to the complex and interrelated processes surrounding sexual behavior may help public health practitioners develop realistic and feasible AIDS-prevention programs. Using threatening messages to motivate people into action may be the first step in a complete and well thought-out AIDS prevention program.

An alarming and unanticipated finding in this study concerned the definition of safer-sex behavior. It appears that a significant minority of college students think in terms of pregnancy, and not AIDS or STDs, when it comes to safer-sex behavior. For example, when asked if changes were made in safer-sex behaviors, several respondents marked yes and wrote: "Birth control pill" (subject 69); "Thought about it but I didn't, she was on the pill" (subject 100); "I only practice safe sex to avoid pregnancy" (subject 58); and "She said she was protected" (subject 64). It is clear that public health practitioners must make their definitions of "safer-sex" clear and explicit, if their goal is to prevent AIDS.

Implications for AIDS Prevention

This study, which replicated the threat-by-efficacy interactions found in other health domains such as alcohol misuse [49] and cigarette smoking [50], strongly suggests that both threat and efficacy must be at high levels if persuasive messages are to be used to promote safer-sex behaviors. Threat must be high so that people are motivated to protect themselves from AIDS. Efficacy must be high so that defensive motivation is not induced and maladaptive responses are not elicited. The trick appears to be to make people feel vulnerable to AIDS (most already acknowledge its severity), *and* to make them feel able to prevent it. Increasing perceptions of self and response efficacy appears to be deceptively simple. Most people would agree that they are able to use condoms and that condoms prevent AIDS. However, when they find themselves in a romantic situation, more often than not, "one thing leads to another" and condoms get overlooked. Indeed, the open-ended responses on the follow-up questionnaire indicated that this happened often. Thus, skills training that focuses on how one might act in a romantic encounter (especially in a spontaneous romantic encounter), and how one might bring up the topic of condoms, would be a valuable experience for many people.

This study contributed not only to the practical problem of AIDS prevention, but to the theoretical advancement of how people process persuasive messages. Specifically, the extended parallel process model's (EPPM) predictions so that 1) too high threat coupled with too low efficacy would lead to maladaptive responses, and that 2) high threat coupled with high efficacy would lead to adaptive responses, were supported. Additionally, EPPM's proposals that maladaptive and adaptive responses are inversely related was supported. Overall, the model is useful for applied practitioners in that it offers specific and practical guidelines for public health campaign message development.

APPENDIX 1. THE DEPENDENT VARIABLES

1. Attitudes toward using condoms
   "My using condoms during the next 4-6 weeks would be:"
   "Bad—Good"
   "Undesirable—Desirable"
   "Unfavorable—Favorable"
   "Not Pleasurable—Pleasurable"
   "Not Safe—Safe" (dropped from follow-up—no variance)
   "Not Effective—Effective"
   "Not Romantic—Romantic"

2. Intentions to use condoms

"Do you intend to buy condoms to prevent AIDS during the next 4-6 weeks?"

   "Definitely no"—"Definitely yes"

"Do you intend to talk to a sexual partner(s) about using condoms during the next 4-6 weeks?"

   "Definitely no"—"Definitely yes"

"Do you intend to use condoms at all during the next 4-6 weeks?"

   "Definitely no"—"Definitely yes"

"Would you use condoms during the next 4-6 weeks if you were to have sex with someone you didn't know very well?"

   "Definitely no"—"Definitely yes"

"I plan to use condoms during the next 4-6 weeks _____."

   "Not at all"—"Every time I have sex"

3. Defensive Avoidance

"The message used in this study made me:"

"*Want* to think about AIDS"—"*Not* want to think about AIDS."

"*Want* to do something to keep myself from getting AIDS"—"*Not* want to do something to keep myself from getting AIDS"

"*Want* to protect myself from AIDS"—"*Not* want to protect myself from AIDS"

"How much time did you spend thinking about the message you read?"

   "I didn't think about it at all"—"I thought about it very often"

"How frequently have you thought about the message since you read it?"

   "Not at all"—"Most of the time"

4. Message Derogation—Reactance

"This message is:"

"Exaggerated-Not at all Exaggerated"

"Distorted—Not at all Distorted"

"Overblown—Not at all Overblown"

"Boring—Interesting"

"Overstated—Not at all Overstated"

5. Perception of Manipulation—Reactance

"This message deliberately tried to manipulate my feelings"

   "Strongly Disagree"—"Strongly Agree"

"How do you feel about the message?"

   "Not at all Manipulated"—"Extremely Manipulated"

   "Not at all Exploited"—"Extremely Exploited"

6. Behavior

"I changed my behaviors since I first participated in this study in order to prevent AIDS."

   "Strongly Disagree"—"Strongly Agree"

"Did you plan to use condoms since you first participated in this study?"
    "No, never . . . "—"Yes, planned and used them . . . "
"Did you talk to a sexual partner(s) about using condoms since you first participated in this study?"
    "No, did not talk . . . "—"Yes, talked frequently . . . "
"Did you and a partner(s) use condoms?"
    "No, never . . . "—"Yes, frequently . . . "
"Did you practice any safe sex skills since you first participated in this study?"
    "Definitely no"—"Definitely yes"

REFERENCES

1. G. Kolata, Experts See AIDS Epidemic among Teens as Next Crisis, *The Orange County Register*, p. A8f, October 8, 1989.
2. H. D. Gayle, R. P. Keeling, M. Garcia-Tunon, B. W. Kilbourne, J. P. Narkunas, F. R. Ingram, M. F. Rogers, and J. W. Curran, Prevalence of the Human Immunodeficiency Virus among University Students, *The New England Journal of Medicine, 323*, pp. 1538-1541, 1990.
3. D. S. Burke, J. F. Brundage, M. Goldenbaum, L. I. Gardner, M. Peterson, R. Visintine, and R. R. Redfield, Human Immunodeficiency Virus Infections in Teenagers: Seroprevalence among Applicants for US Military Service, *Journal of the American Medical Association, 263*, pp. 2074-2077, 1990.
4. S. Y. Chu, J. W. Buehler, and R. L. Berkelman, Impact of the Human Immunodeficiency Virus Epidemic on Mortality in Women of Reproductive Age, United States, *Journal of the American Medical Association 264*, pp. 225-229, 1990.
5. T. J. Coates, Strategies for Modifying Sexual Behavior for Primary and Secondary Prevention of HIV Disease, *Journal of Consulting and Clinical Psychology, 58*, pp. 57-69, 1990.
6. C. E. Koop, *Understanding AIDS: A Message from the Surgeon General*, U.S. Department of Health and Human Services, Washington, D.C., 1988.
7. L. K. Brown and G. K. Fritz, Children's Knowledge and Attitudes about AIDS, *Journal of the American Academy of Child and Adolescent Psychiatry, 27*, pp. 504-508, 1988.
8. R. J. DiClemente, J. Zorn, and L. Temoshok, Adolescents and AIDS: A Survey of Knowledge, Attitudes and Beliefs about AIDS in San Francisco, *American Journal of Public Health, 76*, pp. 1443-1445, 1986.
9. D. P. Fan and C. L. Shaffer, Use of Open-Ended Essays and Computer Content Analysis to Survey College Students' Knowledge of AIDS, *Journal of American College Health, 38*, pp. 221-223, 1990.
10. A. J. C. King, R. P. Beazley, W. K. Warren, C. A. Hankins, A. S. Robertson, and J. L. Radford, *Canada Youth and AIDS Study*, Social Program Evaluation Group, Queen's University at Kingston, Kingston, Ontario, 1988.

11. D. T. Manning, N. Barenberg, L. Gallese, and J. C. Rice, College Students' Knowledge and Health Beliefs about AIDS: Implications for Education and Prevention, *Journal of American College Health, 37*, pp. 254-259, 1989.

12. S. B. Thomas, A. G. Gilliam, and C. G. Iwrey, Knowledge about AIDS and Reported Risk Behaviors among Black College Students, *Journal of American College Health, 38*, pp. 61-66, 1989.

13. Q. C. Thurman and K. M. Franklin, AIDS and College Health: Knowledge, Threat, and Prevention at a Northeastern University, *College Health, 38*, pp. 179-184, 1990.

14. J. Brooks-Gunn, C. B. Boyer, and K. Hein, Preventing HIV Infection and AIDS in Children and Adolescents, *American Psychologist, 43*, pp. 958-964, 1988.

15. E. M. Katzman, M. Mulholland, and E. M. Sutherland, College Students and AIDS: A Preliminary Study of Knowledge, Attitudes, and Behavior, *Journal of American College Health, 37*, pp. 127-130, 1988.

16. L. Strunin and R. Hingson, Acquired Immunodeficiency Syndrome and Adolescents: Knowledge, Beliefs, Attitudes and Behaviors, *Pediatrics, 79*, pp. 824-828, 1987.

17. D. Manning, P. M. Balson, N. Barenberg, and T. M. Moore, Susceptibility to AIDS: What College Students Do and Don't Believe, *Journal of American College Health, 38*, pp. 67-73, 1989.

18. S. M. Kegeles, N. E. Adler, and C. E. Irwin, Sexually Active Adolescents and Condoms: Changes over One Year in Knowledge, Attitudes and Use, *American Journal of Public Health, 78*, pp. 460-461, 1988.

19. C. E. Irwin and S. G. Millstein, Biopsychosocial Correlates of Risk-Taking Behaviors during Adolescence: Can the Physician Intervene? *Journal of Adolescent Health Care, 7*, pp. 82s-96s, 1986.

20. R. W. Rogers, Cognitive and Physiological Processes in Fear Appeals and Attitude Change: A Revised Theory of Protection Motivation, *Social Psychophysiology*, J. Cacioppo and R. E. Petty (eds.), Guilford Press, New York, pp. 153-176, 1983.

21. J. A. Catania, S. M. Kegeles, and T. J. Coates, Towards an Understanding of Risk Behavior: An AIDS Risk-Reduction Model (ARRM), *Health Education Quarterly, 17*, pp. 53-72, 1990.

22. W. DeJong and J. A. Winsten, *Recommendations for Future Mass Media Campaigns to Prevent Preteen and Adolescent Substance Abuse*, Center for Health Communication, Harvard School of Public Health, Boston, Massachusetts, November, 1989.

23. T. Edgar, V. S. Freimuth, and S. L. Hammond, Communicating the AIDS Risk to College Students: The Problem of Motivating Change, *Health Education Research, 3*, pp. 59-65, 1988.

24. K. Witte, *Putting the Fear Back into Fear Appeals: Reconciling the Threat Appeal Literature*, Paper presented at the annual meeting of the Speech Communication Association, Atlanta, Georgia, October, 1991.

25. M. H. Becker, D. P. Haefner, S. V. Kasl, J. P. Kirscht, L. A. Maiman, and I. M. Rosenstock, Selected Psychosocial Models and Correlates of Individual Health-Related Behaviors, *Medical Care, 15*, pp. 27-46, 1977.

26. I. L. Janis, Effects of Fear Arousal on Attitude Change: Recent Developments in Theory and Experimental Research, in *Advances in Experimental Social Psychology, 3*, L. Berkowitz (ed.), Academic Press, New York, pp. 166-225, 1967.
27. H. Leventhal, Findings and Theory in the Study of Fear Communications, in *Advances in Experimental Social Psychology, 5*, L. Berkowitz (ed.), Academic Press, New York, pp. 119-186, 1970.
28. R. W. Rogers, A Protection Motivation Theory of Fear Appeals and Attitude Change, *Journal of Psychology, 91*, pp. 93-114, 1975.
29. R. S. Lazarus, Cognition and Motivation in Emotion, *American Psychologist, 46*, pp. 352-367, 1991.
30. H. Leventhal, Fear Appeals and Persuasion: The Differentiation of a Motivational Construct, *American Journal of Public Health, 61*, pp. 1208-1224, 1971.
31. J. E. Maddux and R. W. Rogers, Protection Motivation and Self-Efficacy: A Revised Theory of Fear Appeals and Attitude Change, *Journal of Experimental Social Psychology, 19*, pp. 469-479, 1983.
32. I. Ajzen and M. Fishbein, *Understanding Attitudes and Predicting Social Behavior*, Prentice-Hall, Englewood Cliffs, New Jersey, 1980.
33. M. Fishbein and I. Ajzen, *Belief, Attitude, Intention, and Behavior: An Introduction to Theory and Research*, Addison-Wesley, Reading, Massachusetts, 1975.
34. American Red Cross, *Teenagers and AIDS*, The American Red Cross, 1988.
35. S. Broder, *AIDS: Modern Concepts and Therapeutic Challenges*, Marcel Dekker, Inc., New York, 1987.
36. P. Ebbesen, R. J. Biggar, and M. Melbye, (eds.), *AIDS: A Basic Guide for Clinicians*, W. B. Saunders Company, Philadelphia, Pennsylvania, 1984.
37. C. F. Farthing, S. E. Brown, and R. C. D. Staughton, *Color Atlas of AIDS and HIV Disease* (2nd Edition), Year Book Medical Publishers, Inc., Chicago, Illinois, 1988.
38. H. Leventhal, "Tetanus" messages, *American Documentation Institute*, #9011, 1965.
39. UCI AIDS Program, *Let's Talk Sex: Avoiding AIDS*, Health Education Office, University of California, Irvine, California, undated.
40. U.S. Dept. of Education, *AIDS The Education of our Children: A Guide for Parents and Teachers*, 1988.
41. H. Leventhal, R. Singer, and S. Jones, Effects of Fear and Specificity of Recommendations upon Attitudes and Behavior, *Journal of Personality and Social Psychology, 2*, pp. 20-29, 1965.
42. P. A. Rippetoe and R. W. Rogers, Effects of Components of Protection-Motivation Theory on Adaptive and Maladaptive Coping with a Health Threat, *Journal of Personality and Social Psychology, 52*, pp. 596-604, 1987.
43. C. Hovland, I. Janis, and H. Kelly, *Communication and Persuasion*, Yale University Press, New Haven, Connecticut, 1953.
44. G. E. Dallal, *PC-SIZE: A Program for Sample Size Determinations* (Version 2.0). USDA Human Nutrition Research Center on Aging, Tufts University, 711 Washington Street, Boston, Massachusetts 02111, 1985.
45. B. G. Tabachnick and L. S. Fidell, *Using Multivariate Statistics* (2nd Edition), Harper Collins, New York, 1989.
46. W. L. Hays, *Statistics* (3rd Edition), Holt Rinehart, Winston, New York, 1981.

47. N. D. Weinstein, The Precaution Adoption Process, *Health Psychology, 7*, pp. 355-386, 1988.
48. S. Saltzman, A. Stoddard, J. McCusker, and K. Mayer, *Factors Associated with Recurrence of Unsafe Sex Practices in a Cohort of Gay Men Previously Engaging in "Safer Sex"*, poster presented at the V International Conference on AIDS, Montreal, Canada, June 1989.
49. M. C. Kleinot and R. W. Rogers, Identifying Effective Components of Alcohol Misuse Prevention Programs, *Journal of Studies on Alcohol, 43*, pp. 802-811, 1982.
50. R. W. Rogers and C. R. Mewborn, Fear Appeals and Attitude Change: Effects of a Threat's Noxiousness, Probability of Occurrence, and the Efficacy of the Coping Responses, *Journal of Personality and Social Psychology, 34*, pp. 54-61, 1976.

[The reported experiment was part of a larger project examining the role of threat, fear, and efficacy, on AIDS prevention. Support of this project by a National Institute of Mental Health Fellowship (training grant #1 F31 MH10029) is gratefully acknowledged.]

II
VOICES OF DISSENT

CHAPTER 7

The Viral Model for AIDS: Paradigmatic Dominance, Politics, or Best Approximation of Reality?

Paul E. Pezza

In January 1995, the *New England Journal of Medicine* featured two reports of research focused on healthy long-term survivors of infection with the virus believed to cause immune system deficiency in humans. One of these articles concludes by saying "Long-term survivors of HIV-1 infection provide a ray of hope indicating that it is possible to live with the virus for prolonged periods without harm" [1]. The other report ends with the observation that "It remains unclear what are the relative contributions of host factors . . . and virologic factors . . . in these subjects" [2]. These statements underscore the fact that the AIDS epidemic is still poorly understood and that it continues to be frustrating. They also call to mind an issue raised several years ago and one which is succinctly summarized in the assertion "HIV is not the cause of AIDS." This statement constitutes the title of an article which appeared in *Science*, the Journal of the American Association for the Advancement of Science [3], in 1988; and it represents the most extreme position of those who take exception to the conventional wisdom regarding AIDS etiology.

This view is not new. Indeed, it is as old as our awareness that a cluster of atypical pneumonias had appeared among gay men in the United States [4]. At that time in 1981 a non-infectious disease hypothesis was offered by the Centers for Disease Control (CDC) to explain the phenomenon. Although quickly supplanted by the viral hypothesis and largely ignored by professional and media sources, that view has persisted.

This chapter does not propose to resolve the question of AIDS etiology. Its purpose is to raise the question of why one explanation for the epidemic of immune system suppression has dominated the discourse on AIDS, despite the anomalies attributed to it by the proponents of other viewpoints. Alternative responses to the question are set forth drawing upon ideas regarding the impact of dominant paradigms in the conduct of science [5-7] and the influence of problem definition and problem ownership on public policy formulation [8-10]. Finally, some discussion is provided of what the consequences may be if one of the contrarian hypotheses proves to be the closer approximation to the truth about AIDS etiology.

THE CONVENTIONAL WISDOM

For many years clinicians, public health practitioners, and health policy analysts have accepted the belief that the epidemic of acquired immune deficiency syndrome (AIDS) in the United States and abroad is attributable to a transmissible viral agent. Indeed, because of its apparent role, the virus has been labeled the human immunodeficiency virus (HIV). A number of consequences have followed from this supposition. We have, in the first decade of the epidemic, witnessed the emergence of fear and discriminatory attitudes and practices in schools, workplaces, and patient care settings. Opinion polls of nationwide samples have shown majorities favoring quarantine of individuals diagnosed with AIDS and the criminalization of blood donation by those at risk for the syndrome. Mandatory identity cards for those infected was supported by one-half of respondents in one survey, with 15 percent advocating tattooing as a more effective means of identification [11]. Policy makers and legislators have entertained, if not promoted and implemented, regulatory proposals ranging from premarital testing for HIV and whole population screening for the virus to universal in-hospital precautions and limitations on the practices of HIV infected clinicians. We have also seen programs mounted for needle exchange on the streets and condom distribution in the schools. The most widespread communication of the HIV-AIDS connection had to be the distribution by United States Surgeon General C. Everett Koop of a mailing, based on the viral hypothesis, to every household in the United States [12].

Public awareness of AIDS was virtually complete by 1988, with 99 percent of those polled by the Gallup organization saying that they had heard or read of the syndrome [13]. Successive opinion polls have shown that the U.S. public has for some time regarded AIDS as the most important health problem facing this nation [14-16]. Recent knowledge assessments indicate that the conventional view has reached almost everyone, with 85 percent in 1992 specifying the virus as the agent of disease and death and only 4 percent disagreeing [17].

ALTERNATIVE VIEWPOINTS

There is, however, an array of viewpoints about the cause of AIDS in the scientific community. At one extreme would be the now orthodox and widely held view that HIV is the transmissible viral agent responsible for the epidemic of immune system suppression. At the other extreme would be the position taken by retrovirologist Peter Duesberg of the University of California at Berkeley. Duesberg argues on the basis of successive meta-analyses of available epidemiologic and laboratory data that HIV is only coincidentally associated with AIDS [3, 18-20]. Indeed, he argues further that given its nature, the virus cannot be responsible for immune system suppression. Duesberg charges that science has been abandoned in the search for the cause of AIDS insofar as the time-honored approach of ruling out alternative explanations by controlling for potentially confounding variables has not been followed. Duesberg believes that a far more reasonable hypothesis to explain AIDS, given the pattern and dynamics of the epidemic in the developed world, is that a toxic agent is at work. The best candidates for such agents are, he thinks, the psychoactive drugs which have been used on an epidemic scale since the 1960s, with certain of these used as muscle relaxants and aphrodisiacs by numbers of gay men [20].

Further along on this spectrum of viewpoints regarding AIDS etiology is Robert Root-Bernstein, professor of physiology at Michigan State University and author of *Rethinking AIDS: The Tragic Cost of Premature Consensus* [21]. As with Duesberg, Root-Bernstein has examined the role of HIV in light of the fact that the association of this virus with the syndrome is not complete and may be confounded by numerous other influences. He makes the case that among those factors not yet adequately considered are several that cause immunosuppression independently or in synergistic combinations and in the absence of HIV [21]. These immunosuppressive factors include undernutrition, multiple, concurrent infections, surgical intervention, anesthesia, the transfusion of blood and blood products, the use of drugs both medicinal and recreational, and autoimmune reactions. Root-Bernstein's own hypothesis proposes that an autoimmune response directed at T-cells and other tissues adds to or may actually cause the immune suppression underlying AIDS. It is the belief of his research group that the antigens presented by an appropriate combination of infectious agents, blood proteins, and sperm provoke the immune reaction. In this view, although HIV antigen may be involved, it is neither necessary nor sufficient to cause the autoimmune response.

The significance of concurrent infections in disabling the immune system is given added emphasis by Nobel-laureate, Kary Mullis. He notes the "catastrophic accumulation of an evolutionarily unprecedented burden of latent infection in some humans," and adds that the gay bath house "could not have been more efficiently organized if maximum exposure to the world's supply of diverse viruses had been actively sought" [22].

Somewhere in the middle of this array of perspectives on AIDS etiology would be Luc Montagnier, the man credited with identifying the virus dubbed HIV. Montagnier has stated that he now thinks that HIV alone is insufficient and must cause AIDS only with the cooperation of other microbes [23, 24]. The same conclusion was arrived at by Shyh-Ching Lo of the U.S. Armed Services Institute of Pathology [24, 25]. The idea of non-infectious as well as infectious co-factors at work as etiologic agents has gained some ground with even one of the staunchest of advocates of the HIV hypothesis, Robert Gallo, head of a research laboratory at the National Cancer Institute (NCI) [21].

Although it was only a small minority, some forty or more scientists and practitioners formed in 1991 an international coalition called the Group for the Scientific Reappraisal of the HIV-AIDS Hypothesis and called for debate on the question of what causes AIDS [26]. Two years later this organization had a reported membership of over 150 [27]. A similar group, calling itself "HIV Connection?" has also been established [21]. Critics of the orthodox position believe that "mainstream research" has violated "the basic principles of objective study: blind protocol of experiment, relevant randomization of samples, and use of matched control," [28] and that the evidence for HIV is "circumstantial" [29].

Notwithstanding that there are responsible and reputable scientists holding a contrarian viewpoint or reserving judgment, and that major figures in the mainstream have also modified their positions on the role of HIV, the idea that HIV causes AIDS prevails among scientists, professionals in medicine and public health, and the public. And this conventional view continues to govern judgments at the level of national health policy formulation as well as at the level of individual behavior. But why does this one viewpoint so dominate the others, even in the face of responsible criticism?

THE DOMINANCE OF THE VIRAL HYPOTHESIS

As in other fields, one can see in public health the dominance of a limited number of perspectives over others at the levels of theory, research, measurement, and practice. Of interest here is how the prevailing theoretical paradigm regarding AIDS etiology may have limited the field's consideration of other perspectives and why. And what public health issues arise as a consequence of a commitment to the viral theory, if it is not correct.

Paradigms

Ideas about what a paradigm is range from that of an epistemological gestalt to that of a political ideology. Thomas Kuhn, in his essay entitled *The Structure of Scientific Revolutions*, speaks of paradigms governing the conduct of science and defines these as "universally recognized scientific achievements that for a time provide model problems and solutions to a community of practitioners," [5]. Related to the paradigm of Kuhn is Lakatos' "research program" and Laudan's "research tradition" [6, 7]. Paradigms, as defined by Kuhn, restrict research efforts and practice traditions in such a way as to permit science to proceed and practice to develop. This restriction is, however, not without some cost as suggested by Burke: "A way of seeing is also a way of not seeing—a focus upon object A involves a neglect of object B" [30]. And such restriction is not without some elements that are arbitrary:

> Observation and experience can and must drastically restrict the range of admissible scientific belief. An apparently arbitrary element, compounded of personal and historical accident, is always a formative ingredient of the beliefs espoused by a given scientific community at a given time [30].

Paradigms can be thought of as organizing reality, using language even in such a way as to indicate what is important and what is irrelevant [31]. To speak of "health behavior," for example, makes the individual an object of analysis and a likely target for intervention efforts. Thus paradigms can be thought of as providing the focus required to proceed while fettering the imagination.

For the most part the literature in public health deals only implicitly with the concept of what is a paradigm, its operation, and its influence. Explicit discussions of paradigms governing the development of health education theory and practice reveal that what is a paradigm is variously defined and applied [32-36]. Some of these ideas are useful when assessing the issues raised in this article about the determination of AIDS etiology.

One explicit discussion of paradigms at work in health education begins with the following two statements:

> Paradigms and their underlying assumptions provide the context, or gestalt, in which research is conducted and knowledge is accumulated.
> The concept of paradigm is important in order to understand the intellectual tradition, results, and directions of activities in a given natural or social science [33].

The first of these statements specifies the role of the paradigm as an epistemological model that guides and that, according to Kuhn, constrains the research endeavor [5]. The second statement elaborates by indicating the power of the paradigm which is in place and the value of considering its role. Green emphasizes further the power of research paradigms to influence professional decisions and societal expectations of public health practice [37].

Paradigm "choices" may be imposed by the research traditions and practice traditions in which we are acculturated and by the way that we are socialized [5, 38]; they may also be the result of serendipitous accident as with the determination of the structure of the DNA molecule in the field of molecular biology [39]. In every instance, paradigm choices are made in a larger context which may well feature political influence.

According to Kuhn, a paradigm tends to be dominant or influential only as long as it is functional [5]. In what appears to be a paradox, it is the very dominance or influence of the prevailing paradigm that should be its undoing. It is the paradigm's power to attract resources and focus attention and activity that fosters the discovery of anomalous phenomena which then so challenge the paradigm that it fails. "Scientific revolution" follows when a "profession can no longer evade anomalies that subvert the existing tradition" [5]. Resolution of what was anomalous by the new paradigm brings the process to completion.

APPLICATION TO THE QUESTION OF WHAT CAUSES AIDS

The foregoing discussion of paradigms and paradigm change can be useful in understanding the dynamics of the limited debate about AIDS etiology and in framing the outcome should the conventional view prove to be wrong.

The Anomalies

Duesberg, Root-Bernstein, Montagnier, and others cite several inconsistencies between the viral hypothesis and available data [19, 21, 24, 25, 40, 41]. Among these are the observation that AIDS risks among HIV infected Americans differ widely based on gender. While HIV appears to be evenly distributed among seventeen to twenty-four year olds, AIDS has occurred far more frequently among men [19]. In New York City and in the United Kingdom for "females (and their infants) outside risk groups, the incidence of AIDS after ten years is negligible," [42]. This is quite unlike the almost even gender distribution of conventional sexually transmitted diseases [19] and raises the question of why AIDS in females occurs at all [42]. According to epidemiologists, Egger and Weyer, "the spread of AIDS does not behave like the spread of a disease caused by a single sexually transmitted agent" [43]. Ninety-five percent of men with AIDS are intravenous drug abusers (IVDAs) or homosexuals. This pattern suggests that it is these behaviors that are risky rather than HIV infection [19]. Such abnormal health risks correlate directly with the incidence of AIDS diseases with only 3 percent of all AIDS cases in the United States having come from groups without behavioral or clinical health risks. Risk group associated, co-factor involvement is further suggested by an extensive literature review conducted by Root-Bernstein [44]. He found that the average interval between infection with HIV and subsequent AIDS is over twenty years for mild hemophiliacs, ten to fourteen years for severe hemophiliacs, ten years for homosexual men, six years for transfusion patients, two years for transplant patients, and six months for perinatally infected infants and concludes that "these differences can only be explained in terms of risk-group associated cofactors" [44].

As indicated earlier, a major criticism of the orthodox view is that it is subject to confounding. Quite reasonably, Duesberg and others point out that one cannot say that the twenty-five conventional diseases (none of which are new) that may define AIDS are attributable to HIV infection without first ruling out a variety of health risks as alternative explanations for the epidemic. Accomplishing this requires comparing the incidence of these diseases in an HIV positive population to their incidence in an HIV negative population. This has not been done, according to critics, because the CDC has reported and recorded these disease outcomes as AIDS only in cases where the virus has been present [45]. Thus, there is no opportunity for applying controls in assessing the association between the virus and the syndrome. Stewart describes the resultant situation as "muddled" and the idea that AIDS is uniquely caused by HIV as "flawed a priori . . . by circular argument . . . and contrived classification" [42].

Proponents of the viral hypothesis see AIDS in hemophiliacs as providing direct support for the role of HIV [46]. However, for hemophiliacs, other recipients of blood transfusions, children of drug-addicted mothers, drug addicts, and male homosexuals with AIDS, competing causes or confounders have not been ruled out in attributing the outcome to HIV. Transfusions of blood and blood factors and intrinsic deficiencies associated with hemophilia may be sufficient to cause the diseases used to refine AIDS [19, 42, 46]. Among non-hemophiliacs receiving transfusions, 50 percent die within one year and 60 percent within three years of the conditions necessitating the transfusion [19]. This obviates prospective follow-up of 60 percent of any sample, clearly a problem in assessing the idea that AIDS is due to a virus with a long latency period. In his reviews of the literature, Duesberg found no study of HIV and blood transfusions that controlled for the conditions necessitating the transfusion [19]. He did find that all hemophiliacs with immunodeficiency had received treatment with factor VIII contaminated by foreign protein, a perfect correlation, while 416 of 1,186 immunodeficient hemophiliacs were free of HIV [46]. Others have raised the question of whether HIV is even transmitted via transfusion. They conclude that "the published data do not prove the hypothesis that such (HIV) transmission occurs" [47].

Among children with AIDS in the United States about 95 percent were subject to pathogenic conditions other than HIV exposure. These conditions were typically drug abuse during pregnancy by the mother or deficiencies in the child requiring blood transfusion. In one controlled investigation of the AIDS risk over time in a population of 297 asymptomatic, HIV positive IVDAs, a threefold higher risk of AIDS was demonstrated by those who persisted in their drug usage as compared to those who abtained [19]. The clear suggestion is that it is the presence of drugs in one's system that is of etiological significance and not the route of administration. Few studies of the association of HIV infection and AIDS in homosexuals have sought to control for the use of the amyl and butyl nitrates as aphrodisiacs and muscle relaxants used to facilitate anal intercourse, and these have been largely focused on Kaposi disease as an outcome.

Again, we have the suggestion that it may be a chemical rather than viral agent that suppresses immune system function. Also pointing in this direction are the widely divergent latent periods, ten years or more in adults and two years in children, said by critics to be inconsistent with the idea that a single pathogenic agent is involved [19, 21] and more typical of outcomes due to long-term exposure to toxic substances [19]. In agreement with this view, recreational and pharmaceutical drugs are among the possible etiologic factors cited by Stewart [48]. That such exposures occur chronically among male homosexuals has been documented [49].

Reviews of the AIDS literature note that in all groups at risk for AIDS the diseases defining the syndrome are seen in individuals with no indication of HIV infection [19, 28, 42, 45]. For example, severe immunodeficiency has been seen in approximately half of those hemophiliacs who are HIV negative as well as half of those who are HIV positive. Kaposi sarcoma is seen in HIV negative homosexuals; neurological deficiencies have been observed in both HIV infected and uninfected infants of drug-addicted mothers; and among twenty-one heroin addicts, only two of whom were HIV positive, immune system function was found to decline over thirteen years time in a manner typical of AIDS [19]. In all, some 5000 cases of HIV-free AIDS-defining diseases and immunodeficiencies have been discerned [46]. If the diseases defining AIDS occur in AIDS risk groups in the absence of HIV, the virus would not be a necessary cause for these conditions.

An additional argument mounted by Duesberg against the conventional wisdom is based on the fact that one can only be HIV positive if an antibody response has been made. He offers the observation that "there is no precedent for an infectious agent that causes disease only years after it is neutralized by antibodies" [19]. Biochemist Mullis adds that to cause AIDS, HIV would have to be a most unusual retrovirus insofar as humans play host to numbers of retroviruses and survive [25]. As already noted [1, 2], some HIV positive individuals continue to be healthy although it has been years since their infection with the virus.

As an alternative to the viral hypothesis, Duesberg proposes that "either drug consumption (frequently associated with malnutrition) by recently established behavioral groups or conventional clinical deficiencies and their treatments are necessary and sufficient to cause indicator diseases of AIDS" [19]. He postulates that the epidemic of immune system suppression in Africa is attributable to chronic malnutrition, repeated and multiple infections, and, possibly, to antibiotic treatment for repeated and multiple infections. Root-Bernstein and Stewart agree that these factors are potentially significant [21, 48], with Stewart adding a consideration of drug "contaminants and impurities which cause refractory infections and dysregulate immunity" [42]. Fisher attaches particular significance to the over utilization of antibiotics [24], and Koliadin specifically cites "the massive use of wide-spectrum antibiotics in order to prevent sexually transmitted diseases" [28].

Radiation is another non-infectious factor not controlled for in the association of HIV and AIDS. Andre Sahkarov first proposed in the 1950s the idea of population exposure to radionuclides as a cause of widespread immunosuppression [50]. Gould and Sternglass have recently emphasized such exposure as a possible explanation for the AIDS epidemic. Their analyses of changes in age-specific mortality between 1983 and 1988 indicate an "anomalous" increase in the twenty-five to forty-four-year-old category in those areas where radiation exposure earlier in life was highest and move them to conclude that "HIV infection may be a symptom rather than a cause of AIDS" [51]. Regarding Africa, Gould and Sternglass note that in the region where AIDS first appeared, strontium 90 in human bone was higher than in any other country in the 1950s.

Echoing Burke on the power of the paradigm in place (cited earlier), Stewart states "despite the overwhelming consensus (HIV/AIDS), or perhaps because of it, there are many uncertainties and flaws of reasoning in this hypothesis on epidemiolocial, clinical, and microbiological grounds." He concludes that "The (HIV) hypothesis has not offered an adequate defence against competent criticisms . . ." [42].

Bolstering the Dominant Model

An effort has been made by the HIV-only proponents to attend to the anomalies noted. These responses include the invocation of "unknown mechanisms" of pathogenesis [25], "silent infections" [52], "paradoxical" antibody responses [21], and modification of the mainstream model for AIDS etiology to include co-factors. In striving to incorporate the concept of a cofactor or cofactors at work, the proponents of what has been the dominant paradigm for explaining AIDS may be making an effort to extend their model of the epidemic and better approximate reality. Instead, it may be illustrative of a prevailing paradigm flexing under stress by coopting dissonant ideas as a means of accommodating anomalies [31], a "mopping up operation" in the words of Kuhn [5].

TRANSITION AND RESISTANCE

A recent review article in the *New England Journal of Medicine* opens with the estimate that "HIV is probably the most intensively studied virus in the history of biomedical research"; and, although the article is based on the assumption that the virus is the cause of AIDS, it concludes that "The immunopathogenic mechanisms of HIV infection are complex and not well understood" [53]. Yet within the field of public health the HIV model has been theoretical bedrock and continues to guide health policy formulation and day to day practice. It would appear that the public health community has been reticent to consider alternative viewpoints. Perusal of the literature in the field will rarely turn up the names of Duesberg and Root-Bernstein, for example, in this context. Further, while the most widely circulated journal in the field of public health, the *American Journal of Public Health*, has in recent years devoted two of twelve issues annually to AIDS as a special topic, only one parenthetical mention [54] has been made of any disagreement regarding the agent responsible for AIDS in those special editions or any others.

There has been an exchange of viewpoints published in *Science* [3, 55] and via letters appearing in a small number of journals, principally *The Lancet* and *Nature*. This discourse is focused entirely on Duesberg's position and is precious little in the way of debate, given the magnitude and severity of the AIDS problem. Proponents of the viral hypothesis charge Duesberg with "selective reading of the literature" [55], yet provide no rebuttal comparable in scope to the detailed and extensively documented positions that he and others have taken.

There appears to have been only one direct response to Duesberg's invitation to others that evidence be provided to contradict the hypothesis for drug use as the etiological factor in AIDS. Ascher, Sheppard, and Winkelstein at the University of California/Berkeley report no drug effect when using data from the San Francisco Men's Health Study, a cohort study, and controlling for confounding variables [56]. In a letter to *The Lancet*, Schechter and colleagues at the University of London offer additional support for this conclusion [57]. Duesberg responds that the work from Berkeley failed to employ adequate controls for drug usage by sero-positives and to consider the problems inherent in self-reported data; he interprets the results as actually supportive of his view [58, 59]. More general support for the drug hypothesis comes in a letter which appears in *Nature*. Its author states that:

> The reasoning behind Duesberg's theory occupies 60 pages of text and refers to more than 600 papers by other authors. The attempt to prove that the theory is wrong, based on references to a few studies by Duesberg's opponents, is not persuasive: there are no criteria to estimate these as more authentic than those to which Duesberg refers [60].

Coordinator of AIDS research at the National Institutes of Health, Anthony Fauci, explains the reluctance of "many scientists" to engage Duesberg in debate "because it pits you against somebody who in many respects is so far off from reality" [61]. John Maddox, editor of *Nature*, defends his publication's denial of Duesberg "a right to reply" saying "it may conflict with the journal's obligation to provide authentic information to its readers"; he adds that Duesberg forfeited the right to expect answers (to his questions) by his "barely tolerable . . . rhetorical technique" [62]. The journal's action followed Duesberg's use of the term "fabrication" [58] in describing the categories employed by Ascher's group in reporting their work done to refute the drug hypothesis.

Beyond the pages of the scientific and professional journals the exchange has, in at least one instance, been reduced to name-calling. Reportedly, an organizer of the 1993 Frontiers in HIV Pathogenesis meeting in the United States planned to have a button made reading "It's the Virus, Stupid" [63]. Adam Meyerson of the journal *Policy Review*, writes that "There has been a rush to judgment implicating HIV . . . and a distressing politicization in the scientific community that refuses to even entertain contrary views" [64]. This assessment accompanied the journal's publication of an exchange of viewpoints between those advocating a reexamination of the viral theory and those in the mainstream.

In eschewing the hypotheses featuring agents other than HIV, medicine and public health may be denying what are said to be the anomalies generated by the, now decade long, dominance of the viral model. That the non-HIV models have been essentially ignored rather than evaluated, found wanting, and discarded suggests that this is so. Additionally, part of the explanation for the hegemony of the HIV theory may lie in the realm of politics.

The Politics of Paradigm Choice

The adoption of new perspectives may be impeded for reasons unrelated to scientific viewpoint. To the extent that power, prestige, and income are derived from a commitment to the status quo, paradigm choice and paradigm change will be influenced. Clearly, the AIDS epidemic has spawned an industry, and it is one which is heavily invested in the conventional wisdom regarding the cause of the syndrome. It is reasonable to expect that those with careers ranging from fund-raising to research to counseling to book sales will be at least skeptical of maverick perspectives which conflict with their own.

Ideological leanings must also be considered. Tesh analyzes the competing ideologies which, over the last century, have shaped the agenda for research and practice in medicine and public health. The essential idea that "statements about causality implicitly assign responsibility for disease (prevention) to some people and excuse others" [65] provides some insight into why one view may hold sway over another. The choice of a paradigm for AIDS etiology featuring a virus that in so many of those affected is said to be contracted as a consequence of unprotected anal intercourse or intravenous drug abuse may be more readily made because it fixes blame for the epidemic on individuals considered deviant and may suit the moral requirements of those doing the choosing.

For lack of opportunity, inclination, or preparation, those who are not able to closely follow AIDS research may find an infectious disease model, particularly one involving a single powerful agent, appealing because it is more familiar and more readily understood than multi-factor models featuring a still uncertain interplay of environmental forces, biological predispositions, and behavioral choices.

It also holds some promise for a simple solution. For those who are dependent on others to interpret and assess the research, the mainstream position is reinforced by summary statements in support of that view made by trusted authority figures. James Curran, director of the AIDS program at CDC, has, for example, said that "there is not AIDS without HIV" [21] and, regarding the HIV-AIDS connection, that "the evidence just hits you in the face" [61]. It is also easier to dismiss a challenge to the conventional wisdom when a figure like Anthony Fauci, coordinator of AIDS research at the National Institutes of Health, describes Duesberg's position as "absolute and total nonsense" [61].

It is from such understandings and commitments that the political context in which the policies determining research priorities, budgeting, and public health practice is formed. That the epidemic of immune system suppression is not itself immune from the negotiation of competing interests, is to be expected. Contemporary science is not done in a vacuum. It is an enterprise dependent on large amounts of external funding, and the business of funding takes place in a still larger arena. What may be surprising is the extent to which AIDS has become politicized. A well-supported case has, for example, been made elsewhere to the effect that many of those who have something to gain from misrepresenting the situation with respect to AIDS among heterosexuals, the "conservative alarmists" and the "liberal democratizers," have done just that [66]. These figures are among the players in that arena where what is the AIDS problem and how to handle it are negotiated.

Problem Definition and Problem Ownership

A set of ideas, implicit in much of the foregoing and useful in understanding the politics of paradigm choice, is that of problem "definition" and problem "ownership" [8]. According to Stone, the "core substance" of problem definition is the "process of imaging making, where images have to do fundamentally with attributing cause, blame, and responsibility" [9]. In this theoretical perspective, competing interests will strive to manipulate the imagery which defines a problem. This extends to the fashioning and promotion of what are called "causal stories" or "causal ideas," important in policy formulation "because they locate the burdens of reform very differently" [9].

Rochefort and Cobb elaborate on these ideas, stating that "To claim ownership of a problem is to seek control over how it is thought of and acted on within the public arena . . . the problem's owner is the one who comes to speak with recognized authority and shapes the direction of public intervention" [67]. These analysts suggest that two alternative motivations for claiming problem ownership are self-interest and the promotion of "an impartially researched and reasoned assessment of an important public issue" [67]. With these ideas in mind, it cannot be said that in 1984, when Secretary of Health, Education, and Welfare Margaret Heckler endorsed the orthodox view of AIDS etiology on behalf of the United

States government, there was sufficient evidence to support a reasoned assessment of all hypotheses; Gallo's paper on the subject had not yet been subject to peer review, let alone publication and subsequent evaluation [21]. What has been said by critics is that the abandonment of an hypothesis featuring a toxic agent by CDC and its adoption of the viral hypothesis fostered the interests of the biomedical research establishment and the pharmaceutical industry [68-70]. If the definition of AIDS as infectious in its etiology is an anomalous theoretical paradigm, its persistence clearly can serve the interests of those owning that definition.

In a discussion specific to AIDS policymaking, Rochefort and Cobb state that "to name a problem's cause is to . . . turn in the direction of certain kinds of remedies and away from others" [71]. The definition of AIDS as a problem due to the transmission of a viral agent has dictated public policy on coping with the epidemic. That such policy may serve the various needs and interests of those who "own" the associated definition is clearly possible. Indeed, sometimes "it is solutions that determine problem definition" and that "predispose the identification of causes" [10]. That is, programmatic agendas and preferred strategies may precede rather than follow problem definition and causal attribution. The religious right, for example, seeking to promote lifestyle change and abstinence may welcome the opportunity to define AIDS as transmitted via sexual activity and IVDA. In the same way, the public health community, with its interest in promoting birth control, may be supportive of a definition of AIDS which specifies condom use as a solution.

Insofar as adopting a new perspective which redefines the epidemic may require surrendering ownership of the AIDS problem and all the advantages of proprietorship, resistance is understandable. Resistance to the idea that AIDS may be attributable to non-infectious agents can be expected from those who own the orthodox definition of the problem and who have, for example, an investment in HIV antibody testing, condom production, or the sale of abstinence.

Stone states that "in politics, causal theories are neither right nor wrong," and that "conflicts over causal stories are, therefore, more than empirical claims" [9]. That the question of AIDS etiology transcends science may well account for the manner in which the debate over the role of HIV is playing out. Causal theories do, however, lead to right or wrong policy as measured by health outcomes and social cost.

CONCLUSION

The infectious disease model, implicating HIV as the agent for AIDS, is the theoretical paradigm that dominates public health research and practice. If it is correct then we may be doing the best that we can as a scientific community and as a society in dealing with a major public health problem. If, on the other hand, we are wrong about the cause of AIDS, it would be difficult to understate the consequences. Although it may be argued that it is better to have made the error of being too cautious in considering alternative perspectives, such a judgment ignores the costs associated with adherence to the view that HIV plays a causal role. If an infectious agent, transmissible in the ways specified by the conventional view, is not the cause of AIDS then we have at the very least made a very large population unduly fearful and anxious by drawing an equation between sexual activity and death. Uncertainty and misunderstanding have extended this to the spectre of contracting AIDS from classmates, co-workers, health practitioners, toilet seats, kitchen utensils, and mosquitoes [72]. Further, the controversies over condom distribution, the abortion of potentially HIV positive embryos, the distribution of syringes, population screening, contact identification and tracing, immigration and tourist policies, and the timing, content, and form of education for prevention would have been engendered without the intended benefit. To these entries on the cost side of the ledger may be added the issues surrounding medical, dental, and nursing practice, practitioner choice of specialty and locus of practice, health insurance coverage, the untoward effects of AZT and other drugs, the acceleration of new drug approval, and the diversion of research talent and resources from other areas. Still other costs involve the potential erosion of the credibility of science and government alike and the dollar expense of acting on the belief that HIV causes AIDS. The latter includes the cost of any liability assigned for action taken or not taken on the basis of the viral model. All of that is quite a lot to pay if we have lingered too long with an inadequate theory. And if we have lingered too long for what are essentially political reasons, then some have benefited at great expense to many others.

This chapter has sought to raise the profile of an all too quiet debate and of the political context in which it occurs. It is hoped that the discussion will stimulate a critical consideration of how it is that we choose the paradigms which guide us as we frame the problems to be researched in public health, determine what methods to employ in discovering solutions, and strive to bring the best solutions to bear most effectively and equitably. While progress may require that we "force nature into the conceptual boxes supplied by professional education" [5], let's be mindful of this kind of restriction and not pause any longer than is necessary at any one stage in the development of the bases for public health practice. The challenge is to embrace the insights gained by utilizing old models, yet allow new paradigms to emerge and exert their influence in moving us to a closer approximation of the truth and a more valid basis for public health practice.

REFERENCES

1. Y. Cao, L. Qin, L. Zhang et al., Virologic and Immunologic Characterization of Long-Term Survivors of Human Immunodeficiency Virus Type 1 Infection, *The New England Journal of Medicine, 332*, pp. 201-208, 1995.
2. G. Pantaleo, S. Menzo, M. Vaccarezza et al., Studies in Subjects with Long-Term Nonprogressive Human Immunodeficiency Virus Infection, *The New England Journal of Medicine, 332*, pp. 209-216, 1995.

3. P. Duesberg, HIV is Not the Cause of AIDS, *Science, 241*, p. 514, 1988.
4. *MMWR*, Atlanta: Centers of Disease Control, *30*, pp. 250-252, 1981.
5. T. Kuhn, *The Structure of Scientific Revolutions*, University of Chicago Press, Chicago, 1970.
6. I. Lakatos, Falsification and the Methodology of Scientific Research Programs, in *Criticism and the Growth of Knowledge*, I. Lakatos and A. Musgrave (eds.), Cambridge University Press, Cambridge, pp. 91-196, 1970.
7. L. Laudan, *Progress and Its Problems*, University of California Press, Berkeley, 1977.
8. J. Gusfield, *The Culture of Public Problems*, University of Chicago Press, Chicago, 1981.
9. D. Stone, Causal Stories and the Formation of Policy Agendas, *Political Science Quarterly, 104*, pp. 281-300, 1989.
10. D. Rochefort and R. Cobb, Problem Definition: An Emerging Perspective, in *The Politics of Problem Definition: Shaping the Policy Agenda*, D. Rochefort and R. Cobb (eds.), University Press of Kansas, Lawrence, pp. 1-31, 1994.
11. *New York Times*, Poll Indicates Majority Favor Quarantine for AIDS Victims, p. 27, December 20, 1985.
12. C. Koop, *Understanding AIDS*, U.S. Government Printing Office, Rockville, Maryland, pp. 1-8, 1988.
13. *Gallup Report*, AIDS: 35 Nation Survey, *273*, pp. 2-73, June 1988.
14. E. Singer, T. Rogers, and M. Corcoran, The Polls—A Report: AIDS, *Public Opinion Quarterly, 51*, pp. 589-595, 1987.
15. R. Blendon, K. Donelan, and R. Knox, Public Opinion and AIDS: Lessons for the Second Decade, *Journal of the American Medical Association, 267*:7, pp. 981-986, 1992.
16. L. Hugick, 1992 Presidential Campaign, *Gallup Poll Monthly, 319*, pp. 2-6, 1992.
17. C. Schoenborn, S. Marsh, and A. Hardy, AIDS Knowledge and Attitudes for 1992, *Advance Data*, Centers for Disease Control and Prevention, Atlanta, February 1994.
18. P. Duesberg, Human Immunodeficiency Virus and Acquired Immunodeficiency Syndrome: Correlation But Not Causation? *Proceedings of the National Academy of Sciences, 86*, pp. 755-764, 1989.
19. P. Duesberg, AIDS Epidemiology: Inconsistencies with Human Immunodeficiency Virus and with Infectious Disease, *Proceedings of the National Academy of Science, 88*, pp. 1575-1579, 1991.
20. P. Duesberg, The Role of Drugs in the Origin of AIDS, *Biomedicine and Pharmacotherapy, 46*, pp. 3-15, 1992.
21. R. Root-Bernstein, *Rethinking AIDS: The Tragic Cost of Premature Consensus*, The Free Press, New York, 1993.
22. K. Mullis, A Hypothetical Disease of the Immune System that May Bear Some Relation to the Acquired Immune Deficiency Syndrome, *Genetica, 95*, pp. 195-197, 1995.
23. F. Bruni, Is AIDS Acting Alone? *Detroit Free Press*, pp. 1B-2B, February 25, 1992.
24. J. Fisher, *The Plague Makers*, Simon & Schuster, New York, 1994.
25. C. Farber, Fatal Distraction, *Spin, 8*:3, pp. 36-91, 1992.
26. T. DeLoughry, 40 Scientists Call on Colleagues to Re-Evaluate AIDS Theory, *The Chronicle of Higher Education*, pp. A9-A15, December 4, 1991.

27. G. Kolata, Debunking Doubts that HIV Causes AIDS, *The New York Times*, March 11, 1993.
28. V. Koliadin, Critical Analysis of the Current Views on the Nature of AIDS, *Genetica, 95*, pp. 71-90, 1995.
29. R. Strohman, Letter, *Science*, p. 157, January 13, 1995.
30. K. Burke, *Permanence and Change*, New Republic, New York, 1935.
31. M. Vlahos, *Center Report: Thinking about World Change*, United States Department of State/Foreign Service Institute, Washington, D.C., 1990.
32. L. Kolbe, D. Iverson, M. Kreuter, G. Hochbaum, and G. Christensen, Propositions for an Alternate and Complementary Health Education Paradigm, *Health Education*, pp. 24-30, May/June 1981.
33. L. Green, National Policy in the Promotion of Health, *International Journal of Health Education, 22*:3, pp. 161-168, 1979.
34. G. Parcel, Theoretical Models for Application in School Health Education Research, *School Health Research*, pp. 39-49, 1983.
35. M. Minkler, Health Education, Health Promotion, and the Open Society: An Historical Perspective, *Health Education Quarterly, 16*:1, pp. 17-30, 1989.
36. E. Fee and N. Krieger, Thinking and Rethinking AIDS: Implications for Health Policy, *International Journal of Health Services, 23*:2, pp. 323-346, 1993.
37. L. Green, The Changing State of Science in Health Education, *Focal Points*, U.S. Department of Health, Education, and Welfare, April 19-23, 1980.
38. R. Merton, *The Sociology of Science: An Episodic Memoir*, Southern Illinois University Press, Carbondale, 1979.
39. J. Watson, *The Double Helix*, Signet, New York, 1968.
40. L. Benitez-Briesca, Are the HIV Viruses Really the Causal Agents of AIDS? *Gac-Med-Mex, 127*:1, pp. 75-84, 1991.
41. H. Rubin, Is HIV the Causative Factor in AIDS? Letter, *Nature, 334*, p. 201, July 21, 1988.
42. G. Stewart, The Epidemiology and Transmission of AIDS: A Hypothesis Linking Behavioral and Biological Determinants to Time, Person, and Place, *Genetica, 95*, pp. 173-193, 1995.
43. H. Eggers and J. Weyer, Linkage and Independence of AIDS Kaposi Disease: The Interaction of Human Immunodeficiency Virus and Some Coagents, *Infection, 19*, pp. 115-122, 1991.
44. R. Root-Bernstein, Five Myths about AIDS that Have Misdirected Research and Treatment, *Genetica, 95*, pp. 111-132, 1995.
45. P. Duesberg, Infectious AIDS—Stretching the Germ Theory Beyond Its Limits, *International Archives of Allergy Immunology, 103*, pp. 118-127, 1994.
46. P. Duesberg, Foreign-Protein Mediated Immunodeficiency in Hemophiliacs With and Without HIV, *Genetica, 95*, pp. 51-70, 1995.
47. E. Papadopulos-Eleopulos, V. Turner, J. Papadimitriou, and D. Causer, Factor VIII, HIV, and AIDS in Haemophiliacs: An Analysis of Their Relationship, *Genetica, 95*, pp. 25-50, 1995.
48. G. Stewart, Uncertainties about AIDS and HIV, Letter, *The Lancet*, p. 1325, June 10, 1989.
49. L. Pifer, Y. Wang, T. Chiang et al., Borderline Immunodeficiency in Male Homosexuals: Is Lifestyle Contributory? *Southern Medical Journal, 80*:6, pp. 687-697, 1987.

50. A. Sakharov, Radioactive Carbon from Nuclear Explosions and Nonthreshold Biological Effects, *Soviet Journal of Atomic Energy, 4*:6, pp. 757-762, 1958.
51. J. Gould and E. Sternglass, Nuclear Fallout, Low Birthweight, and Immune Deficiency, *The International Journal of Health Services, 24*:2, pp. 311-335, 1994.
52. W. Haseltine, Silent HIV Infections, *The New England Journal of Medicine, 320*:22, pp. 1487-1489, 1989.
53. G. Pantaleo, C. Graziosi, and A. Fauci, The Immunopathogenesis of Human Immunodeficiency Virus Infection, *New England Journal of Medicine, 328*:5, pp. 327-335, 1993.
54. E. Fee and N. Krieger, Understanding AIDS: Historical Interpretations and the Limits of Biomedical Individualism, *American Journal of Public Health, 83*:10, pp. 1477-1486, 1993.
55. J. Cohen, The Duesberg Phenomenon, *Science, 266*, pp. 1642-1644, December 9, 1994.
56. M. Ascher, H. Sheppard, W. Winkelstein, and E. Vittinghoff, Does Drug Use Cause AIDS, *Nature, 362*, pp. 103-104, 1993.
57. M. Schechter, K. Craib, J. Montaner, T. Lee, M. O'Shaughnessy, and K. Gelmon, Letter, *The Lancet, 341*, pp. 1222-1223, 1993.
58. P. Duesberg, HIV and the Etiology of AIDS, Letter, *The Lancet*, pp. 957-958, April 10, 1993.
59. P. Duesberg, Letter, *Science, 268*, pp. 350-351, April 21, 1995.
60. V. Koliadin, Letter, *Nature, 364*, p. 96, 1993.
61. W. Booth, A Rebel without a Cause of AIDS, *Science, 239*, pp. 1485-1488, 1988.
62. J. Maddox, Has Duesberg a Right of Reply? *Nature, 363*, p. 109, May 13, 1993.
63. J. Cohen, Keytsone's Blunt Message: "It's the Virus, Stupid," *Science, 260*, pp. 292-293, 1993.
64. A. Meyerson, Is HIV the Cause of AIDS? *Policy Review*, pp. 70-83, Fall 1990.
65. S. Tesh, Disease Causality and Politics, *Journal of Health Politics, Policy and Law, 6*:3, pp. 369-390, 1981.
66. M. Fumento, *The Myth of Heterosexual AIDS*, Basic Books, New York, 1990.
67. D. Rochefort and R. Cobb, Framing and Claiming the Homelessness Problem, *New England Journal of Public Policy, 8*:1, pp. 49-65, 1992.
68. B. Werth, The AIDS Windfall, *New England Monthly*, June 1988.
69. C. Farber, Sins of Omission, *Spin*, November 1989.
70. J. Lauritsen, *The AIDS War: Propaganda, Profiteering and Genocide from the Medical-Industrial Complex*, Asklepios, New York, 1993.
71. D. Rochefort and R. Cobb, Instrumental versus Expressive Definitions of AIDS Policymaking, in *The Politics of Problem Definition: Shaping the Policy Agenda*, D. Rochefort and R. Cobb (eds.), University Press of Kansas, Lawrence, pp. 159-181, 1994.
72. D. Dawson, AIDS Knowledge and Attitudes for July 1988: Provisional Data from the National Health Interview Survey, *Advance Data from Vital and Health Statistics*, No. 161 DHHS Pub. No. (PHS) 89-1250, National Center for Health Statistics, Public Health Service, Hyattsville, Maryland, 1988.

CHAPTER 8

AIDS Communication: What Predicts Health Professionals' Decisions?

D. F. TREADWELL

The persuasion/health communication literature has provided a variety of different theoretical models which compete in the marketplace of ideas. These models have identified many questions such as message appeal, audience attributes, and channel characteristics that need to be answered as a prerequisite to designing any successful AIDS communication program, but many of them are divergent with respect to focus and to specific recommendations.

Generally, the models differ on the emphasis to be placed on such components as rationality/information, external social appeals, internal motivational appeals, demonstration of the behaviors to be emulated, and benefit/cost ratios of the behaviors to be adopted. Program designers must make a number of judgments as to which of these elements and their specific components should be selected and communicated to effectively promote AIDS-preventive behaviors.

A second problem with many models is the lack of emphasis on source attributes in predicting program success. Some models emphasize message-related attributes such as source credibility, but there is usually less than full consideration of other source attributes that might explain program impact. For example, organizational culture, structural constraints, and institutional inertia may explain the final nature of a communication program as much as any theoretical predisposition of its designers.

This article outlines some current theoretical models of health communication, and examines which of these are most heavily drawn upon when health professionals translate theory in practice. These decisions are then related to source attributes thought to explain some of these decisions.

BACKGROUND

Health education models have evolved over time. For example French and Adams identify three types of health education: behavior change, self-empowerment and collective action [1]. These translate in practice into providing messages that will persuade people to change their health behavior, providing skills that allow people to modify their own behavior, and organizing some kind of group or community action that will allow changes to be made in aspects of social structure that are inimical to health.

While health education has developed a number of health-specific models, notably the Health Belief Model [2], and communication theory has developed models of behavior change not specifically related to health, there are a number of areas where the two have come together. For example, Manoff has argued for the application of marketing communication principles to health promotion [3]. Network analysis [4] and diffusion/innovation theory [5] have been applied in health programs as have Fishbein and Ajzen's Theory of Reasoned Action [6], and Bandura's Social Cognitive theory [7].

As a result, health communication faces a diversity of models ranging from a focus on individual information processing, through theories of diffusion and adoption focusing on the relationship between the individual and relevant sources of information in the adoption process, to "social transformatory" theories focusing on political processes and resource allocation [8].

Such models have suggested a number of specific decisions campaign planners need to address, for example the role of opinion leaders, the influence of social norms, the need to show explicit behaviors if behavioral change is desired, and the need to show the cost/benefit advantages of the advocated behavior. Green et al.'s PRECEDE model emphasizes predisposing, enabling and reinforcing conditions, which invoke media for awareness, the provision of needed services, and the reinforcement of support for participants from health service personnel [9].

The problem for practitioners is to determine which specific models or components of models should underpin a program. Several theories call for recognition of social influences in addition to information about the problem. For example, social expectation models argue that the media or social groups establish an expectation of a particular behavior in the target audience—for example that condoms will be used. But Fishbein and Ajzen argue for assessing not just social norms but individuals' evaluation of those norms [6]. In other words the idea that most people practice "safe sex" is only germane when an individual has respect for the opinion of "most people." Similarly, pointing out the consequences of a behavior (use of condoms can prevent AIDS) is only relevant when an individual is actually concerned with preventing AIDS.

The Health Belief Model identifies as key components individual's perceived susceptibility to a problem, perceived severity of the problem, and perceived cost/benefit of adopting a given health behavior [2, 10]. (For example, is the benefit of protection that a condom offers worth the decrease in sexual pleasure than using one may mean?)

Social cognitive theory emphasizes two further components [7]. First, people require relevant skills, which must be taught if necessary. For example, people must know how to buy and use condoms if they are going to adopt the behavior of using them. Franzini, Sideman, Dexter, and Elder are specific that "individuals must be given the skills to communicate effectively with their partners about their unwillingness to engage in certain risky sexual practices" [11, p. 314]. Second, people must believe in their ability to do the particular action. (Individuals will go to a store and buy condoms only if they are confident that they are capable of doing this.)

The Precaution Adoption model suggests that people go through five stages of becoming knowledgeable about risks of a disease, acknowledging that there are risks for other people, acknowledging that there are personal risks, deciding to take precautions to reduce risks, and outlining the steps taken to reduce risk [12].

Other theoretical components include knowledge/awareness, risk assessment, and behavioral rehearsal. For example, DiClemente, Forrest, and Mickler suggest that AIDS prevention education for college students should include not only didactic instruction, but also self-appraisal of risk-taking behaviours and provision of social skills training needed for behaviour change [13, p. 210].

Other perspectives focus on structural impediments to health. These may be individual impediments such as income or education, or social-structure impediments such as provision of clinics or services.

While there is increasing interest in such latter approaches, health communication in practice essentially has had to wrestle with the questions of what message/method combinations will work most effectively with a given audience, in the light of potentially contradictory theoretical advice.

For example, the health belief model, which identifies specific theoretical components such as perceived perceptibility to a problem, perceived severity of the problem and the cost/benefit of adopting new behaviors has been criticized for not providing specific suggestions for persuading respondents how to modify their health behavior or for suggesting a plan for how the behavior change might be brought about [14].

The theoretical implications of some models have even been argued to be counterproductive. For example, one element of the Dual Process Model is a "message that elicits fear and attracts attention to the threat . . ." [15]. While some studies support the use of fear appeals [16], others argue that they are ineffective. For example Brecher argues that scare publicity associated with anti-drug campaigns in the 1970s resulted in the popularization of the relevant drug—i.e., a boomerang effect [17].

Considering message content alone, options theoretically range from fear through social support to specific instructional messages. Similarly, we find theoretical conflict over communication methods. For example, accepting the argument that the locus of control for individuals has shifted from the family, school or group and that the mass media have become the predominant socializing force in society leads to an assumption that mediated communication is most appropriate, and yet many theoretical models continue to invoke social influence as a major foundation [18].

Historically, there has been an ebb and flow of opinion with respect to mass media effects. Hyman and Sheatsley argued for minimal effects, citing "public apathy" [19]. Lazarsfeld and Merton proposed that the power of the mass media was greatly exaggerated [20]. Klapper suggested that reinforcement rather than change was the primary role of the mass media [21]. Rogers [5] suggested that the mass media can increase knowledge, but that attitude change is more likely through interpersonal channels and opinion leadership, an idea reinforced by Zucker [22].

Dependency theory suggests in summary that the less experience one has with something, the more dependent one will be on the media for information about it, suggesting that as community awareness of AIDS increases, the media will play a less significant role in informing individuals [23].

With respect to communication campaigns, Mendelsohn argued that while the mass media by themselves may be relatively powerless to bring about significant change, they could be rendered more effective by social science input in terms of determining appropriate targets, themes, appeals, and media vehicles [24].

FINDING APPROPRIATE MEDIA MESSAGE COMBINATIONS

Out of the diversity of theoretical options available, there is some convergence. While traditional approaches to health communication have favored informative messages based on print media and perhaps persuasive messages based on advertising media, there is evidence that more recent, theoretically-derived campaigns geared to specific behavioral outcomes have successfully influenced health behavior. For example, the Stanford Heart Disease Prevention Program (SDHPP) suggests that an emphasis on behaviour per se rather than a primary focus on knowledge or attitude change is desirable, and that a combination of personal counseling, instruction and mass media may produce changes more effectively in the short term [25].

But within these broad guidelines there is still a problem of deciding on a specific theoretical basis. At risk of oversimplifying, health communication decisions can be thought of as selections from a matrix of possible message types (e.g., fear, social appeal) and communication methods (mass, group, interpersonal) that will effectively reach a specific audience. Theory, however, may have a unidimensional focus, for example looking at individual message processing without regard to how messages reach a particular individual. Practice may be similarly unidimensional. For example, pretesting of television PSA's generally tests for the message with the medium as a constant and ignores possible vehicle effects—that is, that focus groups may be responding to the effect of television per se.

Similarly, pretests asking people simply to select one communication method over another or to select an ideal method are unrealistic. Chaffee for example argues that use of information channels is not an either/or proposition. Mass and interpersonal channels interact as in the case of family television viewing [26]. Nor do individuals respond to communication methods unidimensionally. For example, Cline and Engel found that for college students mass-mediated sources clearly dominated others with respect to amount of information provided, but that they were conspicuously less prominent in terms of their acceptability to respondents [27].

While media selection is usually based on considerations such as audience reach or perceived utility, such variables as source, message, and channel need to be considered simultaneously. Indeed, Neuwirth and Dunwoody argue that not only communication variables, but also noncommunication variables need to be simultaneously assessed [18]. Such research is not always done. For example, Sumser, Gerbert, and Maguire found significant differences in attitudes and perceptions about AIDS related to reliance on different media for information about AIDS, but there was no apparent assessment of the perceived content of those information sources [28]. Similarly, Cline and Engel found no systematic relationship between the credibility of a source and students' reports of having obtained information from that source, but the study does not address the perceived content of these sources, so that while respondents are asked to assess the perceived credibility and likelihood of use of different media, there is no specific check on whether these media may be providing different types of information about AIDS [27].

Program designers drawing on theory thus face two problems. First they may have to address variables on which any one theory may not provide guidance. A communication program hypothetically could then end up being based on multiple theoretical bases with, for example, messages being based on notions of risk or cost/benefit and communication methods being based on notions of opinion leadership and diffusion of innovations. This alternative, drawing on multiple theories simultaneously, raises the second problem—the prospect of conflicting advice.

Collectively, health communication models suggest a variety of approaches that might promote behavioral change. For example information about AIDS, messages showing specific skills needed to deal with the disease or its prevention, awareness of majority or relevant others' response to the problem, fear appeals, social support, and support for the individuals' self-confidence and ability to deal with the issue in practice are all suggested if behavioral change is to occur.

In practice, some elements have to be preferred or rejected, and becomes important then to find the theoretical preferences underpinning programs and to understand some of the reasons behind any given communication design.

THE STUDY

The specific interest of this article was to locate the theoretical issues most pertinent to health and health communication professionals and to explain these in terms of relevant source attributes. Two research questions guided the study:

RQ1: What theoretical aspects predominate in the design of AIDS communication programs?

RQ2: What attributes explain the preference for any given theoretical base?

Two main groups of respondents were used in this study. A group of health and health communication professionals was asked to respond to the problem of how best to communicate to college students in a way that would effectively promote AIDS-preventive behaviors. As a point of reference, a group of college students also was asked to address the same question.

The rationale for focusing on this latter group is well summarized by Cline and Engel [27]. With one in 500 college students found testing positive for HIV, several thousand college students nationally may be infected. Cline and Engel point out the significance of this statistic to the college age population in terms of the latency period of the HIV virus. "The prevalence of AIDS in the age groups 25 to 29 and 30 to 34, in conjunction with an average latency period of eight to ten years, likely puts the traditional college-age population in the midst of an age group at highest risk for infection" [27, p. 2]. Furthermore, "despite being well-informed about AIDS, few college students have changed their behavior in meaningful ways due to the threat of AIDS" [27, p. 3].

DiClimente, Forrest, and Mickler found that college students have a high level of HIV-related sexual risk-taking behavior [13]. They report that a substantial proportion of college students report being sexually active, having multiple sexual partners and practicing unprotected sexual intercourse; that a large proportion of students have not modified their sexual practices and that "alarmingly, a small proportion of students report increasing HIV-related behaviors" [13, p. 208].

Respondents

To determine the models of AIDS communication operant among health and communication professionals working in the AIDS field, respondents were drawn from medical, nursing, and communication personnel at a regional medical center, from medical and nursing staff at two campus health services, and from the membership list of a regional health education association. To represent the target group, a group of twenty-six undergraduate communication majors was selected on the grounds that the vocabulary of communication would be comfortable to them as well as the relevance of the AIDS topic itself.

Method

Because message content and communication methods interact, a method must be found which assesses respondents' perceptions of these holistically. For example, a decision to demonstrate a particular behavior implies the use of visual media, but the medium per se will also influence response to a message—the so-called "vehicle effect." Medium and content form what Groswiler calls "elements of a hybrid relationship rather than isolated factors" [29, p. 68]. Therefore a research method must be found which allows respondents to react to the complexity and relatedness of different methods and content simultaneously.

Not only should program components be tested simultaneously on the basis of providing respondents with all available options, research to date requires such assessment on the basis of known interaction effects. For example the debate on appropriate levels of fear [30, 31] has shifted in favor of recognizing interaction effects with other persuasive components. For example, Leventhal, Safer, and Panagis found that fear messages are not effective in the absence of an action plan [15].

The basic method selected for assessing multiple message/method combinations was Q-methodology. The strength of the method is the assessment of respondents' subjective responses to complex issues, and has been used for this reason in the health field [32].

Q-methodology provides a means of analyzing the phenomenological world of the individual without sacrificing the power of statistical analysis [33]. It provides a convenient means of obtaining an objective measure of subjective response to an issue. The basic Q-sort technique described below usually requires items to be rated independently so that the placement or ranking of one item affects the ranking that can be given to other items, an appropriate method in this study where the focus is on perceptions of the relative utility of various communication approaches. Additionally the method allows ready assessment of the relationship between cases, an important consideration given that part of the study focuses on identifying individuals that have a common theoretical perspective.

In this study a special effort was made to identify specific relevant occupations such as student, physician, nurse, and educator, but not to ensure survey-type representatives because the primary task was to assess patterns of thinking about effective AIDS communication. "As with sampling persons in survey research, the main goal in selecting a Q sample is to provide a miniature which, in major respects, contains the comprehensiveness of the larger process being modeled" [34].

To replicate the universe of message/method components available for AIDS communication, seven major themes commonly found in theoretical models were identified. These were:

1. Information/fact statements.
2. Majority approval/social norm statements.
3. Statements about cost and/or benefits of adopting appropriate behaviours.
4. Specific action/behaviour plan statements.
5. Risk statements.
6. Personal self-confidence/self-effectance statements.
7. Fear appeal statements.

For each of the above seven themes five specific messages were written to provide a total of thirty-five different message possibilities.

Communication methods were categorized under a standard mass-group-interpersonal grouping, and for each of these three approaches, five specific methods relevant to college students were generated, giving a total of fifteen method possibilities, and a total of fifty message/method possibilities in all.

Each message statement or method was printed on a separate card and respondents were each given a set of the fifty cards and asked to sort them into seven categories ranging from "least effective way of persuading college students to adopt behaviors that will prevent AIDS" to "most effective way of persuading college students to adopt behaviors that will prevent AIDS."

The distribution for the categories was 4, 6, 9, 12, 9, 6, 4. That is, respondents were asked to put 4 cards into the first ("least effective") category, 6 into the second, 9 into the third and so on. Each category was assigned a score ranging from 1 to 7 so that cards in the "least effective" category received a score of 1, while cards in the "most effective" category received a score of 7.

The Q-sample of 50 test items used here represents the universe or concourse from which respondents form their subjective impressions of AIDS communication. Clearly the concourse of items can be larger in practice, but the Q-sample size stems primarily from the theoretical structure described above. Also, the number of items in the sort is constrained by pragmatic considerations such as the need to administer the sort and related questionnaires within a standard college class period, and to optimize the response rate from other respondents.

Operationalizing communication theories in this way allows identification of 1) theoretical components for which respondents have a preference, 2) whether key aspects of campaigns that seem to explain success have been preferred, 3) clusters of individuals that have the same theoretical predisposition and their attributes.

In addition to the Q-sort, student respondents completed a questionnaire seeking standard demographic information and information on exposure to AIDS information, health risk behavior, and their self-assessment of key theoretical issues on which the card sort was based such as confidence in ability to deal with

AIDS, level of information about AIDS, and fear of becoming infected with AIDS.

Health and health communication professionals completed the card sort as well as a short questionnaire seeking standard demographic information, level and type of education, and experience with AIDS in terms of medical/health or communication work. These respondents were also asked to identify or explain a brief rationale for why they sorted the statements the way they did.

RESULTS

Student Reference Group

The student reference group completed the sort as part of classes, resulting in a 100 percent return. For other respondent groups contacted by mail the percentage of usable returns ranged from 25 to 35 percent.

Typically, Q-methodology seeks to identify only the subjective responses of individuals rather than a verifiable trait. Therefore only the response stability was measured by having a group of student respondents ($n = 9$) complete a second card sort one week after the first. Stability was computed by correlating each respondent's two sorts. Test-retest correlations averaged .65.

Students ranged in age from nineteen to fifty at nearest birthday with a mean age of twenty-two. Eight-one percent were female and 100 percent were white. Sixty-two percent were Roman Catholic, 23 percent Protestant, and 15 percent said they had no religious affiliation. Students reported having between one and fifteen semesters of higher education, with a median of five semesters of education.

In terms of AIDS-risk behavior, no student reported ever having injected any illegal drug. One individual reported having sex with two different people in the last three months, the remainder reported one or no partners. Self-reported frequency of sex in the previous three months ranged between zero and 100 with a median value of one sexual contact. Thirty-one percent said they had drunk alcohol or used drugs before having sex the last time they had sex. Thirty-six percent reported that they or a partner used a condom the last time they had sex. One hundred percent of students responding to the question said their sexual preference was for a person of the opposite sex.

The most frequently listed sources of information for students are shown in Table 1. Almost all respondents cited leaflets, pamphlets, brochures and television as a source of information about AIDS, followed by newspapers and magazines, and then radio, posters and bulletin boards. Only 54 percent cited an interpersonal source such as best friend, physician or other medical professional, and only 50 percent cited families as a source of information. Campus sources of information such as college classes, fraternities, and campus AIDS task force were

Table 1. Most Frequently Listed Sources of Information about
AIDS/HIV for Students

Leaflets, pamphlets, brochures; television	92%
Newspaper or magazines	77%
Radio; poster, bulletin boards	69%
Best friend; physician or other medical professional	54%
Family	50%
College classes, seminars or discussion groups; spouse/lover; health education specialist	23%
Campus groups such as fraternities, sororities, societies; work or study groups	12%
Direct mail; college or university AIDS task force; AIDS hotline or telephone counseling; community groups such as churches or service organizations	8%
Minister of religion, priest, or religious adviser	0%

cited by between 8 and 23 percent of respondents. No one cited ministers of religion, priests or religious advisers.

On a 5-point, Likert-type "Strongly agree—strongly disagree" scale, student respondents had a mean score of 3.08 (SD 1.4) for "I have been taught about AIDS/HIV in school or high school"; a mean of 3.35 (SD 1.2) for "I talk about AIDS/HIV with my parents or other adults in my family," and a mean of 4.12 (SD .86) for "I talk about AIDS/HIV with my friends." Thus, respondents agreed that they talked about AIDS with their friends, but were less certain they had been taught about the topic or that they discussed the topic with their families.

As a point of comparison for the health professional Q-sort, students were asked to construct an "ideal" AIDS communication program by sorting the same fifty statements from least effective to most effective in terms of promoting AIDS-preventive behavior.

Using these data, the fifty items were ranked in order based on the mean scores obtained for this group (see Table 2). In terms of a communication program aimed at persuading students to adopt AIDS-preventive behaviors, the students' most effective messages were items 34, 4, 11, and 24—Say, "AIDS can kill you," Say, "One in 500 college students may be affected with the AIDS/HIV virus." Say, "Casual sex is just not worth the risk of illness and death from AIDS," and "If you are a college student, you can be especially at risk of AIDS."

The next most effective messages were items 2, 36, 31, 35, and 3—"At present there is no cure for AIDS," Say "AIDS can mean loss of your family and friends," Say "Sex with the wrong person can lead to your illness and death from AIDS," and Say "Most people get the AIDS virus (HIV) by sharing drug needles or by having sex with someone who already has the virus." Students added one demonstration/modeling approach, item 19, "Show how to successfully say

Table 2. Ten Top and Ten Bottom Ranked Items
for Students (*n* = 26)

Item No.		Mean	SD
34.	Say, "AIDS can kill you."	5.54	1.45
4.	Say, "One in 500 college students may be infected with the AIDS/HIV virus."	5.42	1.58
11.	Say, "Casual sex is just not worth the risk of illness and death from AIDS."	5.35	1.90
24.	Say, "If you are a college student you can be especially at risk of AIDS."	5.27	1.71
2.	Say, "At present there is no cure for AIDS. "	5.08	1.76
36.	Use television.	5.04	1.31
31.	Say, "AIDS can mean loss of your family and friends."	4.85	1.12
35.	Say, "Sex with the wrong person can lead to your illness and death from AIDS."	4.81	1.50
19.	Show how to successfully say "no" to someone who wants unprotected sex or who wants to share drug needles.	4.73	1.51
3.	Say, "Most people get the AIDS virus (HIV) by sharing drug needles or by having sex with someone who already has the virus."	4.69	1.49
10.	Say, "The majority of people now take precautions to prevent AIDS."	3.23	1.39
7.	Say, "The majority of people always make sure they use condoms if they think that having sex might put them at risk of AIDS."	3.04	1.15
29.	Say, "You can feel good talking with friends or a partner about AIDS—they probably expect you to."	3.00	1.20
33.	Say, "AIDS can mean loss of your job or career."	2.92	1.81
9.	Say, "The majority of people always make sure they get well-informed about their sex-partners' health."	2.92	1.06
32.	Say, "AIDS can mean very expensive and time-consuming medical care."	2.88	1.28
8.	Say, "The majority of people believe that sharing needles if you do drugs is not a smart idea."	2.73	1.28
6.	Say, "The majority of people are getting very well-informed about AIDS."	2.35	1.47
43.	Use community groups such as churches and service organizations.	2.27	1.34
46.	Use ministers of religion, priests or religious advisers.	1.92	1.35

'no' to someone who wants unprotected sex or who wants to share drug needles," and one method recommendation, item 36 "Use Television."

Looking at the items considered least effective, students strongly rejected message items 8 and 6, Say "The majority of people believe that sharing needles if you do drugs is not a smart idea," and Say "The majority of people are getting very well-informed about AIDS"; and rejected items 10, 7, 29, 32, 33, and 9—Say "The majority of people now take precautions to prevent AIDS," Say "The majority of people always make sure they use condoms if they think that having sex might put them at risk of AIDS," Say "You can feel good talking with friends or a partner about AIDS—they probably expect you to," Say "AIDS can mean loss of your career," Say "The majority of people always make sure they get well-informed about their sex-partners' health," and "AIDS can mean very expensive and time-consuming medical care."

The students strongly rejected two sources of information about AIDS—item 46, "Ministers of religion, priests, or religious advisers," and item 43 "Community groups such as churches and service organizations."

In summary, students rejected all the majority appeal items (6-10), and polarized on the threat/fear items. Items 32 and 33 dealing with loss of job/career, or extended medical care were strongly rejected, but items 31, 34, and 35 dealing with loss of family and death were recommended as appropriate messages. The other recommended messages (items 4, 11, 24) were all "risk-related," dealing with the specific risk to college students or the risks from casual sex. Interestingly, television was the only communication medium strongly recommended by students for reaching college students.

Health Professions Respondents

Three different occupational groupings were drawn from four different locations. Education/communication, nursing, and medical personnel were drawn from the staff of a regional medical center and two area campus health services. Education/communication personnel were further drawn from the mailing list of a regional health education association. Respondents included twenty-six medical center nurses, physicians, and communication personnel; twenty-two campus health service personnel, and forty-six respondents drawn primarily from the professional association mailing list. Respondents completed the same 50-item Q-sort as the students together with a questionnaire eliciting standard demographic information.

Respondents' ages ranged from nineteen to twenty-four to over sixty-five; 67 percent were thirty-five to forty-four or younger. Eighty-five percent were female and 97 percent classified themselves as white. The most frequent religions was Roman Catholic (38.3%) with Protestant the next-most cited (29.8%). Educational qualifications ranged from diplomas to doctorates. Doctorates were held by 7.5

percent of respondents; masters by 40.5 percent, and bachelors by 26.6 percent; 6.4 percent of respondents held a medical degree. Eight respondents listed more than one qualification. Respondents reported a mean of 6.4 years involvement with the health/medical aspects of AIDS, and a mean of 5.4 years involvement with education or communication about AIDS.

To find the configurations of thinking about AIDS communication that existed in the group as a whole, cluster analysis was performed based on the Q-sort scores on the 50 message/method variables. Cluster analysis groups together those individuals who are most similar on their configuration of sort scores. Inspection of the cluster schedule and agglomeration coefficients revealed two major clusters—one of sixty-four and one of thirty respondents.

Table 3 shows the most relevant items for each cluster in terms of acceptance. These items can be considered the most vital recommendations each group would make for a communication campaign aimed at college students, and it can be seen that each cluster's campaign has its own "personality."

The two clusters agree on items 19 and 41 "Show how to successfully say "no" to someone who wants unprotected sex or who wants to share drug needles," and "Use college classes, seminars or discussion groups," but beyond that the clusters adopt quite different strategies. For example cluster one has a 50:50 mix of "show" items and "use" items, that is a mix of demonstration/skill-provision and relevant communication methods, whereas eight of the top 10 items for cluster two are "say" or message items, and only one is a "method" item (Use college classes, seminars or discussion groups).

Whereas the strategy for cluster one is clearly a mix of methods aimed at providing students with the skills needed to deal with AIDS/HIV prevention, cluster two focuses on organized methods such as college classes and heavily emphasizes fear, risk and the facts of HIV transmission.

When we look at items rejected by the two clusters, we find a larger number of items in common. Both clusters reject items 6, 7, 8, 9, 10, 27, and 32. (Say "The majority of people are getting very well-informed about AIDS," Say "The majority of people always make sure they use condoms if they think that having sex might put them at risk of AIDS" Say "The majority of people believe that sharing needles if you do drugs is not a smart idea," Say "The majority of people always make sure they get well-informed about their sex-partner's health," Say "The majority of people now take precautions to prevent AIDS," Say "Groups and individuals that are working to fight AIDS will make you feel very welcome," and Say "AIDS can mean very expensive and time- consuming medical care").

Cluster one uniquely rejects items 14 (Say "The cost of AIDS is just too high to risk getting infected"), 26 (Say "There is absolutely no reason to be embarrassed talking about AIDS with anyone"), 30 (Say "You don't have to feel embarrassed about buying condoms. People buy them all the time.")

Table 3. Most Recommended Items for Each of Two Health
Professions Clusters (Mean and *SD* Follow Each Item)

Item No.	Cluster I (*N* = 64)	Item No.	Cluster II (*N* = 30)
19.	Show how to say "no" to someone who wants unprotected sex or who wants to share drug needles. (6.61, 0.92)	34.	Say "AIDS can kill you." (5.83, 1.32)
		2.	Say "At present there is no cure for AIDS." (5.83, 1.15)
18.	Show how to buy and use condoms. (6.13, 1.32)	11.	Say "Casual sex is just not worth the risk of illness and death from AIDS." (5.63, 1.25)
16.	Show how to talk successfully with others about AIDS. (5.75, 1.27)	4.	Say "One in 500 college students may be affected with the AIDS/HIV virus." (5.2, 1.97)
41.	Use college classes, seminars or discussion groups. (5.56, .99)	19.	Show how to successfully say "no" to someone who wants unprotected sex or who wants to share drug needles. (5.5, 1.65)
20.	Show how to access and use AIDS services such as hotlines and counseling. (5.42, 1.33)	24.	Say "If you are a college student, you can be especially at risk of AIDS." (4.97, 1.73)
17.	Show how and where to get information about AIDS. (5.34, 1.25)	41.	Use college classes, seminars or discussion groups. (4.93, 1.05)
44.	Use campus groups such as clubs and societies. (5.03, 1.14)	23.	Say "You may be at risk of AIDS if you don't find out the health of your sex partner." (4.83, 1.39)
36.	Use television. (4.98, 1.08)	3.	Say "Most people get the AIDS virus by sharing drug needles or by having sex with someone who already has the virus." (4.83, 1.53)
47.	Use spouses, lovers, or other people that are physically intimate to get messages to students. (4.95, 1.41)	28.	Say "When it comes to AIDS, there is no such thing as a dumb question." (4.73, 1.76)
48.	Use best friends. (4.92, 1.29)		

Cluster two uniquely rejects items 40 ("Use direct mail to homes, dorms or apartments"), 43 ("Use community groups such as churches and service organizations"), and 46 ("Use ministers of religion, priests or religious advisers").

In terms of least-recommended approaches, both groups reject all of the majority appeal items. Cluster one uniquely rejects items trying to remove embarrassment in dealing with AIDS topics (items 26, 27, 30), and cluster two uniquely rejects a number of method items (items 46, 43, 40). In summary, cluster one proposes a number of methods aimed at providing students with the skills to deal with AIDS or personal communication about AIDS; it rejects messages based on majority appeal and specifically rejects messages aimed at reducing students' embarrassment in dealing with AIDS. Cluster two is heavily message-oriented; it proposes messages focused on "the facts" of AIDS, fear and risk, and specifically rejects a number of possible communication methods.

To determine why these two different approaches to AIDS communication might exist, the two clusters were examined in terms of demographic attributes and showed clear and statistically significant differences.

Analysis of respondents showed that whereas only 14.1 percent of cluster one was hospital-based, 56.7 percent of cluster two was hospital-based. By contrast 59.4 percent of cluster one respondents belonged to the regional health education association, whereas only 23.3 percent of cluster two belonged to this. Both clusters were approximately equally represented by campus health service personnel. This overall distribution is significantly different (parson Chi-square = 23.01, df 4, $p < .001$).

When respondents described their organizational affiliation, 27.4 percent of cluster one versus 20.0 percent of cluster two indicated affiliation with a college or university health service. Cluster one showed 11.3 percent otherwise affiliated with a university versus 0 percent for cluster two. Cluster two showed 63.3 of respondents affiliated with a hospital versus only 27.4 for cluster one. This distribution also approaches a statistically significant difference (parson Chi-square = 16.1, df 10, $p = .10$).

There was no significant difference between clusters in age, sex, or race, but there was a significant difference (Chi-square = 10.80, df 4, $p < .05$) with respect to religion. Cluster one is only 28.1 percent Roman Catholic whereas cluster two is 60 percent Roman Catholic. Cluster one is somewhat more likely to be Protestant (31.3 versus 26.7%), and definitely more likely to be Jewish (14.1 versus 3.3%), or "other or no religion" (26.5 versus 10% respectively).

There was no significant difference between clusters with respect to the amount of time spent dealing with AIDS in a health/medical context or an education/communication context. However, the clusters did differ significantly with respect to level of education. The percentages of bachelors' degrees in each cluster were similar (52% for cluster one versus 48% for cluster two), but cluster one had 82 percent of the masters' degree versus 18 percent for cluster two, and 100 percent of the doctoral degrees. Of the six identifiable physician respondents, five were in cluster one. This distribution difference is significant (parson Chi-square = 19.39, df 5, $p = .002$).

Cluster two also had sixteen of the twenty identifiable hospital-based nurses. Only three of the thirty respondents in this cluster named health education as an academic specialization, and only three named health education or health promotion as an occupational specialization.

In summary, educational level, religion and institutional affiliation predict the type of communication program designed by respondents. It appears that programs using multiple methods, client involvement, and focusing on skill development are more likely to come from individuals with an academic affiliation and higher academic qualifications.

Another, qualitative, explanation is available in the rationale that respondents were asked to provide when completing their Q-sorts. The two clusters agree on a number of areas. A number of respondents from both clusters said that they tried to put themselves in the role of college students when sorting the cards (e.g. "I tried to put myself back in college when we were all invincible and immortal.") A number also agreed that scare tactics and cost/benefit appeals would not be successful. (e.g., "People don't respond to 'scary messages'," "Cost is not important to students," "Placed as low effectiveness (are) those that cite $/time as 'cost' in cost/benefit; more salient cost to students has to do with rejection or isolation." A number of respondents (rather more from cluster 1) raised students' feelings of invincibility (e.g., "College students believe they will live forever").

While the clusters express some similar sentiments about taking the students' perspective, not using fear or cost/benefit appeals, and trying to deal with attitudes of immortality, the clusters clearly differ with respect to theoretical foundations, use of scare appeals, and communication methods.

While cluster one cites Fishbein and Ajzen's paradigm of persuasion, Durkheim/Hirschi Social Bond Theory, Cultivation Analysis, the Health Belief Model (twice), and Social Learning Theory (twice): nobody from cluster two provided such citations.

Cluster one was more likely to oppose fear tactics. For example:
- "Scare tactics do not work."
- " 'It will kill you' is not working because they think that (they) are immortal."

Cluster two comments tended to favor a direct approach. For example:
- "The more frightening or grim the message the more impact, especially if it relates to the person's own well-being";
- "I felt that it is very important to say how it is. There is no cure . . . "
(This respondent also suggested changing the statement "One in 500 college students may be infected to "One in 500 ARE infected . . .).

The clusters are also clearly different when talking about communication methods. Almost every cluster one respondent making a comment had something to say about approach, and it centered on active, participative, skill-oriented methods:
- "Using close friends and doing some role-playing are great ways to convey messages";
- " . . . experts/educators have demonstrated that role playing, hands on demos and being 'frank' about sex with partners seem to be the most effective types of communication";

- "I believe the best way to learn about something is to experience it—thus cards that 'show' received a higher efficacy rating."

Some cluster one respondents cited authorities from the communication theorists mentioned above through generic 'experts' to Confucius (What I hear, I forget; What I see, I remember. What I do, I understand"). No experts were cited by cluster two.

Methodologically, cluster two comments were clearly in favor of direct teaching:

- "students need to be repeatedly told . . . ";
- ". . . they respond better to visual and audio short bursts of information";
- "I felt it is very important to say how it is";
- "Strong factual messages are the most important";
- "The message should be strong and forceful, making college students take notice . . . They should be taught the facts."

In summary, there is a clear qualitative difference with respect to communication methods, use of fear appeals, and theoretical citations.

Given that a number of respondents said that they tried to "put themselves in the students' shoes" when they did the card sort, a test of this explanation was computed.

Intuitively, message recipients have ideas of what for them are most effective methods of communication and how effective messages should be phrased. This has been manifested most obviously in the initiation of communication programs that bypass existing services and are designed and operated by AIDS activists themselves [35]. Such communication may or may not be theoretically elegant, but using communication models that most approach the intuitive reasoning of message recipients theoretically should result in greater resonance with them and predict a more successful program outcome.

A test of this thinking by respondents was constructed by using the composite "ideal sort" of the students (see Table 3 for students' top-rated items) and measuring how closely the other respondents came to this in their own sorts. To do this, squared Euclidean distance, a dissimilarity measure, was computed between the "ideal sort" and every other sort (excluding students). This gives a measure for each health profession respondent of how similar they are to the composite student sort—the higher the score, the more different their sort and vice versa.

A T-test between the squared Euclidean distance scores for each cluster showed a significant difference. The means for cluster one and two were respectively 185.06 ($SD = 51.01$) and 151.73 ($SD = 37.37$); t (pooled variance) = 3.2 (df 92), $p = .002$). Thus cluster two produced sorts significantly more similar to the composite student sort indicating that cluster two individuals are more likely to design a program that is closer to student expectations of a successful program.

DISCUSSION

The study focused on respondents likely to have a professional concern with AIDS—either from a health/medical point of view or from an education/communication point of view. Within this group there are two divergent views on how most effectively to communicate about AIDS prevention. The large group favors a multi-method approach aimed at providing students with the skills and abilities to deal with AIDS prevention. The smaller group has a greater focus on providing facts, information about the risk students face and possibly some fear appeal in a more formal, directive manner. The two clusters clearly epitomize what Devine and Hurt call "behavioral-based" and "message-based" theories respectively [36].

The variables that predict this difference are religion, institutional affiliation, level of education, and a constructed measure of closeness to student thinking on the subject. The larger group has an overall higher level of education, and is less likely to be associated with a hospital or to be Catholic. They are also more likely to cite a theoretical basis for their reasoning, but less likely to agree with the student target group on how the ideal communication campaign should be designed. The smaller group while being closer to the student ideal in this latter respect, does not cite any theoretical base for its thinking.

This suggests that in developing persuasive campaigns, individuals may use the theoretical grounding that stems from their education or institutional affiliation but in the absence of such a grounding, place themselves intuitively in the shoes of the target audience and attempt to develop a persuasive strategy on this basis.

Further evidence for this is provided by looking at the areas from which the top ten items were drawn for each cluster. Of the seven different message orientations offered respondents, cluster one recommended message items from one area only—the action/behavior items (items 16-20) which were intended to operationalize social-cognitive theory. No other message types were recommended at all.

These five items were balanced 50:50 with five method items. Cluster one in this sense has a specific theoretical focus on providing relevant skills as emphasized in social-cognitive theory. Cluster one follows the SDHPP guidelines previously discussed and can be categorized as French and Adams' "self empowerment" approach. On the other hand, cluster two drew its recommended messages from all seven theory categories approximately equally and recommended only one communication method item.

This pattern is less clear cut with respect to rejected items. In fact the two clusters are almost in agreement in rejecting the majority/social appeal items. There is a clear difference between clusters in that cluster one does not specifically reject any communication method, whereas cluster two specifically rejects items 46, 43, and 40 (Table 3). Interestingly, the student "ideal sort" also specifically rejects items 43 and 46.

With respect to communication methods, Table 2 shows that students list the mass media as their most common sources of information about AIDS, and television is the only method showing in their top ten items. Cluster one recommends television but only as part of a method mix which also includes peer-based and campus-based methods. Cluster two by contrast has only one method in its top ten and that is college classes. This cluster appears not to have recognized the media students use and recommend, in spite of being closer to the student ideal overall.

The question arises of whether one approach is more likely than the other to predict actual communication success. The study does not permit a direct answer to this question, but from a theoretical point of view Wallack argues that mass media programs have two major components: a theory or theoretical model of how to obtain their goal and a method for implementing a program rooted in this theory or model [37]. If either or both of these prove to be incorrect, program failure may result.

In general terms, cluster two does not cite specific theory and is much less frequent in citing communication methods. If Wallack is correct, cluster two's chances of a successful campaign are less even though they are perhaps intuitively more in tune with their target audience. On the other hand, there is some argument that convergence between recipients' views of the ideal communication program and the program in practice should predict a greater resonance with recipients and greater likelihood of success [38].

The area in which all three groups agree is the rejection of the "majority appeal" variables. It is unclear whether this is a rejection of social influence theories, the credibility or accuracy of the statements per se or of the validity of majority opinion. All statements were written rather generally to be relevant to all respondents and because they were not written in any particular vernacular they may have been rejected by the student group as less that credible, but this does not seem to explain why all three groups rejected these items.

It seems that institutional attributes play a part in communication thinking. The smaller cluster is more likely to be associated with a hospital and with respect to its clients may be less likely to have preventive opportunities than, say, college health service employees. Thus the communication designs may be a function of respondents' institutional experience with AIDS. Also, communication decisions may stem from some corporate culture that sees some messages or media as just more appropriate than others [39].

The significant difference between the two groups on religious affiliation, however, suggests that personal predispositions toward AIDS as well as institutional attributes explain individuals' selection of communication methods and messages.

The study limitations are in not providing respondents with all the possibilities that might theoretically be available and in oversimplifying what may be subtle theoretical distinctions. For example, students polarized on the fear appeal items (31-25). They recommended items 31, 34, and 35, but rejected items 33 and 32. In so doing they may have operationalized a distinction between fear and threat, which has been shown to be theoretically important [40], but is not explicit in the study design.

In more general terms, the study does suggest that one component of an older mechanistic "source-message-channel-receiver" model of communication—the source—needs revisiting. The evidence suggests that communication programs are clearly not designed only with a particular theoretical base or audience in mind, but are clearly also a function of individual and institutional source attributes.

REFERENCES

1. J. French and L. Adams, From Analysis to Synthesis, *Health Education Journal, 45*:2, pp. 71-74, 1986.
2. M. H. Becker, The Health Belief Model and Personal Health Behavior, *Health Education Monographs, 2*, pp. 324-511, 1974.
3. R. Manoff, *Social Marketing: New Imperative for Public Health*, Praeger, New York, 1985.
4. E. M. Rogers and D. L. Kincaid, *Communication Networks: Toward A New Paradigm For Research*, Free Press, New York, 1981.
5. E. M. Rogers, *Diffusion of Innovations*, Free Press, New York, 1973.
6. M. Fishbein and I. Ajzen, *Belief, Attitude, Intention, and Behavior: An Introduction To Theory and Research*, Addison-Wesley, Reading, Massachusetts, 1975.
7. A. Bandura, *Social Foundations of Thought and Action. A Social Cognitive Theory*, Prentice-Hall, Englewood Cliffs, New Jersey, 1986.
8. H. Homans and P. Aggleton, Health Education, HIV Infection and Aids, in *Social Aspects Of Aids*, P. Aggleton and H. Homans (eds.), pp. 154-176, The Flamer Press, London, 1988.
9. L. W. Green, M. W. Kreuter, S. G. Deeds, and K. B. Partridge, *Health Education Planning: A Diagnostic Approach*, Mayfield, Palo Alto, California, 1980.
10. N. K. Janz and M. H. Becker, The Health Belief Model: A Decade Later, *Health Education Quarterly, 11*:1, pp. 1-47, Spring 1984.
11. L. R. Franzini, L. M. Sideman, K. E. Dexter, and J. P. Elder, Promoting AIDS Risk Reduction Via Behavioral Training, *Aids Education and Prevention, 2*:4, pp. 313-321, 1990.
12. S. Mendez-Mendez, *Communication Dimensions of Aids Research: The Puerto-Rican Problem*, unpublished, Presented at Central Connecticut State University, September 23, 1992.
13. R. J. Diclemente, K. A. Forrest, and S. Mickler, College Students' Knowledge and Attitudes about AIDS and Changes in HIV-Preventive Behaviors, *AIDS Education and Prevention, 2*:3, pp. 201-212, 1990.

14. K. Siegel, P. B. Grodsky, and A. Herman, AIDS Risk-Reduction Guidelines: A Review and Analysis, *Journal of Community Health, 11*:4, pp. 233-243, 1986.
15. H. Leventhal, M. A. Safer, and D. M. Panagis, The Impact of Communication on the Self-Regulation of Health Beliefs, Decisions, and Behavior, *Health Education Quarterly, 10*, pp. 3-31, 1983.
16. C. A. Insko, A. Arkoff, and V. M. Insko, Effects of High and Low Fear Arousing Communications upon Opinions toward Smoking, *Journal of Experimental Social Psychology, 1*, pp. 256-266, 1965.
17. E. M. Brecher, *Licit and Illicit Drugs*, Little Brown and Company, Boston, 1972.
18. K. Neuwirth and S. Dunwoody, The Complexity of Aids-Related Behavioral Change: The Interaction between Communication and Noncommunication Variables, *AIDS and Public Policy Journal, 4*:1, pp. 20-30, 1989.
19. H. H. Hyman and P. B. Sheatsley, Some Reasons Why Information Campaigns Fail, *Public Opinion Quarterly, 11*, pp. 412-423, 1947.
20. P. F. Lazarsfeld and R. K. Merton, Mass Communication, Popular Taste and Organized Social Action, in *Mass Communications* (2nd Edition), W. Schramm (ed.), University of Illinois Press, Urbana, Illinois, 1948.
21. J. T. Klapper, *The Effects of Mass Communication*, The Free Press, Glencoe, Illinois, 1960.
22. H. G. Zucker, The Variable Nature of News Media Influence, *Communication Yearbook II*, pp. 225-240, Transaction, New Brunswick, New Jersey, 1978.
23. S. Ball-Rokeach and M. Defleur, A Dependency Model of Mass Media Effects, *Communication Research, 3*, pp. 3-21, 1976.
24. H. Mendelsohn, Some Reasons Why Information Campaigns Can Succeed, *Public Opinion Quarterly, 37*, pp. 50-61, 1969.
25. N. Maccoby and D. S. Solomon, Heart Disease Prevention: Community Studies, in *Public Communication Campaigns*, R. E. Rice and W. J. Paisley (eds.), pp. 105-126, Sage Publications, Beverly Hills, California, 1981.
26. S. H. Chaffee, Mass Media and Interpersonal Channels: Competitive Convergent, or Complementary, in *Inter-Media*, G. Gumpert and R. Cathcart (eds.), pp. 57-77, Oxford University Press, New York, 1982.
27. R. J. Cline and J. L. Engel, College Students' Perceptions of Sources of Information about AIDS, *Journal of American College Health, 40*:2, pp. 55-63, 1991.
28. J. Sumser, B. Gerbert, and B. Maguire, *The Impact of Reliance on Different Information Sources on Attitudes about AIDS: A Media Comparison Study*, presented at The International Communication Association Annual Meeting, Chicago, May 1991.
29. P. Grosswiler, Some Methodological Considerations on the Use of Multimedia Q-Sample Items, *Operant Subjectivity, 15*:3, pp. 65-80, 1992.
30. K. L. Higbee, Fifteen Years of Fear Arousal, *Psychological Bulletin, 72*, pp. 426-444, 1969.
31. B. Sternthal and C. S. Craig, Fear Appeals: Revisited and Revised, *Journal of Consumer Research, 1*, pp. 22-34, 1974.
32. K. E. Dennis, Q Methodology: Relevance and Application to Nursing Research, *Advances in Nursing Science, 8*:3, pp. 6-17, 1986.

33. T. D. Stephen, Q-Methodology in Communication Science: An Introduction, *Communication Quarterly, 33*, pp. 193-208, 1985.
34. S. R. Brown, Q as Qualitative Method: 3. Q Samples. In Comserve@Vm.Its.Rpi.Edu. 1991.
35. San Francisco AIDS Foundation, *Media Resource Guide for AIDS Information in San Francisco*, San Francisco, 1987.
36. P. Y. Devine and E. R. Hurt, Message Strategies for Information Comparisons. A Social Psychological Analysis, in *Information Campaigns: Balancing Social Values and Social Change*, C. T. Salmon (ed.), pp. 229-258, Sage, Newbury Park, California, 1989.
37. L. M. Wallack, Mass Media Campaigns: The Odds against Finding Behavioral Change, *Health Education Quarterly, 8*, pp. 209-260, 1981.
38. E. G. Bormann, Symbolic Convergence: Organizational Communication and Culture, *Communication and Organizations: An Interpretive Approach*, L. Putnam and M. E. Pacanowsky (eds.), pp. 99-122, Sage, Beverly Hills, 1983.
39. D. F. Treadwell, Organizational Analysis in Health Education Planning, *International Journal of Health Education, VI*:2, pp. 29-32, 1987.
40. K. Witte, Putting the Fear Back Into Fear Appeals: The Extended Parallel Process Model, *Communication Monographs, 59*:4, pp. 329-349, 1992.

CHAPTER 9

Another Crack in the Mirror: The Politics of AIDS Prevention in Mexico

Héctor Carrillo

Since 1983, when the first case of AIDS in Mexico was identified in a Mexico City hospital, thousands of Mexicans have been diagnosed with the syndrome (called "SIDA" in Spanish) and thousands more have been infected with HIV. To attempt to stop the epidemic, a variety of groups have responded: the Mexican government, nongovernmental groups, and individuals interested in the prevention of HIV transmission. Although the general response to AIDS in Mexico resembles, at least in principle, the efforts developed in other countries like the United States, it is flavored by the particular characteristics of the local culture, social organization, economics and politics.

This article presents a broad analysis of the social context in which AIDS prevention takes place in Mexico. The premise is that, to understand the role of prevention, to analyze the feasibility of its methods, and to project the possibilities of its success, public health practitioners must consider broader social forces in the formulation of their strategies. The distinctive epidemiological characteristics of AIDS in Mexico, the relationship between common people and the state, the role of civil society in the resolution of social problems, attitudes toward difference and social diversity, and the availability of funding are all factors that may influence the success or failure of public health interventions.

In more general terms, the case of AIDS prevention in Mexico exemplifies the importance of politics, society and culture in the design of educational interventions. As a result, the case should also illustrate the fact that prevention efforts cannot be planned without contact with the community, but rather must be shaped and molded according to the social conditions of the people whom they intend to serve.

THE NATURE AND SCOPE OF THE AIDS
EPIDEMIC IN MEXICO

As of January 1993, Mexico had reported to the World Health Organization (WHO) 12,540 cumulative AIDS cases [1].[1] This figure put Mexico in eleventh place worldwide in terms of the number of AIDS cases, and third place in the American continent (after the U.S. and Brazil). The official number of cases, however, is considered to be but a fraction of the actual total. The Secretariat of Health (SSA), the agency that compiles epidemiological data in Mexico, has estimated a rate of underreporting of more than 50 percent that would yield a more realistic figure of about 19,000 cases. Other studies have projected a total of around 25,000 cases by the end of 1993 [2].

Based on the number of yearly cases since 1983, the SSA has stated that the increase in number of cases was slow between 1983 and 1986, exponential between 1987 and 1990, and moderate since 1991, tending to stabilization. Yet, although it is true that the number of cases reported in 1992 (3,219) was just slightly higher than that reported in 1991 (3,166), it is too early to predict that the epidemic is stabilizing. In fact, before 1991, the number of yearly cases reported had been 2,400 or less, so any figure above 3,000 is considerable.

The majority of AIDS cases in Mexico have been reported in large urban areas and tourist resorts. The number of cases per million is highest in Guadalajara (523), Veracruz (488), Mexico City (462), Cuernavaca (448), and Mérida (379). The total number of cases is highest in Mexico City (33% of all cases) and the states of Jalisco (22.6%), Mexico (which borders Mexico City) (4.8%), and San Luis Potosí, Michoacán and Yucatán (4.0% each). Most of the cases have affected middle class people; however, the proportion of cases among lower income groups is growing [3]. There is increasing concern about the potential for an epidemic in rural areas, particularly in towns that have a large number of seasonal agricultural migrants to the United States.[2] In fact, officials have detected what appears to be a shift in regional patterns: the increase in the number of cases in large cities appears to be slowing down, while smaller cities and towns with fewer cases have increasingly higher rates.

In urban areas, as in most other countries, some social groups have been affected disproportionately. Following an epidemiological pattern similar to that in the United States, the first cases were detected among homosexual men. Currently, of 10,425 adult men with AIDS, 87.7 percent acquired HIV sexually: 40 percent have been homosexual, 27.7 percent bisexual, and 20 percent heterosexual. The transmission mode of the remaining cases is thought to be blood

---

[1] All statistics related to the number of AIDS cases in Mexico in this section are provided by INDRE [1].

[2] In Michoacán, one of the states with largest migration to U.S., of 323 cases reported, 110 are among people returning from the United States [4].

transfusions (6.2%), professional blood donation (2.7%), hemophilia (1.3%), and IV drug use (0.8%). No risk information is available for 15.3 percent of the men, while 1.3 percent are categorized as both homosexual and IV drug users.

Among adult women, the distribution is very different. In general, it is thought that most women with AIDS have acquired HIV from blood transfusions (57.9% of 1,726 women), or through heterosexual sex (38.8%). Other risk factors are donating blood (2.6%), and IV drug use (0.5%). No risk information is available for 14.2 percent of the cases among women. Contrary to popular perceptions, as of 1991 there were more cases of AIDS among housewives than among female prostitutes [5]. Studies of HIV seroprevalence among Mexican female prostitutes have yielded results of between 0 and 5 percent [3, 6].

In terms of age, a majority of cases have affected men and women between twenty-five and thirty-four years old (40.6%). The number of pediatric cases is 389, of which 51.7 percent acquired HIV from their mothers, 28 percent from blood transfusions, 18.3 percent due to products to treat hemophilia, and 2.0 percent from sexual abuse.

The picture that emerges from these data is one of an epidemic with characteristics different from those of the AIDS epidemic in the United States. Not unlike the United States, homosexual and bisexual men in Mexico are the group most affected by the disease (57% of all cases in the United States, and 67.7% in Mexico) [7].[3] However, while in the United States almost 23 percent of the cases are among IV drug users, in Mexico IV drug use accounts for only 0.7 percent.[4] As in the United States, AIDS in Mexico has affected more men than women. However, compared to the United States, the role of heterosexual transmission in Mexico appears to be greater (22.7% of all cases in Mexico versus 6.4% in the United States). As time passes, an increasingly larger number of women are being diagnosed with AIDS in Mexico, in comparison to men. In 1984, there were twenty-five new cases among men for every new case affecting a woman. By 1992, the ratio had dropped to only 5:1.

The consensus among officials and AIDS activists is that bisexual behavior is a "bridge" that has brought HIV from homosexual men to women. As a result, Mexican officials have been careful to distinguish between homosexual *and* bisexual men in their statistics. Yet, no studies have fully demonstrated that "bridge." And a comparison with the United States is difficult, given that U.S. epidemiological statistics lump together homosexual and bisexual men in one single category.

---

[3] All statistics about the number of AIDS cases in the U.S. are provided by the Centers for Disease Control and Prevention [7].

[4] Recently, there has been an increase in the number of people with AIDS who acquired the infection through IV drug use, particularly in border cities such as Tijuana and Mexicali and in the three largest cities: Mexico City, Guadalajara and Monterrey [8].

Another interesting comparison is the number of women with AIDS who acquired HIV from blood transfusions in Mexico. Not only is blood transfusion the main cause of infection among women with AIDS, but there are many more women infected in this way than men with AIDS (894 versus 611). Mexican officials explain this disparity as caused by the high number of women who receive blood transfusions during labor. However, in the United States the relationship is the opposite: 3,036 men versus 1,994 women with AIDS who acquired HIV from a blood transfusion. Although it is possible that, proportionally speaking, more women receive transfusions during labor in Mexico, one could speculate that an additional factor could be medical reluctance to diagnose risk as sexual among women, given the level of stigma attached to women's sexuality in Mexico. However, only a study could determine the cause of this disparity.

A common perception is that blood transfusions have been responsible for a greater problem in Mexico than in the United States. However, the number of transfusion AIDS cases per million in Mexico is 16.7 compared to 21.3 in the United States. Nevertheless, the perception of higher risk in Mexico might be related to the existence of less stringent and consistent procedures to protect the blood supply from contamination with HIV.

Also in relation to blood, there has been an unusual form of HIV transmission in Mexico that was not present in the United States. A large number of Mexican professional blood donors acquired HIV in the blood banks. This happened because many commercial blood banks reutilized syringes when they collected blood samples. As a result, in places such as Nezahualcóyotl, a working class suburb of Mexico City, entire families of paid blood donors became HIV-positive [9]. Some studies have found HIV-infection of up to 20 and 30 percent in samples of blood donors [10, 11]. However, due to the closing of all commercial blood banks in 1987, the number of new infections through blood donation has been greatly reduced.

All the statistics quoted above are based on the total number of diagnosed AIDS cases. Few studies in Mexico have been conducted about the number of people who are infected with HIV. Thus, there are no accurate estimates of the number of asymptomatic HIV-positive persons in Mexico. In 1988, the SSA estimated a 24:1 ratio between diagnosed cases and asymptomatic infection. For that year, the use of this ratio yielded 115,000 cases of HIV infection. Around the same time, Gonzalez Block estimated the number of HIV-positive people to be anywhere between 35,000 and 70,000 [12]. Other officials at SSA used similar figures (between 31,600 and 97,700) [13]. If the rate is applied today, using the official number of cases, the number of HIV-positive people would be 300,960. If we account for underreporting, that number would jump to 457,440. Some activists have used the WHO ratios of 1:50 to 1:100 in estimating between 660,400 to 1,320,800 HIV-positive people [14]. However, none of these figures can be scientifically substantiated.

A few seroprevalence studies with homosexual and bisexual men have yielded high proportions of HIV infection in that population. Valdespino and García report that the findings vary from 2 percent to 35 percent in Mexico City, 36 percent and more in Puebla, and lower in other cities [3]. Hernández et al. found a seroprevalence rate of 34 percent among homosexual men and 21 percent among bisexual men in a sample of 2,314 homosexual and bisexual men in Mexico City, between 1988 and 1989 [15]. A recent study in Monterrey found 93 percent seroprevalence in a sample of 100 homosexual men. However, this is the only study that has yielded such high seroprevalence levels [16].[5]

These data on AIDS cases suggest the broad contours of the epidemic in Mexico. However, to understand how to prevent the further spread of HIV, we need to analyze the social and political environment in which the AIDS epidemic has unfolded.

THE FIRST RESPONSE TO AIDS

Although the first news about AIDS in the United States arrived in Mexico early in the 1980s, few people had heard of the disease until 1985. The announcement of Rock Hudson's diagnosis, and the subsequent series of newspaper articles about the existence of AIDS cases in Mexico, brought the disease out of the closet. As Mejía points out, the first attempts by Mexican reporters to cover AIDS were tainted by moralism and by a condemnation of sex and particularly of homosexual practices [12]. These early articles also openly blamed people with HIV for acquiring the disease.

Between 1983 and 1985 there were no statements about AIDS made by Mexican government officials. However, as a result of the publicity that AIDS received in 1985, and the rumors about an epidemic that was out of control, public health officials were forced to break their silence about AIDS in 1986. A report by the Secretary of Health read:

> Mexicans have *no reason to be alarmed* by the acquired immunodeficiency syndrome that has reached high incidence in other countries because, of 63 detected cases, only 17 have been confirmed (quoted in [12], p. 31, my emphasis and translation).

The official view was that the disease did not represent a problem for Mexicans, and the commentary aimed to justify the lack of state response to confront it. This view was confirmed by the opinions of other prominent physicians and public health officials, who stated that most Mexicans were not at risk because

---

[5] This study does not report how the subjects were selected. Other studies have recruited homosexual and bisexual men who seek HIV testing.

"the population of Mexico does not belong to the risk groups."[6] Given that there were few cases, "it makes no sense to distract large amounts of economic and human resources . . . to combat the malady when there are other diseases [to attend to]."[7]

Also in response to the news about AIDS, a wave of anti-homosexual rhetoric and actions took shape. Stereotypical views of homosexuals, combined with ignorance about the disease, promoted a discourse of condemnation of people with AIDS [12]. Fear of the disease resulted in discrimination against people with AIDS. In fact, these fears have later resulted in the systematic violation of the human rights of people with HIV in hospitals, clinics and their work places. There are multiple reports and testimonials about doctors and nurses who would refuse to come close to a person with AIDS, would deny treatment and care, and, in extreme cases, would leave patients without any sanitary care or food for days for fear of catching HIV [17-19].[8] There have also been many cases of people who were fired from their jobs after being tested for HIV antibodies, many times without having given consent for the test. These cases have occurred in banks, private corporations, and state companies such as PEMEX, the state's petroleum company. In one legal case involving PEMEX, after months of legal battles, a federal court ordered that the worker be reinstated in his job, establishing an important legal precedent [21, 22].

In September of 1985, the attention to AIDS was displaced by another unexpected disaster. An earthquake measuring 8.5 in the Richter scale shook about half of the country's territory causing major damage in Mexico City and killing several thousand people.

The earthquake was a pivotal event in Mexico that influenced many spheres, including AIDS. Many analysts see it as the trigger for the real earthquake that was still about to happen [23]. Governmental confusion and lack of preparedness for the event, and the repression of thousands who sought to help in the rescue efforts, made many Mexicans aware of the limited participation of civil society in political decision making. Many potential volunteers felt indignation when the military prevented them from reaching collapsed buildings due to the federal government's fear of a popular uprising. However, despite the controls, extensive popular organizing took place during the months after the earthquake, which taught many Mexicans the value of civil participation in issues normally controlled by the state [23].

Politically speaking, the consequences were many. Calls for democratization and for an end to the unquestioned sixty-year-old power of the official party

---

[6] Dr. Martha Céspedes, quoted in [12], p. 31, my translation.

[7] Dr. Guillermo Ruiz Palacios, quoted in [12], p. 31, my translation.

[8] For reports of human rights violations in AIDS see [20] and *Sociedad y SIDA*, a monthly supplement of the Mexico City newspaper *El Nacional* where many cases have been documented.

gained renewed popularity [23].[9] Another example is the government's recent acknowledgment of human rights violations in Mexico. This development, which was partly a result of community organizing and political pressure, has stimulated and validated the involvement of nongovernmental groups in the investigation of cases, including those cases affecting people with AIDS.[10] From the perspective of AIDS prevention, what seems most important about the earthquake is the emergence of a new consciousness about the role of civil organizations in public life. The earthquake provided the leeway for the formation of new nongovernmental organizations (NGOs) attending to a variety of social problems, including AIDS [24, 25]. The politics of AIDS prevention in Mexico have been greatly influenced by the relationship between the state and NGOs, and the NGOs' demands for government accountability.

CONASIDA AND THE NON-GOVERNMENTAL AIDS GROUPS

After the initial denial about AIDS in the Mexican government waned, international pressure from the World Health Organization resulted in the first official effort to combat the spread of the disease. In 1986, the Mexican government created CONASIDA—the National Council of AIDS—which was made official by presidential decree the following year [12]. WHO had asked that governments establish national AIDS councils, which would administer international prevention funds channeled through its AIDS program [26]. CONASIDA was to become the recipient and administrator of the bulk of the international money for AIDS prevention that flowed to Mexico.

Parallel to the creation of CONASIDA, a number of existing groups around the country (labelled *grupos civiles*), and some newly created ones, began independent efforts to fight AIDS in their own communities. The development of these NGOs had three stages:

1. The first civil groups to respond were those of homosexuals who had been actively fighting for their rights since the late 1970s. *GHOL* (Homosexual Liberation Group), *Colectivo Sol* (Collective of the Sun), *Círculo Cultural Gay* (Gay Cultural Circle), FHAR (Homosexual Revolutionary Action Front), and *Guerrilla Gay*, among other groups, had organized political rallies, marches, cultural events in support of homosexual liberation. Because

[9] In the 1988 presidential elections, Carlos Salinas de Gortari received merely 52% of the popular vote and won through actions that many analysts classified as the most complicated fraud in Mexican electoral politics [23].

[10] As a result the government created a National Human Rights Commission that includes a number of prominent intellectuals and activists to officially conduct the investigations [23].

AIDS was mostly affecting homosexual men, most of these groups initiated prevention activities and advocacy for the rights of people with AIDS.

2. Other new community-based groups were formed with an exclusive focus on AIDS. Most of these NGOs were run by homosexuals and lesbians, prostitutes, blood donors, or people with HIV and their relatives [24]. As in other countries, the people responding to AIDS were those already affected or those who could see the threat of the disease close at hand. Several of these groups grew as a result of the renewed emphasis on nongovernmental action after the 1985 earthquake, and some, like *Brigadistas Contra el SIDA* (Rescue Workers Against AIDS), had originated from the homosexual participation in the post-earthquake rescue efforts [24]. Among the AIDS NGOs were the *Fundación Mexicana para la Lucha contra el SIDA* (Mexican Foundation for the Fight Against AIDS), *CHECCOS* (Humanitarian Committee of Shared Efforts Against AIDS in Guadalajara), *Azomalli, Ave de México* (Mexican Volunteer Educators/Friends), *GIS-SIDA* (Social Investigation Groups for AIDS and Human Rights), and *Organización SIDA Tijuana* (Tijuana AIDS Organization).

3. Soon after the initiation of civil efforts against AIDS, many groups realized that there were two fronts: On the one hand, CONASIDA was emerging as a large organization with resources to fund programs. On the other, the NGOs were small, independent and with no coordination in their efforts. Leaders of some of the groups began thinking about the need for consolidation that would create a stronger NGO front. Several efforts were undertaken to create networks of NGOs, including the formation of *Mexicanos contra el SIDA* (Mexicans Against AIDS), which had 22 member groups nationally in 1992 [27] and the *Red Nacional de Comunicación y Solidaridad Contra el SIDA* (National Network of Communication and Solidarity Against AIDS) with three member groups [28]. Consolidation has proven to be very difficult, however, due to several barriers. One is ideological differences among the groups. Galván et al. identify the political persuasions of the NGOs as ranging from the far left and anarchism to center-left and democratic liberalism [29]. A second problem that these authors note is that many of the groups to be consolidated have very poor organizational structures and programs. In the absence of performing effective AIDS prevention work, each group's legitimacy becomes peculiarly dependent upon the public perception that they are in the vanguard of the struggle.[11] To consolidate, then, is to surrender their identity

---

[11]This issue is not made explicit in most of the writings about AIDS in Mexico, because the writers tend to be sympathetic to NGOs and to present them as a front that opposes the government. However, the reality of leadership conflicts has emerged repeatedly in conversations with the heads of different groups both in Mexico City and Guadalajara, who furiously claim their leadership and minimize the importance of the work of other NGOs.

and popular appeal. Furthermore, when groups actually have joined together to create umbrella structures, the result is merely a new name while the weaknesses in programs remain [29].

THE POLITICS OF FUNDING

Underlying all the programmatic difficulties of NGOs is the problem of financing that most of them face. This is in striking contrast with the strength and level of funding available to CONASIDA. As mentioned before, WHO channels its own and other international funds for AIDS prevention to CONASIDA. Until recently, these funds were CONASIDA's only source of support, and the agency has the power to decide either to administer them or to use them to fund other projects. The agency, however, has mostly used the funds to support its own programs.

Overall, most NGOs have survived on the little money provided by their members and from small donations collected at events. Generally speaking, few of these groups have any significant experience in grant writing and development, and, until recently, they had been able to attract only small international donations and in-kind donations of condoms and brochures for their outreach. As a result, their programs have been very limited and in some cases almost nonexistent. As Galván Díaz et al. point out, only some of these groups (the ones they call "mature organizations") have been capable of establishing effective programs, while others have been mostly fancy labels for good intentions with no practical results [29].

Some of the NGOs, however, have begun to be the recipients of larger sums of international money. *Colectivo Sol*, for instance, has received several grants from renowned foundations, including Ford and MacArthur, that amount to almost half a million dollars in less than three years. Among its programs are the publication of *Acción en SIDA*, an AIDS newsletter for Latin American NGOs; a Latin American networking program for human rights and advocacy; an education program to promote sexual health; a clearinghouse for AIDS related materials, annotated bibliographies, reference lists, and technical assistance for bibliographical consultation; and the publication of *Del Otro Lado*, a magazine for homosexual men and women. Colectivo Sol currently has a staff of twelve and six volunteers.[12]

Juan Jacobo Hernández, the group's director, explains their success as resulting from a recognition of the need for professionalization. He emphasizes that most NGOs in Mexico focus on political activism to the exclusion of organizational planning, and this prevents them from accessing international funding. In his opinion, the international funds of the kind received by *Colectivo Sol* have always been available, but the NGOs have not had the grantwriting expertise, and have not adequately followed the guidelines established by foundations for grant

---

[12]Personal communication with Juan Jacobo Hernández, director of *Colectivo Sol*, on July 29, 1993.

proposals. In the case of *Colectivo Sol*, an initial grant that was offered to them during a site visit served as a springboard for additional fundraising to ensure continuation and expansion of their efforts. Today, the group writes its own grants and has built up a resumé that ensures a name for itself among new potential funders.

Yet, although this success story represents the future directions available to NGOs in Mexico, it is atypical. Even today, the contrast between the more common experience of Mexican AIDS NGOs and their counterparts in the United States is striking. In the United States, the NGOs created to fight AIDS have been capable of attracting private funding, first from middle class gay donors, and later from the community at large and private foundations. In Mexico, there has been no tradition of giving among the middle class. This has prevented any systematic efforts to capture individual donations. In addition, the conservative character of most large local foundations has prevented access to large private donations. And, third, the NGOs themselves have had little access to learning the skills needed to organize fundraising from private sources [25]. In the United States, for instance, fundraising courses for non-profit organizations are readily available, and AIDS groups have effectively organized major fundraising events such as the AIDS Walk and the AIDS Dance-a-Thon in San Francisco that, together, raise almost three million dollars every year. But, ultimately, the main barrier that Mexican NGOs face is the overall financial crisis of the country as a whole, which makes fundraising events like those in San Francisco nothing but a dream.

Another major difference in funding patterns is the role that the U.S. government plays in the allocation of funds to NGOs. Unlike CONASIDA in Mexico, most U.S. government agencies involved in AIDS prevention have assumed the role of coordinating and directing civil efforts through the distribution of federal and local funds [30]. While the Mexican government was more aggressive and direct in establishing AIDS prevention programs, the U.S. government has distributed more funds to community-based groups. The funding role of government has been even stronger at the local level in U.S. cities. Cities that were heavily impacted by AIDS, such as San Francisco, have taken a strong role in developing funding programs for local nonprofit organizations.

In Mexico, no such tradition exists. In fact, the power of the Mexican state since the revolution of 1910 has been characterized by the centralization and administration of all public funds by the government, which is seen as the ultimate provider of services [23]. Having access to services is not, however, an automatic right. The state has created a complex system of patronage by which groups, usually clustered by occupation, must organize and demand services to receive them, and in turn offer their political support to the regime. This system has been labelled "corporatism" by political analysts [23]. In practical terms, this means that the state controls the bulk of funds for social services, and their distribution has a very strong political undertone: the funds are overtly used to extract votes and to pacify oppositional forces. A second consequence is the pervasive dependency of civil society on the state and the resulting absence of strong nongovernmental institutions created by common people.

CONASIDA is a somewhat anomalous case in that it explicitly tried to move away from assuming a role as the dispenser of funds. In an interview in 1991, CONASIDA's director declared that "CONASIDA does not distribute funds for people to implement their ideas" [31, p. 5]. He added that the organization was considering the possibility of funding new projects, but he did not clarify whether any of those projects would take place outside of CONASIDA. This lack of funding, combined with what many NGOs perceived as the inability of CONASIDA to serve their particular communities, created confrontational relationships between the agency and community-based groups. Although the agency had effectively avoided establishing a paternalistic relationship with the NGOs, by monopolizing international funds CONASIDA had also limited their channels to seek international funding independently.

The NGOs, on the other hand, have been split in their opinion about what to do about CONASIDA's funds. Some openly advocated for the governmental agency to dispense money to civil groups [32]. Some others insisted that CONASIDA should use the available funds in its own programs but should also be held accountable for that use [29]. While both approaches involve some risk, the latter seems particularly problematic in so far as it reinforces the subordination of civil society to the state.

This tension between NGOs and the state was evident not only at the federal level, but also at the state and local levels. In Guadalajara, for instance:

> the NGOs . . . asked that the director of COESIDA [the State AIDS Council] resign arguing that the prevention campaigns are poor and that COESIDA spends only 20% of its budget on prevention. The rest, they say, is spent in administration or to improve the director's image . . . Without denying the work performed by NGOs, [COESIDA's director] Díaz Santana says that those organizations are sometimes more worried about financial support than about concrete work. Although he did not provide names, he stated that more than one [NGO] is looking for a solution for its financial problems rather than doing true educational campaigns [32, p. 3, my translation].

From this quote, it is evident that although the problems between the state and the NGOs were strongly motivated by the distribution of financial resources, they extended to the level of the programs themselves. While the NGOs perceived that the government was not being effective with the money that it spent on AIDS prevention, the government charged that by demanding funds, NGOs were oriented to self-benefit rather than service. In Díaz Santana's comment there is the assumption that an NGO does not need to have a comfortable financial situation to do its work, let alone pay a salary to its full time members.

Beginning in 1992, with a new administration in CONASIDA, the working relationship between the organization and the NGOs appears to be becoming closer. Some of the groups have begun to receive "seed funding" to initiate their efforts. In one instance, the organization has worked closely with one of the NGOs in the development of an educational video for bisexual men.[13] The Mexico City AIDS hotline, TelSIDA, has also coordinated efforts with an NGO, *Voz Humana* (Human Voice), which provides telephone information during evenings.[14] These examples may indicate a greater willingness of all parties involved to work together toward common goals. However, because of the differences in funding and organization that remain, CONASIDA's ability to implement prevention efforts still contrasts sharply with that of the NGOs. The characteristics of the educational programs for AIDS in Mexico is the topic of the next section.

INTERVENTIONS TO PROMOTE SAFE SEX

CONASIDA has conducted mass media campaigns that include billboards, posters, brochures, radio and TV commercials. The campaigns are tied to a hotline in Mexico City where volunteers answer 3,000 calls monthly. CONASIDA also coordinates information centers and anonymous testing, and maintains CRIDIS (Regional Center for Exchange, Documentation, and AIDS Information), a library of academic and educational AIDS related materials.

Except for family planning campaigns, the Mexican government has no previous experience promoting behaviors in areas directly related to sexuality. In fact, when the government began to speak up about AIDS, its first actions were devoid of references to sexuality: the emphasis was on control of the blood supply. However, soon after its inception, CONASIDA began addressing openly condom use and safe sex. Around 1988, condoms were visible in billboards and TV ads and became a common household word for the first time in Mexican history. CONASIDA embraced condom use as the center piece of its educational message. In a fashion similar to the AIDS education that was taking place in the U.S. and Europe, its model was strongly influenced by social marketing techniques and by theories about dissemination of information. Interestingly, in direct contrast to the U.S. government response during the Reagan and Bush administrations, CONASIDA's efforts have been bolder and less conservative, and have successfully shattered the taboo against condom advertising in television and the mass media in Mexico. In fact, perhaps motivated by the precedent set by CONASIDA,

---

[13]Personal communication with Dr. José Antonio Izazola, Conasida's Research Director, on June 10, 1993.

[14]Personal communication with Ms. Elvira Carrillo, Director of TelSIDA, on July 15, 1993.

Mexican television now accepts advertising by condom manufacturers (which U.S. television networks do not).

With far fewer resources, the efforts of the NGOs concentrated on grassroots approaches for the dissemination of information. Outreach, for most groups, consists of distributing donated brochures and condoms, giving safe sex talks, and providing one-on-one safe sex counseling. In some instances, the NGOs have specialized in performing outreach in specific places and with specific populations, and have been adventurous enough to do AIDS prevention in places like the public baths where many men go to have sex.

Street outreach, however, has not been without its problems. There are reports of police repression against AIDS activists for what the police perceive as an attack on morality. In one instance in Zapopan, a suburb of Guadalajara, AIDS educators were harassed by policemen, who threatened to arrest them for passing out brochures and condoms in the main plaza and proceeded to escort them to the town limits. AIDS activists have strongly protested these actions as a violation of the constitution and of their rights. However, no official action was taken against the police [33].

The NGOs have also attempted to gain some access to the media. Most commonly, they have ensured their participation in talk shows and interviews. However, their efforts have also included the development of a *"radio novela,"* an AIDS soap opera written by a member of *"Mexicanos Contra el SIDA"* who successfully gained the support of a radio station in Mexico City and the collaboration of a famous TV soap opera actress [34, 35]. Another example is the publication of a monthly AIDS supplement, called *Sociedad y SIDA*, in one of the major newspapers in Mexico City. *GIS-SIDA*, an NGO that works mostly in the area of human rights, compiles and supplies the articles, and the newspaper publishes and distributes the supplement. The NGOs have also begun printing some educational materials and, as I indicated above, are beginning to successfully tie together homosexual liberation and AIDS prevention in the publication of magazines targeting homosexual men and women.

Similar to CONASIDA, the NGOs operate under the assumption that condom use should be the central focus of prevention and that behavior change can be achieved through the dissemination of information. However, not all in Mexico agree with these assumptions. From the viewpoint of the political right, for instance, there should be no dissemination of information about condoms at all. Behavior change, for them, consists of a return to traditional values and sexual abstinence. For AIDS activists who are more oriented toward popular education and community organizing, the issue is whether dissemination of information is enough to ensure behavior change. AIDS activists are also concerned with the selection of target populations and the exclusion of homosexual men in mass media campaigns. In the following two sections, I will address the perspectives of the political right and AIDS activists' concerns about methods of prevention.

OPPOSITION FROM THE POLITICAL RIGHT

As in other countries, the political right in Mexico has reacted vehemently against AIDS education messages that speak openly about sex and that promote condom use. Immediately after the release of the first safe sex campaigns, the Catholic church, the National Action Party (whose Spanish acronym is PAN), and a group that opposes family planning called Provida (Pro-life, mocked as "ProSIDA" by AIDS activists) strongly condemned the governmental AIDS program as promoting homosexuality, promiscuity and social degeneration. As an alternative, they offered abstinence, strengthening of the traditional family, the good influence of parents to prevent the development of homosexuality in their children, and the need to praise the sanctity and moral soundess of the monogamous heterosexual marriage.

This reaction is not different from the opposition of U.S. fundamentalist groups toward AIDS prevention. However, what is different is the force with which the Mexican government counteracted this opposition and disregarded the right as being out of touch with Mexican reality. While in the United States the position of right wing groups was used to justify government inaction, in Mexico the right was much less effective in opposing more liberal educational efforts. Mexico has not had a Jesse Helms or a William Dannemeyer with enough power or political clout to actually prevent the federal government from spending funds on the promotion of condom use and safe sex.

There are several possible reasons for this phenomenon. The main one might be the historical separation between church and state in Mexico instituted in the 1850s by president Benito Juárez, who broke official relations with the Vatican, and took away the church's right to own property, and the priests' right to preach in public places or run for public office [23]. After the Mexican revolution of 1910, the relations between the church and the state became even more fully severed, resulting in the revolt of the "Cristeros"[15] in the 1920s and the emergence of civil conservative organizations that survive even today [38]. These groups and the Catholic church, however, remained somewhat marginal to the mainstream political life of Mexico in subsequent decades. Their only organized political party, the PAN, was considered until recently to be a minor force in opposition against the PRI, the party in power.

Yet, the efforts of the political right in Mexico cannot be ignored, especially as their power grows. President Salinas de Gortari has recently introduced changes in policy that have given the right greater power and new impetus for organizing. One of such changes was the restoration of diplomatic relations with the Vatican,

---

[15]The "Cristeros" were a guerrilla movement of ultraconservative Catholics who organized several revolts in central Mexico during the 1920s. Their efforts were repressed by the federal government and ultimately controlled. Recently, 26 Cristero leaders were beatified by Pope John Paul II, an event that caused controversy in Mexico [36, 37].

and the reinstallation of the Church's rights to preach in public places, to rally, and to own property [23, 36, 39, 40]. The PAN has also emerged as a strong political force that has claimed the government of two Northern states (an unprecedented phenomenon given that the official party, the PRI, had held power in all the states for the last sixty years).

The question is whether the political right will be instrumental in preventing any significant progression in the development of AIDS prevention efforts. Although the work of CONASIDA and the NGOs has managed to reduce the constant misinformation of sensationalist media, the potential for new waves of intolerance should always be considered. When the opposition to the condom campaigns occurred, CONASIDA struck back, defending its approach and lashing out against tolerance and "backward" ideas. AIDS activists claim, however, that CONASIDA has suffered from the pressure of the right and has given in by shying away from the bold messages that it used in the past [12, 29].

An example of this change is the shifting tone of CONASIDA's campaigns. A series of TV spots in 1989 used the popular drawings and cards of the Mexican lottery (bingo). A group of people dressed in costumes similar to characters in the cards sits around a table playing. (In the game, the cards are drawn one by one and their names are read aloud.) In the TV spot, the reader gets to the card that represents death (a skull), and the group shivers. The card that follows is a new one in the game, labeled by CONASIDA "The Lifesaver," which portrays an unrolled condom. The metaphor suggested that playing lottery cards was similar to taking chances in life, and that the only safe chance to take against death was the condom. The characters, men and women, represented a diversity of ages, social classes, and ethnicities, using symbols embedded in the original game cards themselves. The result was a very culturally specific message that was charged with implicit sexuality and a clear promotion of condoms.

In contrast, a more recent campaign was much more subtle. In 1992, CONASIDA's TV ads showed a child asking questions about AIDS while a parent reads a newspaper (his face hidden behind the newspaper). When the parent puts the newspaper down, the viewer sees that his eyes are covered by a blindfold. The slogan that follows reads "take off the blindfold" meaning "open your eyes" and suggesting that parents should call TelSIDA, the national AIDS hotline in Mexico City for information. The message was that it was a responsibility of parents to become informed in order to answer their children's questions. The message, however, said nothing about condoms or safe sex.

Some writers argue that CONASIDA' efforts have been co-opted by the influence of the political right [41]. They see the change as a symptom that CONASIDA is not willing to put out bold messages anymore, and as a sign of a return to conservative family values. Furthermore, they criticize CONASIDA for the absence of positive references to homosexuality in their campaigns. However, from a different perspective this campaign has been one of the most successful ones, because it has made AIDS a relevant topic for a great number of families by using a challenging and visually striking message. In fact, the campaign has generated great interest that has translated into a large number of calls to TelSIDA, where the callers' concerns may be discussed openly and with explicit reference to condoms and safe sex. However, examples such as this one fail to indicate a consensus about what type of messages should be disseminated: For whom should the information be intended? What are the methods that should be used? This brings us to a discussion about the design of AIDS prevention messages.

WHAT TYPES OF AIDS PREVENTION?

Throughout the last decade, AIDS educators in the United States faced the dilemma of whether to acknowledge that some population groups have a higher risk for HIV, and thus to risk their stigmatization, or whether to emphasize that everyone is at risk if they practice certain behaviors. The advantage of the second approach is that it softens the perception of "risk groups" and focuses on risky behavior. The first approach, however, allows for specific communities to be alerted about the problem and to claim the need for targeted education.

AIDS activists in cities like San Francisco and New York, strongly advocated for the de-homosexualization of AIDS as a way to create awareness in the general community that would reduce the stigma attached to the disease [42]. However, after successfully getting across the message that everyone is at risk, activists discovered that funds for education of gay men began to wane. It seemed easier for many foundations and for the government to give funds to educate families, for instance, than to educate gay men. AIDS groups then began to emphasize that, although it is true that everyone is at risk, gay men are at a specially higher risk and have more educational needs regarding AIDS prevention [42].

These issues have been present in Mexico as well. After 1985, the media published multiple articles about the "pink pest" and attributed the disease to homosexuals and degenerates, proclaiming that social avoidance of such people would prevent the disease and calling for mandatory testing of people who were known to be homosexual. In fact, some cities in Mexico conducted raids of homosexuals and prostitutes [43], and in a town in Veracruz the local government went to the extreme of shaving the heads of gay men to ensure that everyone could recognize them and avoid them [12]. The president of CONASIDA at the time, Jaime Sepúlveda Amor, declared:

> The Secretariat of Health strongly condemns the persecution that homosexuals are suffering due to AIDS. We have utmost respect for the sexual preference of every person. Ignorance about the causes of the disease and its transmission have resulted in the false notion that AIDS is caused by homosexuality, which creates the potential for exacerbation of antihomosexual attitudes [12, p. 45, my translation].

His voice was joined by those of intellectuals, defenders of human rights, and by one of the more progressive political parties.

After the popular perception that AIDS is connected to homosexuality was softened, if not eliminated, the official messages in mass media campaigns began to address the general population: first, by moving away from the concept of risk groups and emphasizing behavior, and second, by conveying the sense that anyone could get AIDS. In fact, although AIDS has affected homosexual and bisexual men disproportionately, CONASIDA has never launched a mass media campaign addressing that population or printed materials that show two men together in their graphics. And, because they lacked the funds, NGOs had also not been able to do it. In practical terms, what this has meant is a lack of educational materials for one of the groups at highest risk for HIV. There are indications, however, that this might be changing: CONASIDA has recently produced safe sex videos for homosexual men and for bisexual men, one of them in collaboration with an NGO in Mexico City, a type of project that would be unimaginable for the U.S. federal government to undertake or fund.

On a more general level, although there have been posters and materials targeted at other groups such as women, students, and prostitutes, it is unclear whether using those media is effective in achieving behavior changes in those populations. Many U.S. AIDS activists have recognized that the dissemination of information by itself does not guarantee a change in behavior. Several barriers that may strongly interfere with intentions to assume healthy behaviors have been identified, particularly among educators working with people of color [44-49]. The effects of poverty, inequality in sexual relations, and the oppression of women and homosexuals, among others, are social problems that may come in the way of AIDS prevention. Common examples of the effects of these problems are the inability of many Latinas—given their relative powerlessness in relationships with men—to convince their male partners to use condoms, the agreement of male hustlers to not use a condom when their clients offer to pay them more that way, and the coercive exchange of sex for crack between sellers and female users.

In Mexico, some officials and health educators have recognized similar local barriers to safe behavior. However, little has been done to find alternative AIDS education methods that address such social barriers. In an interview in 1988, Gloria Ornelas, executive director of CONASIDA at the time, declared: "it is not enough to provide information. That does not guarantee a change in conduct. We have launched mass media campaigns, but unfortunately they lack the credibility that we wish they had" [26, p. 309]. But the alternative that she offers is the provision of information in face-to-face interaction—a solution that fails to address those problems of power and inequality.

Rosas comes closer to the recognition of the social barriers for AIDS prevention [50]. He bases his analysis on his experience teaching condom use in places where men go to have public sex. He describes an appalling lack of knowledge about sexuality: people who learn about sex through trial and error and with no previous exposure to any sex education. He also addresses the effects of homophobia, and the difficulties of being an AIDS educator in an erotophobic environment. These two factors are not only barriers to effective AIDS prevention in Mexico but can even make the work of AIDS educators potentially dangerous. Last year, a prominent AIDS activist was murdered with two other homosexual men in his apartment in Mexico City. Since then, there have been more than thirty unexplained murders of homosexuals throughout Mexico, including the slaying of a transvestite leader in Chiapas [51-55].

Rosas's article concludes with a series of recommendations for the future of AIDS education in Mexico: First, he argues that AIDS educators in Mexico must stop using foreign educational models that ignore cultural differences. Second, he criticizes the tendency to use Freirian educational methods in a superficial way, and insists upon a true commitment to social change [56]. Third, he points out that no studies have assessed the efficacy of mass media campaigns in Mexico. Fourth, he calls for the integration of methods of community education in AIDS prevention. Finally, he emphasizes the difficulties faced by middle class educators doing AIDS prevention with working class communities that may operate with different cultural codes, and he notes how difficult it is to gain entry into those communities.

As this summary illustrates, questioning the indiscriminate use of U.S. AIDS prevention methods is an essential task in Mexico. A more in-depth analysis of the social and cultural conditions of AIDS in Mexico, in contrast to those of the United States, might provide a path to adapt and modify the methods. Furthermore, because many of the barriers to AIDS prevention in Mexico are probably influenced by broader social problems such as poverty, discrimination, and social inequality, a consideration of popular education, community organizing, and other methods for social change might prove to be useful in developing new AIDS prevention methods.

The need for the connection between AIDS prevention and social change is stated even more clearly by those who acknowledge that many Mexicans assign a low priority to AIDS in the list of everyday problems that they face:

> Street children are more concerned with having something to eat; sex workers are most preoccupied with having work to support themselves and their children; for young people, exploring sex takes precedence over any concerns about disease [57, p. 6, my translation].

However, even these authors fail to recognize the far-reaching implications of their statement and end up recommending that community organizing be used to disseminate more information about the disease. What is missing is the link between the broad political and social problems and the effects of those problems on the lives of individuals and communities. Rather than using community organizing solely to disseminate information, prevention aimed at behavior change could be integrated into larger efforts to achieve cultural and social changes that are badly needed. What this requires, among other possible strategies, is an effort to coalesce with broader political causes and to question Mexican society and culture at a deeper level: to promote open discussion about sexuality, homosexuality, and women's rights, even if the results are controversial; to confront rightist ideology and question the anti-AIDS prevention policies of the Catholic church; and to encourage street activism as a way to raise a voice that reaches the society at large.

CONCLUSION: THE CHALLENGES AHEAD

In this chapter, I have touched upon a number of broad social issues and epidemiological patterns that affect both the development of effective AIDS prevention and the individuals' potential for implementing behavior changes. In my opinion, the key to the success of AIDS prevention in Mexico lies in the fulfillment of two large social and political projects: 1) a greater participation of the civil society accompanied by a greater intersection of AIDS prevention with other struggles for social change, and 2) the careful evaluation of current methods and the creation of new ones that are more responsive to Mexican society, in two senses—avoiding the simple importation of methods developed for other cultures; and transcending the current narrow focus on the provision of information.

Preventing AIDS in Mexico appears to be much more complex than what the simple dissemination of information about condoms can achieve. I have tried here to identify some of the issues to be considered, but there are many unanswered questions about the specific changes that would make AIDS prevention more effective.

In the area of civil participation, for instance, there seems to be a clear need for actions that improve the conditions of the NGOs, including their level of funding, stability, and programmatic quality. However, the possibilities for such actions are wide open. What can CONASIDA and the NGOs do to increase available funding for AIDS educational programs? CONASIDA might decide to be a catalyst to ensure funding for NGOs, aid them in developing grant-writing skills, and encourage them to bid directly to international foundations. Conceivably, the NGOs themselves might decide to pursue the development of a culture of funding from the state and other private sources from in and outside Mexico, including the organization of fundraising events.

Another set of questions pertains to the development of administrative and programmatic skills in the NGOs. How can the groups focus their attention on the development of new educational strategies and longer term planning for their activities? How can they begin to address the barriers to behavior change and develop new educational methods? And, on an even broader political level, how can the survival of a progressive approach to AIDS prevention be ensured? The boom of political rightist ideology, and the recent violations of the human rights of homosexuals, people with AIDS, and AIDS activists, indicate the possibility of greater repressive actions against AIDS prevention. The question is whether the NGOs and CONASIDA will be able to defend against conservative forces if there is a larger wave of anti-AIDS education attacks. Most importantly, can stronger NGOs have a better chance of organizing and forming coalitions to combat homophobia, repression of prostitutes, inequality of women, and violations of human rights, among other political goals?

The evaluation of AIDS methods implies a fundamental research task. First, the increasing awareness of the problems with importing foreign methods could be used as a departure point for the development of research about sexuality, gender relations, the effects of poverty on AIDS, and other topics in the Mexican context. Second, the experience of popular organizations in Mexico can provide a foundation for research about the expansion of AIDS education methods. Ultimately, the goal would be to include community empowerment and social mobilization as vehicles for behavioral change, rather than relying simply on the provision of information. A research agenda in these two broad areas might provide much needed data for the reformulation of AIDS education strategies.

Despite all the challenges described in this article, Mexico might be better equipped than other countries to develop innovative AIDS prevention methods. The robust governmental response to AIDS, the experience that the NGOs are gaining in community work, the incipient collaboration between CONASIDA and the NGOs, and the long tradition of popular education that exists in Mexico, for instance, might be a strong starting point to reevaluate existing programs and define new ones. For innovation to happen, however, AIDS educators and researchers must unleash their creativity and be willing to allow the fight against larger social maladies to take its part in their work.

AIDS prevention has already created a small crack in the political mirror of Mexico. A close inspection of the social factors that currently limit educational efforts may prove to be crucial in ensuring that future interventions achieve a greater impact in the control of the epidemic and the betterment of the Mexican population.

REFERENCES

1. INDRE—Instituto Nacional de Diagnóstico y Referencia Epidemiológicos, *Boletín Mensual de SIDA/ETS*, México, 7:2, pp. 2356-2373, February 1993.
2. S. Ruiz Velasco and F. Aranda Ordaz, Short-Term Projections of AIDS Cases in Mexico, *Human Biology, 64*:5, pp. 741-755, 1992.
3. J. L. Valdespino y M. de L. García, Epidemiología del SIDA en México. Logros y Nuevos Retos [AIDS Epidemiology in México. Accomplishments and New Challenges], *Sociedad y SIDA, 14*, pp. 8-9, November 1991.

4. AIDS: Growing Problems and a Search for More Effective Answers, *Notimex*, April 21, 1992.
5. AIDS Detected in 2,200 Mexican Women by 1991, *Notimex*, January 26, 1992.
6. A. Pérez López et al. Prevalencia de la Infección por Virus de la Inmunodeficiencia Humana (VIH) y Relación con Otras Enfermedades Transmitidas Sexualmente en un Grupo de Prostitutas en Huixtla, Chiapas [HIV Prevalence and Relationship With Other Sexually Transmitted Diseases in a Group of Prostitutes in Huixtla, Chiapas], *Revista de Investigación Clínica, 43*, pp. 45-47, 1991.
7. Centers for Disease Control and Prevention (CDC), *HIV/AIDS Surveillance Report*, February 1993.
8. R. Morales, Migración y VIH. Algunos Factores Explicativos [Migration and HIV. Some Explanatory Factors], *Sociedad y SIDA, 28*, p. 5, January 1993.
9. Health Minister Compares Mexican AIDS Problems With Those of Africa, *Notimex*, May 16, 1992.
10. E. Vázquez-Valls et al. Efecto de la Legislación Sanitaria Contra el VIH en la Donación de Sangre en Guadalajara, México [Effects of Sanitary Legislation Against HIV in Blood Donation in Guadalajara, Mexico], *Salud Pública de México, 32*:1, pp. 38-42, 1990.
11. C. Avila et al., The Epidemiology of HIV Transmission among Plasma Donors, Mexico City, Mexico, *AIDS, 3*, pp. 631-633, 1989.
12. M. Mejía, SIDA: Historias Extraordinarias del Siglo XX [AIDS: Extraordinary Stories of the 20th Century], in *El SIDA en México: Los Efectos Sociales*, F. Galván Díaz (ed.), Universidad Autónoma Metropolitana, México, D.F., pp. 17-57, 1988.
13. J. L. Valdespino Gómez, et al., Patrones y Predicciones Epidemiológicas del SIDA en México [AIDS Epidemiological Patterns and Predictions in Mexico], *Salud Pública de México, 30*:4, July-August 1988.
14. R. Morales, Sexo con Plenitud a Pesar del VIH/SIDA [Sex With Fulfillment Despite HIV/AIDS], *Sociedad y SIDA, 13*, pp. 1-3, October 1991.
15. M. Hernández et al. Sexual Behavior and Status for Human Immunodeficiency Virus Type 1 among Homosexual and Bisexual Males in Mexico City, *American Journal of Epidemiology, 135*:8, pp. 883-894, 1992.
16. M. S. Flores-Castañeda et al., Anticuerpos Anti-virus Linfotróficos de Células T Humanas en Sujetos de Alto Riesgo Para la Infección por VIH en Monterrey [HTLV-1 Antibodies in Subjects with High Risk for HIV Infection in Monterrey], *Revista de Investigación Clínica, 44*, pp. 37-42, 1992.
17. R. Alvarez, Pacientes y Médicos. Entrevistas [Patients and Physicians. Interviews], in *El Sida en México: Los Efectos Sociales*, F. Galván Díaz (ed.), Universidad Autónoma Metropolitana, México, D.F. pp. 161-169, 1988.
18. L. Cárdenas, Dramatismo, Esperanza y Frustración. Dos enfermos de SIDA. Entrevistas [Drama, Hope and Frustration. Two People with AIDS. Interviews], in *El Sida en México: Los Efectos Sociales*, F. Galván Díaz (ed.), Universidad Autónoma Metropolitana, México, D.F. pp. 173-179, 1988.
19. Robledo Valencia, Luz Adriana, Para Mi Fue un Poco Morir, Casi el Fin. Testimonio [For Me It Was Like Dying. Almost the End. Testimony], in *El Sida en México: Los Efectos Sociales*, F. Galván Díaz (ed.), Universidad Autónoma Metropolitana, México, D.F., pp. 183-190, 1988.

20. F. Galván Díaz (ed.), *El Sida en México: Los Efectos Sociales* [AIDS in Mexico: The Social Effects], Universidad Autónoma Metropolitana, México, D.F., 1988.

21. F. Galván Díaz y F. Luna Millán, Walter Vs. PEMEX ¿Prevalecerá el Derecho? [Walter versus PEMEX: Will the Law Prevail?], in *Sociedad y SIDA, 24*:1, September 1992.

22. G. Pereyra, Caso PEMEX. SIDA y Derechos Humanos [PEMEX Case: AIDS and Human Rights], in *Sociedad y SIDA, 27*:1, December 1992.

23. T. Barry (ed.), *Mexico. A Country Guide*, The Inter-Hemispheric Resource Center, Albuquerque, New Mexico, 1992.

24. A. Díaz Betacourt, De la Lucha Contra el SIDA: Ser y Quehacer de las ONGs en Mexico [About the Fight Against AIDS: Identity and Tasks of the NGOs in Mexico], in *Sociedad y SIDA, 6*:5, March 1991.

25. P. Preciado, ONG's contra el SIDA a Debate [For Debate: NGOs Against AIDS], in *Sociedad y SIDA, 4*:7, January 1991.

26. L. Pérez Franco, El Centro Nacional de Información de CONASIDA: Entrevista con Gloria Ornelas [CONASIDA's National Information Center: Interview With Gloria Ornelas], in Galván Díaz, Francisco (ed.), *El SIDA en México: Los Efectos Sociales*, Universidad Autónoma Metropolitana, México, D.F., pp. 309-325, 1988.

27. *Mexicanos Por La Vida Contra el SIDA Newsletter*, July 1, 1992.

28. Red Nacional de Comunicación y Solidaridad Contra el SIDA, in *Sociedad y SIDA, 6*:8, March 1991.

29. F. Galván Díaz, R. González Villarreal, y R. Morales, Del SIDA en México. Aspectos de Gobierno y Sociedad [Of AIDS in Mexico. Aspects of Government and Society], Appendix in Lumsden, Ian, *Homosexualidad, Sociedad y Estado en México* [*Homosexuality, Society and State in Mexico*], Solediciones, México, D.F., 1991.

30. D. Altman, *AIDS in the Mind of America*, Anchor Press, Doubleday, Garden City, New York, 1986.

31. D. A. Murillo, Dr. Manuel Ponce De León (interview), in *Amigos Contra el SIDA, 1*:1, pp. 5-7, September 1991.

32. A. Y. Reyes, EL VIH en Jalisco. ONG's y COESIDA [HIV in Jalisco. NGOs and COESIDA], in *Sociedad y SIDA, 29*:3, February 1993.

33. Policia de Zapopan: Luchar Contra el SIDA es Atentar a la Moral [Zapopan's Police: To Fight Against AIDS is to Attempt Against Morality], *Sociedad y SIDA, 4*:15, January 1991.

34. M. Palet, La Radio y el SIDA [Radio and AIDS], in *Sociedad y SIDA, 8*:6, May 1991.

35. A. Sánchez, Radio Novela [Radio Soap Opera], in *Sociedad y SIDA, 10*:3, July 1991.

36. Mexican Church-State Relations Modified in 1992, *Notimex*, December 28, 1992.

37. Catholics Celebrate Beatification of Cristero 'Martyrs', *Notimex*, November 22, 1992.

38. F. Barbosa Guzmán, *La Iglesia y el Gobierno Civil* [The Church and the Civil Government], Series "Jalisco desde la Revolución" Vol. VI, Universidad de Guadalajara, Guadalajara, 1988.

39. Mexican Clergy React Positively to Salinas' Address to Nation, *Notimex,* November 2, 1992.

40. Mexico's Renewed Relations With Vatican Meet With General Approval, *Notimex,* September 21, 1992.

41. Taller Documentación Visual, Jueces, Acusados y Abogados. SIDA y Culpabilidad [The Judges, the Accused, and the Attorneys: AIDS and Guilt], in *Sociedad y SIDA, 24*:1, September 1992.

42. R. Bayer, *Private Acts, Social Consequences. AIDS and the Politics of Public Health*, The Free Press, New York, 1989.

43. C. Monsiváis, SIDA y Homofobia: Furia Represiva [AIDS and Homophobia: Repressive Fury], in *Sociedad y SIDA, 5*:1, February 1991.

44. E. Guerrero Pavich, A Chicana Perspective on Mexican Culture and Sexuality, *Journal of Social Work and Human Sexuality, 4*, pp. 47-65, 1986.

45. H. Amaro, Considerations for Prevention of HIV Infection among Hispanic Women, *Psychology of Women Quarterly, 12*, pp. 429-443, 1988.

46. A. Carballo-Diéguez, Hispanic Culture, Gay Male Culture, and AIDS: Counseling Implications, *Journal of Counseling and Development, 68*, pp. 26-30, September 1989.

47. V. M. Mays, and S. D. Cochran, Issues in the Perception of AIDS Risk and Risk Reduction Activities by Black and Hispanic/Latina Women, *American Psychologist, 43*:11, pp. 949-957, November 1988.

48. C. Texidor de Portillo, Poverty, Self-Concept and Health: Experience of Latinas, *Women and Health, 12*:3-4, pp. 229-242, 1988.

49. V. De la Cancela, Minority AIDS Prevention: Moving Beyond Cultural Perspectives Towards Sociopolitical Empowerment, *AIDS Education and Prevention, 1*:2, pp. 141-153, 1989.

50. F. Rosas, Lecciones de Trabajo Comunitario [The Lessons of Community Work], *Sociedad y SIDA, 27*:10, December 1992.

51. U.S. Researchers Report Murders of Gays in Latin America, *Notimex*, March 10, 1993.

52. New Gay Killing Reported in Chiapas, *Notimex*, November 5, 1992.

53. Chiapas Governor Promises Investigation on Killings of Gays, *Notimex*, September 15, 1992.

54. Human Rights Groups Protest Wave of Gay Killings, *Notimex*, September 10, 1992.

55. Recent Murders Alarm Mexico's Gay Community, *Notimex*, September 4, 1992.

56. P. Freire, *Pedagogía del Oprimido (Pedagogy of the Oppressed)*, Siglo XXI, México, 1970.

57. F. Rosas and J. J. Hernández, El SIDA y Nuestra Comunidad [AIDS And Our Community], in *Sociedad y SIDA, 24*:6, September 1992.

CHAPTER 10

HIV/AIDS in Asian and Pacific Islander Communities in the U.S.: A Review, Analysis, and Integration

Gust A. Yep

Asians and Pacific Islanders[1] (A/PI) are the fastest growing cultural groups in the United States. Their population more than doubled in the 1970s and doubled again during the 1980s [1]. At present, they are the third largest racial or ethnic group in this country after African Americans and Hispanics [2]. Within this A/PI category, there is a lot of diversity; there is no single "Asian/Pacific Islander community" [3]. In fact, there are forty-three Asian and Pacific Islander groups including Chinese, Filipino, Japanese, Korean, Vietnamese, Cambodian, Indonesian, Malaysian, Thai, Hawaiian, Samoan, Tongan, among many others [4].

As HIV "began its horrific pandemic march, spreading with surprising efficiency in just a few years to virtually every country on the face of the earth" [5, p. 23], AIDS is still invisible to Asian and Pacific Islanders in the United States. For example, Albrecht and his associates found that being Asian or Hispanic and of lower educational levels were significant predictors of individuals who reported not having heard about AIDS by 1987 [6]. Further, HIV/AIDS is not only invisible to A/PI community members but to public health officials at local, state, and federal levels [3]. Several years later, AIDS continues to remain largely

---

[1] According to the U.S. Census Bureau, there are over forty Asian and Pacific Islander groups from over forty countries and territories, who speak more than 100 different languages (some unwritten). It is recognized that each group has a distinct culture and heritage. The term "Asian/Pacific Islander" is a label of convenience used by government agencies including the Centers for Disease Control (CDC) and the author does not intend to imply cultural and linguistic homogeneity.

hidden and this situation is creating increasing concern for several reasons. First, although incidence of HIV infection among A/PIs is relatively low, there is evidence that Asian AIDS cases are increasing rapidly [3, 7-10]. For example, Mandel and Kitano, and Woo and his associates reported that new AIDS cases in San Francisco are disproportionately increasing among Asians and Pacific Islanders [8, 9]. Second, premarital sexual behavior has been documented among A/PI adolescents and young adults. For example, past research found Asian-American college students to be no different than their non-Asian counterparts in terms of prevalence of premarital sexual behavior [11]. Another report observed the increasing acceptance of premarital sexuality among A/PIs [12]. Such behavior—premarital sex—amplifies the risk of HIV infection for this population. Third, heterosexual Asian Americans are engaging in high-risk sexual practices—for example, sexual intercourse without a condom. In their study assessing rates of sexual activity and patterns of intimate behavior in a group of young, unmarried, heterosexual Asian Americans, Cochran, Mays, and Leung concluded:

> Once sexually active, [sexual] behavior [of Asian Americans] appear to be similar to their non-Asian counterparts and facilitative of HIV infection. . . . This underscores the need for HIV prevention interventions directed toward this ethnic minority group despite current low rates of HIV infection [13, p. 381].

In terms of HIV/AIDS education and prevention for Asians and Pacific Islanders, very little is known [3]. This situation is further exacerbated by the scarcity of resources available for research, training, education, prevention, and service delivery programs. In the AIDS crisis, Asian and Pacific Islander communities are faced with a classic Catch-22. They receive limited, if any, funding for services or research because there are relatively few reported Asian AIDS cases, but no one can financially, socially, and ethically afford to wait for an explosion of HIV infection in these communities.

Because knowledge about HIV/AIDS education in A/PI communities is limited, the present review attempts to partially fill this gap. More specifically, this article will: 1) examine, analyze, and integrate past research related to HIV/AIDS education for Asians, and 2) address the implications of these findings for HIV education and prevention programs for Asian and Pacific Islander communities in this country. To review, analyze, and integrate such diverse body of literature, the AIDS Risk Reduction Model (ARRM), postulated by Catania and his colleagues [14, 15], is used as the organizing framework.

AIDS RISK REDUCTION MODEL

Integrating elements from several models of health behavior change including the health belief model [16, 17], self-efficacy theory [18, 19], fear arousal and attitude change [20, 21], theory of reasoned action [22, 23], diffusion of innovation model [24], and help-seeking models [25, 26], Catania and his colleagues [14, 15] presented a framework for examining people's efforts to reduce their risk to HIV infection. Their psychosocial AIDS Risk Reduction Model has been applied to gay and bisexual men, unmarried white and ethnic heterosexuals, individuals attending antibody testing centers, and adolescent women attending family planning centers. This model is a useful framework for understanding sexual behaviors related to HIV transmission and efforts to modify those behaviors. Catania and his associates explained, "ARRM organizes predictors of health behavior in general (e.g., susceptibility beliefs) and sexual behavior specifically (e.g., sexual enjoyment), and also incorporates some unique influences created by the AIDS epidemic (e.g., personal contact with [a person with AIDS])" [14, p. 247].

The model consists of three stages: 1) labeling, 2) commitment, and 3) enactment [14, 15]. Labeling, the first phase, is the recognition that one's sexual behavior is problematic—they are high risk for contracting HIV—because such behaviors are associated with the transmission of HIV (transmission knowledge), related to a personal sense of risk for HIV infection (personal susceptibility), and associated with the belief that HIV and AIDS are undesirable (social norms). Commitment, the second stage, is the individual's intervention to decrease high risk sexual encounters and increase low risk practices by understanding risk reduction behaviors (knowledge), their benefits (response efficacy), their degree of gratification (perceived enjoyment), their proper enactment (self-efficacy), and their endorsement by others (social support and group norms). Enactment, the last phase, involves taking action to reduce one's high risk sexual behavior by attempting to find solutions (help-seeking behaviors), and acquiring the necessary interpersonal (sexual communication) and behavioral skills (behavior enactment) to perform such solutions.

The model conceptualizes behavior change as a fluid process. The stages may be viewed as indicators of this process and they are not invariant, unidirectional, or irreversible. From a theoretical and community intervention viewpoint, Catania and his colleagues observed:

> ARRM emphasizes the goal of understanding why people fail to progress over the change process. From an intervention standpoint, it is imperative that we understand the different conditions that influence the outcomes of the various stages of the change process. Achieving this goal is important to the task of identifying intervention strategies that facilitate movement towards change for people at different points in the process. Failure to correctly identify the position a person occupies in the change process may waste intervention resources [15, p. 56].

To understand the changes in high risk behavior and to identify proper intervention strategies for HIV/AIDS prevention in Asian and Pacific Island communities, this review utilizes the AIDS risk reduction model as an organizing framework to assess past research with such population. Thus, prior work associated with each of the three stages posited by ARRM is examined with respect to their location in the change process in the context of the HIV/AIDS epidemic.

STAGE ONE: LABELING

Labeling, the first stage of the model, involves recognition and identification of current sexual behaviors as risky in terms of HIV infection. At this stage, individuals begin to perceive their behavior as hazardous and problematic. According to Catania and his associates, this labeling process is influenced by: 1) knowledge of behaviors associated with HIV transmission, 2) perceived vulnerability to the virus, and 3) social networks and norms influencing the individual's perception of the problem [15].

Transmission Knowledge

Transmission knowledge is the accurate understanding of the risk factors associated with the spread of HIV. It includes factual information about the modes (for example, exchange of bodily fluids) and behaviors (for example, unprotected sexual intercourse) associated with HIV transmission. In this review, several studies were identified with various Asian populations including adolescents [27-29], college students [30], adults in San Francisco [31-33], and gay men in California [34-36].

In a large-scale survey, DiClemente and his colleagues examined knowledge, attitudes, and beliefs related to HIV/AIDS by assessing 1,326 adolescents residing in San Francisco [27]. The findings demonstrated ethnic differences in knowledge: Asians were found to be the least informed about HIV/AIDS. More specifically, Asians reported significantly lower overall mean scores than Euro Americans and African Americans. When length of residence in the San Francisco Bay area—a major HIV/AIDS epicenter in the country—was taken into account, DiClemente et al. concluded: "Asians, in general, not only had the lowest [knowledge] mean scores, but those who lived in the Bay area the shortest period of time also had the lowest within-group mean scores" [27, p. 225].

In another large-scale survey, Siegel and his associates surveyed 1,967 inner city, junior high school students in Northern California [28]. Approximately one-third of the sample was Asian, and a substantial proportion of respondents reported high-risk behavior including sexual intercourse and drug use. More African Americans than Asians reported sexual activity and more whites that Asians indicated drug use. Ethnic differences in general knowledge about HIV/AIDS were also detected: Asians had lower knowledge levels than African Americans, Latinos, and Euro Americans. Although no ethnic breakdown was reported, misconceptions about casual transmission of HIV—for example, likelihood of becoming infected from shaking hands with an infected person—were common in this population. This study confirmed earlier findings [27] with respect to Asian adolescents: They are the least informed about HIV/AIDS when compared to their other ethnic counterparts.

Investigating adolescents' knowledge, beliefs, behaviors, and perceptions of risk for HIV infection, Strunin tested two groups of teenagers in Massachusetts, one in a random digit dial telephone survey and the other in a self-administered questionnaire in the Boston school system [29]. Although the number of Asians was small in both studies, Asian students were the least knowledgeable about casual, sexual, and drug use transmission of HIV when compared to their Euro American, African American, and Hispanic peers. For example, over 30 percent of the Asian adolescents did not know about HIV transmission by sperm, semen or vaginal fluids. Similarly, over 30 percent of the same group believed that HIV can be transmitted by sharing eating and drinking utensils or by being in the same room with someone who is infected or has AIDS. Finally, Asians were the least aware of the risks of HIV transmission associated with the sharing of needles.

In their baseline survey of HIV/AIDS knowledge, attitudes, and behaviors in the Chinese communities of San Francisco, Ja and his associates interviewed 192 adult residents of Chinese descent [32]. Their findings indicated that almost everyone correctly identified all known methods of HIV transmission; however, most respondents were misinformed or unsure about transmission through casual contact. For example, over 70 percent of the participants believed that HIV can be transmitted through kissing or sharing a drinking glass with an infected individual. Similarly, over 50 percent of the Chinese in the sample believed or were uncertain about transmission through blood donation, hospital needles, or being close to a gay man. The results also indicated that the best informed subjects were single, college graduates, English speaking, earn a higher annual income than their less informed peers, and know someone with AIDS. Conversely, the least informed respondents were those with less education—most of them had a high school education or less, those interviewed in Chinese, those with lower annual income, and those who did not know anyone with the disease. These findings suggest that sociodemographic variables such as educational level, income, and primary language have a significant effect on knowledge about HIV.

In another baseline survey of HIV/AIDS knowledge, attitudes, and behaviors, Ja and his associates interviewed a sample of 200 adult Japanese residents of San Francisco [33]. Over 95 percent of the respondents demonstrated accurate under-standing of HIV transmission through sexual contact, sharing of needles, and blood transfusion. An almost equally high percentage of participants correctly identified transmission through anal intercourse and from infected mother to unborn child. However, most respondents were misinformed, uncertain, or con-fused about casual transmission. For example, 56 percent of the sample believed that transmission was possible through hospital needles. A substantial number of respondents (40%) believed or were uncertain about HIV transmission through kissing or mosquito bites. Additionally, over one-third of the group was misinformed about transmission through sharing a drinking glass with a person who is seropositive or living with AIDS. The demographic profile of the most informed individuals in the sample was as follows: 1) higher educational level, 2) primarily English speaking, 3) knowledge of someone with AIDS, and 4) mostly male.

In a population-based household assessment to measure HIV/AIDS knowledge, attitudes, beliefs, and behaviors in the Filipino communities of San Francisco, Gorrez and Araneta interviewed 400 respondents for their baseline survey [31]. Their findings indicated that knowledge was low as demonstrated by an overall mean of 58.2 percent correct on the HIV/AIDS knowledge questionnaire. Over 50 percent of the sample indicated lack of accurate knowledge regarding transmission through sharing toothbrushes with HIV-infected individuals, receiving blood transfusion after 1985, or through hospital needles used for vaccinations or medical laboratory tests. Additionally, more than one-third of those surveyed believed that HIV can be transmitted by blood donation or mosquito bites. Adult Filipinos who were never married, born in the United States, and with reported behavioral risk factors for HIV infection were significantly more knowledgeable about HIV transmission than their counterparts. As opposed to the findings in the Japanese communities of San Francisco [33], HIV/AIDS knowledge scores in the Filipino communities did not vary by gender [31].

In her exploratory assessment of high-risk behavior associated with HIV transmission, Kitano tested a self-identified group of 123 gay adult men of Filipino and Chinese descent in San Francisco [34]. Although this study was not representative of the gay Asian community, it provides preliminary findings for this population. HIV-related knowledge was examined in several areas including transmission, prevention, cure, affected groups, and etiology of AIDS. Her findings indicated that her sample exhibited fairly good levels of overall knowledge with low to moderate misconceptions about HIV. Because her sample consisted of responses from openly gay men, Kitano noted that this group is more knowledgeable about HIV than their "closeted" peers—presumably the majority of homosexual Asian men—because of their access to educational materials in the gay community.

More recently, Yep examined HIV-related knowledge in a group of self-identified gay and bisexual Asian men in Los Angeles [35, 36]. Like Kitano's sample [34], his respondents were also volunteers who were fairly open about their sexual orientation, and therefore, not truly representative of the gay Asian community in Southern California. HIV-related knowledge was assessed in two areas: 1) operant—information about history and etiology of AIDS and the most affected populations, and 2) contagion—information about ways in which an individual can become infected. His findings indicated that overall knowledge was high—with respondents averaging above 80 percent correct on a knowledge test [35]. However, caution must, once again, by used to interpret these results. Most of the respondents reported being active in the gay community unlike their non-gay identified counterparts, who may be practicing high-risk behavior without any access to educational resources in the gay media. Because of homophobia and cultural stigma, "closeted gays" are extremely difficult to identify in Asian and Pacific Islander communities.

In sum, it appears that most A/PIs, with the exception of self-identified gay/bisexual men, have lower knowledge scores than their ethnic peers. This lack of accurate knowledge appears to be particularly true in the area of casual transmission, e.g., dry kissing, sharing of eating utensils with someone who is infected, blood donation, among others.

Perceived Susceptibility

Perceived susceptibility is the personal belief about one's degree of vulnerability to HIV. It encompasses perceptions of likelihood of HIV exposure as compared to individuals in A/PI and other ethnic communities. Such beliefs are related to perceptions of community ownership of the health crisis. In this review, perceptions of vulnerability to HIV were examined in Asian-American adolescents [27-29] and college students [10]; Chinese [32] and Japanese [33] households in San Francisco, and self-identified gay men [34-36].

As indicated earlier, DiClemente and his colleagues found Asian adolescents to be least knowledgeable about HIV among all major ethnic groups [27]. They also observed a significant negative correlation between perceived susceptibility and knowledge about HIV/AIDS; in other words, higher levels of perceived vulnerability to HIV were likely to be related to lower knowledge scores. More specifically, they found 57.3 percent of the Asian sample, as compared to 45.3 percent of the Euro American, 48.2 percent of the African American, and 49.6 percent of the Hispanic American sample, reporting a high perceived susceptibility score.

In a more recent study, Strunin also reported that Asian adolescents were least knowledgeable about casual, sexual, and drug use transmissions of HIV [29]. In terms of their concern about becoming infected, Strunin found Asian and Hispanic students to be most worried about "getting AIDS." For example, 94 percent of the Asian students, as compared to 73 percent of the Euro Americans, 73 percent of the Hispanic Americans, and 69 percent of the African Americans, reported being worried about HIV in the telephone survey. Similarly, in the same survey, 85 percent of the Asians compared to 46 percent of African American and 45 percent of Euro and Hispanic Americans indicated that it was likely that they would become HIV-infected.

Ja, Kitano, and Ebata in their baseline surveys of Chinese and Japanese households in San Francisco, reported some preliminary findings related to perceived vulnerability to HIV/AIDS [32, 33]. Ja and his colleagues [32] found that over 75 percent of the Chinese respondents indicated that they can get AIDS; however, 74 percent of this same group also felt that they could protect themselves against HIV exposure and that AIDS would not be likely to affect them (personal susceptibility). In addition, 37 percent of the respondents expressed some concern that someone in their families would become infected in the next year (others' susceptibility). Similarly, Japanese respondents indicated fairly slight concern about AIDS [33]. More specifically, 90 percent of the Japanese participants indicated that they could protect themselves against HIV/AIDS (personal susceptibility) while 77.3 percent of this group expressed little or no concern about someone in their families contracting the disease (others' susceptibility). In sum, these preliminary findings indicate that Chinese and Japanese adults in San Francisco perceive low personal vulnerability to HIV/AIDS and slightly higher perceptions of vulnerability for their family members.

Kitano [34] and Yep [35] examined perceptions of fear and vulnerability related to HIV/AIDS among Asian gay men in California. Kitano measured denial and fear of AIDS among openly gay Chinese and Filipino adults. Her results indicated that denial of AIDS as an existing problem among Asians and fear of people living with AIDS (PLWA) were low. As expected, Kitano also found a significant positive relationship between denial and fear; that is, higher levels of fear were associated with higher levels of denial and vice versa [34]. In his study, Yep examined personal beliefs associated with vulnerability to HIV infection in a group of gay/bisexual men from various A/PI communities in Southern California [35]. He reported a broad scope of perceptions of personal vulnerability ranging from slight to high with a mean of moderate vulnerability to HIV infection. Yep also observed no changes in perceived susceptibility after exposure to a six-hour community-based HIV/AIDS education program [35]. In sum, these two studies indicate that self-identified gay Asian men, residing in one of the major AIDS epicenters in the country (California), tend to perceive themselves to be moderately to highly at risk for HIV infection.

Investigating the population of Asian American college students, Brown [30] and Yep [10] examined their personal concerns about AIDS. Brown found heterosexual college students with an Asian-Pacific cultural orientation to express less concern about HIV/AIDS than their peers with a North-American cultural orientation [30]. Brown explained this finding (personal concern about AIDS) in terms of differences in cultural orientations. Asian American young adults, following more collectivistic and ingroup-outgroup distinctions, perceive incidence of AIDS in their communities (ingroup) to be low compared to other ethnic communities (outgroup), and such perception appears to be accompanied by reduced concern about the HIV epidemic [30]. More simply stated, the lack of ownership of the HIV/AIDS epidemic in A/PI communities is related to lower perceptions of vulnerability to infection. Yep reported similar findings, although Asian American young adults believe that AIDS is a serious health crisis, they do not perceive themselves as particularly vulnerable to it [10]. He also noted that most Asian Americans perceive AIDS and HIV-related conditions to be a non-Asian epidemic [10].

In terms of perceived susceptibility to HIV infection, past research appears to be inconclusive. For example, some studies reported that Asian adolescents and young adults are more concerned about HIV infection than other ethnic groups [27, 29], while other reports indicate the contrary [10, 30]. One possible explanation for such discrepancy may lie in the operationalization of the susceptibility construct as a single-item variable. There is also a need to clearly differentiate between perceptions of vulnerability ("feeling vulnerable to HIV infection") and general sense of concern ("being worried about AIDS"), personal susceptibility ("feeling personally at risk for HIV infection") and others' susceptibility ("feeling that others—for example, family member or friend—are at risk for HIV infection").

Social Networks and Cultural Norms

Networks and norms are sociocultural factors affecting perceptions of health behavior. For example, social networks and cultural norms can influence labeling of behavior as high risk through disapproval, peer pressure, and social stigmatization. In terms of sociocultural factors, several authors [3, 13, 37, 38] have examined the impact of Asian cultural beliefs, norms and values on risk perception associated with HIV in A/PI communities.

Jue outlined several cultural issues related to HIV education and delivery of services to Asians [38]. First, A/PIs tend to view the AIDS epidemic as a Western phenomenon. Asians believe that if they adhere to the norms and values of their cultural orientation, they will not be affected by HIV [38]. Second, the recognition that HIV/AIDS affects A/PI communities also implies acknowledgment of the existence of homosexuality, bisexuality, and intravenous drug use. Strong negative attitudes toward homosexuality, bisexuality, and drug abuse have been identified in A/PI communities [38]. Third, the family is a powerful social unit in A/PI communities [38]. Like other social institutions, the family can be a source of social, emotional, and financial support as well as tension; for example, a gay Asian person may find himself or herself in the difficult predicament between perpetuating the family name through conventional marriage and seeking personal fulfillment through satisfying same-sex relationship. Finally, the potential for conflict between ethnic, family, personal, and sexual identities are omnipresent, and the outcomes of such conflict may oppose the enactment of health protective behavior.

Aoki and his associates identified several taboo subjects within A/PI cultures which may be associated with the AIDS epidemic [3, 37]. They include: 1) sexual behavior, 2) homosexuality, 3) illness, and 4) death. Sexuality is perceived to be strictly private; public discussion of sexual behavior is inhibited and open acknowledgment is difficult [37, 39]. Homosexuality, as noted earlier, is another taboo topic because it is perceived to oppose traditional Asian cultural values of family, unity, and collectivism [38, 40]. Illness, especially serious and terminal disease, is considered inappropriate for public discourse: "The magical belief that mere discussion of a terminal illness may bring about the occurrence of the illness continues to be a powerful motivating force in certain Asian cultures" [37, p. 5]. As a result of this self-fulfilling prophecy, discussion of death and dying is also prohibited [3, 37].

With respect to sexual behavior, Cochran and her associates indicated that Asian-American young adults tend to be more sexually conservative than Euro Americans, Hispanic, and African Americans in some domains of sexuality [13]. In their study, they observed the presence sexual conservatism in terms of initiation of sexual activity; more specifically, only 47 percent of single, heterosexual, young adults between the ages of eighteen and twenty-five, were sexually active in the Asian-American group compared to 72 percent in the Euro American, 59 percent in the Hispanic, and 84 percent in the African-American groups. However, they cautioned that this should not be mistaken with the absence of risky behavior associated with HIV transmission: In their research, no ethnic differences in HIV-related risk behavior were detected among sexually active participants [13].

STAGE TWO: COMMITMENT TO CHANGE

Commitment, the second phase of the model, involves decision making after perceiving a health threat and before taking action on the problem. Catania and his colleagues defined this stage as "the next step in the process of changing high risk behaviors [which] involves reaching a firm decision to make behavioral changes and strongly committing to that decision" [15, p. 59]. Such process is influenced by: 1) response efficacy, 2) perceived enjoyment, 3) self-efficacy, and 4) social factors and knowledge of the health utility of the recommended risk reduction behaviors. Unfortunately, there is a paucity of studies exploring these variables.

Response Efficacy

Response efficacy is the degree of perceived personal effectiveness of risk reducing behaviors, i.e., the perceived benefits associated with safer sexual practices. In their review, only two studies examined this construct in A/PI populations [10, 35]. In his assessment of the effects of a community-based HIV/AIDS education program, Yep measured response efficacy in a group of self-identified gay/bisexual Asian men [35]. His findings indicated that gay Asian men viewed safer sexual practices as extremely effective for the prevention of HIV infection [35]. Similarly, past research with primarily heterosexual Asian American young-adults reported almost identical findings, that is, most of these young adults indicated that safer sexual practices are very beneficial in HIV prevention; however, this health belief has not necessarily translated into adoption of such health protective actions [10]. Furthermore, no research has been conducted with ethnic-specific communities or other adult A/PI populations.

Perceived Enjoyment

In the context of AIDS, perceived enjoyment involves perceptions of pleasure associated with risk reducing sexual activities—for example, how enjoyable is sexual intercourse with a condom? The underlying assumption is that individuals are more likely to make a commitment to modify their behavior if they perceive the new health action to be greater or equal in enjoyment as the current behavior. In the case of safer sex, attitudes toward condoms may be a significant predictor of behavioral change. Yep reported preliminary results about attitudes toward condom use among self-identified gay/bisexual Asian men [35]. Although there was significant range of responses, his findings indicated that, for the most part, the participants reported favorable attitudes toward condom use [35]. Because the study used a small sample, caution must be exercised in interpreting these research findings.

Self-Efficacy

Self-efficacy measures individuals' perceptions of their ability to perform recommended health protective behaviors—for example, feeling competent about the wearing and disposal of condoms. In his study of perceptions of self-efficacy associated with condom use among gay/bisexual Asian men, Yep indicated that these participants reported feeling moderately comfortable with discussing and using condoms during sexual encounters even before exposure to prevention messages in an HIV/AIDS education program [41]. After participation in the program, their attitude and confidence associated with condom use positively increased as demonstrated by a statistically significant ($t = 2.59$, $p = .01$) pretest-posttest comparison. Because of the tremendous diversity—for example, linguistic, generational, sexual lifestyle—in A/PI communities [3, 4], these positive attitudes toward condom use appear to be restricted to only gay/bisexual Asian men in urban areas.

Social Factors

According to ARRM, social factors may have considerable impact on self-efficacy beliefs and behavioral commitment. Such factors include social support and group norms [37, 38, 40] and social conditions including attitude toward people living with AIDS (PLWA) [34, 41, 42].

As noted earlier, illness, death, sex, and homosexuality are considered taboo topics to be kept outside of the realm of public discourse for many Asians and Pacific Islanders [3, 37, 38, 40]. Social support is normally provided by the family—the primary social unit within the culture; however, such source of support can also be the roots of stress. In this cultural context, a child's behavior reflects upon the entire family and this child has the obligation to maintain the family reputation and to continue the family through marriage and the bearing of children. This cultural expectation is especially problematic for a gay son who is perceived to bring shame and loss of face to the entire group as well as ending the family name if he is the only son [38, 40]. For an HIV-infected A/PI person, the situation is further complicated. Fears of anger, shame, and rejection associated with disclosure of HIV status to family members often lead to inaction. In terms of seeking support outside of the family unit, Aoki and Ja observed, "Irrespective of the specific Asian ethnic group or level of acculturation, many Asians with AIDS or ARC find it difficult to rely upon unrelated friends or community services for the provision of caretaking activities" [37, pp. 7-8]. Such lack of social support exacerbates the individual's feelings of social stigmatization, alienation, shame, and isolation.

Social stigmatization and AIDS-phobia continue to be a serious problem in many segments of society [43-50] including A/PI communities. An exception to such negative attitudes toward people living with AIDS is the group of self-identified gay/bisexual men [34, 41]. Kitano pointed out that individuals who identify themselves as gay/bisexual appear to be more comfortable with their sexual identity, and therefore, exhibit more acceptance toward PLWA than those who are "in the closet" or are heterosexual [34]. More recent research [41] confirmed Kitano's position.

STAGE THREE: ENACTMENT

Enactment is the final stage of the model. According to Catania and his associates, enactment is the process of taking the necessary steps to achieve the goal of behavioral change, i.e., adopting HIV-preventive practices [15]. This stage consists of three phases: 1) help-seeking behavior, 2) sexual communication and safer sex negotiation, and 3) behavior enactment. A review of the literature suggests that little research, focusing on A/PI populations, exists in this area.

Help-Seeking Behavior

Help-seeking behavior refer to the vast array of actions people take to solve their perceived problems. In the context of AIDS, these behaviors may be the types of help an individual needs to facilitate reduction of risky sexual practices. Compared to their Euro-American counterparts, Asians and Pacific Islanders have consistently underutilized health-related services [51]. This pattern in A/PI communities is well documented by previous research [52, 53]. In terms of HIV/AIDS-related services, A/PI individuals—especially if they have recently immigrated to the United States—may even be more reluctant to seek assistance from strangers such as AIDS service providers or volunteer services [37]. Fear of embarrassment is a powerful reason for people to avoid seeking assistance [54].

Sexual Communication

To engage in preventive and risk reducing behaviors, the individual needs to have the necessary skills and abilities to interact with sexual partners effectively. This repertoire of skills is called sexual communication. It consists of talking about sex, safer sex negotiation, and other interpersonal communication processes with intimate partners. However, intimate communication and safer sex negotiation are not simple tasks [55].

In his study of heterosexual Asian young adults, Brown found Asian respondents reporting significantly less AIDS-related interpersonal communication than their North-American counterparts [30]. In particular, Asian young adults were less likely to openly discuss sexuality—either directly or indirectly, seriously or humorously. Similarly, Kitano, in her study of self-identified gay Asian men, found Chinese participants to be significantly less willing to discuss HIV/AIDS with a new sexual partner than their Filipino peers [34]. In general, the gay men in Kitano's study reported moderate levels of apprehension and avoidance of safer sex discussion with intimate partners [34]. Although these studies examined two very distinct segments of the A/PI communities (heterosexual and gay male), their findings confirm the lack of sexual communication between partners.

Behavioral Enactment

The final step in the process of altering high risk behavior is behavior enactment, that is, the individual's skills associated with the proper performance of the new behavior, i.e., knowing how to use condoms effectively. In his assessment of behavioral enactment skills with respect to condom use in a group of self-identified gay/bisexual Asian men, Yep reported that a six-hour community-based HIV/AIDS education program was effective in teaching participants how to use condoms properly [35]. This communication program consisted of a three-step process: 1) discussion of the principles and uses of condoms in HIV prevention, i.e., talk about correct usage; 2) behavioral demonstration of how to put on and take off a condom properly, i.e., watch how correct usage is performed, and 3) supervised behavioral enactment and rehearsal, i.e., practice correct usage with a partner in a simulated situation. After the program, most of the participants (87.88%) exhibited acquisition of the proper skills.

SUMMARY AND IMPLICATIONS FOR COMMUNITY HEALTH EDUCATION

During the first decade of the AIDS epidemic, A/PI communities have been notoriously slow in their response to the crisis. More specifically, they have been behind other minority groups—African American, Hispanic, gay white male—in terms of education, prevention, service delivery, and advocacy. Aoki and his associates observed: "Although there were AIDS cases in the Asian community early in the epidemic (the first Asian case in San Francisco was in 1982), it was only after 1986 that any prevention efforts targeting Asians were established" [3, p. 303]. This situation has important implications for health communication campaigns. Such campaigns include interpersonal (e.g., training, counseling), community (e.g., advocacy, neighborhood group, community-based outreach), and mass media (e.g., television, radio, film, print media) components [56].

According to ARRM, it is clear that many segments of the A/PI communities are still in the first stage (problem perception) of the process. In particular, it appears that the general A/PI population has not fully labeled their current behavior as problematic in relationship to HIV infection. For example, Catania and his colleagues noted that knowledge of HIV is necessary for individuals to determine their personal risk accurately and to develop perceptions of vulnerability to infection [15]. With the exception of self-identified gay/bisexual men, it is a well-documented fact that Asians and Pacific Islanders are less knowledgeable about HIV transmission than other ethnic groups regardless of age (adolescents, college students, and adults), gender, and ancestry (e.g., Chinese, Japanese, Filipino, etc.). For example, it is alarming that a recent survey reported that over 50 percent of the respondents were confused about transmission through blood donation or casual contact [32].

For community health campaigns to be effective, they must address the specific conditions, issues, and needs of the target audience at their stage of the change process (i.e., labeling, commitment, enactment); otherwise, intervention strategies may be wasted. To facilitate movement toward change for different segments of the Asian and Pacific Islander communities, four distinct community health education programs are proposed. They are: 1) General HIV/AIDS Awareness (e.g., targeting all Asian and Pacific Islanders); 2) General HIV/AIDS Information Program (e.g., targeting all A/PIs); 3) Education Program for groups who have higher rates of HIV infection (e.g., targeting A/PI sex workers), and 4) Education Program who those who are already infected (e.g., targeting seropositive Asians). As it will be discussed later, some of these programs are being considered or in the process of being created or implemented by A/PI community-based organizations in major metropolitan centers around the country including New York, Los Angeles, and San Francisco. However, information about such programs has not been completely integrated.

Because the majority of Asians and Pacific Islanders are still in the stage of problem perception (Stage One), education programs should be designed to create a sense of community ownership to the HIV/AIDS epidemic. To accomplish this, two related campaigns should be developed: 1) General HIV/AIDS

Awareness, and 2) General HIV/AIDS Information Program. The major goal of the General HIV/AIDS Awareness Campaign is to increase the understanding that AIDS and HIV infection are present in A/PI communities. For example, Asians and Pacific Islanders who are either HIV-positive or living with AIDS should be featured in media programs to convince A/PI communities of their risk. The General HIV/AIDS Information Campaign is designed to increase knowledge of HIV transmission, prevention, early intervention and treatment. Such campaign may use well recognized health professionals (high authority figures) delivering messages about HIV/AIDS in a non-threatening and non-offensive manner (e.g., language content appropriate for the young and the old, the more and less educated). Taken together, these two campaigns can enhance each other by simultaneously raising general awareness and knowledge in the general A/PI population. To develop these programs, Aoki and his colleagues offered several recommendations: 1) communication campaigns need to be sensitive to the heterogeneity and diversity within A/PI communities, e.g., hotlines, brochures, media presentations should be linguistically appropriate; 2) these programs must contain culturally appropriate messages, e.g., emphasis on health and family values, and 3) they must deemphasize culturally taboo topics, e.g., direct discussion of sexual practices and homosexuality [3].

A smaller segment of the A/PI communities, namely self-identified gay and bisexual individuals, appear to be in the second stage (commitment) of the sexual behavior change process. Such individuals perceive their current behavior as problematic and are making decisions about modifying their current health practices. However, such decisions do not appear to be consolidated. For example, a study found that a number of self-identified gay/bisexual Asian men reported some levels of discomfort associated with condom use (self-efficacy) even though they believe that condoms are highly efficacious in the prevention of HIV infection (response efficacy) [41]. To create a commitment and firm decision to change, a third education program appears to be necessary: HIV/AIDS Education Program for High-Risk[2] Groups. This program is designed specifically for those individuals in the A/PI communities who are at "high-risk" for HIV infection and, therefore, it can address issues of sexuality and sexual practices more openly. In addition, such program must contain persuasive strategies designed to: 1) motivate this target population to change, and 2) teach them specific interpersonal and behavioral skills for the successful adoption of these new behaviors [36]. In other words, it should do more than disseminate HIV information.

---

[2]The term "high-risk" is used by public health organizations including the CDC. The author uses this term to indicate particular segments of a community with high levels of HIV infection and it is not intended to imply blame or judgment of these groups.

For those individuals who are already HIV-infected, there is a need for a fourth type of health campaign: Education Program for Seropositive Asians/Asians Living with AIDS. The major goals of such a program are to: 1) provide social support for those who are infected, their significant others, and their families, 2) disseminate current medical and psychosocial information, and 3) encourage this group to seek early intervention within accepted medical and alternative treatment modalities.

Finally, as we enter the second decade of the AIDS epidemic, community organizing has been crucial in the development of more comprehensive HIV/AIDS programs targeting diverse segments of the A/PI communities. For service delivery to be successful with A/PI clients, trust must be an essential ingredient in the provider-client relationship [38]. Based on the concept of trust, community collaboration, and cultural appropriateness, a number of community-based programs has emerged in cities with large A/PI populations including New York, Los Angeles, and San Francisco. These activities started as "community services" supported by in-kind or small funds from community-based organizations including the New York Chinatown Health Clinic, Asian Health Services, Asian Health Project of T.H.E. Clinic, and the Health Department of Hawaii. The Asian AIDS Project and Newcomer Health Services in San Francisco were some of the few programs which were funded specifically for Asians and Pacific Islanders in the mid-1980s.

According to Aoki and his associates, most of the activities of these programs were aimed primarily at the heterosexual Asian and Pacific Islander communities, and focused on information dissemination through brochures, presentations, hotlines, and media publicity [3]. An exception to the above was the "Stop AIDS Project" of the Asian AIDS Project in San Francisco which had client interaction during the education process and had targeted the gay community. Aoki and his colleagues attribute these conditions to the involvement of Asian health service agencies who have not historically delivered direct services to the gay and lesbian communities [3].

These programs also had several other characteristics. Most of the information disseminated emphasized that Asians and Pacific Islanders were not immune to the AIDS virus. This seemed to be in response to the misinformation common in the Asian and Pacific Islander communities that "some Asians do not get AIDS due to their immunity to the virus." This was probably reinforced by the lack of HIV/AIDS information for Asian and Pacific Islanders and perpetuated the image that "Asians do not catch HIV." In general, Asian HIV/AIDS education brochures and presentations were provided in multi-Asian languages, and de-emphasized issues of sex, sexuality and homosexuality.

During the late eighties—1987 to 1990—there were major changes in the development of A/PI HIV/AIDS education programs. Some funding became available for specific Asian and Pacific Islander communities from federal, state, and county governments and private foundations such as California Community

Foundation and the U.S. Conference of Mayors. In San Francisco, Asian American Recovery Services (AARS) received federal, state and city funds. In Oakland, the Association of Asian Pacific Community Health Organizations (AAPCHO) was funded by the Centers for Disease Control (CDC). In Los Angeles, community-based family planning clinics, T.H.E. Clinic-Asian Health Project, Chinatown Service Center, and Koryo Health Foundation received state funding to provide confidential HIV antibody testing. The Korean Health Education, Information, and Referral Center received funding from the U.S. Conference of Mayors. The Asian Pacific AIDS Education Project, a consortium-based HIV education project supported by the APHCV and Special Service for Groups, was funded by the County of Los Angeles. These grants resulted in the development of brochures for primary HIV education and testing information in A/PI languages, and in the training of Asian bilingual health educators to become HIV counselors. Other organizations also started their HIV education and information services. However, most of these education programs received relatively small funding to make any significant impact on the very diverse A/PI communities characterized by large percentages of newly arrived and conservative populations.

Parallel to the development of these HIV education and information programs for the general A/PI communities, the late 1980s also witnessed a rapid mobilization, development and implementation of HIV awareness and education programs in the A/PI gay, lesbian, and bisexual communities. After years of HIV/AIDS denial and ignorance, groups of men in A/PI gay organizations in San Francisco and Los Angeles began intense, catch-up HIV education programs for their communities. The Gay Asian Pacific Alliance Community HIV Project and the Asian Pacific Lesbian and Gays, Inc., became the front runners in the battle against HIV ignorance and denial. HIV awareness and education programs, direct services and advocacy for Asian and Pacific Islanders were developed and implemented.

A slow but steady bridge building between the A/PI gay and lesbian communities and the general A/PI communities began to materialize and form during this period. In Los Angeles, education on lesbian and gay awareness and sensitivity was incorporated into general HIV education programs. The direct result has been that A/PI community service agencies have hired openly gay and lesbian staff.

In early 1990, while Asian Pacific HIV education programs continued, there seemed to be a growing awareness and realization of the lack of prevention and intervention funding for A/PI communities. Asian and Pacific Islander community-based organizations began to critically examine the effectiveness and the gaps in their programs. Along with a lack of funding for culturally and linguistically appropriate HIV services, there was a recognition of the lack of sufficient numbers of A/PI service providers. There has also been serious consideration for A/PI gays to form coalitions with AIDS service providers from other minority communities.

Compared to early HIV education activities, there appears to be many new characteristics among the A/PI programs. There are some education programs which apply the self-efficacy health behavior change model and shifts from the Asian Pacific "fatalistic" to the Asian Pacific "take positive and constructive steps against HIV" mentalities are beginning to emerge. Among A/PI's, however, most of the motivation for behavioral change, in this model, has not been for their own individual health, but for the health of their significant others, particularly their family members. The underlying message was that the individual can protect their family from HIV infection by using condoms and other safer-sex methods.

The HIV education programs continue to convey basic information regarding HIV transmission modes, prevention methods, infection symptoms, and local antibody testing services and resources. Because of the continual arrival of new immigrants and refugees into the United States, these awareness and education issues remain the major focus of HIV programs. The need for these culturally and linguistically relevant programs continues because most local and national HIV/AIDS campaigns are conducted in the English language leaving many monolingual members of certain A/PI communities uninformed. The programs targeting the gay and lesbian community have become explicit and relevant to their culture. There has also been recognition that A/PI youth are at-risk for HIV infection because of existing cultural norms and attitudes about sex and sexuality that prevent effective HIV education in the general A/PI communities. Education and prevention messages, in brochures and in broad media public service announcements, now include more information on sexual transmission, more explicit safer-sex methods including condom usage, and discussion of sexual orientations.

More recently, the newly formed Asian Pacific AIDS Intervention Team (A/P AIT) started operation in the greater Los Angeles area. The major goal of A/P AIT is to educate about HIV/AIDS infection and to outreach and provide hope, support, advocacy, and resources for women and men of all Asian and Pacific Islander communities, and persons living with HIV infection, their families, and significant others. With the hope that HIV infection can remain relatively small among Asians, community-based organizations and programs continue to be at the forefront of the fight against HIV/AIDS in A/PI communities. However, there is an urgent need to integrate the strategies and efforts of such programs into a singular set of principles—based on theoretically sound concepts and models and practice driven techniques—that can be effectively applied and implemented in various segments of the A/PI communities at different stages of the HIV/AIDS risk reduction process.

To summarize, the A/PI communities have started to respond to the threat of HIV/AIDS; however, much work remains to be done. Culturally appropriate education programs need to: 1) increase community ownership of the epidemic, e.g., use communication strategies to promote the belief that AIDS is an Asian/Pacific Islander problem; 2) raise HIV transmission knowledge, e.g., disseminate information to promote higher levels of knowledge related to transmission, prevention, HIV testing, and early intervention; 3) increase personal perceptions of risk, e.g., use persuasive strategies to heighten perceptions of vulnerability to HIV; 4) modify perceptions of health protective actions including response efficacy, perceived enjoyment, and self-efficacy associated with these behaviors, e.g., use social influence techniques to change and maintain perceptions of condoms as effective, enjoyable, and easy to use; 5) disseminate information about available social support and other psychosocial services based on trust and cultural understanding, e.g., use mediated and interpersonal communication to encourage help-seeking behaviors, and 6) assist individuals in the acquisition of intimate communication and behavioral enactment skills, e.g., use cognitive-behavioral strategies to help target individuals learn to effectively communicate in sexual situations and to engage in protective actions. Finally, evaluation of such programs must be performed at each stage of design and implementation.

Future research must examine the potential utility of theoretical models of health behavior change in these communities as well as assess the effectiveness of current educational efforts. Because cultural factors influence all levels of communication, from social cognition and sexual scripts to public health campaigns, the role of culture and communication must be explicitly incorporated into HIV education models [57]. Additionally, future research must investigate the impact of culture on source, message, channel, receiver, and destination variables in this cultural communication process. Finally, future work must be done to examine culturally appropriate methods of program evaluation including standard assessments, e.g., pretest-posttest procedures and other quantitative testing measures, and process evaluations, e.g., qualitative analysis of outreach workers' journals and field notes. The fight against AIDS, at the research level, requires a multidisciplinary approach, and, at the community level, demands that different segments of the Asian and Pacific Islander population—young and old, gay and nongay, monolingual and multilingual, the more and less educated—come together to prevent further spread of the virus and to support and provide hope to those who are already infected.

REFERENCES

1. J. Ngin, More Asian Children Living in Poverty, *Asian Week*, pp. 1 and 17, June 14, 1991.
2. R. T. Schaefer, *Racial and Ethnic Groups, 5th Edition*, Harper Collins, New York, 1983.
3. B. Aoki, C. P. Ngin, B. Mo, and D. Y. Ja, AIDS Prevention Models in Asian-American Communities, in *Primary Prevention of AIDS: Psychological Approaches*, V. M. Mays, G. W. Albee, and S. F. Schneider (eds.), Sage, Newbury Park, California, pp. 290-308, 1989.

4. D. A. Lee and K. Fong, HIV/AIDS and the Asian and Pacific Islander Community, *SIECUS Report*, February/March, pp. 16-22, 1990.

5. J. E. Osborn, A Risk Assessment of the AIDS Epidemic, in *Primary Prevention of AIDS: Psychological Approaches*, V. M. Mays, G. W. Albee, and S. F. Schneider (eds.), Sage, Newbury Park, California, pp. 23-38, 1989.

6. G. L. Albrecht, J. A. Levy, N. M. Sugrue, T. R. Prohaska, and D. G. Ostrow, Who Hasn't Heard about AIDS? *AIDS Education and Prevention, 1,* pp. 261-267, 1989.

7. Asian AIDS Project, D. Y. Ja, and P. Ngin, *AIDS in the Asian Community: A Review and Analysis,* Bay View Hunter's Point Foundation, San Francisco, California, 1987.

8. J. S. Mandel and K. J. Kitano, San Francisco Looks at AIDS in Southeast Asia, *Multicultural Inquiry Research AIDS Quarterly Newsletter, 3,* p. 7, 1989.

9. J. M. Woo, G. W. Rutherford, S. F. Payne, J. L. Barnhart, and G. F. Lemp, The Epidemiology of AIDS in Asian and Pacific Islander Populations in San Francisco, *AIDS, 2,* pp. 473-475, 1988.

10. G. A. Yep, HIV Prevention among Asian-American College Students: Does the Health Belief Model Work? *Journal of American College Health, 41,* pp. 199-205, 1993.

11. D. Sue, Sexual Experience and Attitudes of Asian-American Students, *Psychological Reports, 51,* pp. 401-402, 1982.

12. A. Slagle-Stello, Premarital Sex Gaining in Popularity among Asians, *Ka Leo O Hawai'i,* p. 4, November 24, 1991.

13. S. D. Cochran, V. M. Mays, and L. Leung, Sexual Practices of Heterosexual Asian-American Young Adults: Implications for Risk of HIV Infection, *Archives of Sexual Behavior, 20,* pp. 381-391, 1991.

14. J. A. Catania, T. J. Coates, S. M. Kegeles, M. Ekstrand, J. R. Guydish, and L. L. Bye, Implications of the AIDS Risk Reduction Model for the Gay Community: The Importance of Perceived Sexual Enjoyment and Help-Seeking Behaviors, in *Primary Prevention of AIDS: Psychological Approaches,* V. M. Mays, G. W. Albee, and S. F. Schneider (eds.), Sage, Newbury Park, California, pp. 242-261, 1989.

15. J. A. Catania, S. M. Kegeles, and T. J. Coates, Towards an Understanding of Risk Behavior: An AIDS Risk Reduction Model (ARRM), *Health Education Quarterly, 17,* pp. 53-72, 1990.

16. J. P. Kirscht and J. G. Joseph, The Health Belief Model: Some Implications for Behavior Change, with Reference to Homosexual Males, in *Primary Prevention of AIDS: Psychological Approaches,* V. M. Mays, G. W. Albee, and S. F. Schneider (eds.), Sage, Newbury Park, California, pp. 111-127, 1989.

17. L. A. Maiman and M. H. Becker, The Health Belief Model: Origins and Correlates in Psychological Theory, *Health Education Monographs, 2,* pp. 336-353, 1974.

18. A. Bandura, Self-Efficacy: Toward a Unifying Theory of Behavior Change, *Psychological Review, 84,* pp. 191-215, 1977.

19. A. Bandura, Perceived Self-Efficacy in the Exercise of Control over AIDS Infection, in *Primary Prevention of AIDS: Psychological Approaches,* V. M. Mays, G. W. Albee, and S. F. Schneider (eds.), Sage, Newbury Park, California, pp. 128-141, 1989.

20. I. L. Janis, Effects of Fear Arousal on Attitude Change: Recent Developments in Theory and Experimental Research, in *Advances in Experimental Social Psychology, 3,* L. Berkowitz (ed.), Academic Press, New York, pp. 166-225, 1967.

21. H. Leventhal, Changing Attitudes and Habits to Reduce Risk Factors in Chronic Disease, *American Journal of Cardiology, 31,* pp. 571-580, 1973.
22. M. Fishbein and I. Ajzen, *Belief, Attitude, Intention, and Behavior: An Introduction to Theory and Research,* Addison-Wesley, Reading, Massachusetts, 1975.
23. M. Fishbein and S. E. Middlestadt, Using the Theory of Reasoned Action as a Framework for Understanding and Changing AIDS-Related Behaviors, in *Primary Prevention of AIDS: Psychological Approaches,* V. M. Mays, G. W. Albee, and S. F. Schneider (eds.), Sage, Newbury Park, California, pp. 93-110, 1989.
24. E. M. Rogers, *Diffusion of Innovation,* Free Press, New York, 1983.
25. E. Fischer, D. Winer, and S. Abramowitz, Seeking Professional Help for Psychological Problems, in *New Directions in Helping: Applied Perspectives on Help Seeking and Receiving,* 3, A. Nadler, J. Fisher, and B. DePaulo (eds.), Academic Press, New York, pp. 163-185, 1983.
26. A. Gross and P. McMullen, Models of the Help Seeking Process, in *New Directions in Helping: Help Seeking,* 2, B. DePaulo, A. Nadler, and J. Fisher (eds.), Academic Press, New York, pp. 45-70, 1983.
27. R. J. DiClemente, J. Zorn, and L. Temoshok, The Association of Gender, Ethnicity, and Length of Residence in the Bay Area to Adolescents' Knowledge and Attitudes about Acquired Immune Deficiency Syndrome, *Journal of Applied Social Psychology, 17,* pp. 216-230, 1987.
28. D. Siegel, N. Lazarus, F. Krasnovsky, M. Durbin, and M. Chesney, AIDS Knowledge, Attitudes, and Behavior among Inner City, Junior High School Students, *Journal of School Health, 61,* pp. 160-165, 1991.
29. L. Strunin, Adolescents' Perceptions of Risk for HIV Infection: Implications for Future Research, *Social Science and Medicine, 32,* pp. 221-228, 1991.
30. W. J. Brown, Culture and HIV Education: Reaching High-Risk Heterosexuals in Asian-American Communities, *Journal of Applied Communication Research, 20,* pp. 275-291, 1992.
31. L. Gorrez and M . R. G. Araneta, *AIDS Knowledge, Attitudes, Beliefs, and Behaviors in a Household Survey of Filipinos in San Francisco: Findings, Summary, and Conclusions,* Department of Public Health, San Francisco, California, 1990.
32. D. Y. Ja, K. J. Kitano, and A. Ebata, *Report on a Survey of AIDS Knowledge, Attitudes and Behaviors in San Francisco's Chinese Communities: Executive Summary,* Asian American Recovery Services, Inc., San Francisco, California, 1990.
33. D. Y. Ja, K. J. Kitano, and A. Ebata, *Report on a Survey of AIDS Knowledge, Attitudes and Behaviors in San Francisco's Japanese Communities: Executive Summary,* Asian American Recovery Services, Inc., San Francisco, California, 1990.
34. K. J. Kitano, *Correlates of AIDS-Associated High-Risk Behavior among Chinese and Filipino Gay Men,* unpublished master's thesis, University of California, Berkeley, California, 1988.
35. G. A. Yep, *The Effects of Community-Based HIV/AIDS Education and Prevention Messages on Knowledge, Attitudes and Behavioral Enactment Skills among Asian Men,* paper presented at the Ninth International and Intercultural Communication Conference, Miami, Florida, May 1992.
36. G. A. Yep, First Asian/Pacific Island Men's HIV Conference, Los Angeles, California, *AIDS Education and Prevention, 5,* pp. 87-88, 1993.

37. B. Aoki and D. Y. Ja, *AIDS and Asian Americans: Psychosocial Issues,* paper presented at the Annual Meeting of the American Psychological Association, New York, August 1987.

38. S. Jue, Identifying and Meeting the Needs of Minority Clients with AIDS, in *Responding to AIDS: Psychosocial Initiatives,* C. G. Leukefeld and M. Fimbres (eds.), National Association of Social Workers, Silver Springs, Maryland, pp. 65-79, 1987.

39. P. R. Abramson, The Cultural Context of Japanese Sexuality, *Psychologia, 21,* pp. 1-9, 1986.

40. S. Wu and S. Pak, The Hidden Minority: Perspectives on Being Asian and Gay, *East Wind, 2,* pp. 22-25, 1989.

41. G. A. Yep, *Attitude toward Condoms and AIDS-Phobia among Gay/Bisexual Asian Men: An Assessment of a Community-Based HIV Education Program,* paper presented to the 79th Annual Meeting of the Speech Communication Association, Miami, Florida, November 1993.

42. K. S. Larsen, R. Elder, M. Bader, and C. Dougard, Authoritarianism and Attitudes toward AIDS Victims, *Journal of Social Psychology, 130,* pp. 77-80, 1990.

43. D. Altman, *AIDS in the Mind of America,* Anchor Press/Doubleday, Garden City, New York, 1986.

44. R. J. W. Cline and M. F. Boyd, Communication as Threat and Therapy: Stigma, Social Support, and Coping with HIV Infection, in *Case Studies in Health Communication,* E. B. Ray (ed.), Lawrence Erlbaum, Hillsdale, New Jersey, pp. 131-147, 1993.

45. G. M. Herek and E. K. Glunt, An Epidemic of Stigma: Public Relations to AIDS, *American Psychologist, 43,* pp. 886-891, 1988.

46. J. A. Kelly, J. S. St. Lawrence, S. Smith, H. V. Hood, and D. J. Cook, Stigmatization of AIDS Patients by Physicians, *American Journal of Public Health, 77,* pp. 789-791, 1987.

47. J. A. Kelly, J. S. St. Lawrence, S. Smith, H. V. Hood, and D. J. Cook, Medical Students' Attitudes toward AIDS and Homosexual Patients, *Journal of Medical Education, 62,* pp. 549-556, 1987.

48. L. S. Lewis and L. M. Range, Do Means of Transmission, Risk Knowledge, and Gender Affect AIDS Stigma and Social Interactions? *Journal of Social Behavior and Personality, 7,* pp. 211-216, 1992.

49. F. P. O'Brien, Work-Related Fear of AIDS and Social-Desirability Response Bias, *Psychological Reports, 65,* pp. 371-378, 1989.

50. J. H. Pleck, L. O'Donnell, and J. Snarey, AIDS-Phobia, Contact with AIDS, and AIDS-Related Job Stress in Hospital Workers, *Journal of Homosexuality, 15:3/4,* pp. 41-54, 1988.

51. K. Murase, Models of Service Delivery in Asian American Communities, in *Social Work Practice with Asian Americans,* S. M. Furuto, R. Biswas, D. K. Chung, K. Murase, and F. Ross-Sheriff (eds.), Sage, Newbury Park, California, pp. 101-120, 1992.

52. H. K. Hatanaka, B. Y. Watanabe, and S. Ono, The Utilization of Mental Health Services in the Los Angeles Area, in *Service Delivery in Pan Asian Communities,* W. H. Ishikawa and N. H. Archer (eds.), Pacific Asian Coalition, San Diego, California, pp. 33-39, 1975.

53. S. Sue and H. McKinney, Asian Americans in the Community Mental Health Care System, *American Journal of Orthopsychiatry, 45,* pp. 111-118, 1975.
54. E. G. Shapiro, Embarrassment and Help-Seeking, in *New Directions in Helping: Help-Seeking,* 2, B. M. DePaulo, A. Nadler, and J. D. Fisher (eds.), Academic Press, New York, pp. 143-163, 1983.
55. T. Edgar and M. A. Fitzpatrick, Compliance-Gaining in Relational Interaction: When Your Life Depends on It, *Southern Speech Communication Journal, 53,* pp. 385-405, 1988.
56. T. E. Backer, E. M. Rogers, and P. Sopory, *Designing Health Communication Campaigns: What Works?* Sage, Newbury Park, California, 1992.
57. P. Michal-Johnson and S. P. Bowen, The Place of Culture in HIV Education, in *AIDS: A Communication Perspective,* T. Edgar, M. A. Fitzpatrick, and V. S. Freimuth (eds.), Lawrence Erlbaum, Hillsdale, New Jersey, pp. 147-172, 1992.

[This project was partially supported by the California Universitywide AIDS Research Program (Grant Agreement C91 APHC001)].

CHAPTER 11

Sociology of AIDS within Black Communities: Theoretical Considerations

Clarence Spigner

This chapter does not present cause and effect behavioral explanations for the lethal acquired immune deficiency syndrome/human immunodeficiency virus (AIDS/HIV) infections in black communities. Instead it provides three social theory frameworks that enable health educators understand behavioral responses to AIDS within black populations. These social theory frameworks, expressed from the discipline of sociology by Turner [1], Collins [2], Scambler [3], and others, are conflict theory, in terms of economic stratification, functionalism, in terms of societal marginality, and interactionism, in terms of deviance or stigmatization. Sociologist Talcott Parsons, as a specific example, used functionalism to make a direct application of medicine to the discipline of sociology [4].

Black or African Americans, as a group, have been shown to be continually overrepresented in several categories of morbidity and mortality [5]. Therefore, any understanding of illnesses and deaths from AIDS should also be considered within social frameworks.

A brief chronology of the AIDS crisis followed by epidemiological data of AIDS is presented. The significance of the discipline sociology to understanding AIDS among blacks is provided, followed by the three theoretical frameworks.

BRIEF CHRONOLOGY OF U.S. AIDS CRISIS

AIDS was not presented as a black health problem when it became acknowledged in America's gay male culture during the summer of 1981. But by October

1986, the Center for Disease Control (CDC) announced that blacks and Hispanics accounted for 25 and 15 percent of the reported AIDS cases, respectively. At that time, blacks and Hispanics accounted for only 11.5 and 6.4 percent of the U.S. population (based upon 1980 U.S. Census). The link between intravenous (IV) drug use and AIDS became evident. In fact by September 1986, fear of AIDS was cited as a reason drug abusers in New York City shifted from heroin to crack and powered cocaine [6]. By 1989, the cocaine drug wars fought largely by black inner-city youths replaced AIDS in the headlines. The disease became less of a "cause celebre." Moreover, health education for AIDS prevention has proven more effective among white gay males than among IV drug users [7].

As of January 1990, CDC charted a total of 121,645 AIDS/HIV cases in the United States. Black Americans represent about 27 percent (33,419) of the total AIDS cases (thus far) while only 12.7 percent of the U.S. population (1988 U.S. Census). Whites are now 56 percent (68,034) of the total AIDS cases [8].

Of the total number of AIDS cases among females (11,052) as of January 1990, black females accounted for over 50 percent (5,719). By comparison, white females made up only 27 percent (2,996). Almost 30 percent (3,297) of black females were exposed to the AIDS virus through IV drug use compared to only 11 percent (1,216) of white women. Sixteen percent (1,801) of black females contracted AIDS through heterosexual contact, compared with only 7 percent (808) of white females [8].

Of the total number of AIDS cases among males (108,538) as of January 1990, black males comprised 24 percent (26,624). Ten percent (11,887) acquired AIDS by homosexual/bisexual contact compared to 48 percent (51,873) of white males. Only 3 percent (3,869) of heterosexual white males contacted AIDS through IV drug use compared with over 8 percent (9,270) black heterosexual IV drug users [8].

Total pediatric AIDS cases as of January 1990 were 2,055 (1.7 percent of total). Among the white children, 53 percent were born to mothers with or at risk for AIDS/HIV infection. But among black and Hispanic children, 91 percent and 85 percent respectively, were born to mothers with/or at risk for AIDS/HIV infections [8].

AIDS cases among blacks (and Hispanics) is presently double their current population in the United States.

THE SOCIOLOGY OF AIDS AMONG BLACKS

AIDS represents yet another socio-behavioral disease that disproportionately affects too many African Americans. In January 1986, the year CDC reported increase of AIDS cases among minorities and IV drug users, the Department of Health and Human Services (DHHS) secretary received a report of "excess deaths" among blacks and other minorities from The Task Force on Black and Minority Health. Using the white rate as a standard, the report found 80 percent of excess deaths (the black death rates above the white death rates) among blacks due to cancer, cardiovascular disease and stroke, chemical dependency, diabetes, and homicide and accidents. The Task Force considered demographics, environment and occupations, nutrition, and stress and coping patterns as important social factors related to the excess death rates [5]. Thus, social factors were recognized as significant. This point is particularly important in understanding the AIDS epidemic in the black community.

The more functional participation in combating AIDS during the 1980s tended to be dominated by whites. The relative lack of black participation is explained in part by their low representation in health professions and higher education. For example, a 1987 DHHS Report of Minorities and Women in the Health Fields [9] indicated that blacks made up only 3 percent of the natural scientist occupations, 3 percent of the health diagnosis occupations, and only 4 percent of college/university teachers. This same report, along with the 1986 Task Force Report to the DHHS secretary, as well as the National Research Council's (NRC) Committee on the Status of Black Americans report [10] all stressed the social consequence of the decline of black enrollments in medical schools and health related institutions.

Hence, the epidemiology of AIDS in the black communities had come to reflect social-economic stratification, societal marginality, and social stigmatization of the society in which AIDS occurred.

Black people's response to AIDS (as well as other health problems) needs to be considered within the social conditions they occur. Some health providers, building upon previous socio-behavioral theories, might attribute AIDS among blacks as the result of Moynihan's "Tangle of Pathology" [11], or Lewis' "Culture of Poverty" [12] theories. Such perspectives view the plight of blacks as more products of their own familial or cultural shortcomings. The external structures which also account for such characteristics are given less consideration. In conjunction is the perspective of Health Promotion, which focuses on individual responsibility for health as voiced by McKeowen [13] and others. Such a view of "individualism" was nurtured in the 1980s by the Reagan-Bush presidential administrations, with their expressed attitudes that the disadvantaged should "pull themselves up by their own bootstraps."

The main theme put forth in this chapter is that many blacks remained at-risk for inadequate health due more to poverty and racism: both societal factors, and less for individual or lifestyle shortcomings. AIDS among blacks can be better understood within the sociological perspectives expressed by conflict, functionalist, and interactive social theories.

SOCIAL THEORIES AND BLACK RESPONSE TO AIDS

Conflict Theory and Economic Stratification

The Conflict perspective for understanding behavior is grounded in the assumption that society is an arena where groups battle over scarce resources in pursuit of their own interests. This is especially evident in capitalist countries such as the

United States. For instance, health scholars Navarro [14], Cooper [15], and Waitzkins [16] have expressed this view from the perspective of political economist Karl Marx (1818–1883).

Evidence consistently show that most people of color within white dominated capitalist societies, even those with more socialized health systems such as England [17] and Australia [18], still tend to have inadequate health status. In the United States specifically, the median income for blacks in 1987 was $18,098, while for whites it was $32,274. Also, 33.1 percent of Blacks were below the official poverty line compared to 10.5 percent of whites [19]. Blacks tend to be overrepresented in high education and in the health professions, concentrated in the inner cities, more victimized by the criminal justice system, and continue to face subtle and blatant forms of racial discrimination a quarter century after the 1964 Civil Rights Act [10].

In accord with conflict or social stratification theory, blacks are not as effectively empowered as whites to respond to AID/HIV health promotion programs because of economic stratification. The eighties decade of AIDS prevalence was exacerbated by addiction to illegal drugs like heroin and then "crack" cocaine. Illness resulting from such illegal drug use drove at-risk populations of blacks still further into the underground and away from mainstream medical treatment, rehabilitation, and cure.

Conflict theory would view the economic position of blacks and their health status as an intentional consequence of capitalism. Blacks, coming from a history of slavery and still one-third (in 1987) below the poverty level would respond to the AIDS crisis as conditioned by their economic positions. Interestingly, black scholars such as William Julius Wilson see race as less significant than economic stratification [20]. Thus, because of class determinants, at risk populations of blacks would not have the economic prerequisites to empower themselves as effectively as whites or white gay males. In fact, the NCR's report found that "Since the early 1970s, the economic status of blacks relative to whites has, on the average, stagnated or deteriorated" [10, p. 61]. Thus it is much more difficult for at-risk populations of blacks to respond as effectively to AIDS health education programs.

Functionalist Theory and Social Mainstreaming

The functionalist perspective of society was conceptually viewed by early sociologists Auguste Comte (1798–1857) and Herbert Spencer (1820–1903) as analogous to an organism made up of interdependent parts, each contributing to the functioning of the whole society [1]. Anthropologists introduced terms like "acculturation," "assimilation," and "marginality" to describe various efforts of distinct racial and ethnic groups to attempt to fit into the social mainstream. Blacks (and other minorities) have exhibited a long history as functional or mainstream seeking behavior.

The desire to fit marginal groups into the social mainstream involved blacks at every societal level. The "social engineering phase" (from 1960–1975) of public health's history described by Green [21] articulated the U.S. government's role after recognition of the social inequalities in health. Government was seen as a mechanism to help fit disadvantaged (or dysfunctional) groups into the functional mainstream. It was no accident that the President Johnson's "War on Poverty" and "New Society" programs also ushered in Medicaid and Medicare government health insurance during the Civil Rights Movement; a movement of integration initiated by blacks demanding fair representation within all levels of the social structure.

However, from this functionalist view, an intimate association with a deadly and mysterious disease like AIDS even a quarter a century since the 1964 Civil Rights Act would detract rather than enhance black movement into the social mainstream. Blacks already marginalized by *defacto* and *dejure* segregation practices may be more reluctant to acknowledge a stigmatizing disease such as AIDS/HIV.

AIDS infections grew among black populations largely because of socio-economic conditions. High risk blacks are more likely to be low-income, dependent on government assistance, minimally or unemployed, have more substandard housing and amenities, inadequately educated, and exposed to more environmental stressors. Their race becomes a disadvantaged social status because of discrimination. As a result, economic status diminishes or stagnates along with feelings of self-inadequacy.

Chemical dependency among some blacks, which is concurrent with AIDS infections, may drive many to illegal acts (if not the use of the drug itself), thus becoming labeled as criminals. Thus they are pushed still further outside the mainstream. Drug dependency often results in sickness. However, the Parsonian concept of illness behavior can't manifest itself because the criminal label puts the individual outside the functional steps of "the sick role" [4].

The sum of all these attributes conceptually produces at risk Blacks as dysfunctional within a society which theoretically desires to integrate everyone into a functional whole.

Interactionist Theory and Stigmatization

Interactionism is concerned with the relationship between the individual and society. Charles Horton Cooley (1864–1929) and George Herbert Mead's (1863–1931) view of the self as a result of social processes are significant [1]. Mutually accepted definitions of things are continually created and recreated through social interaction. Put simply, what people think of themselves is a result of what others think of them.

For example, Conrad and Schneider have shown how the gay rights movement of the early 1970s was highly influential in making the medical establishment—

mainly the American Psychiatric Association, discontinue its diagnostic classification of homosexuality as "sexually deviant behavior" [22]. Thus, the stigma of being homosexual was dealt a decisive blow. Ironically, the "Black Is Beautiful" ideology fostered from the 1960s Civil Rights Movement served as a catalyst for gays becoming more accepting of their own lifestyle. But unlike gays, blacks and other racial minorities have historically had to cope with discrimination based upon race rather than lifestyle. Such shared prejudices against a visible minority by a powerful majority is harder to overcome than expression of sexual preference.

Interactionism, with its symbolic and socio-psychological approach, takes a micro-sociological view of human behavior. Hence, the question became how blacks with AIDS were to be socially or culturally perceived by the greater society. A deeper question was black self concept regarding the prevalence of AIDS/HIV.

Symbolically, the term "black" is associated with bad and evil (e.g., black plague, black magic, blackmail, blackball, black Friday, dark cloud, dark forces, etc.). Black people have been linked with lower intelligence [23], criminal behavior [24], and cultural pathology [11,12]. Since interactionism is a dynamic ever-changing process (recall the pre-1970s view of homosexuality as a medical illness), black American behavior regarding the AIDS crisis could stem from fear of labels of deviance or stigmatization supported by the medical establishment's initial politicalization of AIDS as a social problem.

A major example of such medical politicalization was the linking of AIDS with Haitian immigrants in 1983. Sabatier [25], Vaieira [26], and others have pointed out the political ramifications of AIDS being directly linked with a race and a nationality, two things people have very little control over, rather than a lifestyle, something many health promotion advocates believe people can control. In October 1983, a study in the *New England Journal of Medicine* found the sixty-one Haitians suspected of having AIDS had homosexual relations with Americans. Seven months earlier in March, the American Red Cross named homosexual men, drug users, and Haitians as being at-risk for AIDS and not to donate blood. Two years later, in April 1985, the CDC stopped including Haitians on the list of those considered at greatest risk for contacting AIDS. But by July 1986 due to CDC reports of unusual clusters of the disease showing up in Florida and not matching the pattern anywhere else in the nation, Haitians were the first group named at risk by heterosexual transmission of AIDS [6].

The Haitian-AIDS connection is important to interactionist theory for several reasons. Haitian immigrants, most of whom are black, were initially viewed by the medical establishment as a main force of spread of AIDS to the United States. Haitians were viewed as agents for AIDS/HIV infections initially because they were Haitians and less for any behavior associated with contacting the disease. This view subsequently changed. But this cultural perception of Haitians so angered black University of California professor Michael Leguerre that he wrote, "With innuendoes, racist overtones, and inaccuracies, the popular press has described Haitian immigrants in the United States as illiterate, disease-ridden Voo Doo practitioners, and debated whether Haitians are political or economic refugees" [27].

The Haitian experience resulted in a group of blacks being labeled, treated punitively, and disenfranchised solely because their race and nationality was associated with AIDS/HIV. Such labels, legitimized by the government and the medical establishment, were exacerbated by the reports in the popular press.

Moreover, many in the black community may not trust government sanctioned health projects. Health education scholar Nick Freudenberg [28] and others have cautioned that black communities may be suspicious of government sponsored health programs regarding AIDS because of the forty-year-long Tuskegee Syphilis Experiment conducted by the U.S. Public Health Services. In this infamous study, more than 400 illiterate black men were observed and untreated for syphilis from 1932 to 1972 [29]. Thus, such historical and political events have acted to help shape black people's perception of their minority status in predominant white society.

Overall, the social arrangements of status dictated by the visibility of race kept blacks marginalized outside of the social mainstream of effective health education. Blacks at virtually every social level may have even more reason to fear yet another label when the stigma may act to keep them still further away from adequate health status and health provision. As a specific group of political, economic, and socially vulnerable people, an association with such a mysterious and lethal virus can cause understandable intrepidation.

Health promotion strategies have been more effective among whites (and white gays) because many have the required prerequisites such as adequate education, media identification, high motivation, self efficacy, more leisure time choices, etc. As a result, this group has the political power to influence AIDS policy. Journalist Nat Hentoff describes part of this group as the "AIDS establishment" and "composed of public health officials, gay rights and AIDS advocacy groups, and the American Civil Liberties Union" [30]. Plus, white gays are not as visible as blacks. The unequal distribution of the benefits of society along racial lines continues to exacerbate the occurrence and treatment of AIDS/HIV and related drug dependency among African Americans.

CONCLUSIONS AND RECOMMENDATIONS

This article looked back on the AIDS crisis of the 1980s. The overall conclusion is that blacks were denied equal representation within virtually all segments of American society, and as a consequence, effective health promotion against AIDS was seriously hindered. The present high numbers of blacks with AIDS as well as drug abuse cases, along with the small representation of black health professionals can be viewed within the context of social class (Conflict Theory), lack of social integration (Functionalist Theory), and social stigmatization (Interactionist

Theory). The recommendations below have both short-term and long-term policy implications. Many of these suggestions are already operational, and are thus reemphasized for the 1990s to prevent a repeat of the mistakes of the 1980s.

Political Empowerment and Use of Role Models

Blacks (and other minorities) need to be in visible, responsible, and meaningful roles at every level of the health professions. The underrepresentation of blacks in the top hierarchy of the health system has significant ramifications, DHHS secretary Louis Sullivan, notwithstanding. Blacks need to share proportionally in the power to plan, implement, operationalize, and evaluate health delivery programs at local, state, regional, national, and international levels.

Health policy (thus social change) is grounded in research and mass communications. Some influential works published during the eighties often were critical of Randy Shilts' acclaimed book, *And the Band Played On* (St. Martin's Press: New York, 1987) because, among other things, the book hardly mentioned minorities or women. Another book about health policies in the 1980s was Richard Sorian's *The Bitter Pill* (McGraw-Hill: New York, 1988). A specific chapter devoted to a chronology of the AIDS crisis under the Reagan administration mentioned gays and gay organizations, but not of Blacks or other minorities regarding AIDS policy. Such omissions could be ameliorated by more black representation as journalists and researchers.

Health planner Henrik Blum [31] has suggested the use of minority health professionals as role models at the macro level (between groups, communities, organizations, and institutions). In conjunction, behavioral scientist Albert Bandura [32] has pointed out the efficacy of "modeling" in biobehavioral change at the cognitive or micro level. The point is that individuals who share the life experiences of populations at-risk must be meaningfully involved at every level of the health delivery process. This means a renewed emphasis of Affirmative Action programs in higher education. A study by Keith et al. of a medical school class of 1975 affirmed that Black and Hispanic physicians tended to serve patient populations much like their non-minority colleagues [33]. Similar conclusions were presented in the NCR's Report on the status of black Americans [33].

If Blacks are to be the beneficiaries of health promotion, then a more participatory role and role-models are needed.

Coalitions and Networks

There is a white majority at almost every level and segment of the AIDS and drug dependency crisis. Such *de facto* segregation remains indicative of health research and education efforts regarding the AIDS and now the cocaine epidemic. Black Americans themselves have long tradition of helping one another. The predominant non-minority health educators need to network and build meaningful coalitions for effective interaction in black communities. To help facilitate this, public and private health funding agencies should require documented evidence of racial minority input. Where such input is not evident or meaningful, those agencies should restrict funding.

Race-Specific Health Education

This suggestion may be the most troubling of all, because to some it implies separation. But race-specific strategies are needed to target specific problems and overcome health education barriers (which have resulted largely because of poverty and racism). Such race-specific strategies should be multi-faceted and interdependent while assuring sensitivity for possible stigmatization. Various demographic factors must be articulated in health promotion programs. Moreover, such strategies should be evaluated for race-relevance at the formative, impact, and outcome stages for maximum effectiveness.

No racial minority community is monolithic. Even within specific target populations of black and Hispanic IV drug users who are heterosexual and at-risk for AIDS/HIV, there are various sub-populations which are unique. Wilkinson and King have pointed out the conceptual and methodological problems of using race as a variable [34]. In terms of identification alone there are blacks with Spanish surnames and Hispanics who identify themselves as black. There are blacks from Caribbean, Central America and South America. Some blacks have Asian surnames.

Each of these black sub-groups have important differences in economic, regional, linguistic, and religious orientations which influence health and lifestyle behavior. Any health or disease prevention, intervention, and treatment program must be very sensitive in considering these demographic and cultural factors. Representative participation in health promotion programs will help address this issue.

Sex-specific health education is also a key issue in minority communities. Recall that by October 1986, CDC reported that 70 percent of women with AIDS were Black or Hispanic. By the end of the eighties decade, three times as many black women were exposed to the AIDS virus as white women. Also, just as the teaching of condom use is complicated by "machismo" and the Roman Catholic Church within Hispanic communities, among some blacks, an absence male head of household complicates setting an adequate example of responsible expressions of manhood. Health education needs to consider these and related factors with sensitive and innovative interventions in order to avoid victim-blaming.

In conclusion, blacks have less economic power, are more likely to be viewed as dysfunctional, and run the continual risk of social stigmatization. Strategies which are empowering and are race/ethnic specific are required in addressing the alarming growth of AIDS and chemical dependency among portions of the African American population.

REFERENCES

1. J. H. Turner, *The Structure of Sociological Theory*, Dorsey Press, Illinois, 1978.
2. R. Collins, *Three Sociological Traditions*, Oxford University Press, 1985.
3. G. Scambler (ed.), *Sociological Theory and Medical Sociology*, Tavistock Publications, London, 1987.
4. T. Parsons, Social Structure and Dynamic Process: The Case of Modern Medical Practice, *The Social System*, New York, pp. 428–479, 1951.
5. U.S. Department of Health and Human Service, *Task Force on Black and Minority Health*, U.S. Government Printing Office, August 1985.
6. R. Malinowsky and G. J. Perry, Chronology, *AIDS Information Sourcebook*, Ornyx Press, Phoenix, 1988.
7. W. Winkelstein, Jr., M. Samuel, and N. S. Padian, the San Francisco Men's Health Study: III, Reduction in Human Immunodeficiency Virus Transmission among Homosexual/Bisexual Men, 1982–1986, *American Journal of Public Health, 77*, pp. 685–689, 1987.
8. U.S. Department of Health and Human Services, *HIV/AIDS Surveillance*, (U.S. AIDS cases reported through January 1990), Issued February 1990, Centers for Disease Control, U.S. Government Printing Office, Washington, D.C., 1990.
9. U.S. Department of Health and Human Services, *Minorities and Women in the Health Fields, 1987*, U.S. Government Printing Office, Washington, D.C., 1987.
10. National Research Council, *A Common Destiny: Blacks in American Society*, National Academy Press, Washington, D.C., 1989.
11. D. P. Moynihan, The Negro Family and the Case for National Action, in *The Moynihan Report and the Politics of Controversy*, L. Rainwater and W. L. Yancy, (eds.), M.I.T. Press, Massachusetts, 1967.
12. O. Lewis, *La Vida: A Puerto Rican Family in the Culture of Poverty—San Juan and New York*, Random House, New York, 1966.
13. T. McKeown, Determinants of Health, *Human Nature, 1*:66, April 1978.
14. V. Navarro, *Medicine Under Capitalism*, Prodist, New York, 1976.
15. R. Cooper, Race, Disease and Health, in *Health, Race, and Ethnicity*, T. Rathwell and D. Phillips, (eds.), Croom Helm, London, 1986.
16. H. Waitzkins, A Marxist View of Health and Health Care, in *Handbook of Health, Health Care and Health Professions*, D. Mechanic, (ed.), Free Press, New York, 1983.
17. J. L. Donovan, Ethnicity and Health: A Research Review, *Social Science and Medicine, 19*:11, pp. 633–670, 1984.
18. N. Thomson, Australian Aboriginal Health and Health Care, *Social Science and Medicine, 18*:11, pp. 939–948, 1984.
19. U.S. Bureau of the Census, in *The Universal Almanac, 1990*, J. W. Wright, (ed.), Andrews & McMeel, Kansas City, 1990.
20. W. J. Wilson, The Ghetto Underclass and the Social Transformation of the Inner City, *The Black Scholar, 19*:3, pp. 10–17, 1988.
21. L. Green and C. L. Anderson, *Community Health* (5th Edition), Times Mirror/Mosby, St. Louis, 1980.
22. P. Conrad and J. W. Schneider, *Deviance and Medicalization: From Badness to Sickness*, C. V. Mosby, St. Louis, 1986.
23. A. Jensen, How Much Can We Boost I.Q. and Scholastic Achievement, *Harvard Education Review, 39*, pp. 1–123, 1969.

24. S. L. Hill, *Crime, Power, and Mortality*, Chandler Publishing, Scranton, 1971.
25. R. C. Sabatier, Social Cultural, and Demographic Aspects of AIDS, *Western Journal of Medicine, 147*:6, pp, 713–715, 1987.
26. J. Vieira, The Haitian Link, in *AIDS: Fact and Issues*, V. Gong and R. Rudnick (eds.), Rutgers University Press, New Jersey, 1987.
27. M. Leguerre, *American Odyssey: Haitians in New York City*, Cornell University Press, Ithaca, 1984.
28. N. Freudenberg, Historical Omissions: A Critique of *And The Band Plays On*, *Health/PAC Bulletin*, pp. 16-20, Spring 1988.
29. J. H. Jones, *Bad Blood: The Tuskegee Syphilis Experiment*, Free Press, New York, 1981.
30. N. Hentoff, Up against the AIDS Establishment, *The Washington Post*, p. A2, February 1, 1990.
31. H. Blum, *Planning for Health* (2nd Edition), Human Sciences Press, New York, 1981.
32. A. Bandura, Self Efficacy: Towards a Unifying Theory of Behavior Change, *Psychological Review, 84*:2, pp. 191–215, 1977.
33. S. N. Keith, R. M. Bell, A. G. Swanson, and A. P. Williams, Effects of Affirmative Action in Medical Schools: A Study of the Class of 1975, *New England Journal of Medicine, 313*:24, pp. 1519–1525, 1985.
34. D. Wilkinson and G. King, Conceptual and Methodological Issues in the Use of Race as a Variable: Policy Implications, *The Milbank Quarterly, 65*:(suppl. 1), pp. 56–71, 1987.

CHAPTER 12

AIDS in the African Press

Dana Lear

This study was undertaken to determine the role of mass media in dissemination of information about AIDS in sub-Saharan Africa. It was anticipated that newspapers would undertake an educative role given the lack of resources in most national health budgets. As it is generally accepted that AIDS seriously affects the urban elites of African countries, newspapers were thought to be a potentially effective means of communicating with these groups, and a mirror of their responses to the epidemic.

Several themes emerged to organize the material: how AIDS is portrayed, including the level of complexity of ideas, emotional objectivity and intensity, the amount of space, prominence and frequency of coverage; focus of the periodicals' campaign; the government's response; other content; discrimination, blame, and the role of the media.

METHODS

Newspapers were reviewed for Senegal, Togo, Uganda, Nigeria, Kenya, Botswana, Cameroun, Mali, Zaire, and Zimbabwe. The first five were selected for discussion as representative and because collections were complete between 1985 and 1989. Every available issue was surveyed from first coverage until June 1989.[1] Those reviewed were available at Stanford University or the University of California at Berkeley. All papers were at least majority government owned and

---

[1] With the exception of *The New Vision*, only available until end December 1988.

may not be representative of independent coverage. Varying degrees of party control were evident in content and editorial response.[2]

HOW AIDS IS PORTRAYED

The *Kenya Times* printed the first article among the sample with a large page one headline (October 8, 1985) 'MOI: REJECT AIDS CLAIMS.' It quoted the President encouraging Kenyans not to heed foreign propagandists, and to continue investment in Kenya. Lengthy center page spreads were devoted to information and education in mid-1986. By the end of 1986, however, Kenya became embroiled in the debate about the origin of the disease, a preoccupation reflected in the paper for the next year. The emotional intensity of the issue was marked. By 1988, emphasis shifted to the problem of controlling AIDS in Kenya. *New Vision* (Uganda) initiated coverage with 'Press overplaying AIDS scare' on June 24, 1986, three months after it began publication. The paper has published morbidity and mortality statistics and extensive educational articles. The first coverage of *La Nouvelle Marche* (Togo, September 4, 1986) reviewed the Third International Conference on AIDS in Paris. Subsequent coverage included articles on the worldwide situation, educational articles and information about trainings and seminars throughout the country. The government has neither acknowledged nor denied cases in Togo, but assumed the need for national education. Senegal's paper, *Le Soleil*, began coverage of AIDS in Africa on April 9, 1987 with a rather lurid full page one headline and photo, 'SIDA—LE MAL A NOS PORTES' ('AIDS—the evil at our door'). Inside were six pages of balanced, detailed and largely accurate coverage which set a precedent for future articles. The *Daily Times* of Nigeria began discussing AIDS in early 1987. The paper has not published educational articles, but has mainly reported on governmental activity and printed editorial and opinion pieces.

FOCUS OF EDUCATIONAL EFFORTS

The *Kenya Times'* first educational articles appeared August 27, 1986. Entitled 'AIDS; The Attitudes,' it reported that Nairobi had seen "a change for the better in behaviour." A survey of different parts of the country revealed that myths and misconceptions were still prevalent, that some people thought AIDS overwritten about, and others associated AIDS with ideas about traditional illness. Another center

---

[2] Senegal has five papers. The circulation for *Le Soleil* is given as 30,000. Nigeria has 26 papers. The *Times* is by far the largest, with 400,000. Kenya has 5 papers. The *Times* has a circulation of 36,000, less than the *Nation* (165,000), the *Standard* (49,000) and *Taifa Leo* (57,000). Togo has two papers: *Nouvelle Marche* (10,000) and the *Journal Officiél* (circulation not available). Uganda has 13 papers: the *New Vision* and *Taifa Uganda Empya* have 20,000 and 23,000 circulation respectively.

spread (August 31, 1986) included explanations about incubation time and transmission. Readers were advised that "individuals are responsible for ensuring that they do not contract the disease through indiscriminant sexual activity and the health authorities are responsible for seeing that wananchi do not get it through unsterilized needles or through contaminated blood transfusions."[3] The final article in the series (September 3, 1986) reviewed the situation in Kenya, including an article describing the symptoms of AIDS. This series of three articles were the extent of the *Times'* contribution to education, although extensive discourse developed regarding governmental AIDS-related activities.

La Nouvelle Marche considered that prevention ought to be aimed at following asymptomatic carriers (September 4, 1986) and include broad education for everyone, including information about condoms. The paper ran a series February 19-23, 1987, beginning with a page one headline stating "the situation is not a problem in Togo." An accompanying article gave prevention guidelines. The only piece among the papers directed at those infected advised that a seropositive woman was "obliged to submit herself to contraceptive methods. . . . Seropositive people have a collective and individual moral responsibility. They must follow medical advice and respect all preventive measures." The last article in the series reiterated that "in order to avoid spreading the epidemic, it is necessary for everyone to be informed about the virus, its mode of transmission and to respect all measures of prevention recommended by the health authorities." *Le Soleil* published a similar series (April 9-11, 1987). Le Soleil appeared to be a sophisticated urban newspaper aimed at a well educated readership. Educational information was provided in quotes from key officials. Coverage of the national AIDS committee's prevention campaign has emphasized changing "dangerous" behavior, or using condoms if behavior change is not possible (September 29, 1988). However, dangerous behavior has never been defined, and only the issue of October 10, 1988 gave information in simple language. Both Le Soleil and La Nouvelle Marche (September 5, 1986) have targeted prostitutes as the "principal vector of the virus in Africa." A wire service article in the latter (November 21, 1988) described a World Health Organization conference which emphasized the need for realistic economic and sociocultural alternatives for those engaged in prostitution, noting that the consequence of prohibition would be the formation of a clandestine market. Conference participants supported the use of experienced prostitutes as AIDS educators because of their access to populations at risk.

According to Uganda's ambassador to the United Nations (February 10, 1987), surveillance and education began in that country in 1985 with a multimedia campaign advising people to limit partners and use condoms. A poster campaign,

---

[3] Blood was not screened until mid-1987, and then amid a great deal of controversy. See, for example, June 16, 1987.

reported to have actually created panic, announced "Beware of Slim" (June 24, 1986), listing signs and symptoms, mode of transmission and prevention. In a report on President Museveni's visit to Rakai district, it was reported (February 21, 1987) that the government had decided to emphasize monogamy ("zero grazing") instead of condoms, due to concern about the reliance on foreign aid the latter would entail. A later article (September 14, 1988) criticized the focus of programs which direct prevention at individual behavior change when individuals, particularly women, may not have any choice about the number of partners they or their respective partners have, adding that urban migration and postpartum abstinence may impede campaigns for monogamy.

MOBILIZING GOVERNMENT RESPONSE TO AIDS

Kenya, Senegal, and Nigeria formed national AIDS committees in 1986, followed by Togo and Uganda in 1987. Kenya's committee began some professional education in 1986, with workshops for health personnel throughout the country, who were in turn expected to inform health workers in their districts. The first official statement was issued on August 2, 1986, in which the Chief Nursing Officer, Elisabeth Ngugi, advised that a "stable monogamous sexual relationship is the safest." The first case of AIDS was reportedly diagnosed in Kenya in 1983 (August 31, 1986), although the same expert went on to say that 4 percent of prostitutes were seropositive in 1981. Policy issues of concern at the time included the safety of the blood supply, the need for epidemiological information, and the issue of what to do about asymptomatic carriers.

The government's attitude became increasingly serious by mid-1987. The minister of health (July 31, 1987) "announced that the government has taken practical measures to control the situation," declining a suggestion to quarantine, and advising that in the meantime "people should refrain from promiscuity and excessive sex. Parents must explain to their children the dangers." The research of Ngugi and colleagues was published, stating that three quarters of Nairobi prostitutes were seropositive (March 5, 1988). In an article on Kenya's proposed public education plan (March 7, 1988), the country was described as being "in the heart of the 'AIDS belt' in Africa." The author noted that those affected constitute "the cream of Kenya's educated and economically productive population. The continual decimation of this age group could mean that the country will soon have a large number of old people with no one to look after them." According to Ngugi, "AIDS now offers the greatest single threat to the African family system." The new Minister of Health said AIDS cases were "rampant" in major urban centers. The government's five-year plan committed itself to "organise and mobilise appropriate resources to support individuals, families and communities since AIDS and related infections have the potential to cause physical, social and moral problems of immense dimensions. . . . Kenya has resolved not to fool itself any more about the looming spectre of AIDS" (December 2, 1988). The AIDS control plan was finally launched in 1988, with screening of blood donors and those presenting with AIDS related ailments (February 13, 1988). By 1989, Kenya had officially reported 4300 cases, and was concerned about the growing problem of pediatric AIDS (February 20, 1989).

Public education was similarly slow to begin in other countries: the Minister of Health for Nigeria announced the intention (March 13, 1987) to launch a "Use Condoms" campaign which would focus on "the advantages of remaining faithful to marriage partners," but by September 21, 1987, Nigeria was still "working on a strategy." Some controversy was engendered by a statement of the head of the AIDS committee advocating a "total change in lifestyle" (August 25, 1988); it was labeled "absolute rubbish" by the vice-president of the AIDS Committee on Education (October 24, 1988), who maintained that "Professor Essien said the condom was unacceptable because he is a moralist who is only trying to sell his moralist belief by creating fear in the people." Between 1986 and 1989, Senegal hosted a number of conferences and participated in multilateral epidemiological research, but its education campaign did not begin until 1988. The epidemiological member of the national AIDS committee maintained in December 1986 that "Le SIDA n'est pas une préoccupation majeure en Afrique de l'Ouest" ("AIDS is not a major concern in West Africa").

While similarly assuring that the situation was not pressing (February 19, 1987), Togolese efforts began in earnest in 1987 with presentations to secondary school students near Lome (March 18, 1987), and in the north (May 7-9, 1987), cosponsored by the ministries of public health, women's affairs, and education. July 1987 saw the beginning of the campaign aimed at business leaders, September, unions. Togo's progress was articulated at a seminar held in Lome for family planning representatives of ten countries (January 28-31, 1989). According to the ministry for public health, the campaign included epidemiological surveillance, securing the blood supply, clinical care of those with HIV related illness, information, education and communication to reduce sexual and perinatal transmission.

Uganda's medium term plan on AIDS was established in 1987. Its major components included education and information, blood screening, supply of syringes and condoms, surveillance, procurement of drugs, research, and training of health workers. The government had allocated nearly 10 percent of the national budget for AIDS programs. Nonetheless, lack of hard currency made it difficult to purchase supplies (August 9, 1988). Possibly contributing to iatrogenic transmission was the deterioration of medical services and infrastructure during the years of civil war (June 15, 1988). The vice-chair of the Uganda AIDS Action Fund added that medical personnel and the general public were still unaware of the mechanisms of transmission. The President advised Ugandans to take the threat of the epidemic very seriously, and warned against associating AIDS with witchcraft, which would hinder appropriate behavior change. He admonished people to limit themselves to one partner, and to avoid "unprofessional medical treatment" (July 21, 1987).

CONTENT OF COVERAGE

In addition to educational articles and those monitoring governmental activity, papers discussed common myths about AIDS. *New Vision* reminded readers that HIV is transmitted primarily through sexual contact (June 24, 1986), *Le Soleil* noted that governmental efforts had been impeded by common beliefs that AIDS affected only "bad" people (October 10, 1988). Conversely, papers occasionally passed on misinformation, such as the report carried by *La Nouvelle Marche* quoting the Secretary of the Organization of African Unity that Africans were in danger of contracting AIDS from eating monkey meat (February 26, 1987). A story retracting the theory appeared nearly two years later (January 26, 1989). Throughout the study period *La Nouvelle Marche* published extensive information on the situation in other countries, though statistics for Togo never appeared. *La Nouvelle Marche* also reported on African treatment research (November 25, 1986 and April 15, 1988).

The New Vision published two lengthy articles (July 12-13, 1988) in which an expatriate physician confronted the problem of prevention in the face of taboos about discussing death. *Le Soleil* published interviews (April 13, 1989) with two hospitalized patients who had not been informed of their diagnosis, although the hospital reportedly intended to give the information in stages, planning months to build patients' knowledge while simultaneously educating the family in order to reduce the risk of rejection from those reponsible for the patients' food, clothing and social support. The minister of health for Nigeria was castigated by the *Daily Times* (November 2, 1988) for his stated intention that two patients mistakenly transfused with infected blood would not be informed of their condition. Nigerian attitudes were apparently not as generous as Senegalese: a Gallup poll of thirty-five countries found that only Nigerians believed AIDS sufferers should not be treated with compassion (April 26, 1988).

DISCRIMINATION/ANTI-DISCRIMINATION

In response to the question of the approach to healthy carriers of HIV, the epidemiologist member of Senegal's AIDS committee argued against the quarantine of healthy people, but said he would consider threatening incarceration to curtail prostitutes' activity. An article in *The New Vision* (June 13, 1988) cautioned that unwarranted "xenophobia, intolerance and overreaction" would stigmatize AIDS victims. An editorial on August 31, 1988 stated "We must support AIDS sufferers," in response to the announcement that the communion cup could now be shared. A wire service article in Togo (November 21, 1987) discussed the importance of avoiding discrimination of prostitutes if safer sex practices were to generalize to populations at risk. The editor of the Nigeria *Daily Times* contended in response to testing African students overseas (March 11, 1987) that "the OAU has a duty to ensure that the stereotype (that the black race is the personification of evil) not be allowed to be perpetuated. Accordingly, we suggest that it should call on all African countries to employ the powerful tool of reciprocity." Another editorial called it "imperative that we install AIDS confirmatory screening machines at every point of entry into this country to screen foreigners and Nigerians returning from abroad" (March 20, 1987).

BLAME

Le Soleil did not allocate blame for the epidemic, though it noted that Senegal's original cases were contracted elsewhere. Neither the government nor the paper addressed the issue of testing foreigners, discrimination of Africans abroad, expelling those found to be seropositive, or the origin of the disease. The initial coverage in Togo (September 4, 1986) suggested that AIDS may have been imported, like syphilis or gonorrhea. A later article (September 30, 1988) attributed higher urban prevalence to differing urban morals and rural cases to truck drivers. HIV-2 was said to have originated in Guinea Bissau (December 5, 1988). Uganda printed a double page headline (February 10, 1987) which read "There is no way so devastating a disease could have been ignored or hidden by medical authorities in Africa: AIDS VIRUS STARTED IN THE WEST." In an article on the local situation, it was noted that infected residents of a rural town had all been educated in Kampala.

The Nigerian paper allowed generous amounts of column space for opinion pieces about AIDS, approximately half the total coverage on the subject. Reflecting the Gallup poll results, one writer asked "Why the fuss about AIDS?" (October 19, 1987). He typified the paper's opinion in writing "the question is not whether AIDS is fatal but whether in fact we should really bother about it. After all it is a self-inflicted scourge. A person who in his moral weakness plunges into reckless sex extravaganza should be prepared to bear the consequence of his lustful indiscretion. As a matter of fact, AIDS may turn out to be the panacea for our permissiveness in this country. The elite has over the years become addicted to immoral pastimes in their display of societal arrival and affluence." He condemned "society women, so-called, who paint the town red." Another writer echoed (May 12, 1987), that "these amateur prostitutes are the more dangerous of the two because you can never tell that they are infected. Unlike the professional prostitute, she has a wider choice for her partners and usually goes for the highest bidder. These amateurs could be anyone, ranging from students, workers and even married women. For some promiscuous people prostitution is the best way to combine business and pleasure."

The West came in for its share of blame (May 27, 1987): "the first cases of AIDS were reported in the United States of America in their male homosexual population, and as anyone who has worked in Psychiatric Medicine in such a country would know, quite a number of their homosexuals usually opt to go to sea where they're surrounded by an all-male population all the time, and their abnormality is far less likely to cause them any social embarrassment. . . . It is therefore obvious such people that have brought the AIDS virus to Africa and Nigeria." Some of these men must have been bisexual for he continued, "in Nigeria, specifically, most of the AIDS carriers identified so far have been prostitutes who have had contact with white men." Yet another labelled AIDS "the super power disease" (May 25, 1987). A subsequent piece (June 13, 1987) considered "how AIDS was an attempt to disrupt the Nigerian economy as the Kenyan economy has been damaged . . . a desperate attempt by racist scientists and other anti-Africa so-called Western experts to reinforce their dying myth that AIDS originated from Africa . . . the choice of Nigeria as a new ground to spread AIDS scare after Uganda is no doubt deliberate. Nigeria has the largest population of blacks in the world, therefore, Gallo [of the American National Cancer Institute] and his CIA mentors believe that, in order to infuse new inferiority complex on the black men world over, Nigeria will have to be totally included. [Gallo] "himself is said to be a homosexual, and has his own laboratory very close to Fort Detrick Laboratory in the United States where the virus was said to have been manufactured for warfare purposes," a sentiment repeated in another piece (May 28, 1987) which called HIV a "creation of U.S. scientists in their onerous drive for biological supremacy."

The *Kenya Times* also subscribed to the belief that "American scientists created the killer AIDS virus during laboratory experiments which went disastrously wrong and that massive coverup kept the secret from the world" (June 21, 1987). Like the Nigerian *Daily Times*, it allocated nearly half its articles to the issue of blame. The first (August 31, 1986) refuted the African origin theory. An editorial reviewing the Panos Dossier *AIDS and the Third World*[4] (December 4, 1986) quoted the minister of health's opinion that the document was "inaccurate, misleading and perhaps loaded against Kenya if not Africans." A member of parliament was reported incensed by the implication that AIDS was "rampant," and President Moi told the public to ignore the "malicious propaganda emanating from outside the country that the dreaded AIDS disease was rampant" (February 7, 1987), although the *Times* itself called the problem rampant a month later (March 7, 1987). Another editorial accused the Western press of "irresponsibility, inaccuracy and malice in its wild goose chase of trying to nationalise or apportion a racial identity," particularly the British for having "tarnished the entire Kenya

---

[4] *AIDS and the Third World*, Panos Institute, London, 1986.

nation without any iota of scientific validity" (January 14, 1987). Concerning itself with race, one editorial insisted that "Kenya is NOT infested with AIDS" (February 2, 1987), engaging in its own share of disinformation by labeling a Scandinavian film crew the "ancestors of racist South African Boers." A physician was called an "ill-motivated professional propagandist" (September 1, 1987) for tabling a document at a family planning conference which apparently stated that Kenya was "apprehensive about AIDS reporting" and imposes "general press censorship" (August 31, 1987). Several days' articles, which always referred to the man as "a British doctor of Czech descent," called for his expulsion. The physician left Kenya the first week of September.

DISCUSSION

Early in their coverage of the epidemic, Kenya, Uganda, Togo, and Senegal published extensive information about AIDS which explained the nature of HIV, facts about transmission, epidemiology, risk groups and practices, prevention, and vaccine research. These were published in series form, in full or center page spreads. The information was generally accurate and the quality high. The articles concerning virology and vaccines were often presented in an unfiltered way, however, using technical medical language and a reading level higher than that of the rest of the paper. Unlike the rest, Nigeria has never used the *Daily Times* as an educational tool; nor have the others used newspapers as a primary medium of education. Newspapers are more often used to relay information about governmental activities and programs, although interviews with key figures and reports on governmental activities and programs do often contain educational information. Content has been variously directed to health personnel and the general readership. Government owned papers thus have served as intermediary between the government and the people.

Severe gaps in coverage were noted. Uganda published very little on the subject in 1987, Togo only two articles between May 1987 and July 1988, Senegal none between December 1987 and July 1988; while Kenya printed little of substance in 1988. Only one or two articles have been printed in most countries between January and June 1989. Has the issue of AIDS in Africa been resolved? Governments unanimously stated at one time or another that AIDS was not a priority in their respective countries, and these omissions may have reflected governmental inaction.

Theories about the African origin of HIV were understandably interpreted as racist. Western researchers, including Essex of Harvard and Gallo of NCI, published what amounted to intuition without hard data to substantiate their theories. The Panos Institute repeated the hypothesis that central Africans may have contracted AIDS from eating contaminated monkey meat, that "the virus may have existed in an isolated African tribe for many years." The initial evidence was later retracted by Essex and omitted from a later edition of the Panos Dossier.

A problem parallel to the issue of racism was sexism. The justifiable criticism of the press that racism affected populations studied and projects funded was ignored with respect to women. Prostitutes have been scapegoated as "reservoirs" or "vectors" of disease with little concern shown for their health. Why prostitutes and not journalists or civil servants? News stories reported men seeking ever younger sexual partners, and paying extra to avoid using condoms. One article advocated the use of condoms since it was impossible to expect men to change their behavior. A knowledge, attitudes and practice survey in Uganda revealed that women perceive themselves as suffering disproportionately from AIDS but lacking power to make decisions about sex. The attitude on the part of many educated men has been one of denial. "Why worry? After all, a man only dies once, AIDS or no AIDS" (*Daily Times*, December 1, 1988), is a commonly read sentiment, and an excuse for not changing behavior.

The problem of behavior change is compounded by the persistence of myths concerning AIDS (a problem certainly not unique to Africa). People believe that AIDS is sexually transmitted, but they also believe that only Westerners contract it, or only homosexuals, that it can be caused by witchcraft, and casually transmitted. Some believe it can be cured through sexual relations with an uninfected partner. High risk groups are targeted instead of high risk behaviors. Behavior change is often ill-defined or unrealistic. Given men's refusal to remain faithful, monogamy may be an impossible expectation. Men may not perceive themselves to be at risk when promiscuity is not defined. Alternatives to genital intercourse are also considered impossible; behavior change is assumed to mean either condom use or fidelity.

Religion may have an influence on the epidemic. Christianity is a strong influence in some parts of Africa. The Catholic church has actively discouraged the use of condoms in Kenya and Uganda, insisting instead that parishioners "Love faithfully to avoid AIDS." Organized and traditional religions play a strong role in cultural conceptions of death. The implications are great for testing and prevention when patients are not informed of their diagnosis. It is unclear how the media might affect such deeply held beliefs as these. It is clear, however, that in spite of their potential, the African newspapers reviewed here have yet to be used as an important means of health education about AIDS.

BIBLIOGRAPHY

R. M. Anderson, et al., Possible Demographic Consequences of AIDS in Developing Countries, *Nature 326:*228-233, 1988.

M. Carael, et al., Socio-cultural Factors in Relation to HTLV/LAV Transmission in Urban Areas in Central Africa. Abstract, International Symposium on African AIDS, Brussels, Belgium, November 22-23, 1985.

N. Clumeck, et al., Heterosexual Promiscuity among African Patients with AIDS, *New England Journal of Medicine, 313*, p. 182, 1985.

B. Dagenais, SIDA et Media au Senegal. Abstract E.741, p. 926, V International Conference on AIDS, Montreal, 4-9 June, 1989.

K. Edstrom, *AIDS: Its Implications for Women and Children*, Technical background paper prepared for the International Conference on Better Health for Women and Children through Family Planning, Nairobi, October 1987.

D. Feldman, S. R. Friedman, and D. C. des Jarlais, Public Awareness of AIDS in Rwanda, *Social Science and Medicine, 24*:2, pp. 97-100, 1987.

A. Fleming, et al. (eds.), *The Global Impact of AIDS,* Alan Liss, New York, 1988.

A. J. Georges, et al., HIV 1 Seroprevalence and AIDS Diagnostic Criteria in Central African Republic, *Lancet, 8571*:11, pp. 1332-1333, 1987.

J. K. Kreiss, et al., AIDS Virus Infection in Nairobi prostitutes. *New England Journal of Medicine, 314*:7, pp. 414-418, 1986.

L. Kitchen, AIDS in Africa: Knowns and Unknowns. *CSIS Africa Notes, 74*, July 17, 1987.

J. Mann, et al., Condom Usse and HIV Infection among Prostitutes in Zaire (letter), *New England Journal of Medicine, 316*:6, p. 345, 1988.

P. Martin, et al., *Tentative Determination of AIDS Incidence and Risk Factors in the CAR*, Second International Symposium on AIDS in Africa, Naples, Abstract TH-26, October 7-9, 1987.

N. Miller and R. Rockwell (eds.), *AIDS in Africa: The Social and Policy Impact*, Edwin Mellon, Lewiston, 1988.

E. Ngugi, *Effects of an AIDS Education Program on Increasing Condom Use in a Cohort of Nairobi Prostitutes*, III International Conference on AIDS, Washington, D.C., 5:157, June 1986.

E. Ngugi, Reaching the Target Population: Female Prostitutes, in *AIDS Prevention and Control*, WHO, Geneva, 1988.

C. Obbo, *AIDS and Society in Africa*, UCB, March 11, 1989.

J. Obetsebe-Lamptey, Introduction to Part 3: Health Promotion Programmes for Specific Groups, in *AIDS Prevention and Control,* 1988.

H. Pickering, Asking Questions on Sexual Behaviour, *Health Policy and Planning, 3*:3, pp. 237-244, 1988.

O. Piot, et al., AIDS: An International Perspective, *Science, 239*, pp. 573-579, February 5, 1988.

T. Quinn, et al., AIDS in Africa: An Epidemiological Paradigm, *JS, 234*, pp. 955-963, 1986. Noted in Conant article in Miller, 1988.

Revue Medicale Rwandaise, Numero Special sur le SIDA, Minstere de la Sante Publique et des Affaires Sociales, *Number 54*, 1988.

N. J. Schmidt, *Reports on AIDS in the African Press: An Annotated Bibliography*, African Studies Program, Indiana University, Bloomington, Indiana, 1988.

B. Schoepf, et al., *AIDS and Society in Central Africa: A View from Zaire*, in Miller, 1988.

D. Serwadda, et al., Slim Disease: A New Disease in Uganda and Its Association with HTLV-III Infection, *Lancet, ii*, pp. 849-852, 1985.

World Health Organisation, AIDS Cases Reported to WHO, Appendix 2, AIDS: A Global Perspective, *Western Journal of Medicine, 147*:6, p. 738, December 1987.

World Health Organisation, *AIDS Prevention and Control*, Geneva, 1988a.

World Health Organisation, *Guidelines for the Development of a National AIDS Prevention and Control Programme*, Geneva, 1998b.

CHAPTER 13

Women and the Risk of HIV Infection in Nigeria: Implications for Control Programs

Ademola J. Ajuwon and Wuraola Shokunbi

Sexually transmitted diseases (STDs) pose a threat to the health and well-being of the sexually active population in Nigeria [1-3]. The common STDs in the country are gonorrhea, trichomoniasis, chlamydia, candidiasis, syphilis, human papilloma virus, lymphogranuloma venereum, genital warts, and chancroid [4-6]. Although there is no national data on the incidence and prevalence of each of these infections, most scientists in Nigeria agree that the prevalence of STDs is high and increasing due to inadequately trained health manpower, scarcity of functional laboratories, treatment facilities, and changes in sexual behavior [5].

The consequences of STDs are devastating: infants of infected mothers may have ophthalmic infections (which may later lead to blindness) and pneumonia; chronic pelvic inflammatory disease (PID) may complicate STDs, and patients may develop infertility as a result of untreated infections. STDs are also associated with spontaneous abortion, ectopic pregnancy, and cervical cancer [5, 7]. The management of these complications places a heavy toll on the health care delivery in Nigeria.

The report in Nigeria in 1984 of HIV, and the increasing number of Nigerians infected with the virus, have compounded the problem in that HIV has placed an additional burden on the health care system already overstressed by other preventable health problems.

Heterosexual contact is the main route of HIV transmission in Nigeria [8, 9]. This suggests that there is a parity of risk of infection between men and women. However, we argue in this article that women in Nigeria are more at risk of HIV infection than men. We have described the biological, cultural, and economic conditions which make Nigerian women susceptible to HIV infection and have suggested the intervention strategies that will address them.

THE HIV/AIDS SITUATION IN NIGERIA

The first case of AIDS in Nigeria, involving a sexually active thirteen-year-old girl, was officially reported in 1984 [8]. Since then, the number of persons infected with HIV and those who have developed AIDS has been increasing rapidly. For example, in 1992, 367 new AIDS cases were reported in the country; the number rose to 917 by September of 1993 [10]; and 1,490 at the end of 1994 [9]. The Federal Ministry of Health and Social Services (FMOHSS) projects that between one to three million adult Nigerians will probably be infected with HIV by 1996 [9].

As shown in Table 1, HIV has been reported among a broad spectrum of the Nigerian population. These are apparently healthy persons [11, 12], blood donors [13], clients of STD clinics, tuberculosis patients, long distance truck drivers [9], pregnant women attending antenatal clinics [12], and commercial sex workers (CSW) [9, 10, 14]. Using the HIV prevalence among the antenatal clinic attendants as an index, the FMOHSS has put the national seroprevalence rate of HIV in Nigeria at 3.8 percent of the sexually active population in the country [9].

This figure is low in comparison to 28 percent and 30 percent HIV prevalence reported for a comparable population in Uganda [15] and Kenya [16] respectively. However, the Nigerian figure may not reflect the true extent of the problem because AIDS is under reported due to paucity of HIV screening centers (only 16 out of the 30 states in the country have screening centers), inadequacy of laboratory resources for testing and incomplete reporting from some centers [9, 17]. In addition, the fact that AIDS may mimic other common health problems in Nigeria such as tuberculosis, malabsorption syndrome, and malnutrition may mislead Nigerians to think that AIDS is not a new disease, and, therefore, under report it. Under reporting coupled with the long latency period of HIV suggest that many HIV infected Nigerians may not be detected for several years during which they can transmit the virus to others.

Both HIV 1 and HIV 2 are common in Nigeria [12, 13]. These have been reported in virtually all parts of the country, especially in urban areas with Plateau, Benue, Delta, Lagos, and Enugu states leading (in that order) in the number of reported cases [9]. The explanation for this may be the fact that these states have some features which favor the rapid spread of HIV. Plateau, for example, has a cold climate and is, therefore, a popular holiday resort with a relatively high number of CSW. Delta and Lagos have major sea ports which attract a large influx of sailors who are likely to engage in casual sex during their stay in these states.

Table 1. Prevalence of HIV in Different Populations in Nigeria

Source	Population Screened	Location	No. Tested	No. HIV Positive	% HIV Negative
1. Mohammed et al. (1987)	Healthy persons and patients	Maiduguri, Potiskum, Calabar, Enugu	5,238	12	0.23
2. Chickwem, Mohammed and Ola (1989)	Commercial sex workers (CSW)	Maiduguri	353	18	5.1
3. Williams, Hearst, and Udofia (1989)	Clients of CSWs	Ikom Calabar	133	2	1.5
4. FMOHSS (1991/92)	CSW, Women attending ante-natal clinics (ANC) clients of STD clinics and TB patients	11 sentinel site[a]	11,907	482	4.04
5. Olusanya, Lawoko, and Blomberg (1993)	Healthy business employees	Ogun State	385	3	0.77
6. Shokunbi, Saliu, and Essien (1993)	Blood donors, healthy international travellers, and patients	Ibadan	6,389	41	0.93
7. Nnatu et al. (1993)	Pregnant women attending ANC	Lagos	230	2	0.8
8. FMOHSS (1995)	CSW, women attending ANC, STD, and TB patients, long distance truck drivers	16 sentinel sites[b]	22,569	1,490	6.59

[a]The sites are in Benue, Delta, Lagos, Enugu, Cross-Rivers, Kaduna, Kano, Osun, Edo, Oyo, and Jigawa States.
[b]These are in Plateau, Benue, Delta, Lagos, Enugu, Adamawa, Borno, Cross-River, Kaduna, Kwara, Kano, Osun, Anambra, Edo, Sokoto, Oyo, and Jigawa States.

Despite the wide publicity given to AIDS by the local media, the efforts of governmental and non-governmental organizations (NGOs) to educate the public about the threat of AIDS and the report of the increasing number of persons infected with HIV, a majority of Nigerians continue to engage in behaviors which would increase their risk of exposure to HIV. For example, in a survey on sexual networking in five locations in southern and northern Nigeria, Uche-Abanihe [17] found that 54 percent of men and 39 percent of women have had extra-marital relationships, with 18 percent of men and 11 percent of women having done so during the week preceding the survey. The majority of these respondents had not used a condom which is known to offer protection against sexually transmitted HIV [18, 19]. High levels of unprotected sexual networking has also been reported by other investigators in Nigeria [20-22].

A major explanation for the problem is that many Nigerians perceive themselves to be at low risk of HIV infection, even though they engage in high-risk behavior [23, 24]. Many Nigerians have failed to modify high-risk behavior because of the belief that AIDS is not yet common in the country since they have not yet known or seen any AIDS patients. Others view the danger posed by AIDS with fatalism, arguing that one will eventually "die of something," and so are not prepared to change their sexual behavior because of the threat of AIDS [17]. Under these circumstances and considering the pattern of the AIDS epidemic in other sub-saharan African countries, there is likely to be an exponential rise in the incidence of AIDS in Nigeria in the next few years if the current situation persists.

CURRENT NATIONAL HIV PREVENTION AND CONTROL REPORTS

The Federal Government of Nigeria responded to the threat of AIDS in 1986 by setting up the National Expert Advisory Committee on AIDS (NEACA). This was later reconstituted in 1992 and renamed National AIDS and STD Control Program (NACP). The NACP is located in the Department of Disease Control and International Health of the FMOHSS. Charged with the responsibility of coordinating AIDS prevention and control activities, the NACP is divided into five sections: Programme Management; Epidemiology and Surveillance; Information, Education and Communication (IEC); Laboratory; and Clinical Management and Community-based care [8].

The NACP has recorded some achievements since its inception. For example, it has decentralized its operations by appointing one AIDS coordinator for each of the thirty states and the new capital city, Abuja, whose charge is to oversee ongoing AIDS prevention and control efforts in their respective states. In addition, the NACP has established HIV screening centers in some states to track the incidence and prevalence of HIV and design intervention measures to contain them. To this end, routine anonymous unlinked method of testing is being used to screen six groups: CSW, Clients of STD clinic; TB patients; long distance truck drivers; and women attending ANC [8]. With respect to education, the NACP had developed many IEC materials (posters, brochures, pamphlets), trained some health workers and sponsored several educational programs on the electronic media.

Various individuals, local, and international agencies have complemented the efforts of the NACP through the production of educational materials, training of health workers, education of CSWs, and donation of equipment and HIV screening resources [25-27]. Despite these achievements, however, a number of problems continue to hamper the progress of AIDS control programs in the country.

First, the current number of screening centers is grossly inadequate for the 88.5 million population in the country. The centers are concentrated in towns and cities thus creating an urban bias in the sero-prevalence data in the country. Second, as mentioned earlier, there is incomplete reporting in some centers. For example, some centers do not screen the desired sample from the groups [9]. In addition, vital information such as the sex of clients of STD clinics, TB patients, blood donors, and apparently healthy persons were omitted. As a result, we do not have data on the sex distribution of HIV infected persons in the country.

Finally, current educational efforts have relied heavily on the use of the print and electronic media despite the limitations associated with them. Although the media campaign has raised the level of public awareness about AIDS [28, 29], its impact on behavior is limited because many Nigerians who have heard about AIDS continue to engage in sexually risky behaviors [17, 22, 23].

The cause of the problem is that some of the media messages are too diffuse, hence, they do not address the socio-cultural and economic constraints to behavior change. For example, many educational messages encourage the use of a condom to prevent HIV infection without suggesting how women can overcome the many difficulties they face in convincing men to use it. Such messages are also unrealistic because the cost of the condom may not be affordable to many rural dwellers. Also, campaign messages request Nigerians to stick to one sexual partner without suggesting how women can overcome the economic problems which cause many of them to resort to risk-taking behaviors to survive. Furthermore, messages advocating having one partner, may be quite dicey for a woman in a polygynous marriage. A faithful woman in such a marriage still runs the risk of contracting HIV if her husband or any of the other women have extra-marital affairs with an infected person. Innovative educational interventions are needed to address these issues. We now turn to the discussion of the conditions which make women susceptible to HIV infection.

STDs AS A GENDER ISSUE

The physical differences between men and women affect their risk of susceptibility to HIV infection. Women are three times as likely as men to become infected through sexual intercourse because the vaginal wall is delicate and prone to sores and abrasions, which may create pathways for the transmission of STDs including HIV [30]. Yet, STDs are more difficult to diagnose in women than men [31].

Since STDs are commonly asymptomatic in women they are likely to harbor untreated STDs, some of which are known risk factors for HIV transmission [32-34]. This makes the long-term complications of untreated STDs far more serious in women than men.

In Nigeria, there are some cultural barriers that may prevent infected women from seeking prompt and appropriate treatment for STDS. First, there is the stigma associated with STDs. In Nigeria, it is a serious embarrassment for a woman to be publicly seen attending an STD clinic. As a result, many infected women often seek treatment from traditional healers or patent medicine sellers who are likely to provide confidential but inappropriate treatment for their conditions. Second, the practice of purdar (the system of seclusion of women from public places) which is widespread in many moslem communities in Nigeria, may prevent infected women from seeking prompt and appropriate care, especially in areas where medical units are staffed by male doctors [5].

Nigeria is a male dominated society where women are expected to produce as many children as possible, preferably males. The woman is blamed, therefore, for infertility or reproductive failure, consequently many Nigerian women may value pregnancy more than their health and may engage in sexually risky behaviors which would raise their chances of contracting HIV [5]. The proportion of pregnant women with HIV is estimated to range from 0.5 to 24.8 percent in different parts of the country with a mean of 3.8 percent [9]. These women face a serious dilemma since it has been suggested that they are likely to develop AIDS sooner than other HIV infected adults if they carry their pregnancy to term; they also run the risk of transmitting HIV to their babies [35], thus contributing further to the spread of the virus in Nigeria. Yet many of these women may not have or wish to accept the option of an abortion given the high premium placed on fertility.

CULTURAL PRACTICES AFFECTING THE SUSCEPTIBILITY OF WOMEN TO HIV INFECTION

Genital Mutilation

In Nigeria, women are the unfortunate victims of a range of cultural practices which affect their health and well-being. Of relevance to the issue of risk of HIV infection is genital mutilation of which there are two types: "gishiri cut" and "sunna" circumcision. "Gishiri cut" is a type of mutilation practiced by the Hausa of Northern Nigeria in which the vagina is cut usually by old women using an unhygienic razor blade or knife [5]. The cut is usually done to treat conditions such as infertility, generalized body pain, etc. On the other hand, the "sunna" involves excision of the clitoris of infants and young girls. The practice has persisted in Nigeria despite concerted efforts to eradicate it [36-39].

The "sunna" mutilation is a violation of the rights of the girl-child, but has always been justified by men on the grounds that it prevents promiscuity. The excision of the clitoris is therefore aimed at controlling the libido of the females, thus suggesting that sexual pleasure is the exclusive right of men.

Although there is no research evidence yet that female genital mutilation is a risk factor for HIV transmission in Nigeria, the fact that mutilation and subsequent scarring could result in vaginal tears during intercourse implies that it carries some risks. Such tears could create a pathway for the transfer of HIV during sexual intercourse with an infected person, thus increasing further, the efficiency of male to female transmission of HIV. HIV can also be transmitted to the girl-child through use of unsterile instruments which could harbor bacteria and HIV [36].

Sexual Abstinence, Polygyny, and Divorce

The practice of sexual abstinence by Nigerian women shortly before and several months after delivery has been well documented in the literature [40-42]. Among the Yoruba of Western Nigeria, married couples are expected to abstain from sexual intercourse while the infant is being breastfed, after which they can resume normal sexual intercourse. Sexual intercourse is discouraged during breastfeeding because of the belief that the semen could have an adverse effect on the growth of the infant. Although the duration of post partum abstinence has declined in recent years due to increasing use of modern contraceptives, the practice itself is still quite common especially in the rural communities where access to modern contraceptives is limited [42].

Inherent in this practice is a system of double standard of sexual morality between men and women. Although women are expected to abstain from sexual intercourse while the infant is being nursed, men are not affected by this rule in the sense that they have other sexual outlets. For example, polygynous men could easily turn to other wives and monogamous men could have extra-marital sexual relationships while their wives abstain [42]. Thus, sexual norms in Nigeria promote sexual license for men and sexual purity for women. Whereas the wife is expected to be absolutely faithful to her husband, men have the freedom to philander.

Another aspect of the double standard in sexual relationship is reflected in divorce practices. Under Nigerian customary laws, men are normally granted divorce if it is proven that wives have had extra-marital relationships [42]. Unfortunately, women married under customary and Islamic laws in Nigeria do not have that same opportunity because these laws permit polygyny [43]. An adulterous man can easily justify his action by claiming that he plans to marry the other woman.

Under an ideal situation, wives of adulterous men could encourage their husbands to use condoms as a means of protection against HIV. However, persuading men to wear the condom may be a difficult if not an impossible task for many women because in Nigeria a man will consider a woman "loose" (that is promiscuous) if she requests him to use a condom during sexual intercourse. Women may also encounter problems with the use of the female condom, which is now available but not yet used on a large scale in Nigeria because of its prohibitive cost.

This situation places women at a disadvantage in the sense that they lack the ability to control the sexually risky aspects of the behavior of their spouses and do not have the economic power to take action which would protect them from infection with STDs including HIV. Indeed, many women in Nigeria are expressing concern that their own fidelity may not be a guarantee for safety from HIV, considering the fact that previous researches in Nigeria show that a high proportion of women acquired STDs from their spouses [44].

WOMEN, ECONOMIC CRISIS, AND SEXUAL-RISK BEHAVIORS

The Nigerian economy has been in recession since the early 1980s. To revamp it, the Nigerian government introduced in the last half of the 1980s, the economic structural Adjustment Programme (SAP) which consisted of cuts in public spending, removal of subsidies, trade liberalization, currency devaluation, and retrenchment of workers. These measures caused a tragic decline in real income and living standards of the majority of the population. For example, following the removal of subsidies, inflation got out of control and cost of living in Nigeria doubled between 1986 and 1987 [26, 45].

Women have been particularly hard hit by the crisis. Faced with minimal economic support from their spouses and the need to care for their children, some married women in Nigeria have been compelled to exchange sex for additional material support for themselves and their children. As one rural married woman pointed out during a focus group discussion on the cause of sexual networking, "sometimes we are unable to leave our poor husbands and marry men who are better off because we do not want to abandon our children. Instead we have 'ale' (non-marital male sexual partner) who can assist us financially" [21]. The incidence of non-commercial exchange of sexual favors is also on the increase among young girls in institutions of learning who accept food or money from older men with whom they establish casual sexual relationships [5].

Furthermore, some out-of-school young girls have responded to the economic crisis by entering occupations in which they are vulnerable to being lured or forced to having sexual risk relationship with men. For example, several incidents of sexual exploitation of the itinerant female hawkers (IFH) in the course of their work have been reported in the country [46, 47]. Because of their relatively young ages, and the fact that they earn little income, the IFH in Nigeria are easily lured, harassed, and sometimes raped by men inside the bus/lorry stations where the IFH sell their wares. As public awareness about AIDS is increasing in Nigeria, the IFH have become sexual favorites of men because of the belief that the IFH are not likely to have HIV, are sexually inexperienced, and are not regarded as full-time commercial sex workers [46]. Unfortunately, there are no existing programs in Nigeria that specifically target the AIDS education need of this group.

Another outcome of the economic crisis in Nigeria may be the high proportion of Nigerian women who go into full-time commercial sex work, as a means of survival. This situation is reflected in the changing profile of the CSW in Nigeria in recent years. Previous research shows that CSW were usually older women with limited education who have been separated or divorced from their husbands [48, 49]. However, recent research indicates an increasing number of single, well-educated young women, and even teenagers involved in full-time sex work [50, 51].

Despite the vigorous social marketing campaigns for condoms in Nigeria, many CSW still do not use them [14, 50, 51]. This increases their risk of exposure to STDs, some of which are known risk factors for HIV transmission [32-34]. Another source of risk to CSW in Nigeria is their practice of receiving injections of antibiotics as prophylactics against STDs from patent Medicine dealers who re-use needles and syringes [14, 21]. Intervention measures that address these problems are urgently required to reduce the risk of infection among CSW. We now discuss strategies that can reduce the susceptibility of women to HIV infection.

IMPLICATIONS FOR AIDS CONTROL PROGRAM

The following suggestions are made to reduce risks for women.

Assessment of the Nature and Extent of STDs in Nigeria

Since STDs are risk factors for HIV transmission, their control will have a salutary effect on the prevention of further spread of AIDS in Nigeria. There is currently no national data on the incidence and prevalence of STDs in Nigeria. There is, therefore, a need to assess the current situation to determine the extent of the problem. In addition to clinic-based collection of STD data, there is need to conduct routine community surveys and develop a surveillance system whereby STD trends can be monitored and impact of interventions assessed. The NACP is appropriately positioned to implement this proposal.

Development of Women Specific Interventions

Educational programs specifically designed and targeted at women in Nigeria are urgently needed. The programs should be incorporated into current structure of the NACP. To be meaningful, such programs would sensitize women to the risk they face and address the socioeconomic constraints to behavior change. Women leaders should be charged with the responsibility of planning the programs. Informal associations can exert a powerful influence on behavior of members, therefore, the leaders of the informal women organizations can be trained as peer educators who will mobilize others to take actions that will reduce their risk of infection. Women of privilege who belong to professional associations such as Federation of Women Lawyers, (FIDA), Medical Women Association and the Society for Women and AIDS in Africa (SWAA) can organize additional intervention programs for their less privileged counterparts and complement the efforts of the NACP.

Economic Empowerment of Women

The health and well-being of women need to be improved through education which would enable them to become economically independent from their male partners. Both formal and adult literacy programs need to be organized for women with the assistance of local and international agencies interested in improving the well-being of women in Nigeria. The ability of women to become economically independent can be enhanced by improving their access to seed funds which can be used to set up small scale income yielding business. The Ministry of Women Affairs recently created by the Nigerian Government to improve the conditions of women should be responsible for achieving this goal.

Enlisting the Support of Men

The suggestions mentioned above have policy implications, hence the support of men is required because in Nigeria more men than women occupy important policy-making positions. There is a need to sensitize opinion/policy makers, health care providers, and the media to the nature of the risks women are exposed to and the need to take action to reduce these risks.

CONCLUSION

The epidemic of HIV/AIDS is growing rapidly in Nigeria. Although intervention measures are being implemented in the country to control further spread of AIDS, these efforts have not addressed the factors which place women at risk and the barriers to prevention and control. Women constitute a significant but disadvantaged segment of the Nigerian population, therefore, there is need for innovative interventions aimed at ensuring that they appreciate the problems AIDS poses to their health. There is also need to empower women with skills that will enable them to take actions to protect themselves from becoming infected.

REFERENCES

1. M. C. Asuzu and L. O. Idoko, Incidence and Treatment Seeking Patterns for Venereal Diseases in Jos Metropolis, *West African Journal of Medicine, 13*, pp. 156-159, 1994.
2. M. C. Asuzu, B. A. Omotara, and M. K. O. Padonu, The Epidemiology and Management of Sexually Transmitted Diseases in Maiduguri Metropolis, *Nigeria Medical Practitioner, 23*, pp. 57-61, 1992.
3. L. J. Messersmith, T. T. Kane, A. I. Odebiyi, and A. A. Adewuyi, Patterns of Sexual Behaviour and Condom Use in Ile-Ife, Nigeria: Implications for AIDS/STD Prevention and Control, *Health Transition Review, 4*, pp. 197-216, 1994.
4. L. Brabin, J. Kemp, O. K. Obunge, J. Ikimalo, N. Dollimore, N. N. Odu, C. A. Hart, and Briggs, Reproductive Tract Infections and Abortion among Adolescent Girls in Rural Nigeria, *Lancet, 345*, pp. 300-304, 1995.
5. A. O. Adekunle and O. A. Ladipo, Reproductive Tract Infections in Nigeria: Challenges for Fragile Health Infrastructure, in *Reproductive Tract Infections: Global Impact and Priorities for Women's Reproductive Health*, K. K. Holmes, P. Piot, and R. Wasserheit (eds.), Plenum Press, New York, pp. 297-316, 1992.
6. B. O. Ogunbanjo, Sexually Transmitted Diseases in Nigeria: A Review of the Current Situation, *West African Journal of Medicine, 37*, pp. 854-872, 1989.
7. R. Lande, Controlling Sexually Transmitted Disease, *Population Report, 9*, pp. 3-4, 1993.
8. Federal Ministry of Health and Social Services, *Nigeria Bulletin of Epidemiology, 2*, pp. 10-16, 1992.
9. Federal Ministry of Health and Social Services, *Sentinel Sero-Prevalence Report*, pp. 5-9, 1993-94.
10. World Health Organisation, *Surveillance Report*, Epidemiology and Surveillance Unit, Geneva, 1993.
11. A. Mohammed, J. O. Nassidi, E. E. Williams, J. O. Chickwem, G. O. Harry, O. O. Okafor, S. A. Ajose-Coker, P. Ademiluyi, K. M. Turkei, K. M. De-Cork, and T. P. Monath, HIV Infection in Nigeria, *AIDS, 2*, pp. 61-62, 1988.
12. O. Olusanya, A. Lawoko, and J. Blomberg, Sero-Epidemiology of Human Retroviruses in Ogun State of Nigeria, *Scandinavian Journal of Infectious Diseases, 22*, pp. 155-160, 1990.
13. W. A. Shokunbi, I. Saliu, and E. M. Essien, Incidence of Antibodies to HIV_1 and HIV_2 Gene Products in Seropositive Cases Seen in Ibadan, Nigeria, *Health Transition Review, 3*, pp. 185-188, 1993.
14. J. O. Chickwem, I. Mohammed, and T. Ola, Human Immunodeficiency Virus Type 1 (HIV-1) Infection among Female Prostitutes in Borno State of Nigeria: One Year Follow-Up, *East African Medical Journal, 66*, pp. 752-756, 1989.
15. J. W. McGrath, D. A. Schumann, J. Pearson-Marks, C. B. Rwabukwali, R. Mukasa, B. Namande, S. Nakayiwu, and Nakyobe, Cultural Determinants of Sexual Risk Behaviour for AIDS among Bagand Women, *Medical Anthropology Quarterly, 6*, pp. 153-161, 1992.
16. J. Kiragu, HIV Prevention and Women's Rights: Working for One Means for Both, *AIDS Captions, 2*, pp. 40-46, 1995.
17. U. C. Isiugo-Abanihe, Extra-Marital-Relations and Perceptions of HIV/AIDS in Nigeria, *Health Transition Review, 4*, pp. 111-125, 1994.

18. W. L. Roper, H. B. Peterson, and J. W. Curran, Condoms and HIV/STD Prevention—Clarifying the Message, *American Journal of Public Health, 83,* pp. 501-503, 1993.
19. P. Van de Perre, D. Jacobs, and Spencer-Goldbergers, The Latex Condom: An Effective Barrier against Sexual Transmission of AIDS-Related Virus, *AIDS, 1,* pp. 49-52, 1987.
20. O. O. Ososanya and W. R. Brieger, Rural-Urban Mobility in South Western Nigeria: Implications for HIV/AIDS Transmission from Urban to Rural Communities, *Health Education Research, 9,* pp. 507-518, 1994.
21. A. J. Ajuwon, O. Oladepo, J. D. Adeniyi, and W. R. Brieger, Sexual Practices that May Favour the Transmission of HIV in a Rural Community in Nigeria, *International Quarterly of Community Health Education, 14,* pp. 403-416, 1993-94.
22. I. O. Orubuloye, J. C. Caldwell, and P. Caldwell, Experimental Research on Sexual Networking in the Ekiti District of Nigeria, *Health Transition Working Paper, 3,* pp. 1-19, 1990.
23. B. A. Onile, Facts and Figures on AIDS in Nigeria, *Nigeria AIDS Monitor, 1,* pp. 7-17, 1993.
24. O. O. Osowole, *Perceived Susceptibility to AIDS and Attitude towards Condom Use among Long Distance Truck Drivers in Ibadan,* a dissertation in the Department of Preventive and Social Medicine, University of Ibadan, Nigeria, 1992.
25. Federal Ministry of Health and Social Services, *Nigeria AIDS Monitor, 1,* pp. 1-7, 1993.
26. J. D. Webster and B. E. Nnabugwu, Training of Trainers, Workshops for AIDS Prevention in Nigeria: Lessons Learned, *Hygie, 12,* pp. 16-21, 1993.
27. E. E. Williams, Women of Courage: Commercial Sex Workers Mobilise for HIV/AIDS Prevention in Nigeria, *AIDS Captions, 4,* pp. 19-22, 1994.
28. O. Oladepo and W. R. Brieger, AIDS Knowledge, Attitude and Behaviour Patterns among University Students in Ibadan, Nigeria, *African Journal of Medicine and Medical Sciences, 23,* pp. 119-125, 1994.
29. O. M. T. Odujirin and F. O. Akinkuade, Adolescent AIDS Knowledge, Attitude and Beliefs about Preventive Practices in Nigeria, *European Journal of Epidemiology, 7,* pp. 127-133, 1991.
30. A. Skjelmerud, Women in the AIDS Crisis, *Contact, 144,* pp. 3-5, 1995.
31. W. Cates and K. M. Stone, Family Planning: The Responsibility to Prevent both Pregnancy and Reproductive Tract Infections, in *Reproductive Tract Infections; Global Impact and Priorities for Women's Reproductive Health,* A. Germann, K. K. Holmes, P. Piot, and J. N. Wasserheit (eds.), Plenum Press, 1992.
32. K. J. Pallangyo, Treating HIV Infection Like a Sexually Transmitted Disease, *AIDS Action, 6,* pp. 2-3, 1989.
33. B. K. Johnson and R. S. Pond, *AIDS in Africa, A Review of Medical, Public Health, Social Science and Popular Literature,* a Report Prepared under Contact for Misreor, West Germany, 1988.
34. P. Piot, J. K. Kreiss, D. Jackonia, Nginya-Achola, E. N. Ngugi, J. N. Simonsen, D. W. Cameron, H. Taelmau, and F. A. Plummer, Editorial Review: Heterosexual Transmission of HIV, *AIDS, 1,* pp. 199-206, 1987.
35. R. Sabatier, A New Hurdle for Mothers and Children, *AIDS Watch, 2,* pp. 2-3, 1988.

36. A. J. Ajuwon, W. R. Brieger, O. Oladepo, and J. D. Adeniyi, Indigenous Surgical Practices in Rural South-Western Nigeria: Implications for Disease Transmission, *Health Education Research, 10*, pp. 379-384, 1995.
37. E. Ebomoyi, Prevalence of Female Circumcision in Two Nigerian Communities, *Sex Roles, 17*, pp. 139-151, 1987.
38. S. O. Oduntan and M. O. Onadeko, *Female Circumcision in Nigeria*, report presented at a Seminar on Traditional Practices Affecting the Health of Women and Children in Africa, Dakar, Senegar, 1984.
39. S. K. Olamijulo, K. T. Joiner, and G. A. Oyedeji, Female Child Circumcision in Ilesha, Nigeria, *Clinical Paediatrics, 8*, pp. 580-581, 1983.
40. I. O. Orubuloye, Sexual Abstinence Patterns in Rural Western Nigeria: Evidence from a Survey of Yoruba Women, *Social Science and Medicine, 13*, pp. 667-672, 1979.
41. J. C. Caldwell and P. Caldwell, The Role of Marital Sexual Abstinence in Determining Fertility—A Study of the Yoruba of Nigeria, *Population Studies, 3*, pp. 193-217, 1977.
42. A. J. Ajuwon, *Socio-Cultural Practices that May Favour the Transmission of AIDS in a Rural Yoruba Community: Implications for Health Education*, a dissertation in the Department of Preventive and Social Medicine, University of Ibadan, Nigeria, 1990.
43. R. O. Ekundare, *Marriage and Divorce under Yoruba Customary Law*, University of Ife Press, 1969.
44. T. T. A. Elemile, *Epidemiology of Sexually Transmitted Diseases in a Rural Area, Ilora, Oyo State, Nigeria*, fellowship of Nigeria Medical College of Health Dissertation, 1982.
45. S. O. Alubo, Debt Crisis, Health and Health Services in Africa, *Social Science and Medicine, 31*, pp. 639-648, 1990.
46. I. O. Orubuloye, P. Caldwell, and J. C. Caldwell, The Role of High Risk Occupations in the Spread of AIDS: Truck Drivers and Itinerant Market Women, *International Family Planning Perspectives, 19*, pp. 43-48, 1993.
47. I. Obot, *Sexual Abuse of Children in Calabar, Cross-River State, Nigeria in Child Labour in Africa*, Chuku Printing Company, Calabar, 1986.
48. A. Cohen, *Custom and Politics in Urban Africa: A Study of Hausa Migrants in Yoruba Towns*, University of California Press, Los Angeles, 1969.
49. U. G. Oleru, Prostitution in Lagos: A Socio-Medical Study, *Journal of Epidemiology and Community Health, 34*, pp. 312-315, 1980.
50. M. Adedoyin and A. A. Adegoke, Teenage Prostitution, Childabuse: A Survey of the Ilorin Situation, *African Journal of Medicine and Medical Sciences, 24*, pp. 27-31, 1995.
51. I. O. Orubuloye, P. Caldwell, and J. C. Caldwell, Commercial Sex Workers in Nigeria in the Shadow of AIDS, in *Sexual Networking and AIDS in Sub-Sahara Africa, Behavioural Research and the Social Context*, I. O. Orubuloye, J. C. Caldwell, P. Caldwell, and G. Santow (eds.), Australian National University Press, 1994.

III

INNOVATIONS IN
FIELD PRACTICE

CHAPTER 14

Theory and Action for Effective Condom Promotion: Illustrations from a Behavior Intervention Project for Sex Workers in Singapore

Mee Lian Wong, Roy Chan, David Koh, and Christina Misa Wong

The transmission of human immunodeficiency virus (HIV) between female sex workers and their clients is an important means of heterosexual spread of the virus in many countries [1-3]. Most intervention programs for this target group have focused on use of condoms. An HIV/STD education and intervention project called Project Protect was implemented by the Department of STD Control (DSC) in Singapore in 1992 to control the spread of STDs and AIDS among brothel-based sex workers [4]. The first phase of the project, which comprised one three-hour information-based intervention session improved their knowledge of the seriousness of AIDS and its modes of transmission and decreased their misconceptions. However it did not increase condom use [5]. This is not surprising as behavior change takes time and may require more reinforcement sessions. In addition, many factors other than knowledge influence the complex act of condom use among sex workers, considering that it occurs in an interactive context which requires clients' acceptance and empowerment of sex workers to secure clients' compliance in condom use.

The first phase of the project proved beneficial in serving as a starting point for more intensive interventions to effect behavior change. We subsequently developed a project using behavior change and health education theories to increase condom use in this group. This project which was implemented among

316 brothel-based female sex workers in early 1994 led to a significant increase in condom use that was supported by a relative 75 percent reduction in gonorrhea incidence in the experimental group. The design of the behavior intervention and the preliminary quantitative analysis are described elsewhere [6]. This article describes the project activities to illustrate the application of theoretical principles in increasing condom use among sex workers.

NEEDS ASSESSMENT STUDIES

Studies were conducted on brothel-based sex workers to identify the problems and needs for developing interventions. An epidemiological study on 806 brothel-based sex workers found a moderately strong association of STD risk with the number of clients and percentage of condom users [7]. The majority (> 90%) of sex workers were also well-informed of the seriousness of HIV and AIDS, the modes of transmission, the effectiveness of condom use and were keen to use condoms. However, they succeeded only half the time in getting clients to use them. Perceived barriers and low self-efficacy, rather than lack of knowledge were found to be related to non-condom negotiation and low success in getting clients to use condoms. There were a minority few, however, who claimed that they were able to get all their clients to use condoms [8].

In-depth interviews were subsequently held with forty sex workers with a wide range of success in condom negotiation in order to obtain a broad representation of their perceived barriers and approaches used [9]. The main reasons for not using condoms with clients were found to be lack of confidence to request clients to use condoms and lack of negotiation skills to respond to clients' difficult queries and psychological pressure. For example, they did not know how to respond to the following questions from their clients:

> I am not afraid of death. Why are you afraid? If you are afraid, you should not work in this line.

> Why do you want me to use condoms? Do you suspect me of having AIDS?

> Why do you want me to use condoms? Do you have AIDS?

Other important barriers to condom negotiation included fear of losing clients and annoying brothel keepers who may see them as being fussy which might result in losing work.

Overall they identified four groups of different clients: the young unmarried care-free client who does not think about the repercussions of not using condoms; the older client with no family responsibility and who does not worry about dying from AIDS; the regular client who trusts the sex workers and does not see the need to use condoms; and those who cannot function with condoms.

THEORETICAL BASIS OF THE PROGRAM

Based on the findings of our needs assessment studies, we applied Green's PRECEDE framework [10] and Bandura's self-efficacy theory [11] to develop multiple interventions aimed at equipping sex workers with negotiation skills and providing a supportive environment by gathering the support of brothel keepers and their peers

GREEN'S PRECEDE FRAMEWORK

Using Green's PRECEDE framework, we identified condom negotiation as a changeable and important behavior for intervention. First, we motivated sex workers to negotiate condom use by relating safe sex to what they value. The majority of them were in prostitution out of economic necessity to support family members. Our message stressed the money saved from being free of STD and AIDS. All brothel-based sex workers were required to have biweekly gonorrhea tests and an episode of gonorrhea would result in financial costs incurred from payment for medications, and a few days' loss of earnings due to suspension from work.

Second, we provided training to equip them with negotiation skills to counter clients' arguments and develop assertive behavior. Approaches used by their peers who succeeded in getting clients to use condoms were disseminated to them by means of talks, video presentations, and printed materials.

Third, we provided a supportive environment to facilitate behavior change by getting brothel keepers to display posters and talk to clients about condom use and their peers to always negotiate condom use or refuse unprotected sex if the negotiation process fails.

BANDURA'S SELF-EFFICACY THEORY

Bandura states that one can increase a person's confidence in carrying out a task by getting her to observe or hear from friends who have done it successfully. Next the complexities of the target behavior can be broken down into components that are relatively easier to manage. Using this theory, the act of condom negotiation can be broken down into the non-verbal initiation stage and the negotiation stage (Figure 1).

The first task was to use visual cues such as placing condoms at an easily visible place, for example, near the pillow or wash basin or displaying posters on condom use on the walls to prompt the client. If the client did not respond to the visual cues, the sex workers would then initiate negotiation by giving a condom to the client and telling him of the benefits of condom use. This would lead to compliance among some clients.

With non-compliant clients, sex workers were taught to anticipate questions and queries from them so that she could respond confidently with a counter argument and assert her rights. If the clients still refused to use condoms she

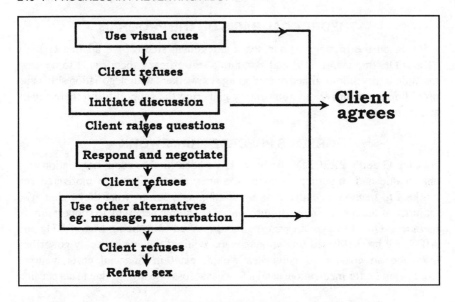

Figure 1. How to negotiate condom use.

would proceed to suggest alternatives such as massage or helping him to mastur-bate. Should this process also fail, she would refuse to take him as a client. Brothel keepers were told to support the sex workers in turning away non-compliant clients. The sex workers were also told to support each other so that clients would have no choice but to use condoms.

THE INTERVENTION PROGRAM

Training of Health Care Providers

Health facilitators (advisors) working at the public STD clinic were trained by the first author in the behavioral and environmental approach to STD/HIV/AIDS control. Training comprised five two-hour sessions covering the following areas: theories on behavior change and their applications; strategies to assess and change sex workers' behavior; and methods and media in health education. The course was task oriented and stressed experiential learning and problem solving. Short lectures were given to deliver the basic principles and these were followed by case study discussions of actual problems identified from baseline studies practical exercises, role-playing, and simulation learning. A handbook was developed and given to participants for easy reference. Nominal Group technique was used to get participants to work collectively and prioritize problems and possible solu-tions for action.

Focus Group Discussion with Brothel Keepers

Focus group discussions were held with brothel keepers to encourage them to support sex workers in condom negotiation and refusing sex without a condom. Discussion was highly interactive and focused on possible solutions to problems raised by them. Some brothel keepers expressed their inability to control the negotiation process between the sex workers and their clients. They were assured that skill development sessions would be conducted for sex workers to increase condom use among them. Brothel keepers were also reminded of the benefits of an STD free brothel and checks by the Department of STD Control on their compliance.

Interventions for Sex Workers

Interventions for sex workers were aimed at motivating them to negotiate condom use, developing their negotiation skills, and increasing their assertiveness in refusing sex without a condom. The following basic messages were delivered: 1) Always use condoms; 2) You have a right to refuse sex and protect yourself from STD and AIDS; 3) Regular clients are not safe; and 4) No one loses and everyone is a winner if all cooperate.

Groups of about sixteen sex workers were organized to provide a heterogenous mix of sex workers with differing attitudes and skills in condom negotiation so as to get them to share their individual polarized views and experiences and provide support to each other under the encouragement and guidance of a health facilitator. Each group was given two two-hour skills training sessions and a booster session. Initially three skills training sessions were planned. At the request of the sex workers the duration of sessions was increased by one hour and the number of sessions reduced to two sessions.

The First Meeting

The objectives of the first meeting were to get sex workers to know each other better, clarify their values and misconceptions, and to demonstrate practical ways of getting clients to use condoms by means of the video. The video presentations consisted of six short video clips in which volunteers among the sex workers role played common problem situations. The video clips (running time: 3 minutes per clip) covered the following topics:

1. First week at work
2. Persuading a young client to use condoms
3. Regular clients need persuading too
4. How about a massage?
5. You have the right to refuse
6. A healthy woman's advice

First Week at Work

This clip shows an inexperienced sex worker getting advice from her seniors on condom use and her right to safe sex.

Persuading a Young Client

This clip shows the use of a positive approach to persuade a young client. The sex worker tells the client he has potential and a bright future ahead and one day he would like to get married and have children. She then emphasizes the point that it is not worth dying from AIDS as a result of not using condoms.

Regular Clients Need Persuading Too

An older regular client is persuaded to use condoms in this clip. The old client refuses to use condoms because he trusts the sex worker to be "clean" and expects the same trust from her. The sex worker then explains that she cannot tell whether her last client has passed STD or AIDS to her and she has asked him to use condoms for his own protection. The client is not convinced and responds that he does not worry about dying from AIDS as he has no family responsibility. The sex worker follows with a counter argument that one does not just die from AIDS but suffers a great deal from it. Also she integrates community values into the message by telling him he may lose "face" and bring suffering and shame to his family (bringing honor to the family is an important value in the Asian community). She then reassures him that he will not lose sensation with the use of condoms. The client finally agrees to use condoms.

How About a Massage?

This clip depicts a situation where a client refuses to use condoms in spite of all the persuasion. The sex worker then suggests a massage to which the client agrees at a discounted rate.

You Have a Right to Refuse

This clip shows a sex worker with a resistant client who refuses condoms and other alternatives. The sex worker politely refuses to take him as a client and returns his money. The client then storms out of the room. The sex worker remains cool, accepting it as part of her work.

A Healthy Woman's Advice

The last clip shows a sex worker persuading her peers to cooperate and use condoms or refuse sex without a condom. She stresses unity and cooperation to fight for their rights against unsupportive brothel keepers and resistant clients.

Each video clip presentation was followed by a discussion of other problems they have experienced and possible solutions. Most groups asked for support from health facilitators to talk to brothel keepers. Sex workers also role-played to increase their self-efficacy and to practice assertive behaviors. They were subsequently asked to keep a log book of clients who refused to use condoms, for three days, with regard to their reasons for not doing so and the difficult queries posed by them when asked to use condoms. The objective of this exercise was to increase the sex workers' awareness of what they were doing, which was a starting point for gaining control.

The Second Meeting

The second meeting was held three to four days after the first meeting. This meeting discussed problems in condom negotiation identified from the self-monitoring exercise. Group members who had succeeded in overcoming similar problems in the past were encouraged to share their experiences with their peers. The health facilitators and group members subsequently helped those with problems to work out a step-by-step approach to deal with difficult clients. For example, one sex worker cited an old client who was not able to carry out the act with a condom. One experienced sex worker shared her techniques on how to help such a client. She further elaborated that she would sometimes tell him not to try too hard as it would be bad for his heart. On most occasions she found the client to be satisfied with her reason and he would agree to a massage without sexual intercourse. Throughout the session the health facilitator praised participants as they provided practical tips and shared experiences. Each group also selected their own peer leader to follow-up on their group members before the next booster session.

Individual Counseling

Individual counseling was given to all sex workers who developed gonorrhea after the intervention to identify possible causes of the infection and to help them overcome perceived barriers. Individual counseling benefited the non-motivated and fatalistic individuals and also those who did not want to share their anxieties in a group. For example one sex worker developed gonorrhea because she held fatalistic views and did not bother to use condoms. She felt she had earned sufficient money for her daughter's education and it would not matter if she passed away from AIDS. The counselor motivated her by relating her non protective behavior to bringing despair and suffering to her daughter should she get AIDS.

The Booster Session

The booster session was held three months after the second session. The objectives of the booster session were to enable participants to assess their progress and discuss further difficulties. It was also used to obtain feedback and provide reinforcement. Condoms were also distributed free to all participants and those who remained free of STD were praised.

PROVIDING PRINTED MATERIALS AS
REINFORCEMENT

Posters with specific messages (Figure 2) directed at clients to always use condoms were distributed to all sex workers and brothel keepers by the Department of STD control to assure them of support.

Comic books designed in an entertaining format that sex workers like to read were also distributed to sex workers. Focusing on personal experiences of sex workers, it was meant to reinforce the video clips and group discussions as sex workers may not recall certain workable approaches. It depicts a story of a sex worker, Mei Ling, who meets her friend Alice at a public STD clinic. Alice has gone there for a gonorrhea injection. Mei Ling, the more experienced sex worker, encourages her to use condoms by telling her the benefits. Alice raises many doubts and problems to which Mei Ling provides practical advice and answers. Alice subsequently tries the approaches that Mei Ling has suggested and finds

Figure 2. Posters displayed in brothels.

them not too difficult after all. The story thus ends with Alice, the younger sex worker gaining her self-esteem.

The story begins in a personalized way by asking questions that sex workers can identify with so that they are encouraged to read further. The cartoon drawings also portray personal experiences and a background very similar to their work setting (Figure 3).

EVALUATION OF THE PROJECT

The design of the behavior intervention program and the preliminary findings are described elsewhere [6]. There were 139 sex workers in the experimental intervention group and 128 sex workers in a demographically comparable control group. In brief this project improved the negotiation skills of the sex workers with a mean success rate in getting clients to use condoms rising from 65.5 percent to 81.9 percent. The proportion of those who always refused sex without a condom rose from 46.4 percent to 65.5 percent. These changes were supported by a significant 75 percent relative reduction in gonorrhea from 9.7 per 100 persons to 2.4 per 100 persons in the four-month period before and after intervention. A control group only showed an improvement of 3.7 percent in negotiation skills and there was no change in behavior outcomes of refusing unprotected sex. Gonorrhea incidence in the control group decreased by a non-significant relative reduction of 39 percent.

The majority (86.7%) found the course useful while 12.7 percent did not know whether the course was useful and only 0.6 percent did not find it useful. Almost all (> 90%) found the video clips useful with the clip on the healthy woman's advice being most highly rated. About half (46.7%) rated this clip as excellent.

CONCLUSION

We have demonstrated the feasibility and effectiveness of behavioral and environmental interventions to control gonorrhea among brothel-based sex workers. Several studies have shown that STD's facilitate the transmission of HIV and a clinic-based intervention consisting of STD control and condom promotion can help in preventing HIV/AIDS.

A few conclusions can be drawn from this project. First it is feasible to apply Bandura's self-efficacy theory in improving negotiation skills among the sex workers. Second, although our targeted group are the sex workers it is important to target interventions toward other groups and the brothels to create a supportive workplace environment to facilitate behavior change. For example, posters were displayed in all brothels to remind clients to always use condoms and brothel keepers were instructed to talk to clients and support sex workers in turning away non-compliant ones. The nominal group technique was used with the health facilitators to get their involvement and commitment in program implementation.

Figure 3. Sample from comic script.

252

Figure 3. (Cont'd.)

253

Figure 3. (Cont'd.)

254

Figure 3. (Cont'd.)

Figure 3. (Cont'd.)

256

Third, the project must address target group needs, which are best determined by a complement of quantitative and qualitative techniques, and by involving the sex workers themselves in project formulation and design of specific messages. Finally the use of a combination of health education methods enables us to meet the differing needs of the sex workers more effectively. The group approach is useful in sharing of experiences and enlisting support. Individual counseling allows the health educator to accommodate individual differences, assess stage of change of the individual's behavior, and provide personalized advice.

This project lends itself to replication among brothel-based sex workers in Southeast Asian communities and other communities with similar sociocultural environments. It may not be replicable in other settings where street-based sex workers predominate. However certain principles which contributed to the effectiveness of this project could be adapted for use in such settings: application of sound theory; use of a complement of quantitative and qualitative techniques to assess target group needs; multiple strategies; and participatory involvement of health care providers and sex workers in planning the interventions. We are following this cohort to assess the sustainability of the behavior change.

[This project was made possible by a grant from Action for AIDS, Singapore.]

REFERENCES

1. J. K. Kreiss, D. Koech, and F. A. Plummer, AIDS Infection in Nairobi Sex Workers: Extension of the Epidemic to East Africa, *New England Journal of Medicine, 314*, pp. 414-418, 1986.
2. J. Mann, D. J. M. Tarantola, and T. W. Netter, *Prevention of AIDS In the World*, Harvard University Press, Cambridge, 1992.
3. B. G. Weniger, K. Limpakarnjanarat, and K. Ungchusak, The Epidemiology of HIV Infection and AIDS in Thailand, *AIDS, 5*:(Suppl 1), pp. S71-S85, 1991.
4. R. K. W. Chan, A. Goh, C. L. Goh, C. Archibald, and M. L. Wong, *'Project Protect'— An STD/AIDS Prevention Intervention Programme for Sex Workers and Establishment in Singapore*, Ninth International Conference on AIDS, Berlin, abstract PO-C14-2904, June 1993.
5. C. P. Archibald, R. K. W. Chan, M. L. Wong, A. Goh, and C. L. Goh, Evaluation of a Safe-Sex Intervention Programme among Sex Workers in Singapore, *International Journal of STD & AIDS, 5*, pp. 268-272, 1994.
6. M. L. Wong, R. K. W. Roy, D. Koh, and J. Lee, Behavioural Interventions for Sex Workers: Impact on Gonorrhoea Rates, *Handbook of Abstracts. IUVDT World STD/AIDS Congress*, Singapore, p. 113, 1995.
7. M. L. Wong, T. C. Tan, M. L. Ho, J. Y. Lim, S. Wan, and R. Chan, Factors Associated with Sexually Transmitted Diseases in Singapore, *International Journal of STD & AIDS, 3*, pp. 323-328, 1992.
8. M. L. Wong, T. C. Tan, M. L. Ho, J. Y. Lim, R. Lim, S. Wan, and R. Chan, Knowledge and Sexual Behaviour Related to HIV and AIDS of Female Sex Workers in Singapore, *Health Education Journal, 53*, pp. 155-162, 1994.

9. M. L. Wong, C. Archibald, R. K. W. Roy, A. Goh, T. C. Tan, and C. L. Goh, Condom use Negotiation among Sex Workers in Singapore: Findings from Qualitative Research, *Health Education Research: Theory & Practice, 9*, pp. 56-67, 1994.
10. L. W. Green and M. W. Kreuter, *Health Promotion Planning, An Education and Environment Approach*, Mayfield, Palo Alto, California, 1990.
11. A. Bandura, *Social Foundations of Thought and Action*, Prentice Hall, Englewood Cliffs, New Jersey, 1986.

CHAPTER 15

Using Theory to Design an Intervention for HIV/AIDS Prevention for Farm Workers in Rural Zimbabwe

Susan M. L. Laver, Bart Van Den Borne, and Gerjo Kok

In Africa the traditional approach to AIDS prevention has been through education. This has been on the assumption that "people will act in their own interest once informed of the risks and benefits" [1] of changing their behavior. In recent years there has been an increasing shift away from expert-driven individually-targeted HIV/AIDS prevention programs toward those which target social change. A variety of primary prevention strategies are used for this purpose. Not uncommonly, however, these strategies are often developed through intuition and in the absence of a thorough problem analysis [2]. It is also not uncommon to find that the theoretical basis for many interventions is still limited to cognitive models which stress the roles of knowledge, attitudes, and beliefs in behavior change. It follows that, where the time and resources are placed on developing cognitive processes within the individual, the benefits of creating change in the community through "reciprocal interaction between cognitive, behavioural and environmental determinants . . ." [1] may not be felt.

The advantage of integrating concepts from different theories to guide the process of behavior change in community-based interventions though not widely practiced, is becoming more widely recognized [3, 4]. For example, interventions which, in addition to targeting cognitive skills and attitudes [5] at an intra personal level, also develop networking skills and response efficacy [6] within the target community, are of value in influencing social change. The strategies by which change is influenced has also attracted considerable debate and in this respect a number of authors [7-10] draw our attention to the seminal work of Paulo Freire [11, 12] whose concept of creating critical consciousness has, according to Glanz [8] added an important dimension to more traditional teaching approaches. In the Freirian model, individual and social change is brought about by developing a climate in which critical thinking, reflection, and problem appraisal is facilitated through a process of listening, dialogue, and action. This approach has been meaningfully adapted for use in many health education projects in first and third world countries [10, 13, 14]. However, as Werch and DiClemente point out, it still appears that "comprehensive programmes founded on multi component, integrative theoretical models, . . . appear to be lacking . . ." [15]. In a similar vein, Wallerstein and Sanchez-Merki remind us that "the challenge exists for us to look (more) objectively towards the theories" that could guide our practice [4].

This article describes how a HIV/AIDS prevention intervention was generated for illiterate farm workers in one district of Zimbabwe using a combination of the social ecology theory [16] and the structured dialogue approach proposed by Freire [12] and later described by Wallerstein and Sanchez-Merki [4], Hope, Timmel, and Hodzi [10]. First we provide an overview of the problem and how it is constructed in farm worker communities. Then we show how theory was combined to generate the methodology for the intervention. The article provides a brief account of the methods that would be used to measure the process and effect of the intervention.

THE PROBLEM

The official estimate of HIV infection in Zimbabwe by early 1995 was estimated around one million people or approximately 10 percent of the population [17]. Loewenson reported in Harare recently that one in five of the productive workforce has HIV [18]. The problem is not confined to the urban areas of Zimbabwe; there is growing evidence of high sero-prevalence levels among rural farm workers who, until recently, have been marginalized in National AIDS Prevention activities [19]. In one study up to 48 percent adults from commercial farms who presented with Sexually Transmitted Diseases (STDs) were HIV +ve [10].

In 1993 we conducted a survey to identify factors likely to place farm workers at risk of STD/HIV infection [19]. Our study arose from a widespread concern that little is known about how the problem is socially produced and maintained in farm worker communities.

Using a structured questionnaire, we interviewed a random sample of 770 male and female farm workers from sixteen randomly selected large scale commercial farms in a district situated from 100 kms north east of Harare where approximately 1,116,928 people or 10.7 percent of the total population of Zimbabwe live [21].

We also collected information through informal discussions with key informants in farm communities.

SUMMARY OF RESEARCH FINDINGS

An adaptation of the Social Ecological Model for Health Promotion [16] guided the conceptualization of the findings at different levels of analysis. The ecological model shows how psychological, psychosocial, organizational, cultural and social, and political theories can be used to guide the targets of behavior change at each level of intervention, i.e., the intra-personal, interpersonal, community, and public policy levels. The findings are presented accordingly: *at the intra-personal (individual) level* characteristics such as knowledge, attitudes, perception of risk etc. of the farm worker are summarized; *at the socio/organizational level* information related to social networks and the organizational culture of the community is presented together with information which relates directly to the community workplace. Finally, information related to regulation is summarized within the *policy level*.

At the intra-personal level, our findings showed that farm communities in our study area were characterized by poor, marginalized workers. Most were second or third generation descendants of families who originated from Malawi, Zambia, and Mozambique. A number of different dialects of the vernacular language were spoken. In sharp contrast to men, women were found to be educationally disadvantaged and illiteracy was correspondingly high.

Exposure to AIDS prevention activities was limited and a high percentage of men and women reported that they "knew very little about AIDS." On selected items of knowledge, misunderstanding about HIV transmission existed. Beliefs that AIDS is brought about by divine/ancestral retribution tended to be upheld by less educated women.

Uneducated women articulated an inability to protect themselves from HIV infection and perceived their risk of contracting HIV to be high. Among more educated men, we found acknowledgment about multi-partnering and that changes in behavior are more likely to come about through changes in normative values. Condom use among men, which is probably the most effective barrier against STD infection was shown to be associated with younger more educated men.

At the socio/organizational level we found that although farm workers live and work together, these communities do not necessarily function as an interdependent group. They lack job tenure and tend to be loosely organized with little decision-making power. Their welfare is generally the concern of the farm owner who is the reference point for most major decisions concerning the workforce. Workers committees had been set up on all the farms in our study sample; however these committees lack the power to bargain or reach decisions of major importance and prove mostly to be a useful reference point for the farm owners. A paternalistic approach to decision making exists and a non-participatory environment generally prevails. The workers felt that there was little that the community could do to prevent the spread of HIV.

We found that there is little recreation for these workers and social groupings tend to mobilize around "farm football," drinking, the church, and handicraft. Free time is also spent in tending to chickens and small plots of vegetables. During times of planting, reaping, and harvest there is an influx of "casual" or "seasonal" workers on many commercial farms. The transitory status of these workers tend to re-enforce their "right" to behave independently of community norms. They are "blamed" for disruptive behavior and prostitution and it was felt that they would be unlikely to participate in a community initiative which promotes the prevention of STD/HIV.

Although no community-based AIDS prevention initiatives were identified on any of the farms in our study, primary health care activities are carried out by Farm Health Workers (FHWs) who are normally women of any age. Selection of FHWs is by their communities; their role is to attend to minor health problems (with very few drugs) and deliver information (without any resources). None had received any training in HIV/AIDS; their approach to health education is usually didactic. Although FHW's are the "official change-agents" with respect to health matters, not surprisingly, they lack recognition and are held in poor esteem by the farm owners and the worker community.

Farm workers are housed as family units in compounds. They do not hold any title to the land and live in dwellings which range from brick to mud and thatch. Some farms have minimum environmental standards of water and sanitation. Few farms had community halls with electricity, but all sixteen farms in our study area had a beerhall, which apart from football was the focal point for recreation. One farm had a public television set but a good number of farm workers owned or shared radios. Newspapers provide an important source of information for literate people, although access is limited and supplies are irregular. Free primary school education was available for children of dependents on eleven farms in our study area.

At the Policy Level

Zimbabwe, like most other African and Western countries, has no laws specifically covering employment-related AIDS issues such as HIV screening [22]. At the time of our study no policy on AIDS for farm workers was in existence. Employers generally retain workers as long as they are able to perform their duties; when a worker dies the farmer helps to pay the funeral expenses. Since deceased workers are likely second or third generation descendants of migrants from neighboring countries, their dependents have no traditional home to which to return. In this context, a generation of orphans, with its attendant problems, is expected to characterize farm communities. Condoms were not freely available on any of the farms in our study; supplies tended to be erratic, cost to the farm owner was a limiting factor, and no policy for accessing or distributing condoms was evident.

In summary, we concluded from these findings that unprotected sex and multi-partnering were the two most important behaviors which placed farm workers at risk of HIV infection. However, we were also cognizant that a wide array of social, organizational, and political forces influenced the problem in farm worker communities. At the intra-personal level women in particular, felt helpless, unable to control their sexuality or reduce the risk of infection with STD/HIV. At the socio/community level the people are dis-empowered and participate only nominally in decision making. At policy level, there are no regulations which enhance accessibility of condoms or protect AIDS sufferers and their dependents. In this context an intervention would need to be sensitive to these issues.

Goal and Objectives of the Intervention

The overall goal of the intervention was to decrease the risk of STD/HIV through unprotected sex and increase farm worker participation in AIDS prevention activities. Our specific objectives included the need to develop a multilevel intervention with a phased participatory methodology which would target change within the individual and the socio/organizational context in which farm worker communities live and work.

In keeping with community organization principles [23] we were cognizant that our intervention should be implemented by persons who were known to, and accepted by, the farm worker communities. We therefore located a cadre of health workers already working in these communities; in Zimbabwe they are known as Farm Health Workers (FHWs).

THEORIES GUIDING THE INTERVENTION

Many authors draw attention to the fact that AIDS prevention interventions commonly fail to shift their focus beyond the cognitive level [3, 24]. McLeroy and his colleagues point out that this incorrectly assumes that "the proximal causes of behaviour lie within the individual . . . rather than in the social environment" [16].

Amaro concurs with this position and says that "human behaviour, especially sexual behaviour, is more complex than models suggest" [3]. The author goes on to stress the need for researchers to locate models and theories which in addition to cognitive change, also target the social context of sexuality and the differences which shape risk behavior between men and women. Taking these issues into account, our attention was focused on the need to conceptualize a prevention program for farm workers in which change could be meaningfully activated beyond a cognitive level. Two models proved appropriate for this purpose. The first concerned the ecological model of health promotion [16]. Although this model was not defined specifically for HIV/AIDS prevention, it is particularly relevant because it focuses attention on individual *and* social factors as targets for change. A variety of intervention strategies are also proposed through the model; these are specific for each level of intervention and range from skills development at the intra-personal level to mass media and regulatory changes at other levels. According to our adaptation of this model however, the intervention would target change at the interpersonal, socio/organizational, and policy levels. None of these levels was considered mutually exclusive.

The second theory of major importance to the development of the intervention was the theory for individual and social change originally developed by Paulo Freire [11] and used extensively in health promotion and social development programs by David Werner [25] and others [4, 7, 10, 14]. In acknowledging the need for interplay between individual and social/organizational change, Freire's work also provides a philosophical framework for the development of *strategies* for interventions. In particular the model had three major advantages for our intervention; first it encompasses a participatory orientation to learning rather than a passive mode of delivering information. In Freire's words, "we simply cannot go to the workers . . . to give them knowledge or to impose upon them the model of the 'good man' contained in a programme whose content we have ourselves organised" [11]. Freire also goes on to say that "it is not our role to speak to people about our own view of the world but rather to dialogue with the people about their view and ours." This was important, given the urgent need to develop and promote a culture of appraisal and dialogue around the issue of HIV/AIDS in farm worker communities. Second, the model incorporates a listening-dialogue-action methodology which is an on-going cyclical process (as opposed to a linear process) appropriate for motivating critical thinking within a target group where there is a need to "re-visit" and "re-appraise" key issues such as lay beliefs throughout the intervention. And third, the model as described by Wallerstein and Sanchez-Merki [4], integrates protection-motivation theory which proposes that decisions to act can be initiated through a variety of information sources [4, 6, 26], thus reducing the dependency on didactics. In addition to the above, we reviewed a number of other theories which we felt to have implications for the intervention at each level of our intervention.

At the intra-personal level, the theory of change is one which primarily concerns individuals. The targets of change include the characteristics of the individual such as knowledge, attitudes, skills, or intentions to change [16]. In conceptualizing the targets of change for our intervention we were initially guided by the Health Belief Model (HBM) [5, 27], described by Amaro [3] as "a cognitive model of behaviour change," which attempts to explain individual behavior according to one's perception of vulnerability, i.e., susceptibility, perceived threat, advantages, and disadvantages of changing behavior and barriers. Since lay beliefs held among people in our target group (e.g., AIDS is a result of Ancestors displeasure; Getting AIDS is a matter of bad luck) were likely to be a barrier to cognitive and attitude change, we considered that an appraisal of HIV in terms of personal threat, vulnerability, and weighing up of advantages and disadvantages of practices (such as not using a condom with girlfriends) should be an ongoing activity at the first level of intervention. In addition to which, the Social Learning Theory in which vicarious learning (modeling) is a central theme, also views behavior as a function of a person's self-efficacy, or the belief that one can successfully execute a behavior in order to produce the outcome (In future, I will be able to ask my partner to use a condom in order to protect myself from getting STD/HIV), was important in our study [28]. In this respect we felt a particular need to develop coping responses (There is something I can do to prevent myself from getting STD/HIV) among women who were shown through our background research to be "helpless" and sexually disempowered.

The Theory of Reasoned Action also had implications for conceptualizing the intervention at the intra-personal level because in addition to beliefs of behavioral outcomes (e.g., using a condom will increase/decrease sexual pleasure or condoms will/will not reduce Sexually Transmitted Diseases), it emphasizes the role of personal intention and attitudes in determining whether a behavior will occur [29, 30]. The theory draws attention to the influence of "normative" beliefs people may have; that is what they think other people—in particular influential people such as peers—would expect them to do in a particular situation. This was particularly important, given attitudes to STD infection and multi-partnering by men (most men expect to have more than one partner; these days men expect to get an STD at least once in their lifetime) which were revealed through our research.

We were cognizant that the models described previously are based on individual conceptualization of behavior. We then focused on the theory of change as it would apply to the tradition of organization in our target community. Many authors propose interesting views on the organizational aspects of community interventions [23, 31]. Minkler describes community organization as "the process by which community groups are helped to identify common problems, mobilise resources and in other ways develop strategies and goals for reaching the goals they have set" [32]. Several key concepts are reported by Minkler to be central to this process [32]. Of particular importance to this study, and central also to the Freirian philosophy were the issues of empowerment which, according to Ross [33] and Freire [11], must increase problem solving, participation and the development of critical consciousness. Minkler says that "in community organisation practice, the concept of empowerment operates on two levels simultaneously. First the individual involved in a community organising effort may feel more support, and . . . such social support may contribute to a more generalised sense of coherence" [32] e.g., a response that the community *can* do something to prevent the spread of HIV.

In emphasizing the role of change agents (Farm Health Workers) in the diffusion process [34, 35], and the linkage approach [36-38] in the social environment, the diffusion of innovations model also removes the focus somewhat away from the individual as the target for change [39]. According to this perspective the intervention would be reenforced at each level through a linkage system made up of Farm Health Workers (the change agents) and Land Owners.

Each of the theories and models presented previously is complex and multimodal. However, there were also many similarities. In examining these models, we tried to keep those components which would enable the attainment of our objectives and permit the flexibility which was required in the conceptualization of the intervention at each level of implementation.

THE INTERVENTION

We proposed that the intervention should be targeted at three levels viz., the intra-personal, socio/organizational and policy levels [16]. The methodology would embrace the Freirian Structured Dialogue Model described by Wallerstein and Sanchez-Merki in which a cyclical listening-appraisal-dialogue-action approach is proposed [4]. Program inputs would incorporate "easy-to-use," replicable, and cost effective methods that could be implemented by Farm Health Workers who would be the change-events.

Since didactic methods have been used more extensively than participatory methods to educate people with AIDS [24], we were aware of the need to train the FHWs to use methods which would be less "teacher dependent." We were also aware of the need to decrease the role of the change agent over time and increase community involvement in AIDS prevention activities. A training program would be developed along with visual materials, such as picture codes and a manual for trainers, to meet these objectives.

The first objective at the intra-personal level of the intervention would be to activate recognition of and personal identification with HIV/AIDS e.g., What is AIDS; how did it get to Zimbabwe; has it reached the rural areas; do STD's lead to the problem, etc. Strategies, such as group discussion which promote active listening and appraisal within the safety of small numbers were proposed. The value of dialogue would be stressed with an emphasis on the importance of the change agent role in facilitation.

This stage would be followed by an appraisal of lay beliefs (e.g., AIDS is a very old disease; Getting AIDS is just a matter of luck, etc.) using a participatory "agree/disagree" activity. A period of threat and susceptibility appraisal would follow (is AIDS really a problem; am I at risk; is my family at risk, etc.). Cognitive changes, for example with respect to instrumental knowledge about STD/HIV/AIDS (mosquitoes do not spread AIDS, a person with STD is at risk of becoming infected with HIV; touching infected people does not cause a person to get HIV, etc.) would be brought about through didactic sessions aided by a flip chart and pictures.

Program inputs would then be oriented toward an appraisal of variables such as self-efficacy (is it possible for women to deny sex to their husbands) and response efficacy (what can we do to protect ourselves) through listening and dialogue aided by "triggers" such as picture codes, which are socially charged pictures that illustrate problems [40]. Personal experience and cultural issues would be used as the basis for the appraisal of social norms (do men expect to have more than one partner these days; is it true that men will only change when their friends decide to do the same, etc.).

This stage would gradually move on to an appraisal of these issues within a societal context (what can we do to involve seasonal workers in AIDS prevention; what can men do; what can women do; what can we as a community do; what can the farm owner do). This phase would be accompanied by a shift in the locus of control from change agent to the community with empowerment, social responsibility, and action (i.e., shown by new initiatives, such as AIDS clubs) as important objectives.

The objective of policy change would mainly target the issue of condom access and distribution within the community, while encouraging critical thought around the problem of AIDS orphans and dependents of sufferers (what can the community do; what should the government do, what should the land owners do).

The locus of control for the intervention would therefore shift from the researcher at the problem definition, materials development, and training stage, to a point at which the project was institutionalized within the community through the change agents. However, given the non-participatory environment in which farm workers have found themselves to be historically, we realized that this may be a difficult objective to achieve. Social action would depend on the support available for change; individual change could become the only possible outcome.

Table 1 provides a summary of the intervention proposal. It shows the principal theories/models which are proposed for each level, the targets of change and the strategies to be employed [16].

MEASURES OF EVALUATION

Although we were aware that behavior change is likely to take place gradually over time, the process of the intervention would be measured throughout the period of implementation and the effect would be measured after a twelve-month period. Process information would be collected by means of:

- Simplified process data forms—to be completed by Farm Health Workers every month. Data pertaining to the following would be collected:
  - reach, i.e.,
    numbers of groups convened
    enquiries from other farm,
    new initiatives within the community

- methods of communication used
- number of condoms distributed
- new condom distribution points
- Sexually Transmitted Disease (STD) incidence data—i.e., number of new STD cases reported to FHW's and catchment clinics within the project area.
- Seasonal data—i.e., data concerning the influx of seasonal workers at different times in the farming calendar, bonus months, leave periods, etc.
- Focus Group Discussions—to collect data from Farm Health Workers
- Follow-up visits to intervention farms and discussions with farm owners.

The effect of the intervention would be measured using the structured interview method. Changes in knowledge, attitudes, perception of threat and vulnerability, self-esteem, social norms, and empowerment would be measured. For comparative purposes, the results from our intervention farms would be compared with randomly assigned control farms.

Table 1. Summary of Intervention Proposal

Level of Intervention (after [16])	Theories of Change	Targets of Change	Phases/Strategies/ Methods (after [4, 11])
Intra-personal level	Health Belief Model [5]	Personal identification with problem Recognition of problem Lay beliefs	Listening Phase Small group discussion
		Vulnerability (i.e., susceptibility, threat, advantages v. disadvantages of behavior change, barriers to change)	Appraisal Phase Agree/Disagree activities Dialogue Phase Flip chart
	Social Learning Theory [28] Theory of Reasoned Action [29, 30]	Cognitive change Attitude change Self-efficacy (empowerment at individual level)	Picture codes Condom distribution
		Social norms	Action Phase AIDS clubs Maintenance of condom supply
Socio- organizational level	Community Organization Theory [32, 34, 35]	Perceived community efficacy (empowerment) Social action	Peer education New community initiatives
Policy level		Perceived support by authority	Organized support by authorities

CONCLUSION

This chapter shows how theory was used to develop an intervention for marginalized farm workers in rural Zimbabwe. It highlights the problem of HIV as revealed through a study of farm workers and goes on to explore relevant theories or models which provided a guide to the development of a methodology for the intervention. It also provides a brief account of the methods that would be used to measure the process and effect of the intervention.

In proposing the intervention we were mindful that, in addition to prevailing factors already described, the receptivity of farm worker communities to our intervention would be determined by many issues. For example, we were aware that farm workers would be at different stages of comprehension about AIDS and not everyone would have an equal opportunity to attend sessions. Some workers would attend some sessions and not others. It was likely that farming activities could disrupt the intervention i.e., when workers were too busy planting or harvesting to spare limited free time for participation in intervention activities. At other times, workers would need to take leave and return to their traditional "homes." We also recognized the need to sustain interest among farm owners especially as it would be unlikely at the outset, that they would see no demonstrable changes in risk taking behavior.

Finally in Zimbabwe, as with many other African countries, a strong culture of didactics exist, especially with respect to education. Workers in particular, expect to be told what not to do; it is unusual for them to be in a learning situation where they are invited to do the talking. The difficulty of proposing a methodology that requires facilitators with limited experience to stand back and listen was not to be underestimated.

REFERENCES

1. S. Fincham, Community Health Promotion Programs, *Social Science Medicine, 35*:3, pp. 239-249, 1992.
2. G. Kok, Health Education and Research for AIDS Prevention, *Hygie-Vol X*, pp. 32-39, 1991/1992.
3. H. Amaro, Love, Sex and Power. Considering Women's Realities in HIV Prevention, *American Psychologist, 50*:6, pp. 437-447, 1995.
4. N. Wallerstein and V. Sanchez-Merki, Freirian Praxis in Health Education: Research Results from an Adolescent Prevention Programme, *Health Education Research. Theory and Practice, 9*:1, pp. 105-118, 1994.
5. M. H. Becker, The Health Belief Model and Sick Role Behaviour, *Health Education Monographs, 2*, pp. 409-419, 1974.
6. R. W. Rogers, C. W. Deckner, and C. R. Mewborn, An Expectancy-Value Theory Approach to the Long Term Modification of Smoking Behaviour, *Journal of Clinical Psychology, 34*, pp. 562-566, 1978.

7. N. Wallerstein and E. Bernstein, Empowerment Education: Freire's Ideas Adapted to Health Education, *Health Education Quarterly, 15*, pp. 379-394, 1988.
8. K. F. Glanz, M. Lewis, and B. K. Rimmer (eds.), *Health Behaviour and Health Education. Theory and Practice*, Jossey-Bass Publishers, San Francisco, 1990.
9. N. Wallerstein and E. Bernstein, Introduction to Community Empowerment, Participatory Education and Health, *Health Education Quarterly, 21*:2, pp. 141-148, Summer 1994.
10. A. Hope, S. Timmel, and C. Hodzi, *Training for Transformation: A Handbook for Community Workers*, 3 Volumes, Mambo Press, Gweru, Zimbabwe, 1984.
11. P. Freire, *Pedagogy of the Oppressed*, Seabury Press, New York, 1972.
12. P. Freire, *Education for Critical Consciousness*, Seabury Press/Continuum Press, New York, 1983.
13. M. Minkler and K. Cox, Creating Critical Consciousness in Health: Applications of Freire's Philosophy and Methods to the Health Care Setting, *International Journal of Health Services*, pp. 311-322, 1980.
14. E. R. Auerbach and N. Wallerstein, *ESL for Action Problem Posing at Work*, Teaching Guide, Addison Wesley, Reading, Massachusetts, 1987.
15. C. E. Werch and J. Diclimente, A Multi-Component Stage Model for Matching Drug Prevention Strategies and Messages to Youth Stage of Use, *Health Education Research. Theory and Practice, 9*:1, pp. 37-46, 1994.
16. K. R. McLeroy, D. Bibeau, A. Steckler, and K. Glanz, An Ecological Perspective on Health Promotion Programs, *Health Education Quarterly, 15*:4, pp. 351-377, 1988.
17. H. Farag, Report on *Zimbabwe Television News, (ZTV)*, January 23, 1995.
18. R. Loewenson, *Sunday Mail Newspaper*, Harare, Zimbabwe, June 18, 1995.
19. J. De May et al., HIV Sentinel Surveillance in Mashonaland West Province: HIV Sero-Prevalence Survey in the Commercial Farming Area of Zvimba District, March-July, A Final Report, *PMD, Mashonaland West Province*, 1992.
20. S. M. Laver, *A Pre-Invention Survey to Determine Understanding of HIV/AIDS in Farm Worker Communities of Zimbabwe*, in press, 1995.
21. CSO, Census Report *Central Statistical Office*, Government Printers, Harare, Zimbabwe, 1992.
22. G. Williams and S. Ray, Workplace against AIDS, Workplace-Based AIDS Initiatives in Zimbabwe, *Strategies for Hope Series No. 8*, Action Aid, AMREF, Kenya, 1993.
23. N. Bracht, Introduction, in *Health Promotion at the Community Level*, N. Bracht (ed.), Sage, Newbury Park, California, pp. 19-25, 1990.
24. S. Laver, AIDS Education is More than Telling People What Not To Do, *Tropical Doctor, 23*, pp. 156-160, 1993.
25. D. Werner and B. Bower, *Helping Health Workers Learn*, The Hesperian Foundation, Palo Alto, California, 1982.
26. R. W. Rogers, Changing Health-Related Attitudes and Behaviour: The Role of Preventive Health Psychology, in *Interfaces in Psychology*, R. McGlyn, J. Maddox, C. Stoltenbury, and R. J. Harvey (eds.), Texas Tech University Press, Lubbock, Texas, 1984.
27. M. Becker and J. Joseph, AIDS and Behavioural Change to Avoid Risk, A Review, *American Journal of Public Health, 78*, pp. 384-410, 1988.

28. A. Bandura, *Social Foundations of Thought and Action: A Social Cognitive Theory*, Prentice-Hall, Englewood Cliffs, New Jersey, 1977.
29. M. Fishbein and I. Ajzen, *Beliefs, Attitudes, Intention and Behaviour: An Introduction to Theory and Research*, Addison-Wesley, Reading, Massachusetts, 1975.
30. M. Fishbein and I. Ajzen, *Understanding Attitudes and Predicting Social Behaviour*, Prentice Hall, Englewood Cliffs, New Jersey, 1980.
31. N. Bracht and L. Kingsbury, Community Organisation Principles in Health Promotion: A Five Stage Model, in *Health Promotion at the Community Level*, N. Bracht (ed.), Sage, Newbury Park, California, pp. 66-88, 1990.
32. M. Minkler, Group Intervention Models of Health Behaviour Change, in *Health Behaviour and Health Education. Theory and Research*, K. Glanz, F. M. Lewis, and B. K. Rimer (eds.), Jossey-Bass Health Series, San Francisco, pp. 253-287, 1990.
33. M. Ross, *Community Organisation: Theory and Principles*, Harper and Row, New York, 1955.
34. E. Rogers and F. Shoemaker, *Communication of Innovations* (2nd Edition), Free Press, New York, 1971.
35. E. Rogers, *Diffusion of Innovations*, Free Press, New York, 1983.
36. R. Havelock, *Planning for Innovation through Dissemination and Utilisation of Knowledge*, Institute for Social Research, Ann Arbor, Michigan, 1971.
37. M. A. Orlandi, The Diffusion and Adoption of Worksite Health Promotion Innovations: An Analysis of Barriers, *Preventive Medicine, 15*, pp. 522-536, 1986.
38. M. A. Orlandi, Promoting Health and Preventing Disease in Health Care Settings, *Preventive Medicine, 16*, pp. 99-130, 1987.
39. J. A. Graeff, J. P. Elder, and E. Mills Booth, *Communication for Health and Behaviour Change, A Developing Country Perspective*, Jossey-Bass Publishers, San Francisco, 1993.
40. S. Laver, Picture Codes in AIDS Education, *World Health Forum, 15*, pp. 39-41, 1994.
41. N. K. Janz and M. H. Becker, The Health Belief Model: A Decade Later, *Health Education Quarterly, 11*:1, pp. 1-48, Spring 1984.

CHAPTER 16

Was the Intervention Implemented as Intended?: A Process Evaluation of an AIDS Prevention Intervention in Rural Zimbabwe

Susan M. L. Laver, Bart Van Den Borne, Gerjo Kok, and Godfrey Woelk

End-point evaluations are still the most common method of assessing the success or failure of interventions. In this respect the questionnaire is very often used to gather information. However, Chambers reminds us that although questionnaires "can be aggregated to give an overall view . . . their penetration is usually shallow, concentrating on what is measurable, answerable and acceptable as a question rather than probing less tangible and more qualitative aspects of society" [1]. The author goes further to say that "conventional questionnaires have many drawbacks if the aim is to gain insight into the lives and conditions of poorer rural people . . . other methods are required, either alone, or together with surveys." Many evaluation theorists, Cook and Campbell [2], Reichart and Cook [3] among others, support this view and advocate the inclusion of quantitative *and* qualitative methods in the data collection repertoire. Increasingly we have come to notice that, in addition to the measurement of outcome or effect of an intervention through quantitative research methods, other methods are recommended for assessing the effectiveness of long-term intervention programs [4].

In this respect, Glanz, Lewis, and Rimer [5], Van Assema [6], and Ingersoll, Bazar, and Zenter [7] advocate the use of well structured and comprehensive *process* evaluation approaches as a means of strengthening assumptions about causality by clarifying the relationships between interventions and outcome. In describing "process evaluation" McGraw et al. [8], say that it ". . . compliments outcome evaluation by providing data to describe how a programme was implemented, how well the activities delivered fit the original design, to whom the services were delivered, the extent to which the target population was reached and factors external to that programme that may compete with the programme effects." Green and Lewis say that "process analyses are useful in large diffuse programmes where the source of programme effects is unclear" [9]. They go on to say that "process analysis helps us to learn as much as possible about how, why, and under what conditions a program brings about certain outcomes (including no effect). It encompasses," he says, "more than the functioning of the program. It answers the question 'what happened' and permits the analysis of unusual failures, successes, or dropouts; close observation of especially effective aspects of the programmes . . . and (it) presents a better picture of how the programme really works."

Recent studies show how process evaluation is used to compliment outcome evaluation in interventions carried out in the United States [8, 10-13]. In a process evaluation study in Canada, Gliksman et al. [14] evaluated the role of alcohol servers in a prevention program; in Holland where the method was used in a school-based smoking prevention project by Dijkstra et al. [15] and an interesting account of a process evaluation of a community intervention project in Bergeyk [6]. Although the authors did not conduct an exhaustive search, there appears to be little documented evidence in easily available sources of process evaluation studies in developing country situations, particularly in respect to community outcomes.

In this article we describe how an STD/HIV/AIDS prevention intervention was generated for farm workers. We show how "process evaluation" was used to describe the events which took place during the intervention period. In particular we report on factors such as seasonal farming activity which affected the process of implementation. We report on the reach of the intervention and methods used. We also report on condom demand during the intervention period, possible effects of labor fluctuation on project implementation, disposable income, and patterns of sexually transmitted disease.

The generation of our process evaluation plan was guided by the experience of McGraw et al. [8] and Van Assema [6].

BACKGROUND RESEARCH

Our intervention was planned against a background of concern about rising HIV infection in workers who live and work on large-scale commercial farms in Zimbabwe. For example a study conducted by De May et al. showed that up to 49 percent of farm workers presenting with STDs at a district hospital in one catchment area were HIV positive [16].

In an effort to examine behavioral factors likely to place workers at risk of STD/HIV infection in farm communities, we conducted a survey by interview [17]; 770 farm workers from seventeen randomly selected commercial farms participated in the study.

The survey showed that at an interpersonal level, farm-workers communities, which are characterized by educationally disadvantaged women when compared with men, have had little exposure to AIDS prevention activities. Our study showed that beliefs that AIDS is brought about by divine/ancestral retribution were upheld by less educated women. A significant association was found with respect to perceived risk to HIV and low self-efficacy among uneducated women who articulated helplessness and an inability to protect themselves from HIV infection. Among more educated men, we found acknowledgment about multi-partnering and that changes in behavior are more likely to come about through changes in normative values. Condom use, which is probably the most effective barrier against STD infection was shown to be very low and associated with younger more educated men.

At a socio-organizational level our findings showed that farm-worker communities are loosely organized, they lack decision-making power and are characterized by extreme poverty. There were no policies or laws in place covering employment-related AIDS issues, and condoms were usually unavailable.

We concluded from these findings that a replicable, low-cost STD/HIV/AIDS prevention program should be designed, implemented, and evaluated in one farming district. A process and impact evaluation would be conducted to measure the effect of the intervention.

INTERVENTION GOAL AND OBJECTIVES

The overall goal of the intervention was to decrease the risk of STD/HIV infection through unprotected sex and increase farm-worker participation in AIDS prevention activities [18]. Our specific objectives included the need to develop a multi-level intervention with a phased, participatory methodology in which dialogue would play a central role. We aimed to target chances such as self-efficacy, social norms, and perceived susceptibility to STD/HIV infection at an intra-personal level. Within the socio-organizational context of the farm-worker community, we aimed to create an enabling climate which would encourage the development of community-based initiatives against AIDS. A further objective concerned policy change with respect to condom distribution and care of AIDS sufferers on farms [18].

CHANGE-AGENTS

In keeping with community organization principles [19] we were cognizant that our intervention should be interpreted by persons who were known to, and accepted by, the farm-worker communities. We therefore located a cadre of health workers already working in these communities; in Zimbabwe they are known as Farm Health Workers (FHWs).

THEORETICAL IMPLICATIONS FOR THE DEVELOPMENT OF THE INTERVENTION

Several theories were reviewed for the purposes of intervention design. Of these, two were especially pertinent to the study. The first concerned the ecological model of health promotion [20]. Although this model was not defined specifically for HIV/AIDS prevention it was relevant because it focused attention on individual *and* social factors as targets for change.

The second theory of major importance to the development of the intervention was the theory for individual and social change originally developed by Paulo Friere [21] and used extensively in health promotion and social development programs by Werner and Bower [22] and others [23-26]. In acknowledging the need for interplay between individual and social/organizational change, Friere's work also provides a philosophical framework for the development of *strategies* for interventions. The model had three major advantages for our intervention; first, it encompasses a participatory orientation to learning rather than a passive mode of delivering information. Second, it incorporates a listening-dialogue-action methodology which is an ongoing cyclical process (as opposed to a linear process) appropriate for motivating change within a target group where there was a need to "re-visit" and "re-appraise" key issues such as lay beliefs, throughout the intervention. And third, the model as described by Wallerstein and Sanchez-Merki [26], integrates protection-motivation theory which proposes that decisions to act can be initiated through a variety of informational sources [26-29], thus reducing the dependency on didactics. Our intervention also combined the constructs of a number of other theories, i.e., the Health Belief Model [30], the Social Learning Theory [31], the Theory of Reasoned Action [32, 33], Community Organisation Theory [19, 34] and Diffusion of Innovations Theory [35].

THE INTERVENTION

Selection of Farm Health Workers

In order for the intervention to have a good chance of success, forty of the "best" Farm Health Workers in the district were selected as change-agents. The selection criteria included their Primary Health Care training record, records of attendance at monthly FHW meetings, commitment to the FHW program, functional literacy, and a willingness to participate. None of the FHWs had received previous training in AIDS prevention; all were female. We randomly assigned twenty FHWs to an intervention group for training in our methodology and assigned twenty to a control. As it would be impractical to follow up twenty FHWs in the intervention group, nine farms were randomly selected from the intervention group for this purpose; eight were selected from the control. Each FHW represented a community of around 300 permanent workers and their dependents.

Materials Development and Training

The FHWs in the intervention group received intensive training which was carried over a period of ten days at a rural district hospital FHW training center. The training was conducted in the vernacular by persons who had already received training in the listening-appraisal-dialogue-action method.

In particular the advantages of a participatory approach versus a didactic approach in information delivery were stressed. FHWs were trained to become "the sharers," instead of the "givers" of information. They learned the importance of "listening" versus "telling" people what was known already. Group work rather than lectures was encouraged. At the conclusion of the training, each Farm Health Worker was equipped with pre-tested resource materials for the intervention. These included posters, picture codes (which are socially charged pictures that illustrate problems), hand-outs which showed color photographs of STDs and an AIDS Flipchart. Our FHWs were also trained in the compilation of process data sheets (Annex A) which would be submitted monthly to the research coordinator. Top-up training was provided at monthly meetings held throughout the intervention period.

A post-training survey indicated that the FHWs had grasped the basic concepts of the listening-appraisal-dialogue-action approach. Their ability to handle small groups and training aids such as picture codes with confidence was measured through practical sessions during and subsequent to their training. They emerged enthusiastic and confident about their new role in HIV/AIDS communication; however, they were also realistic about the barriers which may prevent an attainment of their objectives. These included a lack of "protected" time for education at the workplace, apathy, and disruption by seasonal workers. There was also a clear recognition by FHWs that social action would depend on widespread support for change; individual change could become the only possible outcome.

DESCRIPTION AND IMPLEMENTATION OF THE INTERVENTION

The intervention was carried out according to the phases in our listening-appraisal-dialogue-action model [18, 26]. The process was cyclical and no single phase was discrete.

The Listening Stage

The listening stage targeted active versus passive listening. The issue of AIDS was raised in the farm community by the FHW who encouraged workers to discuss and listen to others discuss the problem. In this stage the FHWs especially aimed to activate recognition of, and personal identification with, HIV/AIDS. Questions such as, What is AIDS/ how did it get to Zimbabwe; has it reached the rural areas; has the problem reached our community, our families, our friends, etc., were raised. Group discussion which promotes active listening and dialogue within the safety of small numbers was used to facilitate this process. This phase lasted about two months.

Appraisal

Since misperceptions and lay beliefs about AIDS were identified as possible barriers to behavior change in farm workers [17], the intervention graduated toward a process of critical appraisal around the issue of vulnerability, i.e., susceptibility to infection, perceived threat, the disadvantages and advantages of changing behavior, and barriers to action. For the initial phase of appraisal, FHWs pooled a number of "trigger statements" which reflected lay beliefs and misunderstandings commonly cited by farm workers, e.g., "AIDS is a very old disease; Getting AIDS is just a matter of luck," etc. The community was invited to participate in "agree/disagree" activities to appraise these beliefs.

This phase was followed by a further period of appraisal which dealt more specifically with the issues of personal threat and susceptibility, e.g., is AIDS really a problem to me; am I personally at risk; is my family at risk, are farm workers at more risk than other people in Zimbabwe, etc. Active listening skills were promoted and empathy, shown to be an important variable for behavior change [26, 36] was encouraged through anecdotes which helped to create and sustain an openness about these issues.

A free, monthly condom supply was offered to FHWs working on intervention and control farms during this phase; many of the control farms did not respond. Supplies were calculated according to the approximate number of males and females permanently resident on the farm and aged between seventeen to fifty-five × fifteen condoms per month. Additional supplies were made available to FHWs on request and more especially during periods when there was an influx of seasonal workers. FHWs were encouraged during this phase, to ensure regular condom supplies at high access points such as beer-halls. The number of condoms distributed each month was recorded on the process data form (Annex A). This phase of the intervention merged with the dialogue phase, although appraisal methods were used throughout the intervention.

Dialogue

In this phase we aimed especially to increase instrumental knowledge about STD/HIV/AIDS (mosquitoes do not spread AIDS, a person with STD is at risk of becoming infected with HIV; touching infected people does not cause a person to get HIV, etc.) and develop critical thought about the social context of the problem (women are at risk; old people and young children will be affected when wage earners die). Teaching resources included a flip chart and color photographs showing STDs. Regular, free condom supplies were maintained through FHWs and volunteer "community-based" distributers.

We also aimed in this phase, to enhance the belief that the sense of vulnerability and helplessness was heightened by low self-efficacy among women. Dialogue and debate was encouraged through discussion and "triggers" such as picture codes which depicted problems of local relevance. Among men, anecdotes provided the catalyst for discussion around social norms which were known to be prevalent (is it true that most men expect to have more than one partner these days; is it true that men only change their ways when their friends decide to do the same, etc.).

Action

The dialogue state gradually progressed in the last months of the intervention to an appraisal of resources available to deal with the problem of HIV/AIDS in a societal context (what can we do to involve seasonal workers in AIDS prevention; what can men do; what can women do, what can we as a community do; what can the farm owner do about the problem). In this phase we expected a shift in the locus of control from change-agent to the community with empowerment, social responsibility, and action (i.e., shown by new initiatives, such as AIDS clubs) as important objectives. Drama was used to promote the concept of change and community-focused action. The objective of policy change in this phase mainly targeted the need to increase access to condoms within the community, while encouraging critical thought around the problem of AIDS orphans and dependents of sufferers (how do children perceive the problem; what can the community do; what should the government do, what should the landowners do).

Process Evaluation Measures

We were mindful that post-intervention community-level changes are difficult to detect within a one-year time frame. In addition to a quasi-experimental post-test study design to measure the effects of the intervention, our process evaluation was designed to answer the question "What happened over time?"

Information was collected through:

- Process data forms—completed by Farm Health Workers every month (Annex A). Data pertaining to the following was collected:
  - methods of communication used
  - reach, i.e.,
    - numbers of groups convened
    - enquiries from other farms
    - new initiatives within the community

- condom demand
- STDs reported to FHWs
- Clinic records, i.e., STD cases reported to catchment clinics within the project area. Cases were identified by farm name, disease type, sex, and age.
- Seasonal activities on farms—i.e., data concerning the influx of seasonal workers at different times in the farming calendar, bonus months, leave periods, etc.
- Focus Group Discussions—to collect mid-point data from Farm Health Workers
- Follow-up visits to farms—discussions with Farm owners

Data Analysis

Qualitative and quantitative data were collected for the process evaluation. The qualitative data was analyzed through content analysis; quantitative data were analyzed using Lotus 1-2-3.

FINDINGS

Process data were collected over twelve months. Figure 1 provides a graphic representation of epidemiological data and condom demand for intervention farms. Figure 1 is also annotated with information pertaining to seasonal patterns of farming activity, seasonal fluctuation of labor, and disposable income patterns observed during the intervention period.

None of the FHWs ($n = 9$) from our intervention farms submitted process data forms (Annex A) every month as planned. Four FHWs completed data forms for eleven months, two FHWs had between four and six months missing. Reasons given for this included illness, leave, forgetfulness, and a bereavement. At the outset of the intervention it was noted that FHWs "inflated" their process data and unrealistic records concerning "reach" were received. This problem resolved as trust was established within the FHW group. Process data was also collected through monthly group discussions with FHWs and a "real" picture of intervention activity was revealed in a way that we could not derive from written reports.

With respect to condom demand (Figure 1), we could not say with any certainty to whom they were issued, i.e., seasonal workers, workers from neighboring farms, or workers from the intervention community. Re-supplies were calculated on a monthly basis according to stock in hand.

Factors Affecting the Process of Implementation

Farming Activities

The intervention was set against a background of farming activity which closely influenced the implementation process in terms of reach and participation.

Off-Season Farming Activities

The "off season" on large-scale tobacco farms, which occurs approximately between July-September, coincided with the "listening phase" of our intervention. We learned from process-data collected during this period that many farm workers were on leave and seasonal workers had moved away from most farms. In theory, fewer people would participate in intervention activities. In contrast to what we expected however, process-data submitted by FHWs for this period showed inflated levels of activity and reach. FHWs later confirmed that this happened because of an anxiety to "please and to show that a good start on the project had been made."

Mid-High Season Farming Activities

The "appraisal-dialogue" phase of the intervention coincided with a period of intensive farming activity from October through April. With the advent of the tobacco planting season, came also an increase in opportunities for seasonal worker employment (Figure 1) and an influx of male and some female casual workers from surrounding farms and communal areas was noted. Wives of permanent workers were employed; school children engaged in after lesson activities such as weeding. It became evident that limited time was available for intervention activities.

On some farms, protected time for the intervention was arranged through the farm owner during working hours. However welcome, time was limited and FHWs reported that activity was mainly restricted to didactic sessions. As expected, men and women preferred to separate for intervention activities. Males-only sessions were more frequent and their exposure to intervention activities during this period was reported to be greater than women who tended to be less visible and harder to reach. In addition to working long hours, women were also committed to domestic chores which precluded the possibility of "after hours" sessions. We also learned that men, and more especially seasonal workers, did not participate in AIDS prevention activities voluntarily during "time-off"; this was said to interfere with social drinking and womanizing at the local beer-halls. One FHW recorded:

> people want to learn but they do not want to spend time learning

Abstracts from FHW process data during this period revealed the following:

> This month I have not had any meetings because people are too busy reaping tobacco (December);

> Due to many hours of working, it is difficult to have meetings. Some do not attend because they are exhausted (April);

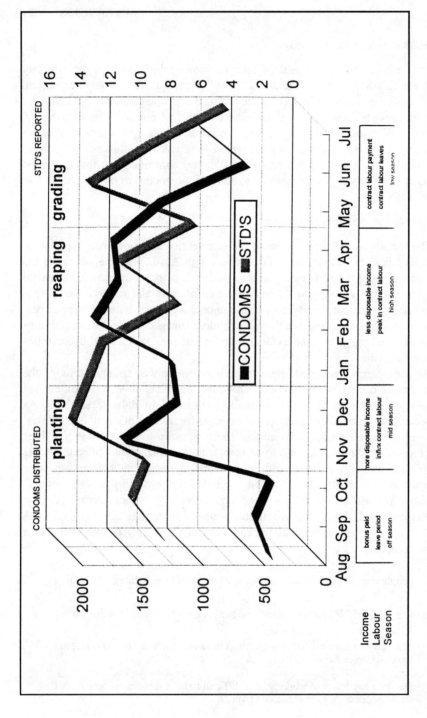

Figure 1. STDs and condom distribution v. season, labor fluctuation, and disposable income on intervention farms (1993-1994).

Women who work do not have equal chance for education activities because they are busy with household duties.

Participation in the intervention by seasonal workers in the high season was described as disruptive. Process data yielded the following comments from FHW's:

They, (referring to seasonal workers) attend when they have nothing else to do; sometimes they are noisy and mostly drunk.

The female seasonal workers are prostituting on our farm.

They care little for the problem of AIDS.

Disposable income on farms increased with the influx of seasonal workers. In the absence of other recreational activities, binge drinking provided a major source of entertainment for men; sex workers were reported to be particularly visible on pay days and interest in AIDS prevention activities was reported to be low.

The Slow Season

A slow season during which tobacco is graded, characterized the period between May-July (Figure 1). This period was marked by the pay-off and a gradual departure of seasonal workers. During this period two major public holidays occurred and an influx of people from urban areas was noted. Our records also showed that the cold weather had an effect on participation in intervention activities at this time:

I am unable to meet people after work this month. The sun sets very early . . . (June);

People want to go straight home after work; it is getting very cold now (June);

I'm behind in "lessons" people are still very busy grading tobacco (May);

This month I did not teach many people because they are away now (June).

METHODS USED

Listening

During the first phase of the intervention process-data showed that FHWs were anxious to proceed from the listening phase to the dialogue phase of the project. One FHW reported:

> The workers had high expectations that I would return from my AIDS training to "teach" not to waste time motivating people to "listen" to others talking about their fears and worries about HIV.

A real fear was expressed that unless FHWs moved ahead quickly with other activities in which visual aids were used, farm workers would soon become disinterested. Key to this phase was the ability of the facilitator to promote listening skills and discussion; clearly there was a conflict between training needs and community expectations.

In spite of these drawbacks the listening phase yielded much information about lay beliefs and among those commonly recorded were:

> People are still saying that AIDS is the same as rukawo.

> It is said that guilty people get AIDS.

> AIDS is thought to be a disease of prostitutes.

> Some men say that they expect to get STDs sometime.

> Women are afraid that they cannot prevent themselves getting HIV.

These statements were collected and used as triggers in the next stage for threat and susceptibility appraisal.

Appraisal-Dialogue

The "agree/disagree" activity in which lay beliefs about HIV/AIDS were debated, proved popular, and aroused interest and participation during this phase. Abstracts from records by FHWs during this period included:

> the people like this activity, it makes them think about another point of view;

> my people ask for agree/disagree all the time;

> men are now attending my sessions—I never saw these men before when I talked about health matters;

> people ask for this activity over weekends;

> at times there is much debate about the truth of these beliefs; and

> the agree/disagree activity makes people participate very well.

In the dialogue phase, a flip chart was used to reenforce instrumental knowledge of HIV/AIDS and picture codes were introduced to encourage problem appraisal and problem solving. The latter was reported to be particularly popular among groups of women. Comments received from FHWs included:

the women especially like the picture codes;

picture codes help to people to talk about real problems and discuss ways of finding a solution;

the picture codes show problems which we were quiet about before this project.

However, FHWs reported that farm workers quickly tired of the same codes; there was a need to rapidly develop new codes as the problems of AIDS was realized in a much wider social context. We responded, but not quickly enough as the need for supplementary codes was greater than we expected. Laminated photographs of STDs were used to convey information in this phase. The pictures aroused much interest particularly among men. Our records revealed that FHWs and resident traditional healers recorded an increase in requests by farm workers for private consultations about STDs around the time that these were first introduced; an increase in condom demand was also recorded. Interestingly, in group discussions with FHWs during this period, we also learned that the pictures also seemed to arouse fear and denial about the problem of STDs.

According to one FHW:

These pictures make some people frightened: they do not want to touch them.

Other FHWs recorded:

Men say that they do not want to think about such things when they see these pictures.

Men ask me privately for these pictures—they prefer to study them alone.

Requests for videos which showed the "real problem" of AIDS were frequently received during this phase of the intervention and farm owners were cooperative in helping to organize public viewing sessions. However, the only locally available videos at that time did not apparently satiate the demand for information about the epidemic as it occurs in Zimbabwe. FHW's frequently reported that the people "wanted to see the real thing."

The action phase was mainly characterized by a move to recruit volunteer farm workers to participate in condom distribution and educational activities. This phase took place at the end of the high season and was reported to be extremely difficult. Little progress was achieved and a number of arguments were put forward by farm workers, i.e.:

we should be paid for our effort;

nothing is for free these days;

what reward can I expect;

people in this community have their own ideas about AIDS;

this problem should be dealt with by the Government;

seasonal workers will spoil our effort;

there is nothing we can do about this problem; and

we have little time for such things.

EFFECTS OF LABOR FLUCTUATION AND AVAILABILITY OF DISPOSABLE INCOME ON CONDOM DEMAND

The pattern of condom demand is shown in Figure 1 together with annotations which refer to seasonal fluctuation in labor supply and disposable income. The peak in condom demand during October 1993 appeared to correspond with an influx of seasonal workers and the return from home leave of permanent farm workers on most farms. A further peak was observed in February 1994 during the high season. However, we could not be sure that these results reflect an increase in condom demand by workers from our intervention farms. One FHW reported:

people from other farms are coming across to take our condoms because they have none of their own.

Further observations included:

People should pay for condoms; they are wasted if they are free.

Free condoms are now being sold in our community.

Bonus pay outs and paydays during the high season (Figure 1) which were reported to be punctuated by binge drinking and an influx of commercial sex workers on many farms, were also thought to influence condom demand from high-access points such as beer-halls. Careless disposal of condoms in these areas were also reported. FHWs noted that condom demand tended to decline significantly with the departure of seasonal workers at the end of the season.

PATTERNS OF SEXUALLY TRANSMITTED DISEASE
DURING THE PROCESS EVALUATION PERIOD

STD incidence data collected from catchment clinics during the intervention period was lower than expected. FHWs reported that people with STD tended to seek treatment either at centers where they would not be recognized or that they gave false names and addresses at catchment clinics. During the period January-April i.e., the busiest time on most farms, a decline in STD reports to catchment clinics was noted. Our process data suggested that it was difficult for workers to take time off during working hours to attend clinics and reports confirmed that farm workers either delayed seeking treatment or consulted Traditional Healers for STD treatment in this period. One FHW recorded,

> many people are using herbs from the bush for STDs at this time; they only go to the clinic later when the sores erupt.

Our findings showed that the most significant peak in STD incidence occurred in November following bonus pay outs and an influx of seasonal workers on our intervention farms (Figure 1). This trend also occurred at district and provincial level.

The increase in the incidence of STDs around May coincided with a decline in seasonal farming activity and the departure of seasonal workers on most tobacco farms.

DISCUSSION

A process evaluation was used to describe the events which took place over one year in an intervention where a listening-appraisal-dialogue-action model was used to raise awareness about STD/HIV/AIDS and stimulate action in farm-worker communities of rural Zimbabwe. The intervention was reiterative; no single phase was discrete.

The extensive nature of the information yielded by the study permitted an insight to the program which may have otherwise been impossible had we relied on an end-point evaluation. First, it helped to explain how the intervention was synthesized over time by the farm-worker communities. Second, and important, it assisted us to respond more readily to the need for additional resources and moral support for our change agents that would have otherwise been impossible.

It also helped us to recognize the limitations imposed by our measurement procedures. We learned, for example, that data related to condom distribution on our intervention farms (Figure 1) may not have been representative of actual demand in those communities since our prevention activities also attracted workers from neighboring farms. Similarly, had we not linked our epidemiological findings to seasonal information we may have erroneously concluded that the decline in STD incidence during the busiest months on our intervention farms was due to the intervention and not—as we learned from the process evaluation—due to a lack of time which limited access to health care during that period (Figure 1). We also learned that while we were cognizant of the need to involve our FHWs in the data collection process, we failed to make the significance of this activity apparent during training and as a result, records were inflated at the beginning of the study. These findings lead us to believe therefore, that the concept of process evaluation should not merely be regarded as an academic activity, but something that is part of training and implementation in every project.

Our study also lead us to question the nature of HIV/AIDS prevention programs in farm-worker communities where reaching a threshold necessary for change is clearly beyond the intervention. We found for example, that in addition to the perspectives held about STD/HIV/AIDS and the ways in which the problem interfaces with culture, fear and stigma among workers, the calibre of the change-agent, and the social and environmental milieu in which the people live and work seem to be equally important in influencing participation and action.

At an organizational level, our data showed that worker communities demonstrated difficulty in responding to the challenge of change even in the face of an epidemic which will place further burdens upon them in the future. While it was hoped that our intervention would encourage people to become organized around an issue as important as HIV/AIDS, it is possible that the lack of previous experience in collective action was a disabling factor in achieving this objective. We also concluded from our observations that, in the face of other problems such as poverty and drought, it was not without reason that workers perceived little sense of purpose in dealing with an "external" threat which will only impact their lives in time.

We therefore questioned the extent to which participation or otherwise, in a community intervention should be used as a valid index of success. In this context we ask whether the desire for participation carries more significance for program implementors than the farm workers themselves? For example, did the intervention uphold and synthesize the perspectives articulated by the community about their inability to participate and their lack of capacity to change? What should the intervention look like the second time around? Although not fully answered by our process evaluation, these questions lead us to believe that while HIV/AIDS prevention programs have a role in generating cognitive and attitude change in farm-worker communities, the motivation to seriously confront and re-pattern risk behavior will possibly best evolve from the people themselves over a much longer period than one year.

We also discovered that the issue of timing and the impact of the farming calendar, for example, to be unexpectedly important factors in influencing program implementation in these communities. In particular, we observed that it was difficult to involve farm workers during the off season and the peak season on farms. When more time was available for intervention activities, fewer people were available because a large number of farm workers took their leave. Conversely in the high season, when more people were available, long working hours precluded intervention activities and fewer farm workers participated. Intervention activities were not ranked as a priority during recreation time. Men preferred binge drinking; women on the other hand, were busy with domestic chores after work. Added to which we found that seasonal workers were disruptive and non-participative during peak periods.

The evaluation assisted in highlighting difficulties experienced by our change-agents in using a methodology where people are not the objects of an educational project, but participants in a process of change. In particular we noted that the culture of didactics which still characterizes health education activities in Zimbabwe, prevailed in spite of intensive training which promoted a participatory approach. This notwithstanding, we also noted that great difficulty was experienced by our FHWs in creating an environment for dialogue and active participation during sessions which were arranged in protected time offered by the farm owner during working hours in the high season. In spite of our implementation plan, we learned that the cyclical nature of the intervention was disrupted throughout the year and our FHWs proceeded during difficult periods, with those methods which they enjoyed using most. On a related issue we also learned that although FHWs were cognizant of the need to promote the concept of self-efficacy, particularly in women, they also acknowledged the problem and real difficulties of influencing cultural norms known to mitigate against the attainment of this concept. We therefore question an approach which is dependent on a single change-agent and suggest that greater support for the intervention may be generated by a group of peers, i.e., men and women who are elected by the farm-worker communities for training in the listening-appraisal-dialogue-action method.

CONCLUSION

Process evaluation receives insufficient attention in community interventions. This study demonstrates however, that process evaluation is as important in measuring "what actually happened" as single end-point measurements which are often used to measure the impact of multi-dimensional interventions. It provided a valuable insight to factors which when aggregated, gave us an overview of a program whose success or failure may well have been determined by issues outside the scope of the intervention. This leads us to our initial question "Was the intervention implemented as planned?" and the answer— only partially.

Process Evaluation Form: Farm Health Workers

Name: _____ Farm: _____
Date: _____

AIDS ACTIVITIES THIS MONTH   **TOTAL**

LARGE GROUPS
  men only   _____
  women only   _____
  mixed—men and women   _____

SMALL GROUPS
  men only   _____
  women only   _____
  mixed—men and women   _____

PRIVATE—FACE TO FACE
  men only   _____
  women only   _____

METHODS USED
  listening survey   _____
  discussion   _____
  picture code   _____
  story   _____
  drama   _____
  talking only   _____
  films/video   _____
  agree/disagree   _____

**NUMBER OF STDs REPORTED
TO YOU THIS MONTH**
  Count Men   _____
  Count Women   _____

**NUMBER OF CONDOMS
DISTRIBUTED BY YOU
THIS MONTH**   **TOTAL**

_____

**OTHER CONDOM
DISTRIBUTION POINTS
ON YOUR FARM**
1. _____
2. _____
3. _____

ENQUIRIES FROM OTHER FARMS
  how many?   _____
  which farms?
  1. _____
  2. _____
  3. _____

**NEW AIDS ACTIVITIES
ON YOUR FARM**
  how many? _____
  what kind? _____

WRITE DOWN ANY OTHER THINGS YOU WISH
TO MENTION

REFERENCES

1. R. Chambers, *Putting the Last First*, Longman Group Ltd., United Kingdom, 1983.
2. T. D. Cook and D. T. Campbell, *Quasi-Experimentation: Design and Analysis Issues in Field Settings*, Houghton Mifflin, Boston, Massachusetts, 1979.
3. C. S. Reichart and T. D. Cook, Beyond Qualitative vs. Quantitative Methods, in *Qualitative and Quantitative Methods in Evaluation Research*, T. D. Cook and G. S. Reichardt (eds.), Sage, Beverly Hills, California, 1979.
4. D. Nutbeam, C. Smith, S. Murphy, and J. Catford, Maintaining Evaluation Designs in Long Term Community Based Health Promotion Programmes: Heartbeat Wales Case Study, *Journal of Epidemiology & Community Health, 47*:2, pp. 127-133, April 1993.
5. K. Glanz, F. M. Lewis, and B. K. Rimer (eds.), *Health Behaviour and Health Education. Theory and Practice*, Jossey-Bass Publishers, San Francisco, 1990.
6. P. Van Assema, The Process Evaluation of a Dutch Community Health Project, in *The Development, Implementation and Evaluation of a Community Health Project*, Universitaire Pers Maastricht, Proefschrift, 1993.
7. G. L. Ingersoll, M. T. Bazar, and J. B. Zenter, Monitoring Unit-Based Innovations: A Process Evaluation Approach, *Nursing Economics, 11*:3, pp. 137-143, May-June 1993.
8. S. A. McGraw, E. J. Stone, S. K. Osganian, J. P. Elder, C. L. Perry, C. C. Johnson, G. S. Parcel, L. S. Webber, and R. V. Luepker, Design of Process Evaluation within the Child and Adolescent Trail for Cardiovascular Health (CATCH), *Health Education Quarterly*, Supplement 2: S5-S26 (Supplement 2) SOPHE, John Wiley & Sons, Inc., 1994.
9. L. W. Green and M. M. Lewis, *Measurement and Evaluation in Health Education and Health Promotion*, Mayfield Publishing Company, Palo Alto, California, 1986.
10. J. R. Flora, C. Lefevre, D. Murray, E. J. Stone, A. Assaf, M. Mittelmark, and J. Finnegan, Jr., A Community Education Monitoring System: Methods from Stanford Five-City Project, the Minnesota Health Heart Programme and the Pawtucket Heart Health Programme, Health Education Research, Theory and Practice, *8*:1, pp. 81-95, 1993.
11. L. A. Lytle, B. Z. Davidann, K. Bachman, C. C. Johnson, J. N. Reeds, K. C. Wambsgans, and S. Budman, CATCH: Challenges of Conducting Process Evaluation in a Multicenter Trial, *Health Education Quarterly*, Suppl 2:S129-142, 1994.
12. C. J. Johnson, V. Osganian, J. Elder, R. V. Luepker, C. J. Johnson, G. S. Parcel, C. L. Perry, and L. S. Webber, CATCH: Family Process Evaluation in a Multicenter Trial, *Health Education Quarterly*, Suppl 2:S91-106, 1994.
13. T. L. McKenzie, P. K. Strikmillar, E. J. Stone, S. E. Woods, S. S. Ehlinger, K. A. Romero, and S. T. Budman, CATCH: Physical Activity Process Evaluation in a Multicenter Trial, *Health Education Quarterly*, Suppl 2:S73-89, 1994.
14. L. Gliksman, D. McKenzie, R. Douglas, S. Brunet, and K. Moffatt, The Role of Alcohol Providers in Prevention: An Evaluation of a Server Intervention Programme, *Addiction, 88*:9, pp. 1195-1203, September 1993.
15. M. Dijkstra, H. de Vries, and G. S. Parcel, The Linkage Approach Applied to a School-Based Smoking Prevention Program in The Netherlands, *Journal of School Health, 63*:8, pp. 339-342, October 1993.
16. P. De May, H. A. Hukuimwe, L. Matsitukwa, B. P. Makasa, and P. De Colombani, HIV Sentinel Surveillance in Mashonaland West Province: HIV Sero-Prevalence

Survey in the Commercial Farming Area of Zvimba District, March-July. A Final Report, *PMD*, Mashonaland West Province, Zimbabwe, 1992.

17. S. Laver, B. Van den Borne, G. Kok, and G. Woelk, A Pre-Intervention Survey to Determine Understanding of HIV/AIDS in Farm Worker Communities of Zimbabwe, Awaiting Publication by *AIDS Education and Prevention*, accepted November 1995.

18. S. Laver, B. Van den Borne, and G. Kok, Using Theory to Design an Intervention for HIV/AIDS Prevention in Farm Workers in Rural Zimbabwe, *International Quarterly of Community Health Education, 15*:4, pp. 349-362, 1994-95.

19. N. Bracht, Introduction, in *Health Promotion at the Community Level*, N. Bracht (ed.), Sage, Newbury Park, California, pp. 19-25, 1990.

20. K. R. McLeroy, D. Bibeau, A. Steckler, and K. Glanz, An Ecological Perspective on Health Promotion Programs, *Health Education Quarterly, 15*:4, pp. 351-377, 1988.

21. P. Friere, *Pedagogy of the Oppressed*, Seabury Press, New York, 1970.

22. D. Werner and B. Bower, *Helping Health Workers Learn*, The Hesperain Foundation, Palo Alto, California, 1982.

23. E. R. Auerbach and N. Wallerstein, *ESL for Action Problem Posing at Work*, Teachers Guide, Addison Wesley, Reading, Massachusetts, 1987.

24. A. Hope, S. Timmel, and C. Hodzi, *Training for Transformation: A Handbook for Community Workers*, 3 Vol., Mambo Press, Gweru, Zimbabwe, 1984.

25. N. Wallerstein and E. Bernstein, Empowerment Education: Freire's Ideas Adapted to Health Education, *Health Education Quarterly, 15*, pp. 379-394, 1988.

26. N. Wallerstein and V. Sanchez-Merki, Freirian Praxis in Health Education: Research Results from an Adolescent Prevention Programme, *Health Education Research. Theory and Practice, 9*:1, pp. 105-118, 1994.

27. R. W. Rogers, C. W. Deckner, and C. R. Mewborn, An Expectancy-Value Theory Approach to the Long Term Modification of Smoking Behaviour, *Journal of Clinical Psychology, 34*, pp. 562-566, 1978.

28. E. Rogers, *Diffusion of Innovations* (3rd Edition), Free Press, New York, 1983.

29. R. W. Rogers, Changing Health-Related Attitudes and Behaviour: The Role of Preventive Health Psychology, in *Interfaces in Psychology*, R. McGlyn, J. Maddox, C. Stoltenbury, and R. J. Harvey (eds.), Texas Tech University Press, Lubbock, Texas, 1984.

30. M. H. Becker, The Health Belief Model and Sick Role Behaviour, *Health Education Monographs, 2*, pp. 409-419, 1974.

31. A. Bandura, *Social Foundations of Thought and Action: A Social Cognitive Theory*, Prentice-Hall, Englewood Cliffs, 1977.

32. M. Fishbein and I. Ajzen, *Beliefs, Attitudes, Intention and Behaviour: An Introduction to Theory and Research*, Addison-Wesley, Reading, Massachusetts, 1975.

33. M. Fishbein and I. Ajzen, *Understanding Attitudes and Predicting Social Behaviour*, Prentice Hall, Englewood Cliffs, New Jersey, 1980.

34. M. Minkler, Group Intervention Models of Health Behaviour Change, in *Health Behaviour and Health Education. Theory and Research*, K. Glanz, F. M. Lewis, and B. K. Rimer (eds.), Jossey-Bass Health Series, San Francisco, pp. 253-287, 1990.

35. E. Rogers and F. Shoemaker, *Communication of Innovations* (2nd Edition), Free Press, New York, 1970.

36. W. R. Millar and S. Rollinick, *Motivational Interviewing: Preparing People to Change Addictive Behaviour*, Guilford Press, New York, 1990.

CHAPTER 17

The Potential of Drama and Songs as Channels for AIDS Education in Africa: A Report on Focus Group Findings from Ghana

Kwadwo Bosompra

The emergence of HIV infection has been of grave concern to most African governments as it has been to others worldwide. In Ghana, since March 1986 when the first two cases of HIV seropositives were reported from the Noguchi Memorial Institute for Medical Research at the University of Ghana, the number of HIV seropositives has shot up dramatically. From data released by the national AIDS reporting system, as of November 31, 1990, the cumulative number of confirmed AIDS cases was 2,148 while HIV seropositives were 4,153 [1]. This situation clearly calls for urgent action.

Already in Ghana, a number of educational programs have been undertaken. The general objective has been to raise Ghanaians' knowledge about AIDS to a level which would help produce changes in sexual behavior and practices to reduce the spread of AIDS. One such program attempts to use drama to catch and retain the attention of a designated audience by simultaneously entertaining and educating the audience—a concept that has come to be referred to in the literature as "enter-educate." But Ghana is certainly not the first country to apply the "enter-educate" concept which has been successfully used to promote desired behavior changes in other parts of the world.

A ready example is the Johns Hopkins University Population Communication Services' "Communication for Young People" Project in Latin America, better known as the Tatiana and Johnny Project [2]. This project used popular music to reach young people aged thirteen to eighteen in eleven Spanish-speaking countries with a sexual responsibility message.

In the West African sub-region, Burkina Faso has for a long time exploited the potential of theater for development. Since 1968, the "Atelier Theatre Burkinabe" (ATB), a troupe dedicated to introducing new ideas to the rural populace through comic drama, has been to all corners of Burkina Faso to promote social development in rural communities [3]. Among its accomplishments, "Atelier" has undertaken performances commissioned by UNICEF and the Burkina Ministry of Health.

In another part of West Africa, specifically in Mali, a traditional format, "Koteba," was selected as an appropriate "enter-educate" vehicle to disseminate family planning messages to the general Malian public because it was seen as a culturally acceptable way of expressing the everyday concerns of the people [4].

In Lesotho, the Marotholi Travelling Theatre (MTT) has used theater as a forum for village discussions about local attitudes toward health, nutrition, agriculture, and social problems [5]. Evaluation results showed that positive attitude change toward the plays' subject matter was high (81% for a play about joining co-operative societies and 77% for one about reforestation). However, actual behavior change varied according to the topic (65% planted trees after participating in the reforestation play, whereas only one villager joined a cooperative as a result of the cooperatives play).

Armed with information about these examples, Ghana's Ministry of Health set up a drama troupe in Accra called "Hewale" to dramatize some AIDS messages in a play entitled "The Bitter Side of AIDS" to a number of communities, churches, factory workers, etc. The popularity of this troupe encouraged the Ministry to set up two others in the Ashanti and Eastern Regions.[1]

To enable the Ministry to assess the play's impact on the AIDS knowledge, attitudes, beliefs and practices of the public, the Health Education Division (HED) decided to undertake a research project in the Eastern Region. This chapter presents the results of the study.

OBJECTIVES

The main objectives of the research project were, among others, to seek answers to the following questions:

1. What were focus group discussion (FGD) participants' levels of knowledge about, and attitudes towards AIDS?
2. Could the play "The Bitter Side of AIDS" make any difference in changing people's beliefs about, and attitudes towards AIDS?

---

[1] Drama has always been a popular means of entertainment in both rural and urban Ghana. Professional drama troupes are popularly referred to as "concert parties." They usually precede their theatrical performances with a lot of good local music and also intersperse the play itself with generous doses of thematically-related songs.

3. Were people likely to change their sexual practices after watching the play "The Bitter Side of AIDS"?
4. Could songs with AIDS-related themes make any difference in changing people's beliefs about, and attitudes towards AIDS?

RESEARCH DESIGN AND METHODOLOGY

The HED selected two locations in the Eastern Region: Koforidua, the Regional capital, to elicit the views of urban dwellers, and Konko, a village about 13 kms from Koforidua, to obtain the views of rural dwellers. In both rural and urban locations, a quasi-experimental design was executed and data were collected using the focus group research approach.

The focus group discussion (FGD) approach is a qualitative research technique that makes it easier to collect data about taboo topics or topics that are difficult to discuss in public. It has been argued that "private group discussions, properly conducted, create an anonymous, relaxed atmosphere of social equality in which participants feel free to describe their actual beliefs and behavior" [6]. Also, when people are of the same sex and belong to the same sub-culture and class, they are generally more willing to disclose and discuss personal information [7].

In this study participants were grouped into males and females, youths and adults, educated and uneducated. Youth referred to those not above twenty-five years of age and educated participants were those who could read news headlines from the weekend paper, *The Mirror*. Discussions were held with people who had watched ("watchers") the play, "The Bitter Side of AIDS," and those who had not ("non-watchers"). Then a month later, a recall study was undertaken which involved only those who had watched the play and who had also participated in the first round of discussions.

Our research design is presented in Figure 1.

For each subset, two separate groups of "watchers" and "non-watchers" of the play were formed except for the recall study which involved only "watchers."

All the discussion groups consisted of a minimum of eight and a maximum of twelve participants. The discussions were facilitated by trained moderators from the University of Ghana using discussion guides designed to elicit responses to our major research questions.

The moderators used tape recorders to record the discussions which they later transcribed to prepare the moderators' reports. These reports were then synthesized into categories of adult and youth "watchers" and "non-watchers" (first round) and "watchers" (recall) for both rural and urban participating groups. The initial (moderators') reports did not show much difference among the various subsets along most of the topics in the discussion guide. Thus, the data analysis addressed all subsets together and specifically identified a subset only when major differences or disagreements occurred.

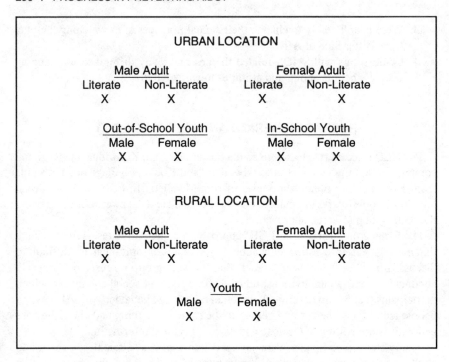

Figure 1. FGD research design.

The analysis was also subdivided into three parts to address the three major areas of interest to this study: AIDS awareness and knowledge, impact of the play, "The Bitter Side of AIDS," and impact of AIDS-related songs, on AIDS-related knowledge and attitudes and sexual behavior of FGD participants.

Zimmerman et al. have cautioned against using qualitative data such as those generated by FGD's to draw statistical conclusions or project responses [6]. They contend that qualitative data are most appropriate, among other things, for gaining insights into behavior patterns about which little is already known. In our case, no study had been done to assess the impact of drama or songs as tools for AIDS education in Ghana.

More importantly, findings from FGDs are not easily generalizable. Thus, our findings need to be interpreted with caution. They certainly can be used to generate hypotheses about the potential of drama and songs as channels for AIDS education in Ghana. Since Ghana's cultural landscape is no different from the rest of Africa, the hypothesis could also be applied, with appropriate adaptations, to other parts of the continent.

FINDINGS
AIDS AWARENESS AND KNOWLEDGE

In both the urban and rural locations of this study, we talked to people who watched the play "The Bitter Side of AIDS" and those who did not watch it, about what they knew about AIDS. Highlights of the discussions are presented.

Health Concerns

Regarding the most important health problem in Ghana, participants tended to identify a wide range of diseases, but the most frequently mentioned were AIDS, malaria, measles, piles and hypertension. The male youth also referred to drug abuse as a major health concern.

However, turning to health problems in their community, the rural participants appeared to consider AIDS to be a distant phenomenon. They rather mentioned guinea worm infection and the lack of medical facilities as their main problems.

The urban dwellers, on the other hand, confirmed that AIDS was a problem and also mentioned guinea worm infection, lack of potable water, *kwashiorkor* and malaria.

What Do You Know about AIDS?

Apart from the rural "non-watchers," all the other groups had heard about AIDS and knew that it was very deadly and did not have a cure.

- AIDS is a killer disease.
- We know that it is a disease which kills people.
- It is a disease you get if you keep changing men. You won't notice it till it is too late.

However, the rural non-watchers contended that AIDS was non-existent in their community, with a few contending that they were not aware of it and some others indicating that they had only heard the name of the disease but did not know anything beyond that.

- I have also heard its name but that is all.
- As for AIDS we have never heard of it here.

Concern about AIDS

Participants were generally worried about AIDS and most of them were discussing its implications. The fear appeared to be based on mutual suspicions between spouses and the incurable nature of the disease.

- It has caused us to fear our wives and our wives also to fear us.

- We are talking more about it and seeking more information to know how the disease could be prevented so that we can be at peace since these days if you have a husband you fear him and the husbands also fear their wives.
- We fear because there is no cure for it.
- If your husband goes to flirt around he can bring it to you and kill you.
- I've got daughters and we advise them to be careful. We are afraid.

However, some rural male youth did not appear to be seriously bothered about AIDS. They did not consider themselves to be at risk because they had stable girlfriends and they could use condoms.

- If your girl[friend] is very stable, you are free. That is why I don't think about it.
- I am aware of the existence of condoms and with that I know I won't contract it.

Some urban [adult] participants were not talking about AIDS because:

- If you warn your friend against it, he will be angry with you so you keep quiet and let them do it.

However, some rural "non-watchers" did not know where to obtain information about the disease.

- We don't know exactly where to seek such information, considering the [rural] nature of our locality.

Causes of AIDS

In both rural and urban locations, participants did not know the causes of AIDS and tended to confuse causes with modes of transmission. There was only one urban male in-school youth (watcher) who could say that "AIDS is caused by a virus that destroys the immune system." The rural "non-watchers," however, admitted that they did not know what caused AIDS.

- As for me I do not know.
- We can't tell. We would rather want to ask you about it.

Mode of Transmission

All participants knew that AIDS could be transmitted through sexual intercourse with an infected person and, therefore, tended to condemn promiscuity. Injection with a contaminated syringe was also mentioned by most participants.

However, apart from the urban youth ("watchers") who exhibited a high degree of familiarity with all the modes of HIV transmission, transfusion with contaminated blood and in vitro transmission from infected pregnant mother to baby were apparently unknown to the other groups.

The urban youth (watchers) said:

- If a man with AIDS donates his blood to a healthy man, the recipient will contract AIDS.
- Sometimes a woman has it, then she gives it to a child she conceives and gives birth to.

The implication here is that AIDS educators would need to pay attention to these less known modes of HIV transmission too. Myths about the mode of HIV transmission were many and these are treated towards the end of this section.

Signs of AIDS

Most participants both rural and urban believed that they could tell whether someone had AIDS or HIV by simply looking at the person. The most common symptoms mentioned were weight loss, chronic diarrhea, loss of appetite, vomiting, fever, boils and sores on the body. However, some of the male youth "watchers" in both rural and urban localities contended that AIDS could not be diagnosed by simply looking at the infected person. The disease, in their opinion, required a medical diagnosis since the symptoms took quite a long time to manifest themselves.

- You can't detect it because it will take over a year before it shows on the physical body.
- Even doctors have to check and test one's blood before they can say that one has AIDS.
- One simply can't tell who has AIDS.

Efforts at AIDS education should, therefore, aim at disabusing people's minds of the idea of doing a visual diagnosis of AIDS.

Cure for AIDS

Participants generally appeared to hold the belief that there was no cure for AIDS although most of them had heard rumors that a Ghanaian herbalist had discovered a cure. They were however, not sure about the truth or otherwise of this rumor.

- It has no cure, if you get it you'll die.
- We have heard that there is a herbalist in Brong Ahafo who has got a cure. As to whether it is true or not we can't tell.
- A fetish priest, Kwaku Firi, in Brong Ahafo has got a cure. It is shown on T.V. a lot of times and he has cured many people.

- It was on the T.V.; there was this traditional African priest with a man and a woman he had cured and who had been proved to be cured at Korle-Bu Teaching Hospital.

The implication here for policy makers is that the Kwaku Firi story needs to be straightened out once and for all, since both rural and urban dwellers have heard about it.

Preventing or Reducing Risk of AIDS

Participants were of the view that avoiding casual sex and using condoms could reduce the risk of contracting AIDS.

- We must not involve ourselves in casual sex.
- As we are students it is better for us not even to indulge in sex.
- If you can't avoid sexual intercourse you can use a condom.

However, some participants expressed reservations about the condom because "as for the condom it can burst." The rural male adults complained that ". . . we don't often see that thing [condoms] or use it." The implication here is that condoms should be made more easily available, at least to adults in both urban and rural areas. Some rural female groups expressed their helplessness and frustration. They agreed that "if you don't trust your husband, give him condoms to use," but at the same time they felt condoms could fail and "can you prevent your husband from having extramarital affairs"? We need to observe here that some married women argued strongly that the use of condoms in the context of marriage was an impossibility. Others did not want to insist on condoms because:

- I will want to have a baby so I'll not even force him to use it.

The urban youth suggested public education especially about the mode of transmission of the disease while urban adults recommended the inclusion in the school curriculum of AIDS education especially relating to the causes, transmission and prevention of the disease.

Some youth felt that:

- If you're getting married then both of you should have your blood tested for AIDS.

Other suggestions were that:

- The government should reduce school fees so that the children can go to school and forget about indiscriminate sex.

How Did You Learn about AIDS

Radio was the most popular source from which participants learned about AIDS. Friends and health personnel were also mentioned. In addition, the urban groups cited television; posters and newspapers were also mentioned.

- I heard it on radio especially, it was on radio that it was publicized.
- The T.V. spoke about it.
- My friends and I discussed it.
- When you go to the hospital they talk about it. At times the nurses talk about it.
- There are posters around.

Which Source(s) Do You Most Trust to Give You Accurate Information about AIDS?

Generally participants tended to trust radio and television to give them the most accurate information about AIDS.

- I think the one on radio because when it is said on radio then it must be true.
- What I see on T.V.
- Doctors and other health personnel were also mentioned because "they have learnt about it and work on it"

What People Need to Know about AIDS

In all FGDs, what participants wanted to know urgently was the mode of transmission of the virus. They also suggested that the symptoms developed by persons with AIDS (PWAs) from the moment of infection to the time of their deaths should be shown on television or cinema to show viewers how deadly the disease could be.

- They should know all about its transmission and prevention.
- They have to show the stages through which AIDS victims go; that if you get it this is what will happen.
- You should show people who have got the disease before; that it was the disease that killed him or her. If this is brought in the cinema it will convince us that Ah, this disease is not good.

Misconceptions about AIDS

In tapping FGD participants' knowledge about AIDS and how the virus was transmitted, a number of misconceptions (combinations of half truths and outright falsehoods), surfaced in both the rural and urban locations of the study. These related to HIV transmission by mosquitoes, through swimming pools, kissing, casual contact and others like gonorrhea and salmon fish! Samples of participants' actual statements are presented.

Transmission of HIV by mosquitoes:

1. Mosquitoes can transmit it by injecting the blood of one person into the blood stream of another.
2. Mosquitoes, too, can cause it since they spread malaria by biting an infected person; in the same way they can spread AIDS.
3. Mosquitoes suck blood from one person to another so they can spread it since AIDS is a disease of the blood.
4. Mosquito is an animal which when biting you, puts something inside you. So when it bites someone and there is a disease in him, it can transmit it to you.

Transmission of HIV through swimming pools:

1. In the swimming pool, too, when a victim urinates in the pool and another person drinks some.
2. It could be spread in swimming pools because the disease comes from women. So if an infected woman enters the pool and washes her private part in it she could contaminate the water with the disease which could be transmitted to others in the pool. (The gender implications of this belief would be worth studying.)
3. From the swimming pool, a victim can urinate into it and another person will drink it. Also the victim could have sores on his body, when the water washes the blood, it can spread to others.

Transmission of HIV through kissing:

1. One can have it through kissing an AIDS infected person, when there is an exchange of saliva.
2. They can kiss you such that you can get a cut on your tongue and blood comes; this can make the man or woman get it.
3. When I have it and I kiss somebody she'll get it.

Transmission of HIV through casual contact:

1. Some people are fond of licking their fingers when eating; when they put their fingers in the mouth, the fingers would be covered with the AIDS water. If the one puts his hand back into the food, the whole dish would be contaminated with AIDS and by that the rest can contract it.
2. If your brother or sister travels to Nigeria or the Ivory Coast and contracts AIDS which is not detected, it can be transmitted to you if you eat together with him or drink from the same cup.

This appears to imply that AIDS is seen as an imported phenomenon. If you do not have a recent history of travel outside Ghana then you cannot have AIDS. The implications of this for AIDS education need to be closely noted.

3. It could be spread through the use of the same cup, for example, the iced-water sellers don't wash their cups very well before serving customers. So if somebody with the disease drinks from the cup and you also do so you could have it.
4. Through sweating, when one person gets in contact with the sweat of a victim.
5. If someone with AIDS get a wound and you use his sponge in bathing you can get it.

Other means of HIV transmission:

1. What brings about AIDS is gonorrhea especially. What made me believe this was that in yesterday's concert I realized that the man first got gonorrhea before the AIDS developed. (This statement was made by a rural participant only.)
2. Through salmon, a sea fish. In the francophone countries bordering Ghana when the AIDS victims die, they are thrown into the sea. The salmon fish eat the body of the victims, contract the disease and swim to the shores of Ghana only to be caught and used as food. (This statement was made by an urban participant only.)

IMPACT OF DRAMA—"THE BITTER SIDE OF AIDS"

This section presents the views of both rural and urban FGD participants who watched the play "The Bitter Side of AIDS." Their views were elicited both the morning after watching the play and a month later. The data are presented below.

What Do You Think the Play was About?

Participants could easily identify the import of the drama as teaching them something about AIDS.

- It is about AIDS; it is about promiscuous sexual behavior.
- It was a warning to the whole student body on how to avoid AIDS.
- They wanted us to be very careful with our sexual habits.

A month later they could still recall that the drama was about the deadliness of AIDS and the need to protect themselves from it.

- It was about how fearful the AIDS disease is.
- How dangerous and deadly the AIDS disease is.

The story line was also clearly recalled.

- It was about a man and a woman who had been friends. After they broke off the woman married another man. The child born out of this relationship had AIDS. The disease was traced to the man of the earlier relationship.

Exact Message of the Play

Participants agreed, and this was also confirmed in the recall study, that the exact message of the play was that AIDS was a killer and was, therefore, to be avoided; and also that AIDS could be prevented by avoiding casual sex and being faithful to one's partner.

- The AIDS is a killer so everybody should avoid it.
- That if you get involved in casual sex you would give it to your partner who sticks to you alone. So it advised us to avoid casual sex.

Was Message Effectively Carried Across?

All FGD participants who watched the play felt that the exact message of the drama was effectively put across.

- They brought out everything clearly; that it [AIDS] is a deadly disease which everybody needs to protect themselves against.
- It was very effectively carried across. It left no doubts in our minds. As for my wife, she got very afraid. This morning many people were discussing that yesterday's play was very frightening.
- Yes, because in the end everyone was very sad even though it was only a play.

Discussion of the Drama

Most participants discussed the content of the drama with their sexual partners, relatives or friends both immediately after the drama and also about a month later as the recall study revealed.

- Yes we discussed it. At the moment it is a cause of worry. It is the only topic we talk about.

The discussion appeared to center around the mode of transmission and preventive measures.

- I discussed it with my boyfriend against going after other girls.
- I discussed it with my friend. She was very concerned about how the people in the play got infected. She asked me how we can protect ourselves from the disease and I replied that we need to look after ourselves well.
- Even a doctor has had it so everyone else has to be really careful.
- My girlfriend protested that she did not have AIDS the first time I attempted to use a condom and it was very difficult convincing her that it was just a protective measure and that I didn't suspect her. After the play I referred her to it.

- I told my unmarried friend that she and her fiance should go and check their blood before marrying.
- My husband being a womanizer, can get it and bring it to me so I told him to advise himself and stop chasing women.
- When I came to watch the play my husband had travelled. When he came back I narrated the story to him.

This discussion has the advantage of keeping the AIDS issue alive on the public's agenda and once a problem remains alive, people begin to think of ways of solving it.

The play appeared to have frightened a number of participants.

- As for me, because of what I saw, I even don't have the desire for women.
- I called my children the night after the show and said "if you get a proposal from any man and you come and tell me, I'll take you for a medical check-up because if you bring this disease here, you will not be accepted.

Lessons from Play

Participants reported learning a lot of useful lessons from the play and a month later they could still remember the lessons. These included the use of condoms as a protective measure, that infected pregnant women could transmit it to their babies and that even medical doctors could also contract AIDS.

- That there is a rubber [condom] that can protect you from getting AIDS.
- I didn't know that if you were pregnant whilst you had AIDS, the baby could be infected but through the play I got to know.
- I didn't know that a doctor or a priest's daughter can get AIDS.
- I didn't know that the disease doesn't kill instantly but takes some time to do so.
- We didn't know that when you get AIDS it will take a really long time before you'll get to know that you have it.
- I got to know that even fat people can be carriers of the AIDS virus.

Behavior Change

Participants confirmed that the play had influenced them to change their sexual behavior and that they had passed a number of resolutions.

- Now I sleep at 6:00 p.m. If my wife asks me why, I refer her to the play.
- I have decided to keep away from women.

- I will stop breaking up relationships at short intervals with men.
- It has influenced me to keep away from women, for example, visiting prostitutes.
- I will wait till I get married.
- I'll stick to the one I've got because I'm used to quarreling and insisting on breaking up.
- If you watch the play and you don't change then it is up to you.

A month later participants still held on to their resolutions:

- I've changed because I'm young and wouldn't like to shorten my life by chasing many women. I used to have at least three girlfriends but now I stick to my wife only.
- I was influenced by it. I have decided to buy condoms myself and give them to my boyfriend because anytime I ask him to buy condoms, he doesn't.
- I've decided to take only one boyfriend.
- I had two girls but I stopped my relations with one after watching the play because she likes going after too many men.
- I'll begin testing for AIDS with my boyfriend.

What Did You Like Best about the Play?

Participants enjoyed the quality of the acting and also the advice the characters in the drama gave.

- They were not shy so they performed very well for us to understand.
- For instance, at a certain point when someone had to cry, the person actually cried.
- I liked the part played by Nana because she was very serious.
- The thing I like is the advice it gave to my sisters and brothers who will not marry but go from here to there.
- The time scheduled for it was perfect because the villagers could come easily with their lanterns and also return safely.
- The duration was okay. It wasn't too long and it wasn't too short.

What Did You Dislike Most about the Play?

Most participants did not have anything against the play.

- We like the whole play.

However, a few made rather tangential comments like the pastor (in the play) being too lax about his daughter's relationship with her boyfriend. Some also said they were saddened by certain parts of the play, a psychological state that they did not particularly wish to be in.

Other Comments about the Play

The tendency to visually diagnose AIDS (i.e., look a person in the face and determine whether the person had AIDS), appeared to be rather strong in some participants. This strong urge led them to request for film shows that would enable them to see the symptoms more clearly.

From the rural youth:

- I thought it will be shown in the form of a film to depict the way the disease makes one grow lean so that we can all see the bony person.

Their adult counterparts added:

- . . . the actors should show us the nature of the disease. This should come in [to the play] so that if one sees someone who is sick with these symptoms, we could say he or she has AIDS.

The urban youth expressed similar sentiments:

- The play should be able to show the signs of the disease on those who had it.
- We should have seen how the baby looked like when she was born.

The implications of these observations are two-fold. First, AIDS education should seek to debunk the popular belief that AIDS can be diagnosed merely by looking at an HIV carrier in the face. Such a tendency could lead to stigmatization and ostracization of unfortunate individuals by society.

Second, if it is considered worthwhile to educate the public on the symptoms of AIDS then the HED should be ready to invest in video and cinema.

Another general observation about the play was:

- I prefer plays which are preceded by music and dancing.

This idea needs to be looked at more closely by the HED since it is the usual format adopted by itinerant drama troupes (concert parties)—popular sources of entertainment especially in rural areas—in the country. To attract, particularly, the rural crowds, the HED might have to go the "concert party" way.

Can People Be Educated through Drama?

After watching the play, FGD participants were all the more convinced that drama could be very effective in AIDS education.

- Yes, because many people attend concert. Every place where a lot of people gather you can teach it. There are people who have not attended school before, so when it is written in the newspapers they can't read but they understand the play.
- Such mobile performances as this, can educate the public a lot.
- When I watch a concert it looks so real to me that I think they are talking to me.
- Drama can educate because sometimes I hear about certain factors about this disease which I don't believe and also can't imagine how it can happen. After watching a play which is a real life situation one can understand the facts and accept them to be true.
- Seeing is believing so drama could effectively carry the message across.
- In places where radio or T.V. can't reach, the concert can be used to tell them how the disease is like.
- Most of the things are explanations which help us understand the disease.
- Drama contains a lot of advice which influence a lot.

Suggestions were put forward as to how best AIDS education through drama could be effectively done.
The urban adults said:

- The play should be performed by such people as Ampadu. When people hear Ampadu is performing, they would go to watch. So a lot of people can be reached through Ampadu and others.

The rural youth observed that:

- The professionals (itinerant drama troupes) have the instruments and microphones so they can speak to the hearing of the people.
- We could form drama groups where we will be taught how to act such plays so that we can also put up performances in other villages.

Suggested Content of AIDS Drama

Most participants favored performing plays on how to avoid AIDS, the effects of AIDS on its victims, and how to care for persons with AIDS.

- How to prevent ourselves from getting AIDS, how AIDS comes about, how to cure AIDS if we get it.
- They should include something that will make students forget about sex and concentrate on their books.
- You will have to tell us how to handle someone who has the disease.

Those who suggested that the drama should show the effects of AIDS on its victims appeared to be interested primarily in fear arousal strategies.

- We should see someone who has got AIDS, how he or she struggles, how he or she will die and be thrown away so that someone will also realize that if you contract AIDS it is dangerous.
- They should let the play be frightening so that people will fear the AIDS more.
- They should let an AIDS patient die in the play. Then people will take the warning seriously.
- They should show people how the disease can affect someone, how uncomfortable she will become, unable to walk and so on, with all the speech defects.

Question and Answer Session

A slight variation on the research design attempted to measure the effect that a question and answer session with health workers after the drama would have on the audience. This was done only for in-school youth due to time and other resource constraints.

The students' comments showed that the session was helpful:

- Formerly I thought mosquitoes could transmit it [AIDS] but after the questions and answers I got to know that mosquitoes could not do that.
- I didn't know that it is only two to three weeks after contracting AIDS that you can transmit it, as the madam (health worker) explained.

If the drama format is adopted by the HED, it might be worthwhile attaching the question and answer session to it. As usual, there would be those audience members who would not ask any questions in public but would sneak to the research team after others had left, to seek clarifications. They also need to be accommodated in any AIDS education program that is drawn up.

IMPACT OF AIDS SONGS

We also solicited participants' views on the potential that songs with AIDS-related themes held for AIDS education. Our findings are presented.

Awareness of AIDS Songs

All the participants were aware of at least one song on AIDS. They mentioned some of the composers as well as the titles.

- Nana Ampadu has played one and Afua Agyepong, too, has played one.

Other names mentioned were Paapa Yankson, C. K. Mann, Kumasi *Nwonkoro*. Most groups could recall the title or some lyrics in Ampadu's song:

- *"Yaree bi aba eye owuo"* (A disease has come it is death).
- " AIDS *enye, se eye wo a ebekum wo"* (AIDS is not good; if it attacks you it will kill you).

Another song they recalled, although they could not remember the name of the artist was:

- *"Yare bone bi aba oman yi mu."* (A certain bad disease has come into this country.)

The general position was that they used to hear the songs frequently in the past but for about the previous three months or more they had not heard any AIDS songs.

- I heard Ampadu's songs often at first but not now.
- We used to hear it but these days we don't hear it anymore.
- It is about three months since we last heard it.
- It is more than three months.

The absence of the songs on the air made some of them think that the disease had been eradicated.

- We thought because they have stopped playing it, they have found a cure for the AIDS and that the disease has stopped.

Source From Which Songs Were Heard

Radio and children were the most popular sources from which participants heard the AIDS songs.

- On radio. GBC 1 and GBC 2 used to play it everyday.
- Children have learnt it by heart and have been singing it.
- The younger children who have just heard the songs sing it on the streets.

Messages in the Songs

Participants said the songs describe AIDS as deadly and that condoms could provide protection against it. Another message from the songs they said, was the need to avoid quack doctors.

- AIDS is a killer disease so we should avoid it by sticking to one partner.
- It is a deadly disease.

- If you by all means have to have sex with someone you don't know, use a condom.
- If you go to any quack doctor for an injection you will have AIDS.

Influence of AIDS Songs on Behavior

Participants generally agreed that the AIDS songs had influenced them to change their sexual behavior.

- I learnt from the songs that we must use condoms to protect ourselves. So just as I heard it I went to buy one box full of condoms and I have been using it because I'm not yet married and I can't also stay there like that.
- I'm very careful now. I don't go about chasing girls.
- Now it is very dangerous to take men friends for money. It can give you AIDS.
- We aren't going to go behind our husbands [no extramarital affairs].
- We are in a village so we've learnt that taking injections [from non-health workers] isn't good.

However, some of the youth from both rural and urban locations reported that the songs had not influenced them in anyway. While the male youth talked about their personal reactions, the females talked about their perception of others.
The males said:

- I have not changed. Because of the availability of condoms I still continue to chase girls.
- I was not influenced.
- As soon as I hear the song I advise myself to stop chasing girls, but when I go outside and see a beautiful girl, I can't control myself.

The female students said:

- They don't take in the words; they just dance to the nice beat.

Some participants compared the effect of the AIDS songs with the play on AIDS:

- They didn't influence me to the extent that the play did.
- In my view the songs didn't change us much but it is the play you performed yesterday that has moved us.

The main reason for this appeared to be that:

- With the song you just hear the words, you don't see with your eyes.

What Do You Like Best About the Songs?

They liked the lyrics because it was educative, gave them advice, and was easy to understand, and also the rhythm because one could dance to it.

- The song is educative, gives advice, and even the rhythm is danceable.
- Concerning the melodies of the song it is pleasing to the ear.
- The music is simply beautiful, especially Nana Ampadu's.
- They contain a lot of advice.
- I'm interested in the point about the use of condoms.
- I like the emphasis they put on the need for men to use condoms because they don't like condoms.
- They're usually in our local languages so we understand them better.
- The voice of the singer is very clear; you can hear all the words.

What Do They Dislike Most About the Songs?

Although most participants said they did not have any dislikes about the AIDS songs, the few (across all groups) who criticized the songs made revealing observations. Some complained that the songs were so good that they could not concentrate on the educational aspect of it.

- . . . the music is too beautiful, it makes you shake to the beat instead of listening to the words.

Other participants said they could not hear the words properly or that there was little information in the songs:

- The instrument part is higher than the words.
- There is not much information.

There were still other participants who were not comfortable with the advice given in the songs. They were playing the ostrich. Once they made up their minds they did not need any advice to create dissonance.

- I don't like Ampadu's advice to "use a condom" because if I use the condom I don't feel it.
- I don't like the advice on condoms. Some of these girls when they see you using it they won't even allow you to do it.
- The use of condoms because if you're poised for sex, any talk about condoms won't work.
- But these condoms he is talking about, some of them have holes in them, and you can't also wear two of them at the same time . . . the condom can fail.

- What I don't like about the songs is that we should use condoms. A condom can easily burst. If this happens it becomes very difficult to remove it from the genital organ of the woman, especially when you're just about to reach orgasm.

The male youth went even further:

- The only time I don't like the AIDS songs is when I've got a girl with me. The songs can dissuade her from having an affair with me.
- These songs could be played on radio in the silence of our rooms. We don't want them being played during dances.

Other views expressed were that:

- I don't like the song; I've three girlfriends and whenever they hear the song they come to me to sue for separation.
- We don't like the idea when it warns us to stick to one woman.

These views appear to indicate that AIDS songs on radio and other electronic media actually serve as important cues to action in the environment. In particular, they appeared to be reminding the females to say no to casual sex and the males to use condoms.

Can Songs Be Used for AIDS Education?

There was divided opinion across all groups, on whether songs held any promise for AIDS education.

- Even snakes like music. They [songs] can certainly be used for AIDS education.
- The songs are good. The rural people can easily understand them.
- Music is a good way. Generally in Ghana we like music.
- On the air, songs get far.
- If a song is well composed it can change people's attitudes.

There was a suggestion on how best AIDS education through songs could be done:

- The should be played like Ampadu's. The melody should be interspersed with narrations which will slowly explain issues regarding the disease.

Others felt the visual impact of television could be harnessed to show some illustrations with the songs:

- Yes, but as for the television, they can show a skeleton after the song.

Those who disagreed that songs could be used for AIDS education contended that people did not pay attention to the lyrics of songs:

- People don't pay particular attention to words in songs.
- People just dance to the songs; they don't even listen to the words.
- Some people, too, are more interested in the instrumental backing than the educative words so it is not very effective.

Parental reaction could also create problems:

- When I was singing the AIDS song my father shouted at me.

CONCLUSIONS AND RECOMMENDATIONS

AIDS Awareness and Knowledge

Whereas the urban participants accepted that AIDS was a health problem in their community, the rural participants tried to distance themselves from AIDS. Thus, AIDS education efforts should stress the reality of AIDS and the fact that everybody is potentially at risk, urban dweller or rural dweller. It is no longer "them" and "us,", it is **"EVERYBODY."**

Most FGD participants had heard about AIDS before and knew it to be a deadly and incurable disease. They were visibly scared of AIDS and were apparently seeking more information about it. Their fear appeared to be based on mutual distrust between spouses and also on the incurable nature of the disease.

Some youth were not worried at all about AIDS because they knew that they could protect themselves with condoms.

A few participants, particularly those in the rural study who did not watch the play, claimed rather limited knowledge about AIDS. This appeared to be consistent with their already reported tendency to distance their community from AIDS. The interesting aspect of their attitude, however, is that they are desirous of obtaining information about AIDS except that they did not know "exactly where to seek such information."

All participants, except urban male in-school youth, appeared to confuse the causes of AIDS with the mode of HIV transmission; this could be a problem of semantics. But perhaps it is not even necessary for AIDS educators to hammer on the viral nature of AIDS since no participant linked it with something like the supernatural or spiritual. This aspect of AIDS education would be more straight forward and better understood if it concentrates on the modes of HIV transmission and associated preventive measures. Participants' own suggestions support this stand.

Most participants were apparently unaware of such modes of HIV transmission as transfusion with contaminated blood and transmission from an infected pregnant woman to her baby during childbirth. The more popular ones were transmission through sexual intercourse with an infected person and the use of contaminated syringes and other such instruments.

AIDS education would, therefore, have to cover the less known modes of HIV transmission as well. In fact FGD participants expressed the agreement that what AIDS information was most needed was the mode of HIV transmission.

Another area that also needs to be addressed is the tendency on the part of most participants to do a visual diagnosis of AIDS. People need to be convinced that they just cannot look at somebody's face and determine that the person is HIV positive. The importance of medical tests must be stressed.

On the discovery of a cure for AIDS, it is important that the "Kwaku Firi story" is straightened out once and for all. Has the man got a cure? How have the Ministry of Health and the nation's medical research institutions reacted to his claims? These questions need to be answered and Ghanaians informed.

Most FGD participants were aware that using condoms could reduce the risk of HIV infection. It is thus recommended that we stop playing the ostrich and make condoms more easily available throughout the country.

Radio appeared to be both the most popular and most trusted source of AIDS information for most participants. The credibility accorded radio by participants appears to explain this. Participants said "when it is said on radio then it must be true." Television and health workers were also mentioned. However, the print media (including posters) were mentioned only as popular sources of AIDS information but not necessarily trusted ones. The implication is that if people are to be convinced about AIDS, then AIDS educators must go for radio, television and interpersonal contact using health workers.

Some misconceptions about the modes of HIV transmission were brought up in the study. These related to transmission by mosquitoes, through swimming pools, kissing, casual contact and others like gonorrhea and salmon fish. These misconceptions should provide more input for AIDS education efforts.

Impact of Drama—"The Bitter Side of AIDS"

Participants appeared to have enjoyed watching the play and it was obvious that the message had been effectively carried across to them. They could easily identify the import of the play and a month after watching it, they could still clearly recall the story line.

Perhaps the strongest point about drama as a vehicle for AIDS education appears to be the apparent success of the play "The Bitter Side of AIDS" in generating discussion about AIDS among spouses. This discussion has the advantage of keeping the AIDS issue alive and once a problem remains alive, people begin to think of ways to solve it. According to our FGD participants, these discussions centered mainly around the mode of HIV transmission and preventive measures. Sexual partners apparently wanted to be reassured of their safety.

Other comments from participants appear to underscore the need for AIDS education to stress counselling on how to introduce condoms into already existing relationships without creating distrust or any other unnecessary tension.

Participants picked a lot of lessons from the play and, in fact, passed resolutions about changing their sexual behavior. They still reported holding on to these resolutions one clear month after watching the play. The change in behavior appeared to be in the direction advocated in the play: cut down on multiple sexual partners, stick to one faithful partner, use condoms etc.

The tendency to visually diagnose AIDS came up again and this presents two implications. First, AIDS education should seek to debunk the popular belief that AIDS can be diagnosed merely by looking at an HIV carrier in the face. Second, if it is considered worthwhile to educate the public on the symptoms of AIDS, then Africa's health educators should be ready to invest in video and/or cinema.

Participants suggested that AIDS drama should be on the following themes: how to avoid contracting AIDS, how to care for persons with AIDS, and the effect of AIDS on its victims. The last of these suggestions appears to underscore the high rating that participants accorded communication strategies that embody fear arousal techniques.

Participants appeared to be of the view that professional itinerant drama troupes presented the finest possibilities for using drama for AIDS education. Thus, health educators would have to adopt either of two approaches.

First, they might consider hiring poplar, crowd pulling professional drama troupes to perform plays with AIDS-related themes or, second, they could use non-professional groups like their own health personnel, but in such cases they would best be advised to adopt the "concert party" format. This usually entails playing a lot of good music before the actual performance commences and also interspersing the play itself with generous doses of thematically related songs. Whichever approach is finally adopted, it would be most beneficial to toss in a question and answer session with AIDS educators at the end of each performance.

Impact of AIDS Songs

Most participants were aware of at least one song on AIDS, with Ampadu's being the most popular. Radio and children were the most popular sources from which FGD participants heard about these AIDS songs. Participants appeared generally to have agreed that the songs had influenced them to change their sexual behavior. An attestation to this was the case of some male participants who reported having problems with their female partners any time a song about AIDS was played.

In direct comparison between the two, participants seemed to prefer AIDS drama to AIDS songs because "with the song you just hear the words, you don't see with your eyes." Another participant put it even more succinctly, "In my view the songs didn't change us much but it is the play you put up yesterday that has moved us." Participants suggested that the visual impact of television could be harnessed to show illustrations of various aspects of AIDS as AIDS songs were being played. It may be worthwhile for health educators to link up with their national broadcasting services to examine the possibility of putting this suggestion into practice.

Overall, the importance of drama and songs as vehicles for AIDS education cannot be understated. People who watched the play testified that they had not only learned a lot of new ideas, but that they had also changed their sexual behavior. If it was not possible to verify the reported change in sexual behavior, at least the knowledge gains were quite obvious and this, in our considered opinion, is what should be the litmus test. AIDS drama DOES increase knowledge about AIDS. It COULD also lead to changes in sexual behavior. Also, songs with AIDS-related themes, if played on radio and other electronic media, could serve as important cues to action in the environment. They could remind their audiences to, for example, say no to casual sex and to adopt safer sexual behaviors.

Ultimately, among those concerned with fighting AIDS worldwide, it is agreed that the best weapon is education that changes people's behavior. In this educational effort, all available channels have to be used. Drama and songs have been found to have a strong potential for changing sexual behavior in both urban and rural locations in Ghana. Ghana's cultural landscape is no different from the rest of Africa. The onus is therefore on health educators in Africa to take a look at these findings and act, for there is no time to waste. If they move quickly enough, the effort expended on this study would have been worthwhile.

REFERENCES

1. Ministry of Health, Accra, "AIDS Report, December 1990."
2. Clearinghouse on Development Communication, 1987, *Popular Music and Sexual Responsibility—Latin American Region*, Clearinghouse on Development Communication, Washington, D.C., Project Profiles, 1988.
3. J. Morrison, On the Road with the Atelier Theatre Burkinabe, *Development Communication Report, 3*:62, pp. 1, 6, 1988.
4. J. Schubert, Family Planning Uses Traditional Theatre in Mali, *Development Communication Report, 2*:61, pp. 1, 15, 16, 1988.
5. Clearinghouse on Development Communication, 1987, *Marotholi Travelling Theatre—Lesotho*, Clearinghouse on Development Communication, Washington, D.C., Project Profiles, 1988.
6. M. Zimmerman, et al., Assessing the Acceptability of NORPLANT Implants in Four Countries: Findings from Focus Group Research, *Studies in Family Planning, 21*:2, pp. 92-103, 1990.
7. E. Folch-Lyon and J. F. Trost, Conducting Focus Group Sessions, *Studies in Family Planning, 12*:12, pp. 443-449, 1981.

CHAPTER 18

Needle Sharing for the Use of Therapeutic Drugs as a Potential AIDS Risk Behavior among Migrant Hispanic Farmworkers in the Eastern Stream

Jerry Lafferty, David Foulk, and Rebecca Ryan

Epidemiological studies have documented that of the AIDS cases in the United States 41 percent are found in ethnic minorities. Latins comprise 6 percent of the nation's population, yet account for 14 percent of AIDS patients, while Blacks, though 12 percent of the United States population, constitute 24 percent of the AIDS cases. Although AIDS affects all racial groups, Blacks and Latins are disproportionately represented [1]. For whatever reason, research has not been directed at identifying risk factors peculiar to this group. Most studies have failed to look at cultural subtleties which may have a dramatic effect on AIDS related behavior. The report to the President's Commission and the void in data concerning ethnic and cultural differences in populations provided the impetus for assembling Georgia Southern University's project staff. This staff then conducted a preliminary fact-finding study on migrant farmworkers in the state of Georgia. This exploratory and descriptive study revealed a number of AIDS risk behaviors and a lack of knowledge about AIDS among migrant workers in Georgia [2].

The Centers for Disease Control (CDC) conducted a national serosurvey of HIV among migrant farmworkers. The results of this study revealed a significant seroprevalence in the eastern stream [3]. The findings of the Georgia Study coupled with the Centers for Disease Control seroprevalence data created cause for great concern [4]. These factors promoted an expansion of the initial Georgia Southern Study.

In the United States intravenous drug use is a major window for heterosexual transmission and a primary source for perinatal transmission of AIDS [5]. The human immunodeficiency virus (HIV) can be transmitted through contaminated blood left in needles, syringes, and other paraphernalia used by drug abusers and nonmedical therapeutic drug users.

AIDS research on conditions under which needle sharing occurs is limited. Two ethnographic studies have identified various situational factors, economic considerations, and social pressures that may lead to needle sharing [6-8]. Anecdotal reports indicate that self-injection of vitamins and antibiotics is relatively common among migrant workers in the United States, as it is in Mexico. These people live in an environment where needle use for self-injection of vitamins and therapeutic drugs is accepted behavior. Depressed income levels and sociocultural acceptance of needle use may encourage sharing in this population. In January 1985, there was a report of a six-month-old Dominican child who was diagnosed positive to HIV. Subsequently, the three-year-old brother was tested and found to be HIV positive, but symptom free. Interviews with the family revealed no known AIDS risk exposure except that the mother gave vitamin injections to first the baby and second to the older brother. After the first injection, the mother wiped the needle with bay rum (an aromatic of about 45 percent alcohol concentration) and injected the second boy. According to this article, needlesticks rarely are associated with seroconversion but this finding suggests that under certain conditions, a small amount of blood left in a needle can transmit HIV [9].

In a study of the Acquired Immunodeficiency Syndrome in Haiti researchers discussed intramuscular injections as a potential risk factor. Pape et al. reported that it is a common practice in Haiti for persons to obtain intramuscular injections when they are "not feeling well." The injections are given by either medical personnel or piqurists (untrained injection givers). Disposable needles and syringes are not readily available in Haiti, so they may be reused without sterilization. Their research indicated that during a five-year period before the onset of AIDS symptoms, intramuscular medications were received by 89 percent of the patients. These patients also received a larger number of injections annually and injections were more likely given by a nonmedical source [10]. In the United States, no other studies have examined self-injection for therapeutic reasons. Consequently, one of the major focal points of this study was to determine socio-cultural influence on needle sharing as a potential risk factor in the transmission of AIDS.

METHODS

The Subjects

This study sought to describe the health knowledge, attitudes and practices of Eastern stream migrant farmworkers relative to AIDS. Data were collected using a sample of 378 migrant hispanic workers. These migrant workers follow a geographic path determined by harvest time for crops. The season begins in Florida in late summer and moves up the coast as crops ripen in Georgia, South Carolina, North Carolina, and ends in late summer in the Delaware, Maryland, and Virginia (Delmarva) peninsula. The timing of this study sought to avoid overlap as workers migrated north. Data were collected by face-to-face interviews. The group studied was a multi-ethnic heterogenous group. Of these, 91.3 percent were male and 8.7 percent were female. The mean age was 28.4 (standard deviation = 10.3). The full distribution of ages which is presented in Table 1 indicates that these workers were at prime ages for AIDS risk. The majority (83.1%) of the respondents were Mexican; 44.4 percent considered Mexico to be their home base and 16.3 percent were U.S. citizens. Almost three quarters (77.1%) of the respondents were Catholic. The majority of the respondents were relatively long-time migrant farmworkers in the United States. Sixty-four percent reported having spent four or more years in this country.

The Instrument

The knowledge items in this instrument were adapted from the National Health Interview Survey (NHIS) which was conducted by the National Center for Health Statistics (NCHS). The survey was composed of both general and critical knowledge items. Seven of the AIDS knowledge questions were constructed as a critical knowledge scale. These are the items that relate to transmission routes and fatality. The National Health Interview Survey is a continuous, cross-sectional household interview survey. To facilitate the use of this instrument with the population of the study, items were modified by adjusting the language level and removing technical terms and references to match the educational and cultural backgrounds of the survey respondents. The survey was printed in English, Spanish, and Creole.[1] To ensure the effectiveness of the questionnaire, interpreters were trained in proper interview technique and a pilot survey of fifty migrant workers was conducted. All interviews in the pilot and eastern stream study were conducted by trained bilingual interviewers.

The Collection of Data

During the months of July, August, and September interviewers went to farm work camps. The majority of the visits were in the evening after the work day had been completed. All residents had an equal opportunity to take part in the study and participation was completely voluntary. Some interviews were also conducted in migrant health clinics. The use of a convenience sample limits the analysis of

---

[1] Copies of the instruments may be requested from the Center for Rural Health and Research, Georgia Southern University, Statesboro, Georgia.

Table 1. Sociodemographic of Hispanics Who Do and Do Not
Self-Inject Drugs for Medicinal Purposes

Characteristics	# Yes	(Percent)	# No	(Percent)	Chi Square
		Self-Inject Medicinals			
Gender					
Male	76	(22.6)	261	(77.4)	Chi Square = 3.01
Female	3	(9.4)	29	(90.6)	p = .082
Marital status					
Married	42	(23.1)	140	(76.9)	Chi Square = 7.69
Unmarried	38	(19.4)	158	(80.6)	p = .3803
Age					
14-18	6	(13.6)	38	(86.4)	
19-25	24	(17.0)	117	(83.0)	Chi Square = 9.24
26-35	24	(22.4)	83	(77.6)	p = .0554
36-44	16	(34.0)	31	(66.0)	
45+	10	(30.3)	23	(69.7)	
Ethnicity					
Mexican	72	(22.9)	242	(77.1)	
Latino	1	(7.7)	12	(92.3)	
Chicano	0		5	(100)	Chi Square = 6.59
Puerto Rican	4	(20.0)	16	(80.0)	p = .7634
Salvadoran	1	(20.0)	4	(80.0)	
Guatemalan	2	(22.0)	7	(78.0)	
Other	0		12	(100)	
Citizenship					
U.S. citizen	10	(16.9)	49	(83.1)	Chi Square = 1.11
Non U.S. citizen	232	(76.8)	70	(23.2)	p = .29
Religion					
Catholic	68	(23.5)	221	(76.5)	Chi Square = 4.11
Non Catholic	12	(13.5)	77	(86.5)	p = .042

the results to exploratory, descriptive interpretation, but the lack of information in this important area makes preliminary research extremely valuable.

Analyses

The analyses utilized Pearson's correlation with dummy variable analyses where appropriate. Recent statistical research has indicated that Pearson's correlation can reasonably be used with ordinal data when the numbers of cases are adequate and when the steps of the score are regular as they are in this case. Chi Square and other descriptive measures were used with nominal level variables.

RESULTS

AIDS Risk Factors

This study explored critical knowledge of AIDS, patterns of sexual behavior, and self-injection for therapeutic reasons. Respondents engaged in a number of AIDS risk behaviors. Sexual intercourse with multiple partners was the major source of risk. The study revealed that 25.4 percent had no sex partners during the past year, 39.1 percent reported only one sexual partner and 35.5 percent reported having two or more sexual partners during the past year. Of the respondents, 26.4 percent reported having multiple partners without the use of a condom. The mean number of sex partners in the past year was 1.7. Anal intercourse was present at insignificant levels. Anal receptive sexual behavior was reported by .8 percent of the male respondents. Anal insertive behavior was reported by .8 percent of the male respondents. Six (1.58%) of the farmworkers reported having taken money for sex, one reported having exchanged sex for drugs. Intercourse with prostitutes was also a major risk factor in this population with seventy (18.5%) indicating that they had paid for sex in the last year.

Use of injectable illegal drugs was relatively low in this study, (2.6% reported injecting drugs such as heroin, cocaine, and speed); but the data did suggest a major incidence of a previously undocumented self-injected drug risk pattern. Eighty of the respondents (21.2%) reported self-injecting antibiotics and vitamins. Twelve (3.2%) reported having injected antibiotics and vitamins with a shared needle.[2] Of the respondents, 22.5 percent indicated that they knew individuals who self-injected antibiotics and vitamins.

As indicated by description statistics in Table 1, those who self-inject medicinal drugs tend to be male, older, and Catholic.[3] Table 2 shows that self-injectors have slightly higher critical knowledge about AIDS and they have a tendency to worry about getting the disease and many frequent prostitutes.[4] The self-injectors do not differ significantly from non-injectors in risk behaviors; however, they do have one tendency toward a positive attitude about condom use and they are somewhat more likely to use condoms with non-spousal partners (Table 3).

---

[2] It seems likely, however, that attempts to clean needles may have been inadequate.

[3] Nonsignificant tendency.

[4] The critical knowledge score is a total of correct answers on the seven knowledge questions specific to AIDS fatality and transmission routes.

Table 2. Migrant Farmworker's Medicinal Self-Injection with AIDS
Knowledge and Fear — Pearson's Correlations (N = 378)

Summary of Questions	r	p
1. Afraid of getting AIDS	.1413	.003
2. Think you might get AIDS	.1423	.003
3. Think you know how one gets AIDS	.1660	.001
4. Critical knowledge	.1311	.005

Note: Items 1 through 3 had yes/no answers coded with yes (high) and no (low). Item 4 used a knowledge scale which is described in the Methods section.

Table 3. Migrant Farmworker's Medicinal Self-Injection with AIDS
Risk Behaviors — Pearson's Correlation (N = 378)

Questions	r	p
1. Feel safe with condoms	.1716	.001
2. Number of sex partners	.0149	ns
3. Hire prostitutes	−.0614	ns
4. Condom use with spouse	−.0071	ns
5. Condom use with non spouse	−.1081	.023

Note: Item 1 (attitudinal questions) and Item 3 were yes/no items coded yes (high) and no (low). Items 4 and 5 were coded: 1 — always, 2 — sometimes, 3 — never.

DISCUSSION

Most of the research on needle sharing as an AIDS-related risk behavior has focused on individuals involved in recreational drug use. Magura et al., stated that intravenous drug use by friends and sexual partners creates a social environment that leads to sharing [6]. Their research supported previous observations that peer behavior strongly influences needle sharing decisions. Though needle sharing is prevalent in the Eastern stream migrant population, it is not perceived by the participants as a negative or dangerous behavior. This study documented that while injections of recreational drugs is present in this population, a more prevailing potential risk factor is self-injection by those using drugs and vitamins as a preventive health behavior. Recreational intravenous drug users represented 2.9 percent of the population while 20.3 percent self-inject drugs and vitamins for medical reasons.

In this Eastern stream study, needle sharing was the potentially most prevalent and dangerous risk behavior for the spread of AIDS found in the migrant population. It was established that the number of individuals who self-injected as a therapeutic behavior and shared needles was greater than those who used recreational drugs and shared needles. The number of therapeutic injectors that share needles was also greater than the number engaged in anal intercourse. There is every reason to believe that the number of individuals using dirty needles to self-inject is vastly under reported. It is very possible that the economic status of migrant workers affords them little discretionary income. Limited funds may force workers to choose between buying new needles and other necessary goods and services. In addition, most workers live in migrant farm work camps located miles from any town making it difficult to purchase new needles. Self-injecting appears to be a culturally accepted behavior in the Eastern stream camps. Twenty-two percent of the respondents reported knowing individuals that self-inject antibiotics and vitamins for medicinal purposes which is very similar to the 22.9 percent that reported self-injecting. It is obvious that this represents a network of people who self-inject and creates a dangerous situation that may lead to needle sharing and an increased potential for spreading AIDS.

The likelihood of contracting AIDS escalates as the number of risk factors increase. The study documents that sharing needles in the migrant population is a serious AIDS risk factor. Self injection of therapeutic agents becomes a greater risk when considered in concert with the other risk factors present in this population. Exposure to additional factors such as sexual promiscuity, frequenting prostitutes, homosexual behavior, and having vaginal or anal intercourse without a condom creates a serious web of causation. These interrelated factors dramatically increase the risk of spreading AIDS in the migrant and seasonal worker population. Hence, each of the individual risk factors may be multiplied and broadcast through the needle risk.

The statistical results of this study were generally consistent with the findings of previous studies that have looked at knowledge of AIDS in different cultures of our population. The migrant farmworker has knowledge about AIDS but many times what they know is not pertinent to the causation or the seriousness of the disease. A high percentage of respondents do not know that AIDS is a fatal disease. It is clear that the migrant workers in this study felt that self-injecting drugs and vitamins for preventive health reasons was a positive behavior. It appears that the migrant population knows it is safe to go to public restrooms, shake hands, drink water from a communal glass but don't know that it is dangerous to share needles while injecting drugs and vitamins for medicinal purposes. General knowledge of AIDS does not motivate migrant behavior as much as critical knowledge and cultural influences.

Although many migrant farmworkers may consider self-injecting a positive health behavior, in reality it is one of the most dangerous risk behaviors in which they could engage. Our present AIDS education programs are sending an incomplete message when they do not consider cultural behaviors such as self-injecting for therapeutic reasons. AIDS education programs that do not take into account cultural assumptions and biases of ethnic groups are missing an important window of opportunity.

REFERENCES

1. D. Hopkins, *Keynote Address: National Conference on AIDS in Minority Populations in the United States*, unpublished report, Centers for Disease Control, Atlanta, Georgia, 1987.
2. D. Foulk, J. Lafferty, R. Ryan, and A. Robertson, AIDS Knowledge and Behavior in a Migrant Farmworker Population, *Migrant World, XVII:3/4*, 1989.
3. J. Narkunas, K. Castro, S. Reig, and Migrant Health Program Collaborative Sites, *Seroprevalence of HIV Infection among Migrant Farmworkers*, Fifth International Conference on AIDS, Montreal, Canada, June 1989.
4. D. Foulk, J. Lafferty, R. Ryan, and A. Robertson, AIDS Knowledge and Risk Behaviors of Migrant and Seasonal Farmworkers in Georgia, *Migrant Health Newsline, 5:4*, pp. 3-4, July/August 1989.
5. D. C. Des Jarlais and S. R. Friedman, HIV Infection Among Intravenous Drug Users: Epidemiology and Risk Reduction, *AIDS, 1*, pp. 67-76, 1987.
6. S. Magura, J. I. Grossman, D. S. Lipton, et al., Determinants of Needle Sharing Among Intravenous Drug Users, *American Journal of Public Health, 79:4*, pp. 459-462, April 1989.
7. S. Murphy, Intravenous Drug Use and AIDS: Notes on the Social Economy of Needle-Sharing, *Contemporary Drug Problem*, pp. 373-395, 1987.
8. D. E. Des Jarlais, S. R. Friedman, and D. Strug, AIDS and Needle-Sharing within the IV Drug Use Subculture, in *The Social Dimensions of AIDS: Methods and Theory*, D. Feldman and M. T. Johnson (eds.), Praeger, New York, 1985.
9. R. D. Koening, T. Gautier, and J. Levy, Unusual Intrafamilial Transmission of Human Immunodeficiency Virus, *Lancet* 2:8507.
10. J. Pape, L. Bernard, T. Franck, et al., The Acquired Immunodeficiency Syndrome in Haita, *Annals of Internals Medicine, 103*, pp. 674-678, 1985.

CHAPTER 19

Enlisting the Support of Traditional Healers in an AIDS Education Campaign in Zambia

B. U. Chirwa and E. Sivile

The first AIDS cases in Zambia were described in 1985. Since then, the number of cases reported to the Ministry of Health has continued to rise. By the end of September 1988 a total of 1,056 cases and 106 deaths were notified. Recognizing that the AIDS epidemic is a problem of extraordinary scope and unprecedented urgency, the Ministry of Health formulated a short-term plan for the control of AIDS in Zambia. Arising out of this was the establishment of the AIDS task force and the National Surveillance Committee.

In the absence of an effective vaccine against HIV the most powerful weapon available in the battle against AIDS is education and information aimed at getting people to make lifesaving choices through changing their behavior and life styles [1]. As a result, an intersectoral health education committee on AIDS was established at the Ministry of Health, and similar committees were set up at provincial and district levels in Zambia.

A national health education campaign began in 1986. A series of posters and a pamphlet containing easily understood messages were widely distributed throughout the country. The two daily papers printed messages on AIDS. Both radio and television programs covered basic issues. AIDS education has been taken to schools through special booklets as well as anti-AIDS clubs. The rural folks have been reached through drama, dance and song.

Realizing that seropositive individuals, patients and their families required more than mere provision of information on AIDS, counseling services have been incepted in clinics and blood screening centers.

These efforts were constrained by lack of support from traditional healers. Getting traditional medical practitioners involved in the AIDS campaign posed a great challenge to health workers. First, some of them did not appreciate that AIDS is a new disease. Second, others hampered the education efforts by publicly claiming that they could cure AIDS or had preparations to prevent HIV infection. Since traditional healers form an important resource group in their respective communities, it was imperative to enlist their support in promoting life styles that will enhance preventive behaviors against AIDS/HIV infection.

ROLE OF TRADITIONAL HEALERS

Most social scientists agree that behavior change requires interpersonal communication [2-4]. The personalized communication becomes even more effective if the sender of the message and the receiver are similar in most attributes such as education, socioeconomics, and culture, the principle of homophilous communication [5]. Liskin et al. have suggested that in order to change behavior of at-risk population it is necessary for educational programs to use credible sources and work closely with intended audiences [6]. In traditional African societies the traditional healer is a credible source who always works closely with the people since he or she is an integral part of the culture. It, therefore, makes a strategic sense to involve healers in AIDS education.

Since the Alma Ata Declaration many health programs have integrated traditional health practitioners in their Primary Health Care activities. Hence, their utilization falls within the framework of recommendation that action against AIDS must be integrated carefully to fit in with existing primary health care priorities and to support existing primary health care strategies [7].

AIDS ACTION has identified traditional healers as a target for education as well as part of the solution, viz their counselling role [8]. Thus, counseling does not have to rely solely on trained professionals. For example, religious leaders and traditional healers have a natural helping or counseling role in society and such individuals should be encouraged to take an active part in AIDS education programs. On the other hand, health education for AIDS needs to focus on the behavior of traditional health practitioners to ensure they use properly sterilized equipment for any treatment which involves piercing the skin.

It is also becoming increasingly clear that in order to involve as many people as possible in the fight against AIDS particularly in developing nations, workshops and enlisting the support of traditional healers will be paramount [9]. Sherr has pointed out that although many people have heard about AIDS through radio and leaflets they complain that they have not been told enough about it [10]. The author recommends workshops and face-to-face discussions where questions and misunderstandings can be dealt with, information and experience shared, and personal involvement and commitment can be encouraged. Workshops can be designed for different areas of educational needs among both health professionals and the public.

WORKSHOP DESIGN

Zambia, a developing nation of 7.2 million, has two systems of health care delivery: modern medicine and traditional. Traditional health practitioners comprise Herbalist, Spiritualist, and Faith healers. From time immemorial the rural population of Zambia has been dependent on traditional health care. It is still very popular, available twenty-four hours a day and not only looks at the disease or organ but at the total human being. It applies some form of holistic approach to solving health problems [11].

Since Alma Ata, the Ministry of Health has made a conscious effort to involve traditional medicine in the health care of the nation. The activities of the traditional health practitioners are coordinated by the traditional medicine unit and the Traditional Practitioners Association of Zambia (TAPAZ). There are approximately 10,000 members registered with the association.

As a first step toward recruiting traditional health practitioners the health education unit entered into a dialogue with their secretariat. Subsequently provincial and district health education officers in conjunction with the local branch of TAPAZ worked out nominations to represent the region at a workshop. This set-up facilitates feedback of proceedings of national events. In addition, the chairman, secretary and two committee members of the secretariat attended the workshop.

The facilitators comprised two health education specialists, a medical doctor in charge of traditional medicine in the Ministry and a psychiatrist with special interest in counseling plus several doctors who have had experience in dealing with AIDS in various settings including community, clinical and school. All had experience working with traditional healers and exhibited a reciprocal relationship with them. Prior to the workshop the various resource persons received orientation on the workshop. This centered on the objectives of the workshop and the process of achieving the same. The main goals of the workshop were twofold: first, to exchange ideas and experience on AIDS, and second, to gain support of traditional healers in the fight against AIDS. To achieve these objectives, a variety of health education methods were employed. Overall, an interactive process involving brainstorming, group discussion and talks with visual aids was employed.

Instrument for Data Collection

In order to assess the impact of the workshop on the knowledge, attitude, and possible practices of participants in relation to AIDS, a pre- and posttest was conducted. The open-ended, as well as multiple-choice style of questionnaire sought information on cause, transmission, treatment, prevention, advice/counseling of the AIDS patient, and finally source of information.

RESULTS

A total of forty traditional medical practitioners from all the nine provinces of Zambia attended the workshop although only thirty-three participants arrived in time to take the pretest. There were more males (65%) than females (35%).

All participants were aware of AIDS and acknowledged its existence in Zambia. Respondents indicated that they had multiple sources of information on AIDS: leaflets accounted for 57.6 percent; radio and television 51.5 percent; discussions with friends, neighbors, and health workers 48.5 percent, and posters 36.4 percent.

The educational principle assumed to be at work was if the health educator respects and is willing to discuss the traditional health practitioners' own beliefs, they in turn may be more receptive to new ideas or perceptions introduced through health education. From Table 1, it can be seen that the main causes attributed to AIDS by thirty-three traditional healers at the beginning of the workshop are abortion (57.6%), lack of cleansing (33.3%), HIV (33.3%), punishment from God (24.2%), and sex with infected persons (12.2%). Response by forty participants after the workshop showed a significant increase for one correct cause, 75 percent for HIV and a significant decrease for one incorrect (5% for punishment from God). Other ideas remained at about the same level.

Some sessions focused on the traditional healers' behavior. Of thirty-three participants who took the pretest 33.3 percent realized that skin piercing instruments, blades used for tatooing/making traditional marks or circumcision could spread HIV infection. At posttest 60 percent of the participants correctly saw the

Table 1. Healers' Ideas of AIDS Cause Before and After Workshop

Cause	Percent Before	Percent After	Z Value	R Value
Abortion	57.6	42.5	1.51	>0.10
HIV	33.3	75.0	3.90	<0.0001
Punishment	24.2	5.0	2.33	<0.02
Sex with infected person	12.1	20.0	0.93	>0.35
Witchcraft	9.1	5.0	—	—
Lack of cleansing rites	9.1	7.5	—	—
Sex with pregnant woman	6.1	7.5	—	—
Others[a]	15.1	0.0	—	—

[a]Others = Poor hygiene, insect bites.
Note: $N = 33\%$ before; 40% after

need to use properly sterilized instruments for any treatment which involves piercing the skin. Only about one-third of participants knew that HIV infection could be transmitted from the expectant mother to her child. Whereas after education, 57.5 percent did. This difference is statistically significant as shown in Table 2.

The participants exhibited correct knowledge of issues which have wide and intense coverage in the national education campaign. A majority of respondents know that the disease could be transmitted through sexual intercourse (87.8%) and blood transfusion (63.6%) at present and remained at that level at the end of the workshop. Similarly, most participants were able to list signs and symptoms relating to AIDS. The recognition factor of symptoms increased. The two symptoms which featured prominently in diagnoses were prolonged diarrhoea (48.4% before and 90% after) and weight loss (82.5% before and 84.2% after). Others are prolonged fever, prolonged cough, weakness, skin rash, and enlarged lymph glands.

Through discussion it became clear that some traditional health practitioners associated some of the common symptoms (e.g., diarrhoea and weight loss) of AIDS to traditionally perceived diseases which they had been treating since time immemorial. To illustrate, "Amakombela" is a disease believed to be acquired by a man who has sexual intercourse with a widow who has not undergone cleansing rites. Among the presenting complaints are progressive weight loss and weakness. "Amakombela" has been known to be treated by traditional healers. An explanation that those symptoms are among the different ways AIDS presents itself created understanding. The participants also indicated that even within the traditional realm there are symptoms common to different diseases. As a result, at the close of the workshop less than half of respondents felt the disease was treatable. Less than a quarter knew that one could be infected without showing any signs or symptoms. Significantly more respondents (68.8%) after the

Table 2. Respondents Knowledge of Transmission of HIV Before and After Workshop

Route of Transmission	Percent Before	Percent After	Z Value	R Value
Sex with AIDS patient	87.9	87.5	—	—
Blood transfusion	63.6	65.0	—	—
Unsterile blades, needles and syringes	33.3	60.0	2.37	<0.05
HIV positive mother to child	33.3	57.5	2.12	<0.05
Others[a]	6.1	5.1	—	—

[a]Others = Touching infected person, insect bites.
Note: N = 33% before; 40% after

workshop knew that one could not tell a patient or an asymptomatic carrier from looks alone.

Most traditional healers recognized ways through which the disease could be spread but they had reservations about contact in daily life with an AIDS sufferer or HIV infected individuals. Their attitude borders on ostracization, as seen in Table 3. Of the thirty-three participants interviewed at the beginning, 54.5 percent would avoid living with an AIDS patient, 48.5 percent would not share bath or toilet, 45.5 percent would not share eating utensils, 27.3 percent would not share clothes, and even less (24.2%) would not shake hands.

Zambia has yet to promote the use of condoms. Amazingly at pretest almost 40 percent of respondents had heard of a condom and that it could be used to prevent transmission of HIV infection. This rose to almost two-thirds of participants indicating the condom as one of the ways of preventing the spread of HIV infection. As expected respondents' knowledge of these topics extensively and intensively dealt with in the campaign was good. Thus, the majority of participants correctly mentioned that spread of HIV infection could be curtailed through fidelity (78.8% at pretest with a slight increase at posttest, 80%).

At the close of the workshop significantly more traditional health practitioners exhibited a positive approach to the AIDS control program, and were willing to participate in it. More participants were sympathetic to an AIDS sufferer after exposure to education and were willing to discuss the problem of AIDS with the patient (55%) than before (6.1%). Similarly, more would recommend AIDS patients and HIV infected individuals refrain from having children (52.5% compared to 27.3% before the education). After the workshop slightly more participants (45%) would discourage polygamy than before (36.4%). Even more important is the fact that more are willing to refer some of their patients to the health institutions. This is depicted in Table 4.

Table 3. Attitude of Traditional Medical Practitioners to
AIDS Patients Before and After Workshop

Idea	Percent Before	Percent After	Z Value	p Value
Not live with AIDS patients	54.5	22.5	2.87	<0.01
Not share toilet	48.5	17.5	2.92	<0.01
Not share utensils	45.5	17.5	2.65	<0.01
Not share clothes	27.3	12.5	1.66	>0.05
Not shake hands	24.2	15.0	0.98	>0.50

Note: N = 33% before; 40% after

Table 4. Healter's Advice to AIDS Patients
Before and After Workshop

Advice	Percent Before	Percent After	Z Value	p Value
Refer to hospital	63.6	82.5	1.83	>0.05
Administer herbs	48.5	47.5	—	—
Avoid polygamy	36.4	45.0	0.75	>0.40
Use condoms	15.5	45.0	2.93	<0.04
Not have children	27.3	52.5	2.28	<0.04
Counseling	6.1	55.0	4.87	<0.0001
Pray to God	3.0	17.5	0.38	>0.40

Note: N = 33% before; 40% after

DISCUSSION

The results of this study indicate that participatory interactive discussion on AIDS is effective in helping healers gain the knowledge and understanding needed to participate in AIDS education in their respective communities. The strength of the participatory approach for education is that small group interaction provides a supportive interpersonal learning environment. Another advantage of small group discussion is that participants are free to raise their concerns and these are dealt with directly. Even more important is the fact that discussion is focused on issues directly relevant to the participating group.

The results of this study have demonstrated that although the national campaign had sensitized the healers to the AIDS problem, issues relating to their beliefs and practices were not addressed. First this reinforces the concept of complementing the mass media campaign with focused education and second, that change in attitude and beliefs requires direct and intensified interpersonal education.

It is also important to point to the interaction that transpired during the workshop. This was based on mutual respect for one another's realm of activity, thereby facilitating exchange of ideas and experiences. In this way conclusions were arrived at through a consensus. This ensured continued future interactions.

Although the number claiming to treat or to know somebody who could treat AIDS dropped from almost three-quarters to less than half after the workshop, about the same number (47.5%) persisted in their claim to possess a cure for AIDS. Subsequently it was necessary for the Health Education Unit to enter into individual discussion with those traditional healers claiming possession of preventive or curative preparations. This was necessary in order to find out more about their treatment. Since modern medicine also does give treatment even if palliative, this supportive therapy be it modern or traditional may help a person cope. So traditional treatment may be useful psychologically. Another important factor to consider is that traditional healing is their livelihood, which can be supported while adding realism. Traditional health practitioners should continue to counsel patients including AIDS patients but should know their limitations and also know when to make referrals to health institutions.

[The workshop was supported by the Norwegian Ministry of Development Cooperation (NORAD).]

REFERENCES

1. London Declaration on AIDS Prevention, in *AIDS Prevention and Control*, WHO and Pergamon Press, Geneva and Oxford, 1988.
2. C. K. Ross, Factors Influencing Successful Preventive Health Education, *Health Education Quarterly, 8*:3, pp. 197-208, 1981.
3. L. W. Green, Determining the Impact and Effectiveness of Health Education as It Relates to Federal Policy, *Health Education Monographs, 6* (Suppl. 1), pp. 28-66, 1978.
4. M. L. Wallack, Mass Media Campaigns. The Odds Against Finding Behaviour Change, *Health Education Quarterly, 8*:3, pp. 209-360, 1981.
5. E. M. Rogers and E. F. Shoemaker, *Communication of Innovations* (2nd Edition), Free Press, New York, 1971.
6. L. Liskin, R. Blackburn, and J. H. Maier, AIDS: A Public Health Crisis, *Population Reports Series L, 6*, pp. 193-228, 1988.
7. J. M. Mann, Control Strategies, *AIDS ACTION, 1*, pp. 4-5, 1987.
8. The Editors, Back to Basic, *AIDS ACTION, 2*, p. 1, 1987.
9. F. Elangot, Uganda on AIDS Control Programme, *AIDS ACTION, 1*, p. 6, 1987.
10. L. Sherr, Running AIDS Workshops, *AIDS ACTION, 3*, p. 7, 1988.
11. W. G. Manyeneng, Community Organization. A Village Health Committee in Botswana, in *Primary Health Care. The African Experience*, R. W. Carlaw and W. B. Ward (eds.), Third Party Publishing Company, California, 1983.
12. Health Education Unit and Traditional Medicine Unit, *Traditional Healers in Zambia*, Ministry of Health, Lusaka, 1987.

CHAPTER 20

The CEPA Project: A New Model for Community-Based Program Planning

David Buchanan, Joani Marinoff, Edna Apostol,
Nancy O'Hare, Dalila Balfour, Maria Rodriguez,
Carmen Claudio, and Carlos Santiago

In recent years, there has been a growing interest in "community-based" approaches to health promotion and disease prevention. A number of authors [1-4] have made a distinction between community-based strategies and what could be termed "social planning" approaches, borrowing from the classic typology by Rothman [5]. In the social planning model, the goals, objectives and implementation activities are identified by public health professionals who design the programs based on their own training and expertise. The pioneering heart disease prevention programs, such as the Stanford three- and five-community studies, the North Karelia project, the Minnesota Heart Health plan and the Pawtucket (RI) project, are well-known examples of the social planning approach to community interventions. But, for a variety of reasons, many people have become disenchanted with expert-driven interventions and have called for new approaches in which lay citizens play a central decision-making role.

There are many reasons supporting a shift from expert-led to citizen-led interventions. First, there is a growing recognition that expert models have been, at best, only modestly successful and not with all populations. Also, there is a sense that, if many public health problems are rooted in community disintegration and anomie (e.g., alcohol and drug abuse, suicide, violence, unsafe sexual behaviors, etc.), then a rekindling of community *civitas* [6] may be necessary to alleviate these problems. This kind of communal rejuvenation is not something that can be imposed by outsiders. Similarly, if a sense of powerlessness contributes to health problems, then a reliance on outside experts may foster or exacerbate feelings of dependency and incompetence.

In the larger picture, many people think government-run programs benefit middle class program managers more than the populations in need. Some authors have gone even further to suggest that bureaucratic programs do more harm than good [4, 7]. Furthermore, there is a growing disillusionment with the ability of positivist social science methods to determine truths about the human condition, and hence, there have been renewed calls for moving away from the idea of a "scientifically-guided" society and toward a "self-guiding" society [8]. Within the field of health education, there have long been injunctions to "start where the people are" [9]. Finally, a powerful democratic impulse provides a moral imperative to open up any processes that might allow people to control the conditions that affect their lives.

Based on the foregoing, the call for community-based health promotion programs is well justified. In this chapter, we present a case study of a new program that has developed an innovative approach to community-based public health programming. The Centro de Educacion, Prevencion y Accion (CEPA) project is designed to break down the barriers between program developers and program recipients to the greatest degree possible. The program described here illustrates both the possibilities and the limitations of intensive citizen involvement. The case study presents some of the lessons learned in the process in hopes that they may be of value to others trying to develop community-based approaches to health promotion.

BACKGROUND

The Centro de Educacion, Prevencion y Accion (CEPA) project is a collaborative endeavor between the Holyoke Latino Community Coalition and the University of Massachusetts School of Public Health. The CEPA program is one part of a larger project funded under the "Community-Based Public Health" initiative of the W. K. Kellogg Foundation. To set the context for the discussion, a brief description of the overall initiative is in order.

The Community-Based Public Health initiative grew out of the recommendations contained in the Institute of Medicine's *Future of Public Health* (1988) report, the "Faculty—Agency Forum" meetings and original thinking from within the W. K. Kellogg Foundation. The initial "request for proposals" was released in March 1991. The Community-Based Public Health initiative was unique in at least two respects. Where both the IOM report and the Faculty-Agency Forum focused on building stronger ties between academic programs and public health agencies (health departments), the Kellogg Foundation thought it essential to include community groups as well in any new efforts to revitalize the field of public health (for many of the reasons cited previously). Hence, they required a tri-partite relationship: academics, professional practitioners, and community-based organizations.

Second, realizing that the creation of viable linkages among these three major partners was going to be an unprecedented and undoubtedly difficult process, the Foundation established a two-stage proposal process. The Request For Proposals (RFP) called for the submission of brief concept papers. From over 100 submissions, the Foundation selected fifteen semi-finalist consortia from across the country to participate in a year-long "Leadership and Model Development" phase. The LMD phase was unfunded (except for travel expenses) and, over the course of five national meetings, culminated in the development of full proposals. The full proposals were submitted in April 1992; seven consortia were awarded funding in September.

The Massachusetts Community-Based Public Health Consortium is composed of five major member organizations: the University of Massachusetts School of Public Health; the Massachusetts Area Health Education Centers (AHEC); the Massachusetts Association of Health Boards; the University of Massachusetts (Worcester) Medical School; and, four communities located in central and western Massachusetts. The project is located in semi-rural New England, with two distinct population groups participating: rural, white, working class communities and rural Latinos (predominantly Puerto Ricans) now living in urban centers.

The initial contact that led to the creation of the Consortium was between the School of Public Health and the Massachusetts AHEC. At that time, the MAHEC had initiated and was staffing three community coalitions. In addition, the Executive Director of one of the local AHEC offices was also the co-chair of the Holyoke Latino Community Coalition. Thus, collaboration with the MAHEC was instrumental in initiating contacts between the university and the community coalitions.

The CEPA program is based in the city of Holyoke, a small city (pop. 42,463) in the throes of industrial decline. Holyoke has experienced large demographic shifts over the last two decades, with a major influx of Puerto Rican migrants who now compose over one-third of the population. Holyoke has among the highest rates in the state for infant mortality, teen pregnancy, children living in poverty, Latinos living in poverty, substance abuse problems and people with HIV and AIDS. In a recent report, the Massachusetts Civil Rights Commission cited Holyoke as one of five cities in the Commonwealth likely to experience widespread civil disturbances in the following years. A summary of select demographic and public health indicators comparing Holyoke with statewide averages is presented in Figures 1-3. By any measure, the health status indicators for Holyoke are grim.

This report describes the first two phases of the CEPA program, the planning and initial implementation phases, which occurred during the first two years of the project.

THE CEPA PROGRAM: PLANNING STAGE

During the Leadership and Model Development stage of the Community-Based Public Health initiative, an extensive needs assessment process was undertaken in each of the participating communities. One of the major advantages of this initiative is that there were no pre-conceived notions about the types of public health problems to be addressed. This opportunity enabled the Consortium to conduct a true community needs assessment, with free rein to pursue whichever community priorities emerged, rather than—as is more commonly the case—responding to funding agency's mandates.

In Holyoke, a faculty member began working with the Health Promotion group of the Holyoke Latino Community Coalition (HLCC). The HLCC was founded in 1984 and is now the longest standing independent community organization serving the health needs of the Holyoke Latino community. The Health Promotion group is one of four action subgroups of the HLCC; the group ranges in size from six to ten members. The Health Promotion group is made up of Latinos who are Holyoke residents or health and human service providers working in Holyoke.

In the planning stage, the Health Promotion group used three methods to gather needs assessment information: focus groups with residents, personal and telephone interviews with providers, and a community forum. The basic protocol for the focus groups, interviews and community forum is shown in Table 1. Information was collected in Spanish or English, whichever language was more comfortable for the participants.

A total of six focus groups were conducted by members of the Health Promotion group. Focus groups were held with: teenagers (two groups), residents in a public housing project, elders, and residents recruited on street corners (two groups). The responses gathered in the focus group interviews are notable for their insight into the health needs of the community. They also serve to illustrate the differences between a community-based approach and standardized needs assessment protocols (such as the CDC's Behavioral Risk Factor Survey).

For example, focus group participants were asked "¿Que cosas necesitan las personas/comunidades para ser saludables?" (What do people/communities need to be healthy?). Among the residents' responses were: "a person you can trust," "leaders who care," and "role models." While these answers may not fit into the response categories of standardized instruments (e.g., seat belt use, low-fat diets, and the like), they do offer insight into the limits of current epidemiological thinking.

In addition to the focus groups, the Health Promotion group conducted personal and telephone interviews ($N = 25$) with representatives from virtually all health agencies located in Holyoke. The use of a community-driven interview protocol, developed and implemented by members of the Holyoke community, again elicited remarkably perceptive responses. For example, in reply to questions about what people need to be healthy, providers answered: "purpose in

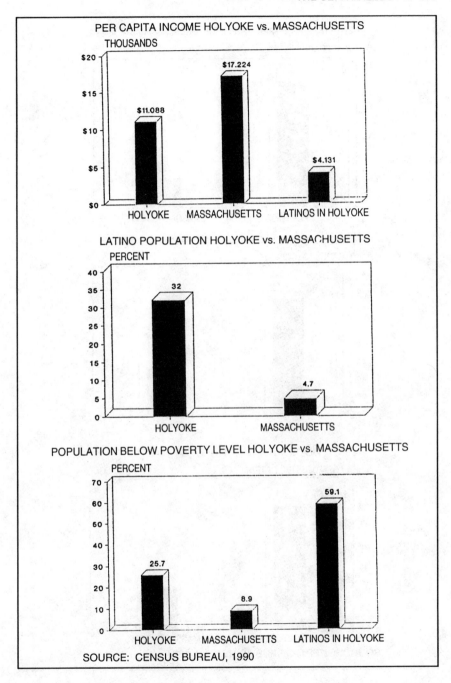

Figure 1. Select Demographic Indicators.

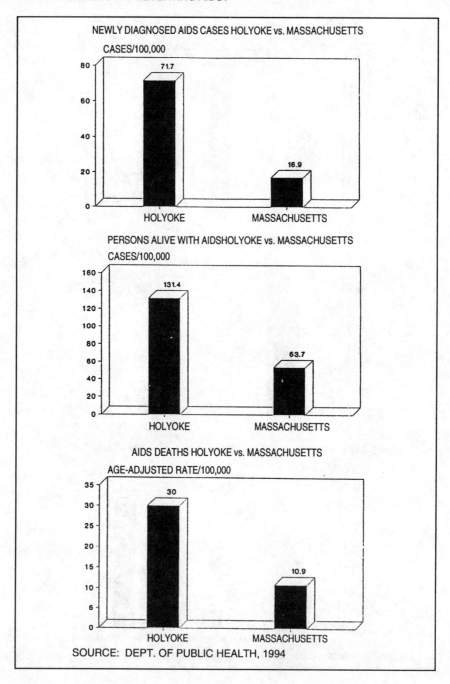

Figure 2. Select Health Indicators.

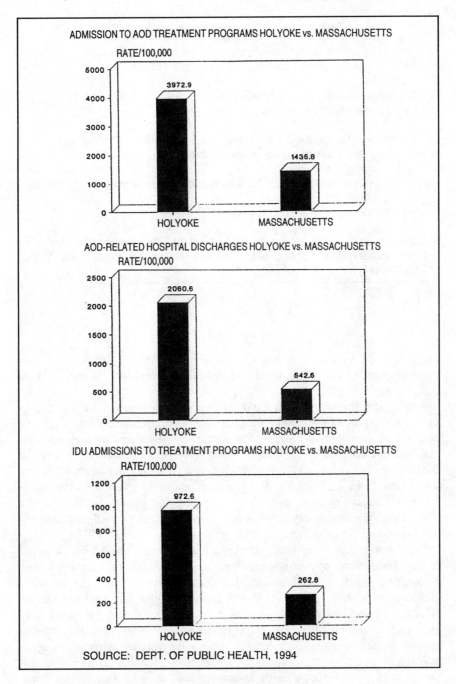

Figure 3. Select HIV/AIDS Indicators.

Table 1. Focus Group and Interview Protocol

1. Que cosas necesitan las personas/comunidades para ser saludables?
   [What things do communities/persons need to be healthy?]

2. Que problemas de salud existen en Holyoke?
   [What are the health problems in Holyoke?]

3. Cuales de estos problems son los tres mas importante?
   [Which of these health problems are the three most important?]

4. Que tipo de programas tu puedes sugerir para ayudar a resolver algunos de
   estos problemas?
   [How can these problems be addressed?]

5. Que tipo de ayuda puede proveer la Escuela de Salud Publica en Holyoke?
   [How can the UMass School of Public Health help with some of these
   problems?]

life," "a sense of moral coherence," "good relationships," "a good basis for spiritual growth," as well as more conventional answers such as non-smoking and exercise.

Finally, the Holyoke Latino Community Coalition organized a community forum to allow other community members the opportunity to provide input into determining priority health needs. The forum was advertised through coalition mailings, the community newspaper, phone calls and flyers distributed in the community. The community forum resulted in a lively discussion about current social conditions in Holyoke. Many pointed questions were directed at the academics regarding their motives for pursuing the project in the Holyoke community. The community forum was tape-recorded, transcribed, and analyzed by a consultant to the coalition.

The focus groups, telephone interviews and the community forum resulted in the identification of four priority issues: 1) HIV/AIDS, 2) substance abuse, 3) domestic violence, and 4) medical interpreting services. Since the first three problems are closely related, the Health Promotion group decided to focus on HIV/AIDS prevention, with the expectation that any program that could have an impact on reducing the risk of HIV infection would also necessarily have to have an impact on issues like substance abuse and domestic violence. The needs assessment results were bolstered by Department of Public Health data that show that Holyoke suffers a vastly disproportionate share of the AIDS epidemic (see Figure 3).

In summary, in using a community-based approach, the CEPA project called on community members to identify their own questions and to collect information from other community members on their own terms. The academic partners played a minor, secondary role. The results of this process were not only robust but in many respects more thought-provoking than standardized, needs assessment protocols.

INITIAL IMPLEMENTATION STAGE

From the community needs assessment, the HLCC Health Promotion group proposed to initiate an innovative, community-based HIV/AIDS prevention program. The HP group (now joined by a faculty member and a graduate student) re-constituted itself as an Advisory Board for the CEPA project. Because of the history of Puerto Rico's colonial status, gross inequalities in economic status, and extensive personal experiences with discrimination, the HP group decided that the CEPA program should be based on a participatory, critical thinking, and empowerment model.

The basic philosophy of the CEPA program is that people in high risk environments know better than anyone else what will be effective in preventing HIV infection given their circumstances. Therefore, the fundamental strategy of CEPA is to reduce the gap between program developers and program recipients to the greatest extent possible. This strategy ensures that program activities will be the most relevant, culturally appropriate and well-suited to meet the needs of those at risk.

To put this strategy into practice, the CEPA program has developed a three-stage process: 1) Conciencization/Education, 2) Planning, and 3) Action (C-E-P-A). The stages are dynamic, not sequential; they overlap and inform one another.

Conciencizacion/Education

In stage one, the CEPA staff (a project coordinator and an outreach worker) participated in an intensive self-led educational process with the Advisory Board. The conciencization/education process [10, 11] focused on community development, community organizing, community empowerment, critical consciousness and participatory education. The Advisory Board thought these topics were essential because of their experiences with discrimination and social and economic disenfranchisement in Holyoke. Particular readings were also identified by the Advisory Board. Sessions were conducted as a process of mutual, self-education and consciousness-raising, with weekly meetings extending over a three month period.

Growing out of the praxis of conciencization, the Advisory Board and CEPA staff developed an eleven-session training program to carry out with community residents. Even though the Advisory Board is composed of community residents and community providers, they felt they needed to get even closer to the population at risk, and hence, work directly with local neighborhood residents.

Like the staff development experience, the resident training program is based on models of empowerment and participatory education. Based on the work of Paulo Freire, the empowerment process has been described by Wallerstein [12]; it consists of listening, dialoguing, problem-posing, and action. As the Advisory Board discovered, the respective models (empowerment and participatory) are not entirely compatible, with an inherent bias toward examining the "root causes" of health problems in the empowerment model and a more open, self-directed approach in the participatory education model [13-16]. The challenges in balancing these approaches will be examined in greater detail in the discussion section.

Planning

In stage two planning, the CEPA staff set out going door-to-door in a neighborhood selected because of its high level of risk factors (i.e., poor, rundown housing stock, high unemployment rates, high numbers of school drop-outs, presence of sex industry workers, and presence of drug dealers and shooting galleries). The staff also met with community agencies, social organizations, church representatives, tenants groups, and so on. They introduced themselves and the program and invited community residents to participate in planning the program.

The objective at this stage was to recruit a small group of eight to twelve neighborhood residents to form a Residents Planning Board. After lengthy discussions, the Advisory Board decided to enlist a planning group as diverse as possible, rather than seek out specific subgroups (e.g., sex workers, adolescents, etc.). Board members were opposed to the idea of recruiting community members according to pre-selected categories. In contrast to expert planning models, they thought that such a process would further fragment the community by stressing differences over more significant, shared commonalities.

Based on a successful outreach effort, a highly diverse group was recruited in the initial round. The ten participants ranged in age from thirteen to fifty-five. There were two men and eight women, two people with AIDS, and one family unit (father, mother, and daughter). They work in a variety of occupations, from insurance, to homemaker, teacher, counselor, unemployed, and student. All are Puerto Rican.

All sessions were planned originally to be conducted in Spanish. As the group evolved, however, they decided to encourage people to speak in whichever language they felt most comfortable, as virtually everyone was bilingual. The residents were stipended for their participation. The stipends are not motivational incentives, but due compensation for the time, knowledge, and labor supplied by the residents.

The community residents then met once a week for two hours in the evening to participate in a series of structured discussions designed by the Advisory Board. At the heart of the community-based approach, these sessions are designed to have people living in high risk environments identify the needs, barriers, and resources they personally experience in trying to respond effectively to the threat of AIDS. The purpose of these discussions is to have those at highest risk decide for themselves the types of services, support, and actions that will best address the causes of their susceptibility.

(To recall the overlapping nature of the three identified stages, these sessions are also clearly a part of the community conciencizacion and education process and a part of the Action of the CEPA project.)

An outline of the objectives for the eleven sessions is shown in Table 2. The planning process took three months to complete. Each session was tape-recorded and each concluded with time for immediate feedback, so the process could be replicated and modified as needed. The end result of these sessions was the identification of the types of services needed for effective community-based HIV prevention. The desired program characteristics were framed in terms of a simple, user-friendly "request for proposals."

Growing out of the planning process, the Residents Planning Board decided that community programs should focus on work with the teenage population. They identified four major goals for community programming. To prevent HIV infection, they said programs should: 1) promote self-esteem, both individually and collectively; 2) promote life-enhancing family values; 3) create a public space for the Puerto Rican community; and 4) promote effective communication skills.

The goals identified deserve a couple of comments. First, it is important to note that the community residents did not think that clinical information about modes of HIV transmission was essential. In contrast to many conventional programs, they understood well that the problem of AIDS was due to more than a simple lack of information. As one member put it, "You have to feel pretty good about yourself to want to protect yourself from HIV."

Second, the goal of promoting life-enhancing family values is a distinct reflection of Puerto Rican cultural values. In contrast to the high value placed on individualism in the United States, Puerto Rican community members situated the issue in the social context of inherent familial relationships. Echoing this priority, participants noted that the name of the project, "cepa," can be translated as "core" or "root," as in family roots of geneological trees.

The Residents Planning Board identified seven additional characteristics or criteria that would make programs more effective: 1) peer (teen) involvement in programming and outreach activities; 2) Persons With AIDS (PWA) involvement in all levels of programming; 3) the appropriation of leadership and guidance roles by program participants; 4) a focus on the strengths within the community; 5) well trained staff; 6) an on-going evaluation process; and, 7) guarantees of confidentiality for participants. They advised that programs should focus on self-esteem, self-determination, community development and the promotion of peer interaction. Typical activities might include after-school activities, summer programs, sports and other team activities, peer support groups and drop-in neighborhood centers.

Table 2. Outline of Resident Training Sessions

Session	Objectives
1	To get to know group members To understand project expectations To understand individual/collective commitment and responsibilities To develop a schedule of next five meetings
2	To continue developing group cohesiveness To review project expectations To review schedule of meetings To introduce the topic of HIV
3	To share personal migration stories To share personal understanding of Holyoke To compare/contrast stories to connect collective experiences
4	To increase knowledge of HIV//AIDS To explore and begin to understand root causes of HIV infection To become more aware about why Latinos, specifically Puerto Ricans, are vulnerable to HIV To understand the social, psychological, and medical impact of HIV
5	To discuss further the root causes of HIV infection among Latinos To establish linkages among causes To illustrate with case studies how these linkages are interrelated
6	To continue discussing the root causes of HIV infection among Latinos To identify and discuss factors contributing to low self-esteem
7	To identify ways by which individuals can take individual and/or collective action to impact systems To identify individual/collective strengths that protect communities from low self-esteem and lack of well-being
8	To facilitate a process by which participants identify effective HIV prevention strategies To emphasize the individual's role as an impetus for change To connect the ideas that will be identified by this process with the resources that are available through the mini-grants
9	To continue the process of identifying the criteria for programs To prioritize the program proposals and ideas
10	To identify a process for announcing, selecting, reviewing, and evaluating the program proposals To identify participants who would like to continue as voluntary members of the advisory board To evaluate the residents' training program
11	To establish a timetable for the RFP and projects To recognize the efforts of the participants To celebrate the planning process

Action

In stage three, a call for community action was issued through the requests for proposals, providing funding for grants up to $5,000. The proposal was widely circulated in the community through flyers, radio programs and announcements, newspaper articles, outreach, handbills, mailings, community parties, presentations in agencies, a press conference, an open house, and word of mouth through informal interpersonal networks.

Members of the Residents Planning Board, Advisory Board, and CEPA staff jointly participated in reviewing the proposals and determining which groups received funding. In line with the project's philosophy, the reviewers decided from the outset to give preference in funding to non-traditional groups or agencies. Residents involved in the planning stage eagerly volunteered for a monitoring role in reviewing the progress of the community grants too.

In the first round, the reviewers decided to fund three proposals. One proposal was to lend partial support to a Latino teen theater troupe focusing on adolescent themes, one proposal was to set up a summer teen drop-in center (submitted and run by teenagers), and third was to fund a mother's group to start dance, music, and basketball lessons for neighborhood teens. As a condition of funding, the CEPA project requested that each group participate in a shortened version of the residents critical thinking process.

At this point, the CEPA project has successfully engaged community members in a substantive role in a community-based program planning process. Whether or not this process will result in more effective HIV prevention efforts is unknown at this time. In collaboration with community members, the Advisory Board will be monitoring the progress of the community grants over the next three years. CEPA is also in the process of replicating the program in two other neighborhoods. Based on the CEPA experience, there are several points for discussion about the prospects for community-based program planning.

DISCUSSION

At this point in the CEPA program, the Advisory Board members are deeply impressed both with the difficulties in creating a fully participatory model (and not slipping into a "banking" mode of education that presumes people need to be filled with the experts' information) and with the benefits of such an approach. The dilemma of reconciling a commitment to a participatory, community-based approach with the aspirations and expectations of the program initiators has become a central theme in ongoing discussions of the CEPA project. Several examples will serve to illustrate this point.

From the outset, the Advisory Board has wrestled with questions about how to define the project. Members were committed to a *process* of involving community members in designing the project. But we also recognized that funding agencies usually require quite specific delineation of the proposed program activities before extending their support. How, then, could CEPA specify the program activities before it had engaged the very people who were to decide which activities were most appropriate?

In the original grant proposal, the Health Promotion group compromised by describing the planned process and listing a number of potential activities. The W. K. Kellogg Foundation accepted the idea. But, when CEPA has sought additional funding, other foundations have responded as expected in demanding to know exactly what they were going to be getting for their money. The idea that program activities would emerge from the process and could take many unforeseeable forms has been difficult to sell (even to some of the other partners in the larger Kellogg CBPH project).

Then, the Advisory Board had to decide how to structure the residents training program. Again, we wrestled with the trade-offs. If the Advisory Board designed the training, then we would be assuming control, telling the participants what we expect them to do, and inevitably reproducing our own assumptions, interests, and biases. But if we did not provide any structure to the discussions, we feared people would think we were unprepared and did not know what we were doing. Again, a delicate, carefully considered compromise emerged as the process proceeded.

In the event, we decided to plan all of the sessions in advance (see Table 2). But during the training, we tried—largely unsuccessfully—to encourage the residents to take over and lead the sessions. We struggled too over revealing the full plan of the sessions. Some of us thought that presenting a completed plan would discourage the residents from realizing they could re-direct the sessions; others thought that failing to tell them what was planned was even more manipulative.

So, as the process was underway, we decided to share plans for the next immediate session and ask the residents for their suggestions and approval. Few changes were made. The feedback from the residents was that they were generally comfortable with the direction of the sessions. But they also expressed concerns— on more than one occasion—that they did not fully understand why we were doing a few particular activities and that they wanted to move more quickly into designing the HIV prevention program.

Two further examples: In planning the sessions, the Advisory Board decided to dedicate one session to a discussion of the historical relationship between Puerto Rico and the United States. Here, the tensions between a critical empowerment model and a participatory model became most apparent. On the one hand, Advisory Board members thought it was important to make clear the connection between the history of U.S. imperialist domination and the present disproportionate share of health burdens borne by the Puerto Rican peoples. On the other hand, Board members wanted just to hear and share personal migration stories and believed that collectively these stories would make the same point. So the CEPA project was again faced with questions about how to proceed.

In the session at hand, the Advisory Board tried to prepare a concise history of Puerto Rico's colonial status. It was of course impossible to cover a complete history in such a short period of time. So, a member of the Advisory Board ended up presenting a long lecture that took up almost the entire time that evening. The community voices were left out, the residents reduced to a passive role of being fed information. More to the point, the session jarred us into thinking about the seductiveness of power and control and about how we too had internalized the banking system of education.

Similarly, we felt obligated to present the clinical perspective about HIV transmission in another session. We invited a guest speaker, but we knew we needed to prepare her for the CEPA mutual teacher-learner educational process. We also thought the standard medical model needed to be balanced with a broader sociopolitical perspective that we could present. But despite the best laid plans, the guest speaker wound up dominating the session and the residents were again treated as empty vessels waiting to be filled.

As was the case after each session, the Advisory Board and staff took time immediately afterwards to process these sessions and reflect self-critically on the experience. Like at many other points in the project, we came face-to-face with the possibilities and limits of community-based program planning. The experience brought home how difficult it is to set up a process that enables people to take control of the conditions that affect their lives and how difficult it is not to assume a powerful, controlling role in telling people what we think they need to know.

We shared our concerns with the residents at the next meeting. Collectively, we decided to repeat the AIDS 101 session, this time, however, listening to the knowledge each of us already had. The candor of the Advisory Board, admitting our mistakes, dropping any pretensions as experts with answers about how people should live their lives, changed the tone and dynamic of the meetings. The distance between program developers and program recipients was narrowed. Community members and board members came a little closer in understanding that answers to questions about how to live in the face of the threat of AIDS could not be dictated, but must be generated through a process of mutual discussion, reflection and dialogue about the kind of community we want to live in together.

The Advisory Board was struck by the possibilities and benefits of this project as well. The most moving experience for everyone involved was a rekindling of pride in our Puerto Rican identity. The sense of confusion and ambivalence around having "dual identities"—and its relationship to a sense of low self-esteem—was openly discussed for the first time for many of us. Discussions about the influence of cultural roles and how they shape perceptions, both positively and negatively, of possible choices and subsequent decisions were frank, deeply personal, and collectively liberating. The experience reconnected each of us with the bonds of community.

In conclusion, the CEPA experience shows how program initiators inevitably make decisions that shape the direction of any resulting community programs. The idea that program developers can totally bracket their assumptions is difficult to maintain. The extent to which a program might be called "community-based" will always be a matter of degree. Hence, rather than presuming they have the best interests of the people at heart, public health professionals might better approach community development work by self-critically examining their own interests and biases first.

But these constraints are not insurmountable. As long as feedback is openly and continuously solicited and incorporated, the gap between program developers and recipients can continue to be narrowed. The CEPA project thus provides a powerful model for maximizing community involvement in issues vital to the health and well-being of community residents.

REFERENCES

1. D. Chavis and P. Florin, *Community Development, Community Participation, and Substance Abuse Prevention*, Bureau of Drug Abuse Services, Department of Health, Santa Clara County, California, 1990.
2. S. Fawcett, A. Paine, V. Francisco, and M. Vliet, Promoting Health through Community Development, in *Promoting Health and Mental Health: Behavioral Approaches to Prevention*, D. Glenwick and L. Jason (eds.), Haworth Press, New York.
3. H. Grace, Building Community: A Conceptual Perspective, *International Journal of the W. K. Kellogg Foundation*, W. K. Kellogg Foundation, Battle Creek, Michigan, Spring 1990.
4. J. McKnight, Regenerating Community, *Social Policy*, pp. 54-58, Winter 1987,
5. J. Rothman, Three Models of Community Organization Practice, Their Mixing and Phasing, in *Strategies of Community Organization: A Book of Readings* (3rd Edition), F. M. Cox, J. Erlich, and J. Rothman (eds.), F.E. Peacock, Itasca, Illinois, 1979.
6. D. Bell, *The Cultural Contradictions of Capitalism*, Basic Books, New York, 1976.
7. C. Murray, *Losing Ground*, Basic Books, New York, 1984.
8. C. Lindblom, *Inquiry and Change: The Troubled Attempt to Understand and Shape Society*, Yale University Press, New Haven, 1990.
9. D. Nyswander, The Open Society: Its Implications for Health Educators, *Health Education Monographs, 1*, pp. 3-13, 1967.
10. P. Freire, *Pedagogy of the Oppressed*, The Seabury Press, New York, 1968.
11. P. Freire, *Education for Critical Consciousness*, The Seabury Press, New York 1973.
12. N. Wallerstein, Powerlessness, Empowerment and Health: Implications for Health Promotion Programs, *American Journal of Health Promotion, 6*:3, pp. 197-205, 1992.
13. CUSO, *Basic and Tools: A Collection of Popular Education Resources and Activities*, CUSO Education Department, Ottawa, 1985.
14. B. L. Hall and J. Kidd (eds.), *Adult Learning: A Design for Action*, Pergammon Press, Toronto, 1978.
15. M. Knowles, *The Adult Learner: A Neglected Species*, Gulf Publishing, Houston, 1978.
16. J. Mezirow, A Critical Theory of Self-Directed Learning, in *Self-Directed Learning: From Theory to Practice*, S. Brookfield (ed.), Jossey-Bass, San Francisco, 1985.

Contributors*

ADENIYI, JOSHUA D., Dr.PH.   University of Ibadan, Nigeria
AJUWON, ADEMOLA J., MPH   University of Ibadan, Nigeria
APOSTOL, EDNA, MPH   Massachusetts Area Health Education Centers
BALFOUR, DALILA   Massachusetts Department of Public Health
BOSOMPRA, KWADWO, MPH   University of Ghana, Legon
BRIEGER, WILLIAM R., Dr.PH.   University of Ibadan, Nigeria
BUCHANAN, DAVID, Dr.PH.   University of Massachusetts, Amherst
CARRILLO, HECTOR, MCP, MPH   School of Public Health, University of California, Berkeley
CERNADA, GEORGE, Dr.PH.   University of Massachusetts, Amherst
CHAN, ROY, M.R.C.P., M.B.B.S.   Department of STD Control, National Skin Centre, Singapore
CHIRWA, B. U., MB.Ch.B., MPH   Health Education Unit, Ministry of Health, Lusaka, Republic of Zambia
CLAUDIO, CARMEN   Centro de Educacion, Prevencion, y Accion, Holyoke
EDEM, CHRISTIANA UDO   Texas Tech University, Lubbock
FOULK, DAVID, Ed.D.   Georgia Southern University, Statesboro
FRANCIS, CLAUDETTE, MA   Caribbean Epidemiological Centre, West Indies
HARVEY, S. MARIE   University of Oregon, Eugene
KOH, DAVID, Ph.D., M.B.B.S.   Department of Community, Occupational and Family Medicine, National University of Singapore
KOK, GERJO   University of Limburg, Maastricht, The Netherlands
LAFFERTY, JERRY, Ph.D.   Georgia Southern University, Statesboro
LAVER, SUSAN M.   Department of Community Medicine, University of Zimbabwe, Harare
LEAR, DANA, M.H.Sc.   University of California, Berkeley
LUX, KATHLEEN, R.N., Ph.D.   The Ohio State University, Columbus

*Current agency affiliations at the time these chapters were submitted for publication.

MARINOFF, JOANI, MPH Centro de Educacion, Prevencion, y Accion, Holyoke
MATSHAZI, DUMISO, MPH San Bernardino, California
MODESTE, NAOMI N., Dr.PH. Loma Linda University, California
O'HARE, NANCY, MPH Baystate Medical Hospital, Massachusetts
OLADEPO, OLADIMEJI, MPH, Ph.D. University of Ibadan, Nigeria
PETOSA, RICK, Ph.D. The Ohio State University, Columbus
PEZZA, PAUL E., Ph.D., MPH, MAT Providence College, Rhode Island
RICHTER, DONNA L., Ed.D. University of South Carolina, Columbia
RODRIGUEZ, MARIA, MSW Holyoke Hospital
RYAN, REBECCA, MPS Georgia Southern University, Statesboro
SANTIAGO, CARLOS, MSW Massachusetts Department of Public Health
SHOKUNBI, WURAOLA, M.B.B.S. University College Hospital, Ibadan, Nigeria
SIVILE, E. Health Education Unit, Ministry of Health, Lusaka, Republic of Zambia
SPIGNER, CLARENCE, Dr.PH. Department of School and Community Health, University of Oregon, Eugene
STEWART, THOMAS J., Ph.D. South Carolina State University, Orangeburg
TREADWELL, D. F. Westfield State College, Massachusetts
VAN DEN BORNE, BART University of Limburg, Maastricht, The Netherlands
WITTE, KIM, Ph.D. Texas A&M University, College Station
WOELK, GODFREY University of Zimbabwe, Harare
WONG, MEE LIAN, MPH, M.B.B.S. Department of Community, Occupational and Family Medicine, National University of Singapore
WONG, CHRISTINA MISA, B.A. Department of Community, Occupational and Family Medicine, National University of Singapore
YEP, GUST A., Ph.D. California State University, Los Angeles

Index

[Public Health Education]
in Asian Pacific American community, 191-197
behavior modification and, 305-306, 311, 312-313
behavioral demonstration in, 8, 142, 143, 144, 145, 146, 148, 191, 193, 247-249, 252-256
community-based, 335-338, 342-350
drama as, 294-309, 315-316, 317
for farm workers, 263-265, 266-267, 268, 276-290
focus groups in, 247, 280, 294-316, 338
in Ghana, 294-317
in Hispanic American community, 211
in Mexico, 161-162, 163, 166-167, 169-172
models of, 134-138, 139
in Nigeria, 235-236
politics and, 126, 127, 160-165, 207-208, 210
program evaluation for, 251, 267-268, 273-274, 279-280, 287-289
scientific paradigms and, 119
for sex workers, 243-257
song as, 295, 309-314, 316-317
in United States, 170, 210-211
for women, 235-236, 245-246
Public policy, 126-127

Radiation exposure, 123
Religion
health communication and, 147, 150, 151
sexually transmitted diseases and, 42, 127, 224
Research, 12-13, 118-120 (see also Health Belief Model)
on community health promotion, 336-338, 342-350
on community sexual practices, 23-31
condom-use intentions in, 60, 61-63, 65-66, 68, 69, 76-84, 92-105, 189
drama in, 294-309, 315-316, 317
focus groups in, 23-24, 247, 294-316, 338
health communication, 138-152

[Research]
health providers in, 338, 342
ideology and, 125
key informants in, 23
newspaper survey in, 215-224
Q-methodology in, 139-140
self-efficacy in, 49, 57, 61-64, 65-66, 97, 100, 103, 189
on sexual attitudes
in adolescents, 48-54, 56-57, 59, 66, 68, 185
in delinquent adolescents, 55-69
in migrant farm workers, 323-324
in university students, 37-45, 76-84, 92-105, 186
song in, 295, 309-314, 316-317
Risk behavior (see High risk behavior)
Root-Bernstein, Robert, 117, 120-121, 122

San Francisco, 164, 170, 180, 182-184, 185-186, 194, 195
Chinese community in, 183, 185-186
Filipino community in, 184
Japanese community in, 183-184, 186
San Francisco Men's Health Study, 124
Scare tactics (see Threat appeals)
Scientific paradigms, 118-120
ideology and, 125
Self-efficacy, 189, 245-249
Senegal, 216, 217, 218, 219, 220, 221, 223
Sex workers (see Commercial sex workers)
Sexism, and HIV, 224
Sexual attitudes
adolescents and, 48-50, 52-53, 56-57, 59, 66, 68, 180, 188
Asian Pacific Americans and, 186-187, 188-189, 191, 196
condom use and, 39, 41, 42, 44, 45, 50, 60, 61-63, 66, 80, 81-82, 306
delinquent adolescents and, 58-59, 60-69
migrant farm workers and, 323-324
university students and, 39, 41, 42, 79-84, 103-105, 180, 186